CU00894831

I would like to dedicate this book to my wife, Sue, and son, Jack, who have had to put up with me working lots of late nights over the past few months and have not had as much attention from me as they deserve. I was in two minds whether to write this book; had it not been for Sue, the book would not now be on the shelves.

Thank you, Sue.

EXPLORER

Personal Oracle8

Richard Fieldhouse

Publisher

Keith Weiskamp

Project Editor

Meredith Brittain

Production Coordinator

Kim Eoff

Cover Design

Anthony Stock

Layout Design

April Nielsen

Marketing Specialist

Jody Kent

CD-ROM Development

Robert Clarfield

Personal Oracle8 EXplorer

Copyright © 1998, by The Coriolis Group, Inc.

All rights reserved. This book may not be duplicated in any way without the express written consent of the publisher, except in the form of brief excerpts or quotations for the purposes of review. The information contained herein is for the personal use of the reader and may not be incorporated in any commercial programs, other books, databases, or any kind of software without written consent of the publisher. Making copies of this book or any portion for any purpose other than your own is a violation of United States copyright laws.

Limits of Liability and Disclaimer of Warranty

The author and publisher of this book have used their best efforts in preparing the book and the programs contained in it. These efforts include the development, research, and testing of the theories and programs to determine their effectiveness. The author and publisher make no warranty of any kind, expressed or implied, with regard to these programs or the documentation contained in this book.

The author and publisher shall not be liable in the event of incidental or consequential damages in connection with, or arising out of, the furnishing, performance, or use of the programs, associated instructions, and/or claims of productivity gains.

Trademarks

Trademarked names appear throughout this book. Rather than list the names and entities that own the trademarks or insert a trademark symbol with each mention of the trademarked name, the publisher states that it is using the names for editorial purposes only and to the benefit of the trademark owner, with no intention of infringing upon that trademark.

The Coriolis Group, Inc.
An International Thomson Publishing Company
14455 N. Hayden Road, Suite 220
Scottsdale, Arizona 85260

602/483-0192
FAX 602/483-0193
http://www.coriolis.com

Library of Congress Cataloging-in-Publication Data
Fieldhouse, Richard, 1969 -
    Personal Oracle8 EXplorer / by Richard Fieldhouse.
        p.   cm.
    Includes index.
    ISBN 1-57610-250-5
    1. Oracle (Computer file)   2. Relational databases.
QA76.9.D3F535   1998
005.75'85 — dc21   98-16071
                                                                    CIP

Printed in the United States of America
10 9 8 7 6 5 4 3 2 1

an International Thomson Publishing company

Albany, NY • Belmont, CA • Bonn • Boston • Cincinnati • Detroit • Johannesburg • London
Madrid • Melbourne • Mexico City • New York • Paris • Singapore • Tokyo • Toronto • Washington

Acknowledgments

I would like to take this opportunity to thank everyone who has been involved with the creation of this book. Special thanks must go to Meredith Brittain, my project editor, for all the help and guidance provided while writing and reviewing the contents of the book. Other thanks must go to the following people who have helped to get this book together: Robert Clarfield, CD-ROM Developer; Kim Eoff, Production Coordinator; Jody Kent, Marketing Product Specialist; Susan Holly, Copyeditor; and Tony Stock, Cover Design.

Special thanks must also go to Michael Ault and Donald Burleson—Mike for the initial introduction to the Coriolis Group and Don for his continued enthusiasm for the book and subject that kept me going through the late nights of the last few months.

About The Author

Richard Fieldhouse (Chippenham, UK) is a freelance Oracle Applications Consultant DBA with over ten years of experience in the Oracle field. Working as the DBA on some of the biggest Oracle databases in the world, Fieldhouse has gained an in-depth knowledge of all aspects of Oracle databases. As a user of Personal Oracle for more than eight years, he has also gained expertise with Oracle on a smaller scale. His email address is Richard_Fieldhouse@compuserve.com.

Table Of Contents

INTRODUCTION

As a programmer or budding developer of Oracle database applications, you're starting at the right place and with the right product by reading this book. I'll show you how you can become proficient in the use, design, and tuning of any Oracle database. This book is written to take anybody who has a basic grounding in the use of a PC and associated software through the maze of Oracle8.

I say Oracle8, not Personal Oracle8, because while this book is based on Personal Oracle8, all of the features are exactly the same in every Oracle8 database, whether it's running on Unix, VMS, Windows NT, or Windows 95. The main difference is that on Windows 95 and Windows NT, the product is more graphically oriented—for example, it uses wizards to create tables. For this reason, when any procedures in this book are shown using graphical tools, I'll also describe how to do the procedure from the command line (which is sometimes the only way of doing things using such operating systems as Unix and VMS).

By reading and understanding this book, you should accomplish four goals:

- Design an efficient database from the ground up, using Oracle's object technology
- Write simple and efficient SQL and PL/SQL code to manipulate the data within a database
- Gain a working knowledge of the Oracle8 database and all its object-oriented features
- Receive a large salary increase

Over the past eight years as a database administrator (DBA), I have looked for books associated with Oracle and have noticed that good books aimed at the intermediate level—those you can pick up and quickly become productive with—are few and far between. For this reason, I decided to write my own book, based on my own experience.

Starting my programming experience with version 5 of Oracle, I came to realize that you have to learn by trying first, then reading later. Because most projects in the workplace are on fairly tight schedules, you need to be able to pick up a piece of software and become as productive as possible in as short a time as possible. This book will be the guide to Oracle8 that I wish had been available when I was learning.

At the time of this writing, no other book is available commercially, outside of the Oracle manuals, that deals with Personal Oracle8 and associated tools from an intermediate perspective. The purpose of this book is to cover the development of applications using Personal Oracle8 in conjunction with the documentation on the Personal Oracle8 CD-ROM.

WHAT IS ORACLE?

Oracle is an extremely complex and high-powered database; in fact, it is the most widely used database in the world. For these and many other reasons, it is generally recognized by computer programmers worldwide as the best. The Oracle database is one of the most technically advanced pieces of software available. One of Oracle's main selling points is that it and its applications are portable across any operating system. This means that an application developed using Personal Oracle8 could quite easily be scaled up and installed on a high-end Unix server with thousands of users accessing the data. One important point to make here is that the Oracle database will run on nearly any commercial operating system, using the same human interface, known as SQL*Plus or PL/SQL.

First, let me take you through the progression of Oracle releases so you can visualize what the Oracle8 database is. Versions 6 and 7 of the Oracle database are relational, meaning that the data stored is referenced by unique identifiers and grouped by relationships. In technical speak, it uses primary and foreign keys (constraints) to enforce referential integrity.

Version 8 is an object-relational database. This means that it still uses the relational theory, but has added extensions of object-oriented theory. In this book, these subjects will be dealt with in more detail, and you will use some of the object theory (even though you might not realize it). The extensions of object-oriented theory add further capability to the Oracle database, in some cases allowing the programmer to apply it more easily to real-life business applications.

INTENDED AUDIENCE

This book is aimed at the programmer or the home-computer hobbyist who wishes to find out more about Oracle. I have designed the book to be used in two different ways:

- You can skim through chapters and just try the demos that appear throughout the book. This will give you a good understanding of how to use the product. You can later return to the related chapters to discover the theory behind the practice.

- You can follow the chapters in order and gradually build up your expertise and overall knowledge, until you have a full working knowledge of how to build applications on Personal Oracle8.

In writing this book, I have assumed that the reader has some knowledge of Windows 95 and has used a database (e.g., MS Access, FoxPro, or dBase). Other people who would benefit from reading this book are:

- Oracle developers who wish to know more about developing/prototyping applications on Personal Oracle

- College students who wish to get a good in-depth knowledge of relational databases

- Other information technology professionals who wish to keep their skills up to date by using Personal Oracle8

PERSONAL ORACLE8

Personal Oracle8, a scaled-down version of Oracle's popular database, is aimed primarily at the desktop market (rather than Oracle's primary market, the high-end Unix or Windows NT servers). The Personal Oracle versions came about because Oracle wanted to give its customers a trial version of the software, which they could easily install and use.

The primary difference between Oracle8 and Personal Oracle8 is that on the Personal version, only single-user access is available as a server—hence, the name *Personal.* Therefore, the software is ideally suited for use as a single-user prototyping tool. Again, because of Oracle's portability, a Personal Oracle database can be easily exported and imported into a large multiuser Oracle platform. This gives users an ideal development platform, because all features available on a high-end server are available to the user on the desktop, including the ability to enable a database for the Web.

Personal Oracle8 is designed to be used in conjunction with Oracle's view of the future in information technology—the network computer (NC). Oracle8 (which according to its subtitle is "The Database for Network Computing") has been specifically designed with the NC architecture in mind. Some of the database's key features are:

- The ability to support any number of users (in the server versions)
- The ability to support any amount of data
- Faster application development
- Increase in cost effectiveness

In reality, what do you get on the Personal Oracle8 installation CD-ROM? You get one of the most technically advanced pieces of software available today, as well as a ready-made development environment for any database application—all in a low-priced, cost-effective database package for Windows 95. The Personal Oracle8 database is way ahead of its competitors in the desktop market. This book will show you how easy it is to use and implement this software, and, more importantly, it will help you understand what is going on in the database and why.

ORACLE'S PRODUCT SUITE

Oracle Corporation produces a lot of software aimed at nearly every type of machine and operating system. A piece of software, which usually has a generic name such as Oracle Server, is available for virtually any type of operating system. The aim of this section is to give you an idea of where the Personal Oracle8 software sits in relation to other Oracle products. A list of Oracle's main product areas follows.

Oracle8 Universal Server

The Oracle8 Universal Server is, as the name implies, a server that will encompass all. The server is the core database, and a number of add-ons provide even more functionality. Some of these add-ons are listed and described here:

- *WebServer Option*—Allows access to your Oracle database from the Web. This will give anyone with a Web browser the ability to access your Web pages. Okay, you say, what's so new about that? This option allows you to tailor your Web pages to react differently to each user accessing them. For example, imagine having a Web page that realizes who you are and, accordingly, lets you access your information from the Internet. This is done by storing your information within the database; then, when you access the Web page, the database knows who you are and can show you relevant information.

- *Spatial Data Option*—Widely used in very large databases, such as data warehouses. This option changes the way the data is stored, allowing for quicker access to data by using a different indexing strategy.

- *ConText*—Basically, a text search engine embedded within the database. This allows you to search unstructured text within the database, because most information is of unstructured text format (e.g., newspaper articles).

- *OLAP*—Stands for online analytical processing of data. This option allows you to store the data within the database in different dimensions. A *dimension* is the way the data is categorized. For a car dealership, for example, a dimension may be the customer name, the type of car purchased, or the amount of money spent. The OLAP option allows you to store your data in either a multidimensional or relational way.

- *Parallel Server*—Allows you to have a single database that is accessed by multiple nodes. The database is stored on a shared disk array available to all nodes. This gives you more power, because a multiple-node database is more fault tolerant. If you have one machine and it fails, then you do not have access to the database. With Parallel Server, you have an instance of the database on each node, so if one goes down the other nodes will carry on. This is extremely useful if the database is mission critical.

- *Video Option*—Allows you to store video and sound within the database. This video and sound can then be played back, in realtime, to anybody on the network. This is the technology behind "video on demand." This will allow multiple users to view the same piece of video whenever they want.

Personal Oracle8 And Personal Oracle Lite

Personal Oracle and Oracle Lite are scaled-down versions of their big brother, Oracle8 Universal Server. They provide access to the Oracle database on the desktop. Oracle Lite is a "lightweight relational database that runs in less than 1MB of RAM," according to Oracle. It is designed for use as a mobile application—i.e., to run on portable computers. Oracle Lite supports bidirectional replication with Oracle Universal Server.

SQL*Plus

All databases accept commands from the user in a common language: Structured Query Language (SQL). Oracle provides a tool, SQL*Plus, which is a standard SQL interpreter; the "Plus" is Oracle's added functionality. SQL*Plus is Oracle's command-line interface to the database. By using SQL*Plus, you can interrogate the database and format the output. SQL*Plus by itself is useful, but when you add the procedural capabilities of PL/SQL, you have a tool that can easily give you access to all of the features of Oracle8. SQL*Plus and PL/SQL are used in the creation of Oracle databases. The Personal Oracle8 database uses wizards to make tasks easier for you by converting your inputs into SQL commands, then executing them against the database.

The procedural option allows you to use SQL*Plus type structures within procedures, giving you the flexibility needed to write simple or complex functions or packages. In this book, you'll see exactly how SQL*Plus and PL/SQL are used to create such procedures and functions.

Oracle8 Enterprise Manager

The Oracle8 Enterprise Manager (OEM) is the tool for managing the whole Oracle environment. The Enterprise Manager includes tools to monitor and interact with the database, job scheduling, and automated backup management facilities. This tool is primarily for systems administration use. Oracle8 Enterprise Manager supports new features of Oracle8—e.g., object partitioning, server backups, and security management. OEM also handles the recovery of a corrupt database by using Recovery Manager. This speeds up the recovery of databases by the database administrator. Database administration tools are available through the Enterprise Manager.

Designer/2000

Designer/2000 is a business-process modeling tool. It gives the user the ability to design complex business objects and rules in an easy-to-understand way. The rules can then be implemented on the server automatically. This data modeling tool allows the designer to model an application independently of the implementation, thus giving the power to implement on multiple platforms from a single model.

Developer/2000

The Developer/2000 package has three main components: Reports, Forms, and Graphics. These components combine to create an easy-to-use application development package.

The easy-to-use Reports tool enables the user to create detailed and complex reports from any Oracle database. You can use Oracle Reports against a Personal Oracle8 database to produce business standard reports quickly and easily. The reports can include embedded graphics and can easily be Web enabled.

Forms is an extremely powerful tool for creating front-end data-input screens. The Forms tool allows the user to create applications very quickly. When this incorporates reports, you can quite easily create and produce a professional application in a relatively short time.

The Graphics tool gives picture representations of data within a database. For example, creating a pie chart from data retrieved from the database is quite easy using Oracle Graphics. If you incorporate this with either Oracle Reports or Oracle Forms, you can build up graphical reports and forms from the database with very little effort.

Object Database Designer

Object Database Designer is aimed at anybody who designs and builds Oracle databases and is specifically helpful when creating object-relational databases, because it includes the ability to use user-defined types within the database model. Once the database model is designed, it can then be automatically implemented, because the Object Database Designer will create the required SQL statements and execute them for you. The advantage of this is that the design is viewed graphically and a change of design can quickly be implemented on the database. The designer is tightly integrated with C++, the most common object-oriented programming language.

THE NEXT STEP

This Introduction gives you an idea of Oracle's history and product line. Now that you know where Personal Oracle is placed in the hierarchy of Oracle software, why not install it? Chapter 1 covers the quick installation of Personal Oracle8.

Quick-Start Installation

This chapter will give the more computer-literate user a fast-track method to install the Personal Oracle8 software and get on with the creation of the demo database. Once you've completed this chapter, you will have installed the standard database (Application Developer option). To install other options—i.e., the Replication option—please refer to Chapter 2. Refer to Chapter 14 for more details on installing to a machine with Personal Oracle7 already installed.

Installing this software could change your career prospects.

HARDWARE AND SOFTWARE REQUIREMENTS

To install Personal Oracle8, you must make sure your system complies with the following minimum hardware and software requirements:

Hardware

Minimum hardware requirements are as follows:

- 32MB RAM for standard installation
- 48MB RAM for installation of the Replication option
- 165MB of available disk space (for the standard installation)
- 200MB of available disk space (for the Replication option)
- A CD-ROM drive

Software

Minimum software requirements are as follows:

- Windows 95 (noncompressed drive)
- A suitable Web browser (to read the online documentation)

INSTALLATION OF SOFTWARE FROM CD-ROM

Insert the CD-ROM into the drive on your computer. This will initiate the Autorun facility of Windows 95 and automatically start up the software. You'll be presented with the window shown in Figure 1.1.

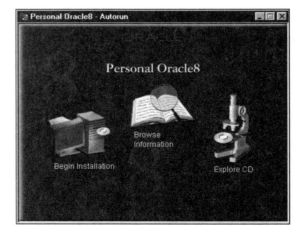

Figure 1.1 *Personal Oracle8 Autorun window.*

Choose the Begin Installation icon. This will execute the Oracle Installer. The Installer will then ask what language you would like the software to be installed with, as shown in Figure 1.2.

Once you've chosen a language and clicked on the OK button, the Installer will prompt you for the installation settings: the company name you wish to register the software under and the directory you want to install the software to, as shown in Figure 1.3. Leaving the default directory at C:\ORAWIN95 is a good idea at this point, as all Oracle products default to this when installed under Windows 95. If you need to change the default directory—if you have other Oracle products installed elsewhere—then click on the folder icon to select a different directory.

When you've selected the installation settings and clicked on the OK button, you'll be presented with the Installation Options screen, shown in Figure 1.4. This is where you decide which type of installation you'll perform. For a quick installation, choose the default (Application Developer). This will install a ready-to-use database and associated tools with the most common options. If you need to install a Runtime or Custom option, read Chapter 2 for guidelines and a discussion of all options available.

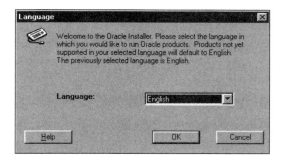

Figure 1.2   *Language window.*

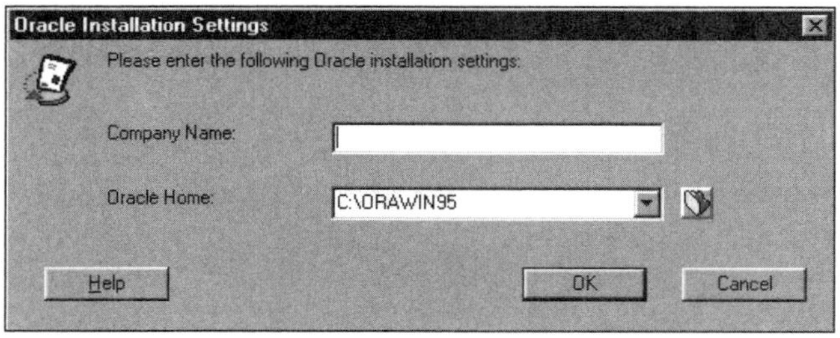

Figure 1.3   *Oracle Installation Settings window.*

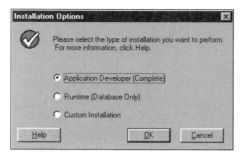

Figure 1.4 *Installation Options window.*

Figure 1.5 *Starter Database Installation Options window.*

Click on the OK button with the default option selected. The Starter Database Installation Options window will be displayed, as shown in Figure 1.5. This selects the type of database to install. For this quick installation, you need a standard database. The installation of the Replication option is covered in Chapter 2.

Once you've clicked on the OK button with the standard database option, the installer will check for other product dependencies. This will be shown on the installer screen with a progress indication bar. After a short time, you'll see the Oracle8 Documentation window shown in Figure 1.6. This is where you choose how to have the documentation installed. The answer here will depend upon how much free disk space you have. The minimum disk space requirement includes the documentation being installed locally on your hard disk drive. If space is at a premium, select the CD-ROM option. This requires that you load the CD-ROM every time you need to access the documentation.

Select the appropriate option and click on the OK button. The Installer will once again analyze the dependencies, and the installation will begin. This may take some time, depending largely on the speed of your CD-ROM drive. The progress indication bar will gradually increase toward 100 percent. The Installer, at this point, is copying the files from the CD-ROM to your hard disk. Other tasks performed by the Installer are as follows:

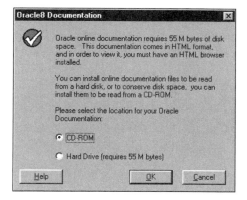

Figure 1.6 *Oracle8 Documentation window.*

- Creates icons on your desktop.

- Installs and creates the starter database.

- Installs the documentation (if selected) to your hard disk.

- Registers the application.

The above tasks are performed automatically. You'll see messages above and below the progress indicator explaining what the Installer is doing. Once the installation is complete, you'll receive a message that the installation was successful, as shown in Figure 1.7.

At this point, you have a working copy of Personal Oracle8. Click on the OK button to exit the Installer. You'll be presented with your Windows 95 desktop, with two new folders: Oracle for Windows 95 and Personal Oracle8 for Windows 95.

The Oracle for Windows 95 folder, shown in Figure 1.8, contains all of the software installed that is common across all Oracle products on Windows 95.

Among the many items created in this folder, the Oracle Installer, documentation, and release notes are some of the most useful.

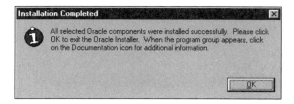

Figure 1.7 *Installation Completed window.*

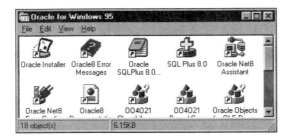

Figure 1.8   *Oracle for Windows 95 folder.*

The Personal Oracle8 for Windows 95 folder, shown in Figure 1.9, contains all the Personal Oracle8 programs and documentation. With the version I am using (V8.0.3.0.0), seven icons are created, which I discuss in the next section.

- Oracle8 Navigator

- Personal Oracle8 Help

- Personal Oracle8 Release Notes

- Start Database

- Stop Database

- The Backup Manager

- The Recovery Manager

Overview Of Personal Oracle8 Icons

Once your software is installed, various icons will appear on your desktop and Start menu bar. The following sections give you an overview of these icons and what they are used for.

Figure 1.9   *Personal Oracle8 for Windows 95 folder.*

Oracle8 Navigator

The Navigator is the graphical user interface tool used to manage and display projects, local database objects, and connections to remote databases. You will use this tool in all aspects of developing the demo database, from creating users and roles to populating tables within the database. The Navigator performs a similar function to the Windows 95 Explorer. If you click on the Personal Oracle8 folder, it will expand to show projects and the local database, as shown in Figure 1.10. Projects are used to store project-related information—i.e., all objects related to products. Projects can also be used to store external files—e.g., reports or spreadsheets. The Navigator is discussed in more detail in later chapters.

Personal Oracle8 Help

This icon will display the Personal Oracle8 help screen. The help file is a standard Windows 95 type of help function. You can choose to look through the contents, an index, or to search for words.

Personal Oracle8 Release Notes

The release notes are the latest information available about Personal Oracle8, including bug fixes and known problems. These may be different on later versions of the software. It is a good idea to look at the release notes right after installation.

Start Database

Use this icon to start the database. When you've finished the installation, the database will be stopped. Your first job is to start the database by double-clicking on this icon. Numerous

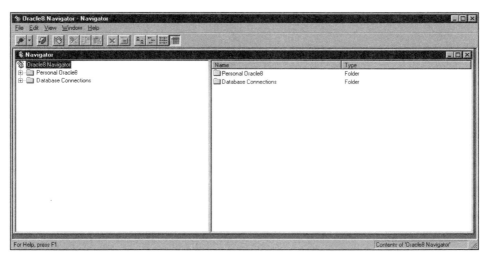

Figure 1.10 *Oracle8 Navigator window.*

messages will appear on the screen, indicating the state of the database. The last message should say "Oracle8 database started successfully." Once this appears, click on the OK button. You'll also notice that a small icon appears on the task bar, showing that the database is running.

Stop Database

Use this icon to stop the database. You should stop it before you shut down your PC to reduce the chance of corruption to the database. You can stop the database in two ways: Click on Start|Programs|Personal Oracle8 for Windows 95|Stop Database, or right-click on the icon on the task bar and then click on the Oracle8 Shutdown option.

The Backup Manager

Use this tool to back up your Personal Oracle8 database. It gives you the option to back up the whole database to disk or tape (if available). I'll fully discuss other available backup strategies in Chapter 15.

The Recovery Manager

The Recovery Manager is used to recover a corrupt database from a previous backup. This program allows various options for recovery. Again, these are discussed fully in Chapter 15.

A DETAILED EXPLANATION

Now that you've used the quick route to install Oracle8, you may want to know more about the options and potential problems involved in the procedure. For a detailed explanation of the installation process, see Chapter 2. If you need to install the other options available with Personal Oracle8 —i.e., replication—also see Chapter 2. Or skip to Chapter 3, where you'll create your first database.

DETAILED START INSTALLATION

Getting the most out of your installation session with the Oracle Installer and Personal Oracle8.

In Chapter 1, I provided a quick trip through the installation process. In this chapter, I'll delve into the issues discussed in Chapter 1 and discuss some of the side issues involved in the installation process. I'll explain the procedure in detail, give you some tips and warnings, and tell you about various options.

INSTALLATION OVERVIEW

This chapter will explain two common ways to install Personal Oracle8 software: from a CD-ROM or downloaded from the Oracle site on the World Wide Web. The installation procedure is very similar for both types of products.

Once the CD-ROM is inserted into the drive or downloaded from the Web, the startup screen will appear. This screen gives you three options:

- Begin the installation.
- Browse the documentation.
- Explore the Personal Oracle8 CD-ROM.

In this chapter, I'll explain what each option entails. The main objective of this chapter is to make you aware of all available options for the installation of Personal Oracle8.

Before You Install

Before you can install the software, you must do the following to ensure an easy and error-free installation of Personal Oracle8:

- *Read the hard-copy release notes*—These notes can contain information that was discovered too late to implement on the CD-ROM; thus, it is the most up-to-date information available for Personal Oracle8. (The release notes are not available if you download a trial copy from the Web.) Although you will not need most of the information in the release notes, in some cases, you'll find them quite useful. The release notes I received, for example, explain how to enable the two-phase commit in a Windows 95 installation. This piece of information would be invaluable if you were to install Personal Oracle8 so other people could connect to your database. The third-party user would not function correctly without a two-phase commit in place.

- *Read the HTML release notes*—Once you've read the hard-copy release notes, read the release notes on the CD-ROM, usually found in the D:\Doc\Relnote directory (if you're using a Web browser). The HTML release notes can sometimes be different from the hard-copy release notes.

- *Check if a previous version of Personal Oracle exists on the machine you are using*—If this is the case, refer to Chapter 14.

HARDWARE AND SOFTWARE REQUIREMENTS

Before you can install your copy of Personal Oracle8, you must ensure your system meets the following minimum specifications.

Hardware Requirements

Minimum hardware requirements are as follows:

- 100-percent IBM-compatible PC with a Pentium processor
- CD-ROM drive (16-speed preferred)
- Network card (optional, only for use with the distributed features)
- Free hard-disk space (see the "Disk Space Requirements" section, below)
- 32MB of RAM (starter database) or 48MB of RAM (Replication option)

Software Requirements

Minimum software requirements are as follows:

* Microsoft Windows 95

* A Web browser to view the Oracle online documentation (Microsoft Internet Explorer or Netscape Navigator is recommended)

* A network protocol installed (if you wish to use the distributed features)—either TCP/IP, SPX, or Named Pipes

Disk Space Requirements

When installing Personal Oracle8, choices you make along the way will determine which sort of installation is performed and may change the disk space requirements. Table 2.1 presents the available choices and the relevant disk space needed for each.

As Table 2.1 shows, Runtime and Application Developer installations are straightforward, but a custom installation can be very large. A custom installation is performed through the Oracle Installer, where you choose exactly which modules you need (i.e., you can install the database, but not the tools). This chapter will include an explanation of all available products for installation from the CD-ROM.

You can install the online documentation on your hard disk drive. This option, which requires an additional 55MB of space, is available during the installation.

One of the main limitations on installing Personal Oracle8 on Windows 95 is the use of compressed drives. Personal Oracle8 will not perform well, if at all, on compressed drives. Personal Oracle8 does not support a database being installed on a compressed drive. The software can be installed to a compressed drive, but not the database. If you try to install the software to a compressed drive, the Installer will ask you to install the database to a non-compressed area. If all drives are compressed, I suggest either buying a larger drive or removing some software and uncompressing the drive. Refer to the instructions for your

Table 2.1   *Disk space requirements.*

Installation Type	Disk Space Required (MB)
Runtime (standard database)	75
Application Developer (standard database)	109
Runtime (replication database)	110
Application Developer (replication database)	144
Custom	393 (maximum)

disk-compression tools for either removing disk compression or freeing up more non-compressed space. You'll need at least 20MB of uncompressed free space to install the starter database; this rises to 40MB for the replication database.

Personal Oracle8 for Windows 95 will require about 20MB of free disk space on the drive where the Windows 95 Virtual Memory page file is located (usually on the C: drive). This space is required in addition to the space needed for Personal Oracle8 program files.

INSTALLATION FROM CD-ROM

Before installing Personal Oracle8 from a CD-ROM, ensure that no other software is running. This may cause problems with your installation. Inserting the CD-ROM will use the Autorun facility of Windows 95 and automatically start up the software. You'll be presented with a window giving you the option to install the software, view the documentation, or explore the CD-ROM.

Choose the Begin Installation icon. Doing so will execute the Oracle Installer, which will ask what language you require the software to be installed with. If you choose a language that is not supported, the software will default to English. If you later install another Oracle product and change the language installed, all existing products will be left with the original language. If you wish to change the installed language, you'll need to reinstall the product.

Once you've chosen a language and clicked on the OK button, the Installer will prompt you for the installation settings: the company name you wish to register the software under and the directory you want to install the software to. The company information is stored within the Installer and used for licensing information. Leaving the default directory at C:\ORAWIN95 is a good idea at this point, as all Oracle products default to this directory when installed under Windows 95. If you do need to change the default directory (if you have other Oracle products installed elsewhere), click on the folder icon to select a different directory.

When you've selected the installation settings and clicked on the OK button, you'll be presented with the Installation Options screen. This is where you decide which type of installation you will perform. For a quick installation, choose the default (Application Developer). This will install a ready-to-use database and all associated tools with the most commonly used options. The products installed are as follows:

- Personal Oracle8
- Oracle8 Navigator
- Oracle8 Utilities

- Oracle Net8 Assistant
- Oracle Net8 Add-on
- Oracle Net8 Client
- SQL*Plus
- Oracle Call Interface
- Oracle Objects for OLE
- Oracle8 ODBC Driver
- Oracle8 Documentation
- Personal Oracle8 Release Notes
- Assistant Common Files
- Oracle Trace Collection Services
- Java Runtime Environment
- Oracle Installer
- Oracle Data Migration Assistant (installed only if a Personal Oracle7 database already exists)
- Oracle Migration Assistant for Microsoft Access
- Required Support Files

Although you may never use some of these products, this is the best installation route for the novice user. Once you become more advanced and wish to add other products from the CD-ROM, you can execute the Oracle Installer to do so.

If you need to install the Runtime option, the number of products installed will be considerably less, therefore consuming less disk space (as shown previously in Table 2.1). The Runtime option installs the following products:

- Personal Oracle8
- Assistant Common Files
- Oracle8 Utilities
- Oracle Trace Collection Services
- Java Runtime Environment
- Personal Oracle8 Release Notes

- Oracle Data Migration Assistant
- Required Support Files
- Oracle Net8 Add-on
- Oracle Net8 Client

Notice that this list includes no development products—e.g., Oracle Objects or Oracle ODBC Driver. You can install these later using the Oracle Installer.

If you choose the Custom option, the Oracle Installer is started immediately. (Read the section in this chapter on using the Oracle Installer, which will allow you to continue with your installation. The following information on installing Personal Oracle8 does not apply to a custom installation.) The Installer lists all of the products available for installation. The full list of available products is the same as for the Application Developer installation, with the addition of the following products:

- Oracle Client Configuration Manager
- Oracle Client Software Agent
- Oracle Net8 Protocol Adapters
- Oracle Protocol Adapters
- Oracle7 Utilities
- SQL*Net Add-on (patch)
- SQL*Net Client

Once you've selected which option to install, click on the OK button. The Starter Database Installation Options window will be displayed. You have three options:

- *Standard*—This will automatically install and configure a database for normal use. With this type of database, you can receive read-only snapshots of data from a master database to use on your Personal Oracle8 database (see Figure 2.1). This is the default installation.

- *Replication*—This will automatically install and configure a database for use with replication. The Replication option allows for the use of updatable snapshots from a master Oracle database (see Figure 2.2). This gives the user a two-way interface to a master database. The use of snapshots will be explained later in this book. If you're an advanced Oracle user, this is the database to install.

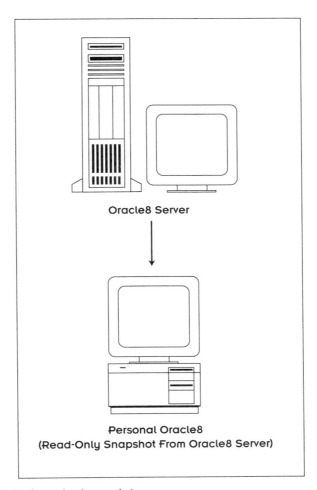

Oracle8 Server

Personal Oracle8
(Read-Only Snapshot From Oracle8 Server)

Figure 2.1 *An example of a read-only snapshot.*

- *None*—This option installs the software only, without creating a database automatically. This is useful if you wish to create your database separately—i.e., on a different drive or spread across several disks. For further discussion of the Replication option, see the "Options For Installation: Replication" section later in this chapter.

Once you've clicked on the OK button, the Installer will check for other product dependencies, shown on the Installer screen with a progress indication bar. After a short time, the Oracle8 Documentation window is displayed. This is where you choose how to install the documentation. Your answer will depend upon how much free disk space you have. If space is at a premium, select the CD-ROM option. This means you must load the CD-ROM every time you need to access the documentation.

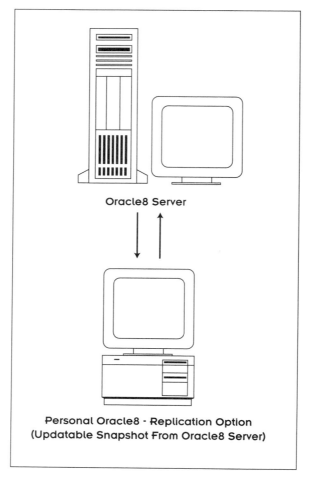

Oracle8 Server

**Personal Oracle8 - Replication Option
(Updatable Snapshot From Oracle8 Server)**

Figure 2.2 *An example of an updatable snapshot.*

Select the appropriate option and click on the OK button. The Installer will once again analyze the dependencies, and the installation will begin. This may take some time, depending largely on the speed of your CD-ROM drive. The progress indication bar will gradually increase toward 100 percent. At this point, the Installer is copying the files from the CD-ROM to your hard disk. Other tasks performed by the Installer are as follows:

- Creates icons on your desktop.

- Installs and creates the starter database.

- Installs the documentation (if selected) to your hard disk.

- Registers the application.

These tasks are performed automatically. You'll see messages above and below the progress indicator explaining what the Installer is doing. Once finished, the Installer will give you a message stating the installation was successful.

At this point, you have a working copy of Personal Oracle8. Click on the OK button to exit the Installer. You'll be presented with two new folders on your Windows 95 desktop:

- *Oracle for Windows 95 folder*—Contains all of the software installed that is common across all Oracle products on Windows 95. Among the most useful items in this folder are the Oracle Installer, documentation, and release notes.

- *Personal Oracle8 for Windows 95 folder*—Contains all the Personal Oracle8 programs and documentation.

Take time now to look at the Personal Oracle8 release notes, which will give you up-to-date information on any known problems or limitations of the software. The release notes also contain any information just released, which was not included on the Web browser documentation.

INSTALLATION FROM THE WEB

Many sites on the Web offer trial software, and Oracle's site is no exception. In fact, most of Oracle's software can be downloaded (on a 60-day trial basis) from its Web site (**www.oracle.com**). Personal Oracle8 can also be downloaded, in one of two forms:

- *One large file*—If you choose this option, once the program is downloaded (which could take some time), you're left with an executable file (which is compressed). Once executed, this file will automatically uncompress itself, giving you many files. One of these files will be called setup.exe.

- *Several small files*—If you choose this option, which gives you about 46 small files, you're presented with a file called runme.bat. Once this file is executed, it will uncompress all of the other downloaded files, giving you a setup.exe file, among others.

Once you execute the setup.exe file, you're given the 60-day trial license information. Click on OK to continue. This then gives you the language-information window. (This may sound familiar if you've read the beginning of this chapter.) From here, the installation is exactly the same as that of the CD-ROM. In fact, the Web-downloaded version is really a compressed copy of the CD-ROM.

OPTIONS FOR INSTALLATION: REPLICATION

According to the online documentation, "Replication is the process of copying and maintaining database objects in multiple databases that make up a distributed database system. Replication can improve the performance and protect the availability of applications because alternate data access options exist. For example, an application might normally access a local database rather than a remote server to minimize network traffic and achieve maximum performance. Furthermore, the application can continue to function if the local server experiences a failure, but other servers with replicated data remain accessible. Oracle Server supports two different forms of replication: basic and advanced replication."

The basic form of replication allows you to use read-only snapshots from a server, which is useful for minimizing network traffic, as the queries can be performed against the local machine without accessing the remote server. This is performed by using *read-only table snapshots* (i.e., snapshots taken from the remote server and downloaded to the local database). Users can then access, but cannot change, this data. If a change is needed, the user must change the server data. Then, the server can propagate the changes to the local environment, but again receives a read-only table snapshot.

The advanced form of replication is the same as basic replication, but with the added ability to update the local database. This then propagates the changes to the remote server automatically. Advanced replication, which has many different configurations, is complicated to maintain. Keep in mind that a change on a local database will have to change on all other databases in the replication chain.

WHAT'S ON THE CD-ROM?

The CD-ROM for Personal Oracle8 includes a number of products for a number of different operating systems. You're allowed to use only those for which you have licenses. This section describes these products.

As you recall, when you insert the CD-ROM into the drive, you see a window giving you the option to begin the installation, browse the documentation, or explore the Personal Oracle8 CD-ROM. When you choose the third option, you're presented with a number of folders. As you're probably aware, a CD-ROM can contain thousands of files. I'll discuss only the top-level directories here (see Figure 2.3) and leave it to you to search through and explore these folders more deeply.

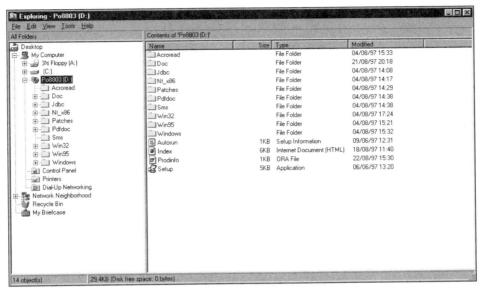

Figure 2.3 *An example of exploring the CD-ROM.*

Exploring The CD-ROM

Acroread

Inside this folder, you'll find one file—Ar32e30—which is a self-extracting installation file for the Adobe Acrobat reader. It is used in conjunction with the help documentation. Adobe Acrobat reads PDF files, which can be found all over the CD-ROM.

Doc

This directory contains all of the online HTML documentation for Personal Oracle8, as well as more information for the Oracle8 server. These are the files installed when you choose to put the documentation on your hard disk.

JDBC

Inside this folder are the JDBC (Java DataBase Connectivity) libraries, which enable Java programs to access the Oracle8 database. Three drivers are available: one for Oracle7 clients, one for Oracle8 clients, and one for applets.

Nt_x86

This folder contains products for the Windows NT installation.

Patches

On the version I am using, two patches are available in this folder. The first—380655—is to correct a Forms V4 compatibility problem. The second—232111—is a SQL*Net patch. For full details, refer to the documentation.

Pdfdoc

This folder contains Oracle's first release of the server documentation in Adobe Acrobat reader format. It is extremely useful, as it is fully searchable. This folder also gives you information on other Oracle products, such as Oracle Video Server.

SMS

The SMS folder includes all of the files needed to distribute the Oracle software using Microsoft's SMS server. For more details, see the README file in this directory.

Win32

Win32 contains all of the software available for installation on a 32-bit operating system. In this directory, you'll find the software you need to install for a Windows 95 implementation. The Oracle Installer reads the PRD file in the Install directory, then installs your selected products from within this folder.

Win95

Some extra installable functions for the Windows 95 implementation are available in the Win95 folder, including the executables for starting/stopping the database and the recovery and backup managers.

Windows

This folder contains all the files for installation on a Windows 3.1 operating system. If you decide to install the Oracle7 client, this directory contains all of the needed information.

Product Descriptions

Java Runtime Environment

The Java Runtime Environment (JRE) is the minimum standard Java platform for running Java programs. It is made up of the following products:

- Java Virtual Machine
- Java core classes
- Supporting files

JRE gives you the environment for executing Java programs. This standard is a prerequisite for any Java development with Personal Oracle8.

Oracle Call Interface

The Oracle Call Interface (OCI) provides programmers with a library of standard database access functions, for use with third-generation languages. This allows third-generation languages, such as COBOL, to access an Oracle8 database without embedding PL/SQL into the code.

Oracle Client Configuration Manager

If you have a network, the Oracle Client Configuration Manager allows you to keep client configurations up to date with new software. It acts as the server, updating any machine with the client agent installed.

Oracle Client Software Agent

The Oracle Client Software Agent sits on the networked PC. It checks what Oracle software is installed on your machine and receives software from the Client Configuration Manager. The Client Software Agent is required for the distribution of software using the Client Software Manager.

Oracle Data Migration Assistant

This is the software that eases the transition between Personal Oracle7 and Personal Oracle8. The migration guide is a good place to discover exactly how this software is used.

Oracle Installer

The Oracle Installer is the software that installs any Oracle product. Detailed instructions for its use are included later in this chapter.

Oracle Migration Assistant For Microsoft Access

This software makes the transition between Microsoft Access and Personal Oracle8 easier. Refer to the migration guide for information about how to use this piece of software.

Oracle Net8

Oracle Net8, which allows Oracle databases to communicate with each other, is required if you use Personal Oracle8 with the Replication option or if you connect your Personal Oracle8 database to any other Oracle database. Products included with Oracle Net8 are Net8 Add-on, Net8 Assistant, and Net8 Protocol. The Net8 Add-on allows Personal Oracle8 to participate in a two-phase commit transaction. The Net8 Assistant helps you configure and administer your Oracle networking files. The Net8 Protocol Adapters allow for the Net8 software to communicate across different network implementations.

Oracle Objects For OLE

Oracle Objects for OLE is a suite of objects that allow for communication between Oracle databases and applications that understand Visual Basic custom controls or OLE automation.

Oracle Protocol Adapters

The Protocol Adapters allow Oracle SQL*Net (version 2.3.3) to communicate across different network implementations. This is mainly for Personal Oracle7 databases running on a Windows 3.1 platform.

Oracle7 Utilities

This software provides a command-line-based utility for use with the database. It can be used for connecting to and administering an Oracle7 database.

Oracle8 Documentation

This is the CD-ROM documentation. If you wish, you can install this separately; it will take up to 55MB of disk space. You need a Web browser to access the documentation.

Oracle8 Navigator

This GUI tool manages and displays projects, local database objects, and connections to remote databases. We will use this tool in all aspects of developing this book's demo database, from creating users and roles to populating tables within the database. The Navigator performs a similar function to Windows 95 Explorer. The online help file takes the format of standard Windows 95 help files.

Oracle8 ODBC Driver

The ODBC (open database connectivity) driver allows other databases to connect and communicate with Personal Oracle8. You need this driver so Personal Oracle8 can interface with other applications, such as Microsoft Access.

Personal Oracle8

This is the actual database and associated tools for Personal Oracle8. It consists of two parts:

- *Oracle8 DBMS*—The actual database, installed automatically when selected in the default installation.

- *Oracle8 Utilities*—Includes such products as Oracle Backup Manager and Oracle Recovery Manager.

Personal Oracle8 Release Notes

You should read the release notes before installing any of the products available on the CD-ROM. These notes contain the latest information on the product being installed.

Required Support Files

On the CD-ROM, you'll find several support files that are automatically installed with any product you choose. The Installer installs the files when it is checking out product dependencies. The support files should not be installed separately, unless specified by an Oracle error message.

SQL*Net Add-On

This patch allows Personal Oracle7 to take part in a two-phase commit transaction.

SQL*Net Client

This software communicates between the network and a Personal Oracle7 database. It cannot be used to connect to a Personal Oracle8 database. For that you need Oracle Net8, described previously in this section.

SQL*Plus

SQL*Plus is the command-line interface for using SQL. This is a common standard among all relational databases.

USING THE ORACLE INSTALLER

The Oracle Installer allows you to complete the following tasks:

- Install Oracle products
- Remove Oracle products

- Find space requirements
- Restore desktop icons

When you insert the Personal Oracle8 CD-ROM into your computer, the Installer will be automatically installed as the first program. It will guide you through the installation of Personal Oracle8.

If you wish to add Oracle software, you can do so through the Installer. To activate the Installer from the Windows 95 task bar, independently of the standard installation, follow these instructions: Click on Start|Programs|Oracle for Windows 95|Oracle Installer. You'll see a screen that looks like Figure 2.4.

The Installer displays the available products on the left-hand side and the currently installed products on the right-hand side. The other windows offer information on the products being installed/removed. The Oracle Installer's various functions are detailed below.

From... Button

You use the From... button to access the drive from which the Oracle software is being installed. The software looks for a PRD file, which lists all the software available for installation

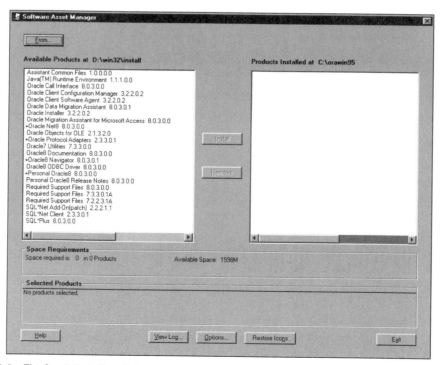

Figure 2.4 *The Oracle Installer window.*

from the medium, usually a CD-ROM. If a PRD file is not found, a dialog box appears directing you to do a search for a PRD file. If none exists, you have no available products to install through the Installer. If this is the case, refer to your installation instructions for the product being installed. The PRD files are usually found in the Install directory.

A PRD file takes one of the following forms:

- *WINDOWS.PRD*—For a Windows 3.1 installation
- *WIN95.PRD*—For a Windows 95 installation
- *NT.PRD*—For a Windows NT installation

The Oracle Installer will search for only the appropriate PRD file. This is determined by the platform the Installer is executing on.

Products Available Window

Once you've found the PRD file, you'll see the Products Available window. It displays the products listed in the PRD file as being available on the CD. Some will be preceded by a plus sign (+), meaning that those products are made up of a group of other products. To see these other products, double-click on the product itself and the list will expand. The + has now changed to a minus sign (-). Clicking on the product now will collapse the list.

You can select products to install in a number of ways. If you want to install only one product, click on the product once to highlight it, then click on the Install button. If you need multiple products, and if they are all in a group, hold down the Shift key, click on the first in the group, then on the last in the group. This will highlight all products in between. Next, click on the Install button. If you need to install several products that are not in one group, hold down the Ctrl key and click on the required products. Finally, click on the Install button.

Products Installed Window

This window shows you which products are already installed on your system. You also use this window to uninstall products. To uninstall any product, select the product, in the same way as described in the previous paragraph. Then click on the Remove button. You may see a prompt asking if you wish to remove any shared products. You should answer no unless you're uninstalling everything from your PC.

Install/Remove Buttons

As described in the previous two paragraphs, the Install and Remove buttons are for installing and removing software from your PC. This is done by selecting from the Products Installed or Products Available windows the products you wish to install or remove.

Space Requirements Window

This area of the Oracle Installer shows the disk space required to install the selected product(s). Clicking on one of the products in the Products Available window will display the disk space required to install that product. If you select multiple products, the display shows the cumulative disk space required for installation. This area also shows the available space on the drive where your Oracle products are installed. If the selected products will use more disk space than is available, the Installer will not allow you to install the products until you deselect some to decrease the cumulative disk space required to less than the available space.

Selected Products Window

This window displays brief information for the product selected for installation/uninstallation. If multiple products are selected, the window displays multiple lines. This window is fully scrollable, so you can see the full descriptions.

Help Button

The Help button does exactly what it says: displays the help information. The help information is in the form of a window. When you click on the area of help required in the top half of the window, the help information is displayed in the bottom half. The information found using the Help button can also be found in the Help window.

View Log... Button

Clicking on the View Log... button displays the Log View window, which shows the information logged to a file while you are installing/uninstalling products. This window displays three levels of detail: summary, brief, and detailed. The log file is searchable. Just enter your search text in the box provided and click on the Search button. The results will appear in the Current Log File window.

Options... Button

Clicking on the Options... button displays the Options window. A number of options are available when using the Oracle Installer:

- *Display Before Installing*—This displays a warning message before installing any product to your hard drive. The default is to install automatically to your hard drive without prompting.

- *Display Before Removing*—This option is automatically selected. It displays a warning message before the removal of any product.

- *Display Additional Message Prompt*—This will display any additional messages while you are installing or uninstalling Oracle software. Even if this option is not selected, any messages that warn of unusual occurrences will still be displayed.

- *Log Installer Actions*—Check this box if you want the Installer to log all of its actions or if you are experiencing problems with an installation. This box is normally left unchecked to increase performance when installing. The log file created is called ORAINST.LOG. You can view this file using the View Log... button.

- *Remember Location Of Available Products*—This option is automatically selected. It allows the Oracle Installer to remember where the last PRD file was. On startup, the Installer will automatically scan this directory for a PRD file.

To select or deselect any of these options, just click on the box alongside the option you need. This will either clear it of a tick mark or place a tick mark in the box. Click on the OK button to keep the changes or the Cancel button to discard the changes.

Restore Icons Button

This useful function of the Installer restores all Oracle product icons that have accidentally been deleted.

Exit Button

This button does exactly what it says. It exits from the Oracle Installer, first asking if you really want to exit.

WHAT IS INSTALLED WHERE AND WHY?

When you install Personal Oracle8 from the CD-ROM, the Installer creates a directory structure on your hard disk (normally, the C: drive). This is the Oracle home directory and is usually, on Windows 95 implementations, called ORAWIN95.

If you read the previous section on exploring the CD-ROM, you know that the Installer has helped to create the contents of the CD-ROM on your hard drive. You should be aware of a few directories in ORAWIN95:

- *Bin*—This is the main directory below ORAWIN95. It contains all of the Oracle executables you see on your desktop—i.e., Oracle Navigator, Import and Export, among others. The Installer automatically adds this important directory to the PC's path environment variable. If you delete any files from this directory, you'll have to reinstall the product.

- *Database*—This is the next major directory. As its name suggests, this is where the default database is created. This directory can be very large, as the files that make up a database can be anywhere from 5K to the size of your hard disk. Do not delete any of these files. If you do, you will have a corrupt database. I recommend creating a directory in another location to store the database. Database and application tuning will be discussed later in this book.

- *Doc*—This directory contains all of the online documentation for Personal Oracle8, if you installed it to your hard disk. This is useful if you wish to look at any information from within a Web browser without going through the Start menu.

The ORAWIN95 directory has many more subdirectories. Looking through these directories and searching for help files or README files often provides more up-to-date information on the products installed.

HINTS AND TIPS

Problems To Watch For

At the time of this writing, there were a few known problems with the Personal Oracle8 software. These are listed in this section. For a more up-to-date listing of problems and bugs, refer to Oracle's Web site (**www.oracle.com**).

Universal Naming Conventions

One of the advantages of Windows 95 is that you can use long file and directory names. At the time of writing, however, these long names cannot be used with Personal Oracle8. This has two implications:

- You must stick with the DOS naming conventions—a maximum of eight characters for the file name and three characters for the file-name extension.

- You must not use the // notation to represent the start of a directory.

Coexistence Of Oracle Databases

You cannot have more than one version of the Oracle database software on your machine at any one time. This means you cannot have Personal Oracle7 installed in C:\ORAWIN and Personal Oracle8 installed in C:\ORAWIN95.

Oracle8 Navigator Date Limitation

The Personal Oracle8 Navigator is limited to dates with 16 characters or fewer.

Oracle Online Documentation

You cannot view the online documentation with a 16-bit browser, such as Netscape Navigator for Windows 3.1. You'll have to use a 32-bit operating system browser to view the documentation. Again, I recommend the use of either Microsoft Internet Explorer or Netscape Navigator.

"Cannot Find BROWSE95" Error

When you access the online documentation you may receive the error message, "Cannot find BROWSE95". This error occurs if you've previously installed Oracle Power Browser on your system. To solve this problem, reinstall the browser you wish to view the documentation with.

Enabling The Two-Phase Commit

When a database is started, it does not automatically configure itself for use with the two-phase commit. This is a distributed feature, which allows any incoming connections to use a two-phase commit. To enable this, first click on the Start button, then the Run button. Next, type "oraconct on". This will enable the two-phase commit. To disable the two-phase commit, follow the same procedure, but type "oraconct off".

Multiple Versions Of SQL*Plus

Multiple versions of SQL*Plus can exist on the same machine. When SQL*Plus version 8.0.3.0.0 (which comes with Personal Oracle8) is installed, it does not remove any other versions. (You may delete other versions of the SQL*Plus software if you wish.)

Switching Between Oracle Homes

In previous versions of Personal Oracle, the software allowed for the switching of Oracle homes so the software could be installed in two different directories (for example, if you have two copies of the software). This feature is not supported on Personal Oracle8 for Windows 95.

16-Bit Client Support

Version 8.0.3 of Oracle networking products does not support a 16-bit client. You can, however, connect to a Personal Oracle8 database from a 16-bit client using a 16-bit version of SQL*Net (versions 2.2 and 2.3). The disadvantage is that no Oracle8 features are available through the 16-bit client.

Memory Leak

At the time of this writing, Personal Oracle8 was leaking memory, but don't worry, it isn't much—only 10K per connection to the database. According to Oracle, "This appears to be caused by a bug in Windows 95 where thread local storage is not properly cleaned up", (whatever that means). Nonetheless, this is only a small problem and not one a developer should worry about. If you have a lot of connections into your Personal Oracle8 database, you should periodically close down and restart the database to correct the problem.

Virtual Memory

The Personal Oracle8 database has a high requirement for memory. For this reason, it uses *virtual memory*—disk space that is used as memory. Sometimes, when virtual memory becomes sparse, Personal Oracle8 starts acting strangely. If you think this is a problem on your machine, do the following:

* Make sure virtual memory is enabled. You can check this through the system icon in the control panel on Windows 95.

* Check that you have some disk space available on the drive that the Windows 95 swap file (virtual memory) is installed on.

No real guidelines exist for how much virtual memory is needed to run Personal Oracle8. Of course, the more memory you have available, the better. If you're short of memory, the best way to free up more is to close down other applications that are executing while you're using Personal Oracle8. You'll know if you have problems with memory when you get the following error numbers when starting or using the database: ORA-09352 or ORA-09242.

The Personal Oracle8 software usually needs about 12 to 16MB of free virtual memory to start or stop the database.

WHAT HAVE YOU LEARNED?

In this chapter, you discovered the contents of the CD-ROM and how they relate to the product you just installed: Personal Oracle8. This chapter has given you the necessary knowledge to install any Oracle product. You can now move to the next chapter, Chapter 3, which explains the concept of a relational database and shows you how to design your own Personal Oracle8 database from the beginning.

CREATING YOUR FIRST DATABASE

CHAPTER 3

To allow you to become as productive as possible with Personal Oracle8, I'll take you straight into the creation of a demo database. This chapter will guide you through the practicalities of creating objects within a database. The database you create will be very basic. Later in the book, you'll enhance the database with added functionality. For a detailed discussion of the theory behind the practice, read Chapter 4 on relational theory.

Before you can create your first database, you need to know some basic database administration skills—i.e., how to start up and shut down the database. You also need to know how to use the Personal Oracle8 Navigator. I'll explain these skills in this chapter. Once you've learned the basics, creating objects through the Navigator will be simple. This chapter will also describe, in detail, how to create your first objects.

Now is the time to create your first database. It's not as difficult as everybody makes out, so enjoy it.

DATABASE ADMINISTRATION TOOLS

You must be aware of certain procedures when using a Personal Oracle8 database. One of the first habits you should learn is shutting down the database before turning off your PC. The database is really just a set of files. The startup and shutdown options update the files with any changes you've made to their structure. For example, if you add a tablespace to your database, the database needs to know this when it is next started up. It reads this information from a *control file*, which is used, as its name suggests, to control the database. When the database starts up, it reads the control file to see which files are a part of the database. It does a lot of other processing as well, all of which is detailed in Chapter 17. For now, all you need to be aware of is how to start and stop the database.

Starting The Database

Once you've created the database, you can start it in two ways—either from the Start menu or through the Oracle8 Navigator.

To start a database from the Start menu, click on Start|Programs|Personal Oracle8 for Windows 95|Start Database. You'll see several consecutive messages on the screen:

- Starting Up Database
- Checking Security...
- Oracle8 Instance Started
- Database Mounted
- Oracle8 Database Started Successfully

Your other option for starting up the database is through the Navigator. All you have to do is try to access the database; as soon as you click on the database icon, it will automatically start itself up.

Stopping The Database

You also have two choices for stopping the database, which you should do before you turn your machine off. You can again access Start|Programs|Personal Oracle8 for Windows 95|Stop Database. The following messages should appear consecutively to indicate a successful shutdown:

- Checking Security...
- Shutting Down Database
- Database Dismounted
- Oracle8 Database Is Shutdown

You can also shut down the database by using the small icon on your task bar. If you move the mouse over the icon and right-click, the menu that appears has one option—Oracle8 Shutdown. If you left-click on this option, your database will shut down.

THE NAVIGATOR

The Oracle8 Navigator is the tool you'll use to get the most out of Personal Oracle8. The Oracle Navigator is similar to the Windows 95 Navigator, so you should find it easy to use. You'll use the Oracle8 Navigator to display information about your database—for example, which tables/views/indexes etc. have been created, who owns them, and who has privileges to use them (see Figure 3.1).

You can also use the Navigator to create tables, views, indexes, etc., through the use of wizards. In addition, the Navigator implements *projects*, a way of grouping information together, equivalent to a schema. This section provides a brief description of these areas of the Oracle8 Navigator. I will cover more of the Navigator's functionality as the book progresses.

Projects

Think of projects as folders for storing all related information. A folder can contain any database objects that are associated with each other. For example, if you had two tables that were used in the same application, you could store them as part of a project—the project would be the application. These database items are all located on the local database. A project can contain any database objects—tables, views, or sequences. Also, only in Personal Oracle8,

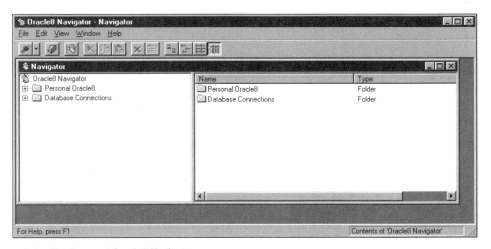

Figure 3.1   *The Personal Oracle8 Navigator.*

a project can contain pointers to other files on your system. For example, you could have an application in the database that stores contract information; you could store pointers to word processing files or spreadsheet information. These objects are what you use to store and organize the data related to your project.

Within a project, you can create, modify, and delete any database object. You have the option to delete from the project only or from the database.

Local Database

The local database is the one situated on your PC—i.e., your local machine. If you click on this icon, as mentioned previously, the Navigator will start the database automatically. You cannot shut down your database through the Navigator.

You will notice a socket-like icon over the local database icon when you have a session connected. This will happen automatically when you click on the local database. Doing so connects you to the database and enables you to view, create, and delete database objects. You'll see a list of object types under the local database. In creating your first database, you'll use some of the more important objects:

- Tables
- Views
- Sequences
- Users
- Roles

Database Connections

The database connections selection on the Navigator window is the part of the Navigator that controls the connections to your local and remote databases, using Oracle's Net8 product (discussed in detail in later chapters). You can create any number of connections to local or remote databases. You can have more than one user connected at any one time. This is a convenient way to organize your users.

THE DEMO DATABASE

By the end of this chapter, you will have created a demo database. This database will be a fairly basic stock-control/order-entry system (such systems lend themselves nicely to object-relational databases). You'll develop the database as you progress through the book.

Database Diagram

Every database has to have a design. The design for the demo database is shown in Figure 3.2. The database is made from five tables (the rectangular boxes), which are joined together by relationships (in this case, arrows). These are one-to-many relationships—i.e., an order can be placed by only one customer, but a customer can place many orders. In the diagram, the pointed end of the arrow represents the many relationship, and the opposite end represents the one relationship.

From this database diagram, you can draw the following conclusions:

- A supplier can supply many products, but a product can come from only one supplier (linked by **Supplier_id**).

- A customer can place many orders, but an order can be placed by only one company (linked by **Customer_id**).

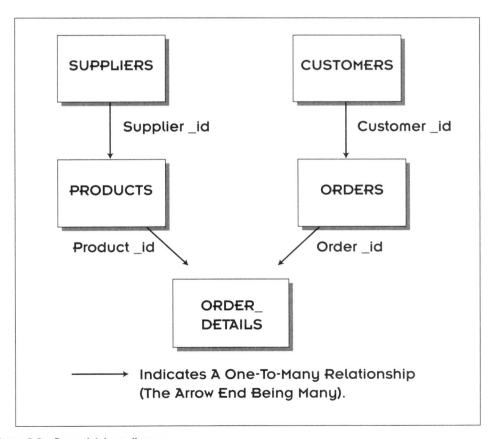

Figure 3.2 *Demo database diagram.*

- An order is made from a number of detail records, but a detail can appear on only one order (linked by **Order_id**).

Now that you have a design, you can start building the database. If you need to know more about design and relational theory, refer to Chapter 4, which deals with the subject in depth.

The next step is to create a new project from within the Personal Oracle8 Navigator.

Creating A Project

From within the Oracle8 Navigator, you can create a new project in a number of ways:

- Click on File|New|New Project.

- From the icon bar at the top of the Navigator, click on the down arrow, or the one with a green plus sign in it. This will give you a list. From this list, click on New Project.

- Right-click on the Projects folder in the main Navigator window, then choose New.

I usually choose the third option, which is easiest and most intuitive. Once you have clicked on the New button, the Navigator asks where you would like to create the file for your project. The best location is the C:\ORAWIN95\Nav80 directory, as this is where the other project files reside. In the file-name box, type in "Demo". You should then see a window that looks similar to Figure 3.3.

Click on the Save button, which creates your new project folder. An empty project folder is displayed in the center of the Navigator window. You don't need this window because you will see all of the required objects just fine by using the Navigator, so click on the top right-hand corner of this new demo project window to remove it. This does not actually delete it, but just removes it from the screen. An extra project is now within the project folder, below the Toolbox and Sample projects. You now have a project you can start to use. The next step is to create a user.

Figure 3.3 *Create Project window.*

Creating A User

I've found that the best way to create a user is to right-click on the Demo project folder, and choose New|User..., as shown in Figure 3.4.

Although you can create new users in other ways, I find this is the best method, because it creates the new user inside your project. This way, you don't have to create a user and then drag the user into your project. (This is the first time I've mentioned the drag and drop functionality of the Navigator; as you'll see later, it can be useful for quickly creating objects within your project.) Once you've chosen to create a new user, you'll be presented with the New User Properties window, shown in Figure 3.5.

This is where you enter your new user's name and password. In this case, both the name and password will be **DEMO**. You'll need to enter the password twice before continuing. This is a confirmation check to prevent typing mistakes. Next, click on the Role/Privilege tab at the top of the window. This is where you give the **DEMO** user its privileges, as shown in Figure 3.6.

When you enter this window, you'll see that the user you're creating, **DEMO** in this case, will already have one role—**CONNECT**—granted to it. This will allow that user to create and delete objects within your own schema. For the purposes of this demo database, you'll also need to grant the **DBA** role to the **DEMO** user. To do so, just click on the **DBA** role in the

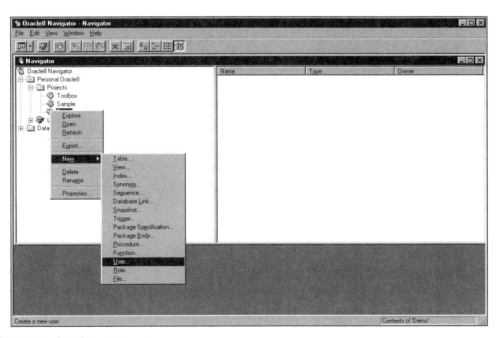

Figure 3.4 *Creating a new user.*

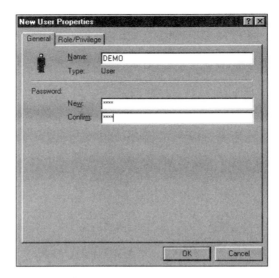

Figure 3.5 *The New User Properties window.*

Figure 3.6 *The Role/Privilege tab.*

right-hand window, the remaining window, and then click on the left chevron (<) sign. You then need to click on the OK button to create your user.

Once this is done, you'll have a user called **DEMO** inside your Demo project. To check this, click once on the Demo project, and on the right-hand side of the screen you'll see your user. You should see a small icon of a man, followed by the name of the user you created, with a type of user.

Creating Tables

To implement the database diagram (refer back to Figure 3.2), you have to create the following tables:

- SUPPLIERS

- PRODUCTS

- CUSTOMERS

- ORDERS

- ORDER_DETAILS

To create a table within your project, start by right-clicking on the Demo project icon and choosing New|Table. This prompts you for the way in which you want to create your table, as shown in Figure 3.7. You can create a table either through the use of a wizard or manually. In this section, I'll show you how to create a table through a wizard. Chapter 6 will describe the creation of a table manually.

Click on the OK button with the Use Table Wizard radio button selected. This will display the Table Wizard - Page 1 of 7 window, shown in Figure 3.8.

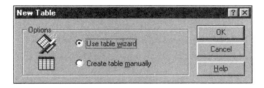

Figure 3.7 *New Table window.*

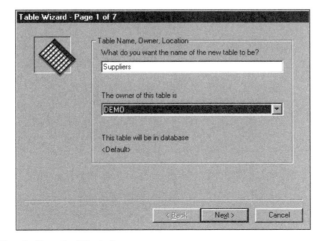

Figure 3.8 *Table Wizard - Page 1 of 7 window.*

In this window, you're asked to give the table a name and show who the owner is. For this first example, you'll create the **SUPPLIERS** table. In the first field, type in "Suppliers" (without the quotes), and in the second field, select the user you have just created, **DEMO**. Then click on the Next button. This will display the second page of the table wizard, shown in Figure 3.9.

This is the window where you specify the columns needed for your table. As you'll see, this window has a number of fields and buttons. The buttons on the bottom row are for navigating between the various pages of the wizard. The row of buttons that start with the << symbol are described as follows:

- <<—Takes you to the first column defined in the table.

- <—Takes you to the previous column defined in the table.

- >—Takes you to the next column defined in the table.

- >>—Takes you to the last column defined in the table.

- New—Creates a new column.

- Insert—Inserts a new column before the current column.

- Delete—Deletes the current column.

The current column is displayed on the left-hand side of the window. This increments as you create more columns. Table 3.1, shown later in this chapter, has the information to enter for the **SUPPLIERS** table. First, enter the column name, "Supplier_id". Note that you cannot have any spaces in the column name; use the underscore character (_) in place of a space. If you try to create a table with spaces in the column names, you will receive an error when you

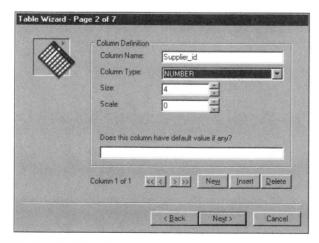

Figure 3.9 *Table Wizard - Page 2 of 7 window.*

reach the last page of the wizard. Once you have entered the column name, you must choose its data type. For this column, choose **NUMBER**, with a size of 4 and a scale of 0 (see Figure 3.9). This column does not have any default values.

You have now entered one column; only seven to go. To enter the next column, click on the New button and enter the required information, which you can find, again, in Table 3.1. After you have entered all eight columns, click on the Next button to take you to the next page of the wizard, shown in Figure 3.10.

In this window, you'll specify some of the key information for the table—such as whether or not the specified column must have information in it and whether that information has to be unique across the table. This helps to define your primary key. The buttons are similar to those of the previous window. Enter the required information into this screen for each of the eight columns—i.e., for the **Supplier_id** column, you should have selected the No, It Cannot Be Null and Yes, It Must Be Unique radio buttons. Once you have finished entering all eight columns, click on the Next button, which takes you to the next page of the wizard, shown in Figure 3.11. You may be prompted to enter the DEMO user password at this point.

This window is used for specifying the foreign keys. For this database, at the moment, we do not want to set up any foreign-key information. Click on the Next button to go straight to the next page of the wizard, shown in Figure 3.12.

This window is where you specify the primary key, which is the main key for the table. Notice that all of the primary keys are specified as being not null and unique. This is necessary to avoid duplicates within the table, by enforcing referential integrity. In this window, just click on the second column of the first row to define this column as the primary key. The number

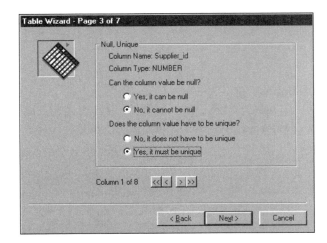

Figure 3.10   *Table Wizard - Page 3 of 7 window.*

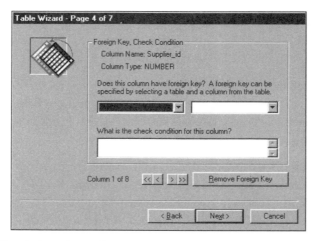

Figure 3.11 *Table Wizard - Page 4 of 7 window.*

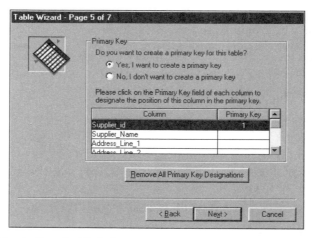

Figure 3.12 *Table Wizard - Page 5 of 7 window.*

1 will appear in this column. This is because it is possible to have more than one column in a primary key. Once you've specified the primary key, click on the Next button again to take you to the next page of the wizard, shown in Figure 3.13.

This window helps you organize the columns you entered, by allowing you to specify the order in which they appear. You should have no need to do anything in this window, as the columns entered are already in the correct order. If you do wish to alter the order of the columns, just click on the column you wish to move, and then click on the Up or Down button to move it. Once you're happy with the order of your columns, click on the Next button to take you to the final window of the table wizard, shown in Figure 3.14.

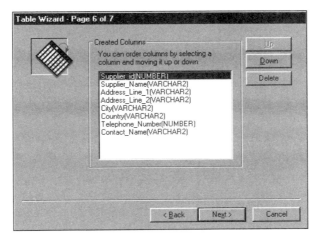

Figure 3.13 *Table Wizard - Page 6 of 7 window.*

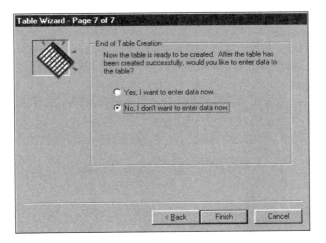

Figure 3.14 *Table Wizard - Page 7 of 7 window.*

This window lets you finish your table. Just click on the Finish button, and the table will be created. You will also find two radio buttons here: One lets you start entering data once the table is created; the other just creates the table. For this example, select the No, I Don't Want To Enter Data Now button. It's easier to enter the data at a later stage. Create the table by clicking on the Finish button. If you receive an error message, go back and check that you didn't create any column names with spaces.

After you've created the table, you're again back at the Navigator window, but this time a new object will be present in the projects window. On the right-hand side, you'll see an entry for the table you've just created. To check the table, right-click on the table icon, then left-click on the Properties... button. This shows you the properties for the table just created. To see the design of the table, click on the Design tab. This will display a window similar to that shown in Figure 3.15.

Now you can create the other four tables of the demo database. If you have any problems, refer to the section just completed. The next section defines all of the tables to be created, including a brief description of what they are and their relationships.

Table Listing

The following sections present a complete guide to the tables being created, including a description of the table, what its relationships are, and the data types associated with the columns. Tables 3.1 through 3.5 show the sizes for all the columns being created for the tables within the demonstration database.

SUPPLIERS Table

The **SUPPLIERS** table holds all of the information needed about the product supplier. This has a relationship to the **PRODUCTS** table—i.e., a supplier can supply many products, but a product can come from only one supplier.

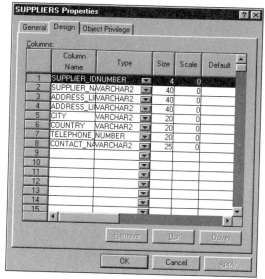

Figure 3.15 SUPPLIERS Properties window.

Table 3.1   *SUPPLIERS* table.

Column Name	Data Type	Size	Scale	Can Be Null?	Unique?	Primary Key?
Supplier_id	NUMBER	4	0	No	Yes	Yes
Supplier_Name	VARCHAR2	40	0	No	No	No
Address_Line_1	VARCHAR2	40	0	No	No	No
Address_Line_2	VARCHAR2	40	0	Yes	No	No
City	VARCHAR2	20	0	No	No	No
Country	VARCHAR2	20	0	Yes	No	No
Telephone_Number	NUMBER	20	0	Yes	No	No
Contact_Name	VARCHAR2	25	0	Yes	No	No

PRODUCTS Table

The **PRODUCTS** table holds information about the products for sale, including the cost and retail price. This table has two relationships: one with the **SUPPLIERS** table and one with the **ORDER _DETAILS** table. A product can appear only once for each record of the **ORDER _DETAILS** table.

CUSTOMERS Table

The **CUSTOMERS** table holds all of the information needed about the customer. This has a relationship to the **ORDERS** table—a customer can place many orders, but an order can be placed by only one customer.

Table 3.2   *PRODUCTS* table.

Column Name	Data Type	Size	Scale	Can Be Null?	Unique?	Primary Key?
Product_id	NUMBER	4	0	No	Yes	Yes
Supplier_id	NUMBER	4	0	No	No	No
Product_Name	VARCHAR2	40	0	No	No	No
Unit_Cost_Price	NUMBER	5	2	Yes	No	No
Unit_Retail_Price	NUMBER	5	2	No	No	No
Units_In_Stock	NUMBER	5	0	No	No	No
Reorder_Level	NUMBER	4	0	Yes	No	No

Table 3.3 *CUSTOMERS table.*

Column Name	Data Type	Size	Scale	Can Be Null?	Unique?	Primary Key?
Customer_id	NUMBER	5	0	No	Yes	Yes
Customer_Name	VARCHAR2	40	0	No	No	No
Address_Line_1	VARCHAR2	40	0	No	No	No
Address_Line_2	VARCHAR2	40	0	Yes	No	No
City	VARCHAR2	20	0	No	No	No
Country	VARCHAR2	20	0	Yes	N	No
Telephone_Number	NUMBER	20	0	Yes	No	No
Contact_Name	VARCHAR2	25	0	Yes	No	No

ORDERS Table

The **ORDERS** table holds information about the orders placed. This takes the form of an order header. The table holds high-level information about the order, such as **Order_Date**, **Customer_id**, and dispatched date. This table has two relationships: one to the **CUSTOMERS** table for the customer information, and one to the **ORDER_DETAILS** table for the low-level details of the order.

ORDER_DETAILS Table

This table holds the low-level information for each order. Composed of many rows per order, this table holds information on the makeup of the order—for example, each item ordered will have a row inserted. Its relationships are to the **ORDERS** table for the order and customer information and to the **PRODUCTS** table for the product and supplier information.

Table 3.4 *ORDERS table.*

Column Name	Data Type	Size	Scale	Can Be Null?	Unique?	Primary Key?
Order_id	NUMBER	6	0	No	Yes	Yes
Customer_id	NUMBER	5	0	No	No	No
Order_Date	DATE	0	0	No	No	No
Dispatched_Date	DATE	0	0	No	No	No
Order_Due_Date	DATE	0	0	No	No	No

Table 3.5 *ORDER_DETAILS table.*

Column Name	Data Type	Size	Scale	Can Be Null?	Unique?	Primary Key?
Order_id	NUMBER	6	0	No	No	Yes
Product_id	NUMBER	4	0	No	No	No
Number_Ordered	NUMBER	6	0	No	No	No
Unit_Price	NUMBER	5	2	No	No	No

After entering all of the previous information, you should see a Navigator screen that looks similar to Figure 3.16.

Entering Basic Information

To enter information into the tables you've just created, you can again use the Navigator. The easiest way is to right-click on the table you wish to enter information into, then click on the Open button. This will open up a blank window with the column headings at the top. This is the form you enter your data into. An example is Figure 3.17, which shows the **CUSTOMERS** table open and ready to receive data.

To enter information into this window, just click on the field in which you want to enter and type the information. Remember to fill in all fields that are necessary—those defined as being not null should have information entered. After you've entered the first line, right-click on the mouse and you'll see a menu bar appear. From this bar you can choose one of several items:

- *Insert Before*—Allows you to insert a line before the current line. This is useful if you are entering data and miss a line. Of course, the database does not care if the data you enter is not in order.

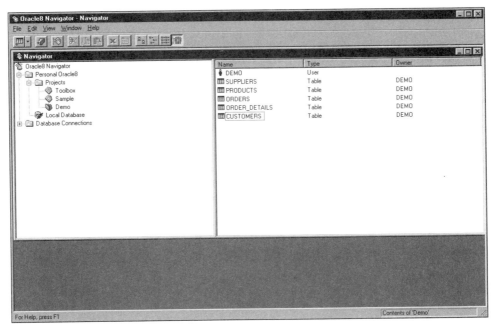

Figure 3.16   *Navigator window with tables created.*

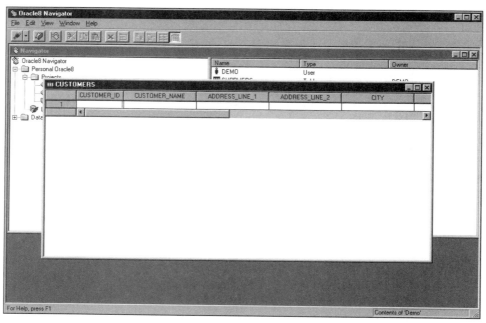

Figure 3.17 *An empty CUSTOMERS table.*

- *Insert After*—Allows you to create the next row. This is the most frequently used of the items, as it allows you to continue entering data into the table.

- *Commit Insert*—Sends the data to the database. This stores the information you supplied within the database. If any problems with the insert occur—say, a field was left empty when it should have been not null—an error message will be displayed. When committing your data to the database, do not commit after every line; you can create all of your rows before committing them.

- *Cancel Insert*—Cancels the current line being inserted. This does not do a commit to the database.

- *Refresh*—Allows you to refresh the information on the screen. For example, if you've entered 50 records in the table and wish to see them in order, you can refresh them. If the form contains any uncommitted information, you'll be asked if you would like to commit it before doing the refresh. Click on either Yes or No, and the table will be refreshed.

The Data To Be Entered

You're now ready to enter the data, which should not take long. The pieces of data are the basic building blocks of our demo database. Enter the data in Tables 3.6 to 3.10 into the appropriate tables.

Table 3.6   SUPPLIERS data.

Supplier_id	Supplier_Name	Add 1	Add 2	City	Country	Tel No	Contact
1001	Test Company Ltd	1 The Street		London	England	1234567890	Mr. Smith
1002	Training Company Inc	2 The Street		London	England	2345678901	Mr. Brown
1003	Widget Design Inc	52nd Street	Fords	New York	USA	3456789012	Mr. Jones
1004	JRF Relational Associates Ltd	42nd Street	Brooklyn	New York	USA	4567890123	Mrs. James
1005	Hardware Ltd	57 The Close	Burstwick	Hull	England	5678901234	Mr. Fieldhouse

Table 3.7   PRODUCTS data.

Prod_id	Supplier_id	Prod Name	Cost	Retail	In-Stock	Reorder
5001	1005	A Nut	1.00	2.00	1000	100
5002	1005	B Nut	2.00	4.00	1000	100
5003	1001	1cm Screw	5.00	10.00	1000	500
5004	1002	1cm Nail	3.00	6.00	1000	200
5005	1004	1mm Washer	0.50	1.00	1000	50
5006	1004	2mm Washer	0.70	1.40	1000	50
5007	1002	2cm Nail	6.00	12.00	1000	200
5008	1001	2cm Screw	10.00	20.00	1000	500
5009	1001	3cm Screw	20.00	40.00	1000	500
5010	1005	C Nut	3.00	6.00	1000	100

Table 3.8   CUSTOMERS table.

Customer_id	Customer_Name	Add 1	Add 2	City	Country	Tel No	Contact
20001	ABC Ltd	1 The Street	Mayfair	London	England	1234455	Mr. Smith
20002	DEF Ltd	2 The Street	Mayfair	London	England	2343213	Mr. Jones
20003	GHI Inc	102W 52nd St		New York	USA	234321	Mr. Brown
20004	JKL Inc	105 5th Ave		New York	USA	111112	Mr. Costelloe
20005	MNO Ltd	5 The Mall		London	England	1234321	Mr. Windsor

Table 3.9   ORDERS table.

Order_id	Customer_id	Order Date	Dispatched	Due Date
100001	20001	01-JAN-1999	10-JAN-1999	31-JAN-1999
100002	20001	02-JAN-1999	11-JAN-1999	31-JAN-1999
100003	20002	01-MAY-1998	09-MAY-1998	31-MAY-1998
100004	20003	01-JUN-1998	03-JUN-1998	10-JUN-1998
100005	20004	28-AUG-1999	29-AUG-1999	30-SEP-1999
100006	20005	28-AUG-1999	10-SEP-1999	31-AUG-1999

Table 3.10 ORDER_DETAILS table.

Order_id	Product_id	Number Ordered	Unit Price
100001	5001	10	2.0
100001	5002	20	4.0
100001	5003	10	10.0
100002	5001	20	2.0
100003	5002	10	4.0
100003	5004	50	6.0
100004	5001	15	2.0
100004	5002	25	4.0
100005	5004	10	6.0
100005	5003	10	10.0
100005	5002	10	4.0
100006	5001	20	2.0

Displaying The Information Entered

After entering all of this information, you'll want to see it in table format. Simply right-click on the table name you wish to view—**SUPPLIERS**, for example—and click on the Open button. This will present you with a window that looks similar to Figure 3.18.

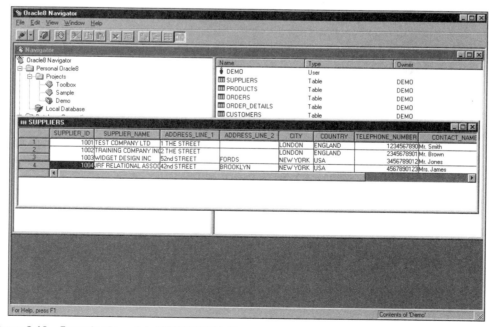

Figure 3.18 Example of populated **SUPPLIERS** table.

You are now ready to learn how to manipulate this information using Personal Oracle8's SQL*Plus.

CONCLUSION

You've now created a working database. In this chapter, you learned how to create a user and used it to create and populate tables. Chapter 5 will explore the possibilities for extracting data from your database using SQL*Plus.

If you wish to know more about relational design, turn to Chapter 4, where it is explained in detail.

Relational Theory

Before you dive into the demo database and create objects, you need to understand the basics of databases. You must also have some idea of what the database is supposed to do and what it will look like, before you can create any objects. This chapter will take you through the design and creation of all the objects required.

The basics behind the database— these are the building blocks of Oracle.

ORACLE8 BASICS

Please read and understand the basics before creating your database. This will give you an ideal grounding for the more advanced topics covered later in this book.

Tables

Tables are the basic building blocks of a relational database. A table is a structure for storing data. It is composed of columns and rows. A table can contain a number of columns that divide the data into specific groups.

A database is made up of a number of tables and their relationships. Personal Oracle8 is an object-relational database.

It still uses tables, as in a relational database, but it can store and use them differently (as objects). You'll find out how to do this later in the book.

A table is a collection of data. All of this data must have the same properties. For example, your address book may contain lots of names and addresses. This information could be formatted into a table, as in Table 4.1.

This table has four columns that group the data. Each column must have the same data type—the telephone number column, for example, would be defined as type **NUMBER**. (Data types are covered later in this chapter.) This is why all data within a table has the same attributes. This table could then be used as a part of a database. Most of the information you keep in your diary could be stored in a database. For the demonstration database, you'll create a number of tables to store all of the data.

Rows

A row is a line of information within a table; Table 4.1, for example, has five rows. A table is made up of a number of rows, and each row is made up of pieces of related data, divided into columns. The only limit on the number of rows allowed within a table is the amount of space you have to store the table. On Oracle7 servers, tables with more than one million rows of data are not uncommon.

Tablespaces

Tablespaces are how Oracle implements the grouping of tables and other objects. When you create a database, you create a number of tablespaces, which hold tables within them. The following three tablespaces are present on nearly every installation of Oracle:

- *SYSTEM*—This tablespace, which must be present on every database, is used for storing all of the tables and associated objects that Oracle needs to maintain. This tablespace contains the data about the data itself. For example, if you create a table in the USER tablespace, the physical makeup of the table you create—the columns and data definitions—is stored within the SYSTEM tablespace.

Table 4.1 *The **ADDRESS BOOK** table.*

First Name	Surname	City	Telephone Number
John	Rowlands	London	1234567890
Andrew	Pickering	Hull	2345678901
Jack	Fieldhouse	Bath	3456789012
Andrew	Habblett	Lincoln	4567890123
Sue	Connell	Crowle	5678901234

- *TEMP*—This tablespace is where Oracle performs sorts and calculations.

- *USER*—This tablespace could be used to store any tables or objects created by a specific user. These user tables should not be stored in the SYSTEM tablespace.

Data Types

A number of data types can be used within an Oracle8 database. They define the data that is stored within a column.

Standard Data Types

The basic data types are:

- *CHAR*—Used to store fixed-length character strings. For example, the column for state code would have a data type of **CHAR(2)**—in other words, a two-character column. **CHAR** data types should be used only for fixed-length strings of text, as Oracle8 stores any data with the **CHAR** data type to the full length of the column. It does so by padding the remainder with spaces, then storing the full string within the database. For example, if you defined the **State** column as being **CHAR(5)**, the data stored for New Jersey would be NJ and three spaces.

- *VARCHAR2*—Used for variable-length text strings. An example of these strings would be a person's full name. The Oracle8 database stores a **VARCHAR2** data type without padding the string to the size of the column with spaces.

- *NUMBER*—A generic data type for storing any format or type of number. It can be given a *precision*, which defines the maximum number of digits to be stored, and a *scale*, which indicates where the decimal point is placed.

- *DATE*—Stores dates, along with all time information. Oracle8 has a number of formatting options for dates. The standard way is to store dates in the full format, so you'll have no problems with year 2000 issues.

Schemas

Databases can organize objects within schemas. A *schema* is just a way of storing all related objects together. After all, it's better to be organized. You can think of a user as a schema—i.e., all objects are organized together. When you create a user, Oracle8 actually creates a schema with the same name as the user.

Users

When you log on to an Oracle8 database, you must provide a username and password. Without a correct username and password combination, Oracle8 will not allow you to access the database. Once you're in the database, you have a strict set of rules governing what you can, and, more importantly, can't do. Oracle8 governs the security of the data through users and roles. (Roles are described in the next section.)

You can easily create a user through SQL*Plus or the Oracle8 Navigator. When you create a user, you need to give the username and password, which will allow default access to the database. This gives the user a connect-only privilege. Roles are an easier way to allow the user to create and delete objects.

Roles

Roles govern security within the database. A role is a collection of database privileges. Rather than giving a user a list of 10 privileges, you just grant access to the role. A single user can have many roles. The default role for a new user is **CONNECT**. On a default installation of Personal Oracle8, the following roles are automatically assigned:

- AQ_ADMINISTRATOR_ROLE
- AQ_USER_ROLE
- CONNECT
- DBA
- DELETE_CATALOG_ROLE
- EXECUTE_CATALOG_ROLE
- EXP_FULL_DATABASE
- IMP_FULL_DATABASE
- RECOVERY_CATALOG_OWNER
- RESOURCE
- SELECT_CATALOG_ROLE
- SNMPAGENT

You can add to these roles by creating your own. Roles are easy to create and are described in more detail later in this book. At this point, you need to know only three roles:

- *CONNECT*—Allows the user to do the following actions within the user's own schema: connect to the database; create tables, views, synonyms, and sequences; create database links; and create data clusters.

- *DBA*—Allows the user to do anything within the database, to any schema. This role is intended for use by an administrator, and should not be given to anybody else.

- *RESOURCE*—Allows the user to do the following actions within the user's own schema: create tables, views, synonyms, and sequences; create data clusters; create procedures, functions, and packages; and create triggers and object types. This role is intended for use primarily by developers.

DESIGNING YOUR FIRST DATABASE

Database Design

Good database design usually takes into account many factors:

- The requirement of the business or customers

- Efficient use of end-user time

- The level and frequency of information requests

- The size of the base tables and views

- Overall machine utilization

- Available or affordable hardware and software

- Available database or programming expertise

- Existing applications

The object here is to produce a good logical representation of the data items in a given system. Given a particular environment, what relations are needed to represent it and what should the attributes of those relations be?

Often, however, such factors mean that the best logical design may not be the best for the given situation. The techniques described here do provide good data designs that are flexible and relatively easy to maintain. They provide a good starting point from which other considerations or restrictions can be applied.

Most of the tables in this chapter are in the Personal Oracle8 database, which is created when you install the software.

Good And Bad Design

What do I mean by good design? Consider Table 4.2.

This design leads to a couple of problems:

- The table shows redundancy; that is, each department's location is shown more than once.

- The design fails to include the locations of any departments without employees.

A good design principle is one fact in one place—i.e., avoid redundancy wherever possible.

Normalization

Normalization consists of a series of steps that are applied to a set of relations to obtain a good logical design.

Normalization theory is based on the idea of *normal forms*. A relation is in a particular normal form if it satisfies a certain set of constraints—e.g., a relation is in first normal (1NF) if, and only if, it satisfies the constraint that it contains *atomic* (single) values only. All normalized relations are in 1NF, because, by definition, their attributes contain values drawn from underlying domains that can contain only single values.

Table 4.2   *An example **EMP** table.*

EmpNo	EName	DeptNo	Loc
1782	CLARK	10	NEW YORK
1934	MILLE	10	NEW YORK
1839	KING	10	NEW YORK
1369	SMITH	20	DALLAS
1788	SCOTT	20	DALLAS
1566	JONES	20	DALLAS
1876	ADAMS	20	DALLAS
1902	FORD	20	DALLAS
1499	ALLEN	30	CHICAGO
1698	BLAKE	30	CHICAGO
1844	TURNER	30	CHICAGO
1900	JAMES	30	CHICAGO
1654	MARTIN	30	CHICAGO
1521	WARD	30	CHICAGO

Types Of Normal Form

There are four types of normal forms, referred to as first (1NF), second (2NF), third (3NF), and Boyce/Codd Normal Form (BCNF). These types are discussed at length later in this chapter.

- If a relation is in 3NF, it is automatically in 2NF and 1NF.

- If a relation is in 2NF, it is automatically in 1NF.

- Boyce and Codd, the forefathers of relational design, proposed a stronger definition of 3NF, known as Boyce/Codd Normal Form, or BCNF. BCNF is usually, but not always, a good target to aim for when designing database applications.

Functional Dependence

Given a relation R, attribute Y of R is functionally dependent on attribute X of R, if, and only if, each X value in R has associated with it just one Y value in R at any one time.

Hands up if the preceding paragraph makes any sense to you. The next paragraph should clear up any confusion.

In the **EMP** table (Table 4.4), attributes **EName**, **Job**, and **Sal** are each functionally dependent on attribute **EmpNo**. This is because, given a particular value for **EmpNo**, there exists exactly one corresponding value of **EName**, **Job**, and **Sal**.

The fact that a particular data item is functionally dependent on another can be written as: R.X. > R.Y. For example, **EMP.EmpNo** > **EMP.Sal** or **EMP.EmpNo** > **EMP** (**EName**, **Job**, **Sal**)—or, put the other way 'round, you can say that attribute **EmpNo** functionally determines attributes **EName**, **Job**, and **Sal**. Once you know a given employee number, that fixes the values of the other attributes.

You've seen that the Y value can be composite (made up of multiple columns)—i.e., **EMP.EmpNo** > **EMP** (**EName**, **Job**, **Sal**).

X values can also be composite. If an employee's salary was completely determined by length of service and job title, then attribute **Sal** would be functionally dependent on the combination of **Hiredate** and **Job**. This could be written as: **EMP** (**Hiredate**, **Job**) > **EMP.Sal**.

Full Functional Dependence

Functional dependence will mean full functional dependence unless explicitly stated otherwise. Recognizing functional and full functional dependence means understanding the precise meaning of each data item and its relationship to other data items.

Beware of misleading or incomplete data item names, such as:

- *Salary*—Weekly, monthly, annual?

- *Name*—Precise format, initials, forenames, etc.?

- *Mgr*—Manager's employee number?

The data dictionary is invaluable in documenting and standardizing data items. Having identified functional dependencies between data items, you will later see how these can be declared in a database schema.

Commonsense Definition Of Third Normal Form (3NF)

A relation R is in 3NF if, and only if, for all time, each occurrence of R consists of a primary-key value that identifies some entity, together with a set of mutually independent attribute values that describe that entity. (Assume for simplicity that each relation has a single candidate key—i.e., a primary key and no alternate keys). For example, relation **EMP** is in 3NF (see Table 4.3). Each department occurrence consists of an **EmpNo** identifying a particular employee, together with two other pieces of information describing that employee: the employee's name and department number. Each of the three descriptive items are mutually independent—that is, the employee table is in 3NF, the primary key being **EmpNo**. The other attributes describing a given employee are independent of one another.

Reducing A Set Of Relations To 3NF

A relation R is in 1NF if, and only if, all underlying domains contain only atomic values.

Consider the relation shown in Table 4.4, which is in 1NF.

In this relation, employees in different departments can have the same employee number. So **EmpNo** is unique only within a given department. This means that to identify an employee uniquely in the company as a whole, the **EmpNo** and **DeptNo** for that employee must be specified—that is, **EmpNo** and **DeptNo** are combined to form a composite primary key.

Table 4.3   *EMP table.*

EmpNo	EName	DeptNo
1001	WARD	10
1002	JONES	10
1003	SMITH	20
1004	BROWN	30
1005	GREEN	20

Table 4.4 *EMP* *table example of 1NF.*

DeptNo	EmpNo	EName	Job	Sal	Loc
10	7782	CLARK	MANAGER	4000	NEW YORK
10	7839	KING	PRESIDENT	5000	NEW YORK
10	7934	MILLER	CLERK	1000	NEW YORK
20	7782	SMITH	CLERK	1000	DALLAS
20	7839	JONES	MANAGER	4000	DALLAS
20	7934	SCOTT	ANALYST	2000	DALLAS
20	7876	ADAMS	CLERK	1000	DALLAS
20	7902	FORD	ANALYST	2000	DALLAS
30	7782	ALLEN	SALESMAN	3000	CHICAGO
30	7839	WARD	SALESMAN	3000	CHICAGO
30	7934	MARTIN	SALESMAN	3000	CHICAGO
30	7698	BLAKE	MANAGER	4000	CHICAGO
30	7844	TURNER	SALESMAN	3000	CHICAGO
30	7900	JAMES	CLERK	1000	CHICAGO

This example introduces the constraint that **Sal** is determined by **Job** (i.e., clerks make $1,000; analysts, $2,000; salesmen, $3,000; managers, $4,000; and the president, $5,000). This relationship can be expressed as: **EMP.Job > EMP.Sal**.

This relation has two drawbacks:

- **Loc** is not fully functionally dependent on the primary key.

- **Sal** and **Job** are not mutually independent.

Problems Resulting From INSERT, DELETE, And UPDATE Operations

There are a number of problems relating to **INSERT**, **UPDATE** and **DELETE** operations, including:

- *INSERT*—You cannot **INSERT** a department until it contains one or more employees. This is because until a department has at least one employee, you have no appropriate primary key value. (Remember my integrity rule #1: No component of a primary key value may be null.)

- *DELETE*—If you **DELETE** the last employee for a given department, you destroy not only that employee, but also the fact that that department is located in a particular town. This is really the same problem as for the **INSERT** case.

- *UPDATE*—If a department changed location, you would have to search for all the rows in which that **DeptNo** appears. Otherwise, the database will be left in an inconsistent state.

Eliminating The Non-Full Functional Dependencies

The solution to these problems is to replace the relation with two relations, as shown in Tables 4.5 and 4.6.

Tables 4.5 and 4.6 are the two relations in 2NF. The location details have been removed from the **DEPT** table. With these two relations we can:

- **INSERT** departments, regardless of whether they have employees in them.

- **DELETE** employees, even the last employee in a department, without erasing the fact that the department is situated in a particular location.

Table 4.5 *Solution to **DEPT** table.*

DeptNo	EmpNo	EName	Job	Sal
10	7782	CLARK	MANAGER	4000
10	7839	KING	PRESIDENT	5000
10	7934	MILLER	CLERK	1000
20	7782	SMITH	CLERK	1000
20	7839	JONES	MANAGER	4000
20	7934	SCOTT	ANALYST	2000
20	7876	ADAMS	CLERK	1000
20	7902	FORD	ANALYST	2000
30	7782	ALLEN	SALESMAN	3000
30	7839	WARD	SALESMAN	3000
30	7934	MARTIN	SALESMAN	3000
30	7698	BLAKE	MANAGER	4000
30	7844	TURNER	SALESMAN	3000
30	7900	JAMES	CLERK	1000

Table 4.6 *Solution from **DEPT** table.*

DeptNo	Loc
10	NEW YORK
20	DALLAS
30	CHICAGO
40	BOSTON

- **UPDATE** a department's location, without having to change all employees in that department.

We have eliminated the non-full functional dependency of **Loc** in the original relation. In the second of the new relations, **Loc** is fully functionally dependent on **DeptNo**. The problem was caused by including location, which is really only relevant to departments, in a relation describing employees.

Second Normal Form (2NF)

A relation R is in 2NF if, and only if, it is in 1NF and every non-key attribute is fully functionally dependent on the primary key. (An attribute is non-key if it is not part or all of the primary key.) These relations are in 2NF. In Table 4.4, the primary key is in the combination of **EmpNo** and **DeptNo**; and in Table 4.5, the primary key is **DeptNo**.

The original relation (Table 4.2) from which these last two were derived is in 1NF.

1NF relations can always be reduced to an equivalent collection of 2NF relations. This is done by replacing the original relation with suitable projections of itself. The original relation can always be reconstructed by taking the natural join of these projections.

Problems With Relations

The relation shown in Table 4.6 is in 3NF, but the relation shown in Table 4.5 still gives rise to problems. Remember that **Sal** is determined by **Job**. **Sal** is, in fact, functionally dependent on the primary key—**EmpNo-DeptNo**—but it is still dependent on it, via **Job**. What is actually happening is that **EmpNo-DeptNo** determines which employee you are talking about, and that determines the **Job**, but it is the **Job** that determines the **Sal**, not the **EmpNo-DeptNo**.

This dependence leads to the following problems:

- You cannot insert the fact that a given **Job** has a particular **Sal** until you have an employee with that **Job**, because until then, you have no appropriate primary-key value.

- If you delete the only record for a particular **Job**, you remove not only the data on that employee, but also the information that that **Job** has that **Sal**.

- The **Sal** value for a given **Job** appears many times. The relation still contains redundancy. To change the **Sal** for **Analyst**, for example, you either have to search the relation for every **Analyst** employee or risk the possibility of producing an inconsistent table.

The solution is to replace the relation from Table 4.5 with two relations, shown in Tables 4.7 and 4.8.

Table 4.7 **EMP** *table in 3NF.*

DeptNo	EmpNo	EName	Job
10	7782	CLARK	MANAGER
10	7839	KING	PRESIDENT
10	7934	MILLER	CLERK
20	7782	SMITH	CLERK
20	7839	JONES	MANAGER
20	7934	SCOTT	ANALYST
20	7876	ADAMS	CLERK
20	7902	FORD	ANALYST
30	7782	ALLEN	SALESMAN
30	7839	WARD	SALESMAN
30	7934	MARTIN	SALESMAN
30	7698	BLAKE	MANAGER
30	7844	TURNER	SALESMAN
30	7900	JAMES	CLERK

Table 4.8 **JOB** *table in 3NF.*

Job	Sal
MANAGER	4000
PRESIDENT	5000
CLERK	1000
ANALYST	2000
SALESMAN	3000

The primary key of the relation seen in Table 4.7 is **EmpNo-DeptNo**; the primary key of Table 4.8 is **Job**.

Third Normal Form [3NF]

A relation R is in 3NF if, and only if, it is in 2NF and every non-key attribute is not dependent on the primary key.

- The relations seen in Tables 4.7 and 4.8 are both in 3NF.

- The relation seen in Table 4.5 is in 2NF.

You can always reduce 2NF relations to an equivalent collection of 3NF relations. You'll lose no information in the reduction, because you can join the projections back together. The

3NF collection, however, may contain information, such as the fact that the salary for engineers is $2,500, that could not be shown in the original 2NF relation.

Note that it is not possible to say whether the relationship among data values in a table is in 3NF simply by looking at them. You need to know the meaning of the data and the dependencies involved before you can say which, if any, normal form the relation is in. Also, the DBMS cannot ensure the relation is maintained in 2NF or 3NF without being informed of any dependencies. For a relation in 3NF, all that is needed to inform the DBMS of those dependencies is a declaration of the attributes forming the primary key. The DBMS then knows that all other attributes are functionally dependent on this attribute or attribute combination, and will be able to enforce this constraint. This is another reason 3NF is a good target to aim for in data design.

BCNF Relations

Let's call an attribute on which some other attribute is fully functionally dependent a *functional determinant*. Then BCNF can be defined as follows: A relation R is in BCNF, if, and only if, every determinant is a candidate key. (Remember, candidate key means possible primary key.) For an attribute or attribute combination to be a candidate key, it must have a different value for each of the records in the relation.

Is the relation seen in Table 4.5 in BCNF?

- Its determinants are: **EmpNo-DeptNo** > (**EName, Job**), **DeptNo** > **EName, Job** > **Sal**.

- Are all of these candidate keys?

EmpNo-DeptNo is in BCNF, because it is different for every employee record. **DeptNo** is not, because it has the same value in more than one employee record. **Job** also has the same value in more than one record. Therefore, Table 4.5 is not in BCNF, because two of the three determinants are not candidate keys.

More Examples Of BCNF Relations

Similarly, Table 4.4 is not in BCNF; it has two determinants: **EmpNo-DeptNo** and **Job**, of which only **EmpNo-DeptNo** has a different value for each employee record.

The relation seen in Table 4.6 is in BCNF, because its determinant, **DeptNo**, is a candidate key. (Note that **Loc** is not a determinant, because we assume it is possible to have more than one department based in a given location). Table 4.6 is in BCNF, because **EmpNo-DeptNo** is the only determinant and has a unique value for each row in the table; it is, therefore, a candidate key.

Similarly, Table 4.8 has one determinant, **Job**, which is a candidate key. (Again, note that **Sal** is not a determinant, because we assume it is possible to have more than one **Job** with the same **Sal**.)

Summary Of BCNF

BCNF eliminates certain problems that can occur with the old definition of 3NF. BCNF is also easier to understand than 3NF, as it does not refer to the concepts of primary key, transitive dependence, and full functional dependence. However, the concepts of full and transitive dependence are useful in practice because they indicate the step-by-step process needed to reduce an arbitrary relation to an equivalent collection of BCNF relations.

Good And Bad Decompositions

Consider the relation seen in Table 4.5 with attributes **EmpNo**, **Job**, and **Sal**, with the following dependencies:

- EmpNo > Job
- Job > Sal
- EmpNo > Sal

The following decompositions are possible:

- Decomposition A: EJ(**EmpNo**, **Job**), and JS(**Job**, **Sal**)
- Decomposition B: EJ(**EmpNo**, **Job**) and ES(**EmpNo**, **Sal**)

Decompositions A and B both give two BCNF projections. You cannot, however, insert in B the fact that **Job** has a particular **Sal** value unless an employee has that **Job**. In Decomposition A, you can make **UPDATE**s to either relation without regard for the other relation, but this is not true of B. The difference is that in A, the decomposition was made according to the functional dependencies (FDs), but in B the second relation is based on a transitive dependency.

UPDATEs to the relations in B must be monitored to ensure that the FD **Job > Sal** is not violated. If two employees have the same **Job** in projection EJ, they must have the same **Sal** in projection ES. Thus, the two projections are not independent of each other.

Repeating Groups

Suppose that within a company there are projects, each of which has a number of people working on it and a number of hardware resources allocated to it. An un-normalized relation can be constructed to describe the relationships between projects, employees, and resources, as shown in Table 4.9.

Table 4.9 *Projects and employees.*

Project	Employees	Resources
INSTALL LAN	(JAMES, SMITH)	(PCs, CABLES)
TUNE DATABASE	(JAMES, FIELD)	(MAINFRAME)
SECURITY	(GREEN, LOMAS)	(PCs, TOKENS, CARDS)

This relation has no functional dependencies. The only operation of a normalizing nature that you can perform is to flatten the structure, as shown in Table 4.10.

In this new relation, each record appears if, and only if, Project P is being worked on by Employee E, and Resource R has been allocated to P. The relation contains a lot of redundancy, which, as usual, leads to **UPDATE** problems—for example, to add the information that a project has had a new resource allocated to it, you must create a new record for each of the employees working on that project. However, the relation is in BCNF, because it is all-key and there are no other functional determinants.

Multivalued Dependencies

The problems in Table 4.9 occur because employees and resources are independent of one another. The situation would be improved if you replaced relation shown in Table 4.9 with projections PE (**Project, Employee**) and PR (**Project, Resource**). These two projections are both all-key and so are both in BCNF. This decomposition has been made on the basis of a multivalued dependency (MVD). This relation has two MVDs:

- Project >> Employee
- Project >> Resource

Table 4.10 *Flattened structure.*

Project	Employee	Resource
INSTALL LAN	JAMES	PCs
INSTALL LAN	JAMES	CABLES
INSTALL LAN	SMITH	PCs
INSTALL LAN	SMITH	CABLES
TUNE DATABASE	JAMES	MAINFRAME
TUNE DATABASE	FIELD	MAINFRAME
SECURITY	GREEN	PCs
SECURITY	GREEN	TOKENS
SECURITY	GREEN	CARDS
SECURITY	LOMAS	PCs
SECURITY	LOMAS	TOKENS
SECURITY	LOMAS	CARDS

The statement R.A >> R.B is read: Attribute R.B is multidependent on attribute R.A, or R.A multidetermines R.B. The first MVD means that though a **Project** does not have a single corresponding **Employee**—i.e., **Employee** is not functionally dependent on **Project**—each **Project** does have a well-defined set of corresponding **Employees**. The second MVD of **Resource** on **Project** works the same way.

The definition of MVD is: Given a relation R with attributes A, B, and C, the multivalued dependency R.A >> R.B holds in R if, and only if, the set of B values matching a given A value/C value pair in R depends only on the A value and is independent of the C value. A, B, and C may be composite. Given the relation R(A,B,C), the MVD R.A >> R.B holds if, and only if, the MVD R.A >> R.C also holds. MVDs always go together in pairs in this way. Both, therefore, can be written as: R.A >> R.B R.C (**Project** >> **Employee Resource**).

Summary Of Normalization

To summarize normalization, we can make the following points:

1. Take projections of the original 1NF relation to eliminate any non-full functional dependencies. This will produce a collection of 2NF relations.

2. Take projections of these 2NF relations to eliminate any transitive dependencies. This will produce a collection of 3NF relations.

3. Take projections of these 3NF relations to eliminate any remaining functional dependencies in which the determinant is not a candidate key. This will produce a collection of BCNF relations.

Steps 1 through 3 can be condensed into the single guideline: Take projections of the original relation to eliminate FDs in which the determinant is not a candidate key.

4. Take projections of these BCNF relations to eliminate any multivalued dependencies that are not also functional dependencies. This will produce a collection of BCNF relations. (Note: The usual practice is to eliminate these MVDs before applying the other steps above.)

At each step, you can use the concept of independent components to guide the choice of which projections to take. The general objective is to reduce redundancy and, therefore, to avoid certain **UPDATE** problems. Remember, however, there are often good reasons for not normalizing all the way, and these should be understood.

Normalization Exercise

This section presents a short exercise in normalization. The solution appears in the next section.

The following list of data items describes projects and the personnel linked to those projects:

- **Project_code**
- **Project_type**
- **Project_description**
- **Personnel_no**
- **Name**
- **Grade**
- **Salary_scale**
- **Date_joined**
- **Alloc_time**

Produce a set of 3NF relations from these data items, taking into account the following assumptions. Indicate the primary and foreign keys in the 3NF relations.

- Each project may have one or more people allocated to it.
- **Date_joined** refers to the date that person joined the project.
- **Alloc_time** indicates the length of time a person is allocated to a project.
- Each person is on a single job grade.
- One salary scale may apply to a number of grades, but a given grade will have only one salary scale.

Solution To Normalization Exercise

Table 4.11 shows the 3NF relations solution.

Table 4.11 *The 3NF relations solution.*

Relation - Projects	
Project_code	Primary key
Project_type	
Project_description	

Relation - Project_Person	
Project_code	Leading part of primary key
Personnel_no	Trailing part of primary key
Date_joined	
Alloc_time	

(continued)

Table 4.11 *The 3NF relations solution (continued).*

Relation - Person

Personnel_no	Primary key
Name	
Grade	Foreign key

Relation - Grade

Grade	Primary key
Salary_scale	

Entity Relationship Diagrams

Entity relationship diagrams (ERDs) are used to design relational databases. These diagrams show in picture format the relationships between tables. Understanding these diagrams is useful when you're creating a database. Figure 4.1 shows an entity relationship diagram.

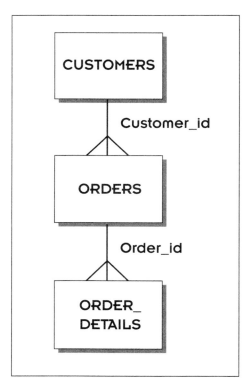

Figure 4.1 *Example of an entity relationship diagram.*

These diagrams are made up of a number of rectangular boxes, each representing a table. These boxes are joined together with relationships. Relationships can be one of two types:

- One-to-many
- One-to-one

Relationships are represented on the entity relationship diagram by using crow's-foot notation. These are the lines between the boxes. A single straight line between one box and another signifies a one-to-one relationship. A single line between two boxes, with three lines touching one of the boxes, represents a one-to-many relationship—the many being the box with the three lines touching it.

Constraints

As a primary key allows any piece of data to be directly referenced by its key value, keeping the integrity of the table is important. One way to enforce the integrity of the table is to use constraints.

Constraints are really rules for inserting data into the table. For example, a constraint is placed on the primary key. This means it must be unique, so if an existing item were inserted into the table, the constraint would disallow the transaction.

Here's another example of a constraint: Some columns in tables may depend on other values existing in other tables. A constraint could be placed on a table to define this. Constraints can be implemented in Personal Oracle8 through the Navigator. This can be implemented at the time of table creation or at a later stage.

Default Values

You can use default values for inserting data into a table when the column is left blank. For example, if your company has an **ORDERS** table, and the order date is left blank when inserting, you can use a default value to insert today's date into the field. This will reduce the number of keystrokes an operator has to make. Default values can also be used in generating primary keys; this is where a sequence number can automatically be generated and inserted as the primary key.

TIME FOR SQL*PLUS

In this chapter, you learned the theory behind creating a useable database. Once you've created the database and normalized all of the tables and data, you're ready to start manipulating the data. To do this, you'll use SQL*Plus, which I'll explain in the next chapter.

Accessing Your Database

Now that you have entered some of the information that makes up the demonstration database, and you know the theory behind the database, this is a good time to learn how to use the data in the database. You'll use SQL*Plus for viewing the information entered.

OVERVIEW

Access your data using SQL*Plus. The data is useless if you cannot see and manipulate it.

SQL*Plus is a character-based query language that enables the user to ask the database questions. These questions are formatted into statements the database can understand, using Structured Query Language (or SQL, often pronounced *sequel*). Examples of the types of simple requests made to a database would be:

- Show me all records in the **PRODUCTS** table.

- Show me all records in the **PRODUCTS** table produced by a specific supplier.

- Show me the company that has the largest order value.

- Show me every order received this month.

We'll cover more complex statements later. This chapter will give you the basics of SQL, enabling you to retrieve some data from the database. This is one of the basic skills you'll need to work with Personal Oracle8, because everything that interacts with the database uses some form of SQL.

SQL is a relational database language that allows the programmer to insert, update, delete, and query the information stored within a database. SQL can be written by itself or inserted into another language, such as COBOL or C; this latter type of SQL is commonly referred to as embedded SQL.

SQL is composed of two different types of language: Data Definition Language (DDL), which is used to define the data within the database; and Data Manipulation Language (DML), which is used to change existing data.

DDL commands include:

- *CREATE*—Creates objects, such as tables, within the database.
- *ALTER*—Alters the structure of the database.
- *DROP*—Deletes objects from the database.

Some example DML statements are:

- *INSERT*—Inserts data into a table.
- *UPDATE*—Updates existing data within a table.
- *DELETE*—Deletes data from a table.

WRITING SQL STATEMENTS

You can write SQL statements in many different ways, but the best course is to follow a standard from the beginning. This will become important in later chapters when you begin writing more complex statements. It will also make it easier to debug any problems with your code.

SQL statements can be written on one line or many lines. In most cases, you'll want to use more than one line, as one-line SQL statements are more difficult to read than multiple-line statements, as shown in Listings 5.1 and 5.2.

Listing 5.1 A one-line SQL statement.

```
select product_name,product_id,supplier_id,unit_retail_price from products;
```

Listing 5.2   A multiple-line SQL statement.

```
select product_name,
       product_id,
       supplier_id,
       unit_retail_price
from products;
```

When you write a multiple-line SQL statement, you will usually want to place the clauses—
SELECT and **FROM** in this case—on different lines.

SQL statements are not case-sensitive. All of the following SQL statements are valid and produce the same results:

```
SELECT * FROM PRODUCTS;
select * from products;
SeLeCt * FrOm PrOdUcTs;
```

You enter your SQL commands at the **SQL>** prompt. All lines of the statement are numbered. If you write a 10-line SQL statement, all of the lines are kept in the SQL buffer. The buffer can hold only one statement at a time. The statement can be executed in a number of ways:

- By placing a semicolon at the end of the last line.

- By placing a slash at the **SQL>** prompt.

- By issuing the **RUN** command at the **SQL>** prompt.

- By using the @ sign to execute a file.

SQL*PLUS

With SQL*Plus, Oracle has extended the SQL standard with extra functionality. In addition to the normal SQL commands, SQL*Plus has extra text-formatting, file-saving, and editing options. To gain access to SQL*Plus, you need a username and password. In Chapter 3, you created a user called **DEMO** with a password of **DEMO**, which you can use to access SQL*Plus. Start SQL*Plus by using the following menu path: Start|Programs|Oracle for Windows 95|SQL Plus 8.0. If the database is down, it will automatically be started when you access SQL*Plus.

When you start SQL*Plus, you'll see the Log On screen shown in Figure 5.1.

Type in your username and password, then click on the OK button. Again, if the database is not started, it will automatically start, and you'll be given the SQL*Plus screen shown in Figure 5.2.

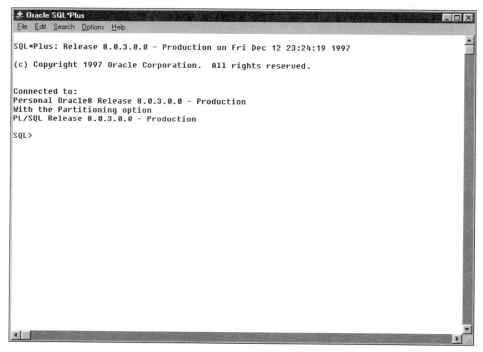

Figure 5.1 SQL*Plus Log On screen.

Figure 5.2 SQL*Plus session on Windows 95.

The SQL Buffer

On gaining entry to SQL*Plus, you'll see the **SQL>** prompt, which shows that the database is ready to accept your commands. You are actually positioned at Line 1 of the buffer. Like any other editing buffer, it allows you to make up the statement before passing it to SQL*Plus to interpret and display the results.

Pressing the Enter key moves you to the next line. To execute the command, place a semicolon at the end of the line, or press Enter and place it by itself on the last line. You can then press Enter to execute the statement. The command will execute and return the information to your screen. The **SQL>** prompt returns after the command has been executed. At this point, the command is still in the buffer, where it can be edited, saved to a file, or re-executed. To re-execute, just type in a slash (/) at the **SQL>** prompt. Table 5.1 displays commands that act upon the contents of the SQL buffer.

The editing commands in Table 5.1 act on the current line in the buffer, with the exception of the **RUN** and **LIST** commands. The current line of the buffer is indicated by an asterisk. For example, in Figure 5.3, the SQL statement in the buffer is listed with the **LIST** command, then Line 3 is listed, followed by Lines 2 through 5.

The semicolon is not written to the buffer. If you have used the semicolon on the last line of the statement, when listing the buffer the semicolon will not be present. The commands in Table 5.2 do not act upon the contents of the SQL buffer.

Table 5.1   *SQL buffer commands.*

Command	Abbreviation	Purpose
RUN	R	Executes the current statement in the SQL buffer
	/	Same as above
APPEND text	A text	Adds text to the end of the current line
CHANGE	C/old/new	Changes old text to new text
CHANGE	C/text/	Deletes text from the current line
CLEAR BUFFER	CL BUFF	Deletes all lines in the SQL buffer
DEL		Deletes the current line
INPUT	I	Adds an indefinite number of lines after the current line
LIST	L	Lists all of the lines currently in the buffer
	;	Lists all of the lines currently in the buffer
LIST n	L n	Lists line number n
LIST n m	L n m	Lists lines n through m

Table 5.2   *More SQL commands.*

Command	Abbreviation	Purpose
EXIT		Exits the SQL*Plus session
QUIT		Same as above
SAVE file name		Saves the buffer to file name
GET file name		Loads the file name into the SQL buffer
START file name	@	Executes the commands in file name
ED file name		Uses the system's default editor to edit file name
DESCRIBE	DESC	Displays database object structures, such as tables

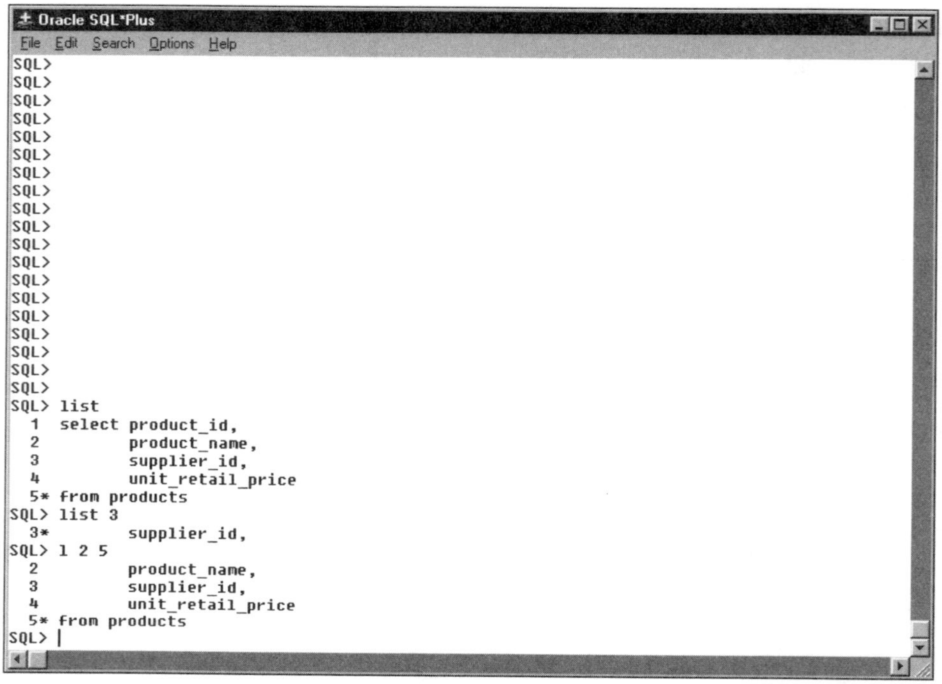

Figure 5.3   An example SQL*Plus session.

SELECT STATEMENT

The **SELECT** statement, which retrieves data from the database, is one of the most important statements in SQL*Plus. **SELECT** has a minimum of two clauses:

- *SELECT*—Tells the database which columns you need to view.
- *FROM*—Tells the database which tables or views to look at.

For example:

```
SELECT column name to be displayed
FROM table(s) that hold the columns;
```

The column names are separated by commas and are not case-sensitive. Listing 5.3 shows an example **SELECT** statement and its output. This and all other examples in this chapter use the data defined and entered in previous chapters.

Listing 5.3   An example **SELECT** statement.

```
SQL> select product_id,product_name,units_in_stock
  2  from products;
```

```
PRODUCT_ID PRODUCT_NAME                                UNITS_IN_STOCK
---------- ------------------------------------------- --------------
      5001 A Nut                                                 1000
      5002 B Nut                                                 1000
      5003 1cm Screw                                             1000
      5004 1cm Nail                                              1000
      5005 1mm Washer                                            1000
      5006 2mm Washer                                            1000
      5007 2cm Nail                                              1000
      5008 2cm Screw                                             1000
      5009 3cm Screw                                             1000
      5010 C Nut                                                 1000

10 rows selected.
```

SQL*Plus has headed each column with its column name; the widths of the columns are taken from the database and were defined when the table was created.

Selecting All Columns

To select all columns in a table, you don't have to specify each column name separately in the **SELECT** statement. You can use an asterisk (*) to denote all columns. They will be displayed in the order they were created in the table. If you need the columns displayed in a different order, you must specify each column in the **SELECT** statement. Listing 5.4 is an example of selecting all columns from a table.

Listing 5.4 *Selecting all columns from the **ORDER_DETAILS** table.*

```
SQL> select * from order_details;

 ORDER_ID PRODUCT_ID NUMBER_ORDERED UNIT_PRICE
--------- ---------- -------------- ----------
   100001       5002             20          4
   100001       5001             10          2
   100001       5003             10         10
   100002       5001             20          2
   100003       5002             10          4
   100004       5001             15          2
   100004       5002             25          4
   100005       5004             10          6
   100005       5003             10         10
   100005       5002             10          4
   100006       5001             20          2
   100003       5004             50          6

12 rows selected.
```

Duplicate Rows

In some tables, you can duplicate some columns—for example, the **Product_id** column in the ORDER_DETAILS table will have duplicate values. If a **SELECT** were done using the **Product_id** column, it would produce the result shown in Listing 5.5.

Listing 5.5 *Selecting one column from the **ORDER_DETAILS** table.*

```
SQL> select product_id from order_details;

PRODUCT_ID
----------
      5002
      5001
      5003
      5001
      5002
      5001
      5002
      5004
      5003
      5002
      5001
      5004

12 rows selected.
```

If you use the **DISTINCT** option of the **SELECT** clause, however, each value will be displayed once, thus eliminating duplicates from the rows returned, as shown in Listing 5.6.

Listing 5.6 *Use of the **DISTINCT** clause.*

```
SQL> select distinct product_id
  2  from order_details;

PRODUCT_ID
----------
      5001
      5002
      5003
      5004
```

If you define multiple columns in the **SELECT** clause, the **DISTINCT** clause works on all of them. You need to specify the **DISTINCT** clause only once. Listing 5.7 is an example.

Listing 5.7 *The **DISTINCT** clause acting on more than one row.*

```
SQL> select distinct product_id,number_ordered
  2  from order_details;
```

```
PRODUCT_ID NUMBER_ORDERED
---------- ---------------
      5001              10
      5001              15
      5001              20
      5002              10
      5002              20
      5002              25
      5003              10
      5004              10
      5004              50
```

```
9 rows selected.
```

Column Aliases

The columns displayed by **SELECT** statements have the column name as the heading when accessed through SQL*Plus. You can create an alternative heading by specifying an alias after the column name in the **SELECT** statement, as shown in Listing 5.8. Enclosing the alias in double quotes allows the use of special characters, such as spaces. Note that a space is left between the column name and the first double quote.

Listing 5.8   Using column aliases.

```
SQL> select product_id "Product Id" from products;
```

```
Product Id
----------
      5001
      5002
      5003
      5004
      5005
      5006
      5007
      5008
      5009
      5010
```

```
10 rows selected.
```

Arithmetic Expressions

You can use arithmetic expressions to manipulate the display of number and date columns. These expressions act upon different columns within the **SELECT** statement. The expressions are:

- The addition operator (+)

- The subtraction operator (-)

- The multiplication operator (*)

- The division operator (/)

The example in Listing 5.9 shows the use of these expressions within a **SELECT** statement.

Listing 5.9   *Arithmetic operators in a SQL statement.*

```
SQL> select order_id,
  2         number_ordered*unit_price
  3  from order_details;

 ORDER_ID NUMBER_ORDERED*UNIT_PRICE
--------- ------------------------
   100001                       80
   100001                       20
   100001                      100
   100002                       40
   100003                       40
   100004                       30
   100004                      100
   100005                       60
   100005                      100
   100005                       40
   100006                       40
   100003                      300

12 rows selected.
```

Multiple operators can act upon one column. For example:

```
unit_price*14/4
```

Priorities are placed on the operators when you use more than one. The multiplication operator has top priority, followed in order by division, addition, and subtraction. If more than one operator of the same priority is used, they are read from left to right. You can change the precedence of the operators by using parentheses.

Combining Columns

The easiest way to combine columns is to use the concatenation operator, represented by two vertical bars (||). This combines two or more columns to be displayed in one column, as shown in Listing 5.10.

Listing 5.10 *The concatenation operator.*

```
SQL> select customer_id||customer_name
  2  from customers;

CUSTOMER_ID||CUSTOMER_NAME
-------------------------------------
20002DEF Ltd
20001ABC Ltd
20003GHI Inc
20004JKL Inc
20005MNO Ltd
```

In this case, the two columns **Customer_id** and **Customer_Name** are combined to display one column. The concatenation operator is usually used to combine a column value with some user-defined text. Adding user-defined text to SQL statements is referred to as using *literals*.

Adding Text To Your Statements

The text you can add to your SQL statements will appear once for each row. Date and character strings must be enclosed in single quotes. Listing 5.11 shows how you would add text to SQL statements to make the output more readable.

Listing 5.11 *Using text literals within SQL.*

```
SQL> select customer_name||' has the telephone number - '||telephone_number
  2  from customers;

CUSTOMER_NAME||'HASTHETELEPHONENUMBER-'||TELEPHONE_NUMBER
---------------------------------------------------------------------
DEF Ltd has the telephone number - 2343213
ABC Ltd has the telephone number - 1234455
GHI Inc has the telephone number - 234321
JKL Inc has the telephone number - 111112
MNO Ltd has the telephone number - 1234321
```

Null Values

Null values are stored in the database whenever a value is not inserted into the database; for example, when you enter the customer address information into the **CUSTOMERS** table, sometimes you have no information to enter for **Address_Line_2**. This is then stored as a null value.

Null values can be used to give columns default values. To do this, you need to use the **NVL** function. Personal Oracle8's many available functions, which allow the manipulation of a column of values, will be explained in detail later in this chapter. The **NVL** command allows you to give default values for any null column. The example in Listing 5.12 shows the replacement of **Address_Line_2** with a series of dashes where the line is null.

Listing 5.12   An example using the **NVL** function.

```
SQL> select address_line_2 from customers;

ADDRESS_LINE_2
----------------------------------------
Mayfair
Mayfair


Burstwick

SQL> select nvl(address_line_2,'----------')
  2  from customers;

NVL(ADDRESS_LINE_2,'----------')
----------------------------------------
Mayfair
Mayfair
----------
----------
Burstwick
```

This function is more commonly used to deal with null number values. If a number is null and you multiply it by another number, the output will be null. You can use the **NVL** function to default any null value to be 0:

```
nvl(commision,0)
```

The best way to think of a null value is to think of it as a value that has not yet been set.

You can use the **NVL** function to convert a null numeric, character, or date value to another numeric, character, or date value. The only proviso is that the column types be the same:

- **NVL(Order_Date,'01-JAN-99')**
- **NVL(Unit_Price,0)**
- **NVL(Address_Line_2,'----------')**

Ordering Your Output

So far, when you've used SQL statements, you've not been interested in the order of the rows returned. When a SQL statement is issued to the database, the rows returned are in the order that they were entered into the database. This is sometimes not the best way to view the output. You can use the **ORDER BY** clause to display the data in a different order, either ascending or descending. This clause should go on the last line of the SQL statement. The default ordering of the **ORDER BY** clause is ascending. If you wish to order the information in descending order, add **DESC** to the end, as shown in Listing 5.13. This option puts numerical output into a more readable format.

Listing 5.13   The *ORDER BY* clause.

```
SQL> select product_id
  2   from products
  3   order by product_id;

PRODUCT_ID
----------
      5001
      5002
      5003
      5004
      5005
      5006
      5007
      5008
      5009
      5010

10 rows selected

SQL> select product_id
  2   from products
  3   order by product_id desc;

PRODUCT_ID
----------
      5010
      5009
      5008
      5007
      5006
      5005
      5004
      5003
      5002
      5001

10 rows selected.
```

Returning Subsets Of Data

All of the previously mentioned SQL statements have been returning every row in the table. In most cases, this is not a good strategy to use. Most production databases have tables with thousands, and in some cases millions, of rows. Returning all of these rows would not be practical. You can reduce the amount of data returned to a more manageable size by using the **WHERE** clause to select only the records you're interested in. This clause enables you to restrict your output to those rows that meet a certain condition. The **WHERE** clause must follow the **FROM** clause.

The **WHERE** clause compares values held in columns, literals, arithmetic expressions, or functions. It contains three elements:

- A column name
- A comparison operator
- A column name, constant, or list of values

Comparison Operators

Comparison operators can be divided into two main groups: logical operators and SQL operators. The logical operators are:

- Equal to (=)
- Greater than (>)
- Less than (<)
- Greater than or equal to (>=)
- Less than or equal to (<=)

The SQL operators are:

- *LIKE*—Matches a character pattern
- *IS NULL*—Matches if the column value is null
- *IN (list)*—Matches if the column value is in the supplied list
- *BETWEEN a AND b*—Matches if the column value is between value a and value b

Logical Operators

Listing 5.14 is an example of a logical operator. You can substitute any of the logical operators with the one used in this example.

Listing 5.14   An example logical operator.

```
SQL> select customer_name
  2  from customers
  3  where city = 'New York';

CUSTOMER_NAME
---------------------------
GHI Inc
JKL Inc
```

Note that the text string that you're searching for—New York—is in mixed case. When using text searches, you should use the correct case, as case is stored within the database (i.e., the database is case-sensitive when searching for text).

You can also compare one column value with that of another column in the same row. However, the columns must be of the same type, and the values will always be in the same row.

SQL Operators

The **LIKE** operator allows you to match on patterns—i.e., parts of a character string. You can also refer to this as a wild-card search. The **LIKE** operator uses two symbols to construct the string that columns are matched against:

- The percentage (%) symbol is used to match zero or more characters. For example, S% would match anything that *begins* with the uppercase letter S, while %S would match anything that *ends* with the uppercase letter S.

- The underscore (_) symbol specifies a single-character position. For example, S_M would match any three-letter string that starts with S and ends with M.

These two symbols can be mixed together on the same line. For example, S_M% would match any string where the first character is S and the third character is M. An example of the **LIKE** operator is shown in Listing 5.15.

*Listing 5.15   An example of the **LIKE** operator.*

```
SQL> select supplier_name
  2  from suppliers
  3  where city like 'New%';

SUPPLIER_NAME
-------------------------------
Widget Design Inc
JRF Relational Associates Ltd
```

The **IS NULL** operator is used, as its name suggests, to match for any columns that are null. An example is shown in Listing 5.16.

Listing 5.16 *An example of the **IS NULL** operator.*

```
SQL> select supplier_name
  2  from suppliers
  3  where address_line_2 is null;

SUPPLIER_NAME
----------------------------------
Test Company Ltd
Training Company Inc
```

The **IN** operator tests for the column value in a specified list of values. The list of values, again, must take note of the data type and use single quotes for character and date fields and no quotes for numeric fields. The example shown in Listing 5.17 uses the **PRODUCTS** table to display products produced by suppliers specified in the list.

Listing 5.17 *An example of the **IN** operator.*

```
SQL> select product_id,product_name
  2  from products
  3  where supplier_id in (1001,1002);

PRODUCT_ID PRODUCT_NAME
---------- -------------------------
      5003 1cm Screw
      5004 1cm Nail
      5007 2cm Nail
      5008 2cm Screw
      5009 3cm Screw
```

The **BETWEEN** operator is used mainly in numeric and date calculations. It tests for values within a high- and low-value range. The range includes the limiting values. For example, the expression

```
between 1 and 10
```

would be the same as:

```
>=1 and <=10
```

Listing 5.18 shows an example of the use of the **BETWEEN** operator.

Listing 5.18 *An example of the **BETWEEN** operator.*

```
SQL> select order_id,order_date
  2  from orders
  3  where order_date between '01-JAN-1999' and '31-DEC-1999';

 ORDER_ID ORDER_DAT
--------- ---------
   100001 01-Jan-99
   100002 02-Jan-99
   100005 28-Aug-99
   100006 28-Aug-99
```

To make certain inquiries against the database, you may want to construct a statement to extract all rows that do not match a given condition. For example, let's say that in a class of 100 people taking an examination, 99 pass. In this case, selecting all rows that do not meet a condition—in this case, the person who did not pass the examination—is often easier than selecting those who do meet the condition. You can do this in SQL*Plus, using the **NOT** or ! operator:

- *!=*—Not equal to
- *NOT BETWEEN*—Outside of the range specified
- *NOT IN (list)*—Outside of the list of values
- *IS NOT NULL*—All values that are not null in the specified column
- *NOT LIKE*—All values that do not match the specified pattern

Be aware of the difference between the ! operator and the **NOT** operator: The ! operator should be used with only logical operators, such as =, <, >, while the **NOT** operator should be used with only SQL operators. Each of the listed **NOT** operators perform the exact opposite when they have ! or **NOT** assigned with them. For example, Listing 5.19 show all orders not dispatched during 1999.

Listing 5.19 *An example of the **NOT** operator.*

```
SQL> select order_id,dispatched_date
  2  from orders
  3  where dispatched_date not between '01-JAN-1999' and '31-DEC-1999';

 ORDER_ID DISPATCHE
--------- ---------
   100003 09-May-98
   100004 03-Jun-98
```

Using Multiple Conditions

Rarely will you perform a query that relies on only one condition. In the commercial world, many applications are written using SQL statements that are hundreds of lines long.

Suppose you want to display all of the orders placed in 1999 by customer number 20001. This would need two conditions: the first to display all orders placed in 1999, and the second to display only those ordered by customer 20001. The SQL code for this appears in Listing 5.20.

Listing 5.20   An example of multiple conditions.

```
SQL> select order_id,customer_id,order_date
  2  from orders
  3  where order_date between '01-JAN-1999' and '31-DEC-1999'
  4  and customer_id = 20001;

 ORDER_ID CUSTOMER_ID ORDER_DAT
--------- ----------- ---------
   100001       20001 01-Jan-99
   100002       20001 02-Jan-99
```

This example uses the **AND** operator on Line 4 to require that both conditions are true for the query to return rows. You can also use the **OR** operator, which states that at least one of the conditions must be true. For example, the same statement as in Listing 5.20 could be rewritten using the **OR** operator with different results, as shown in Listing 5.21.

Listing 5.21   An example of the OR operator.

```
SQL> select order_id,customer_id,order_date
  2  from orders
  3  where order_date between '01-JAN-1999' and '31-DEC-1999'
  4  or customer_id = 20001;

 ORDER_ID CUSTOMER_ID ORDER_DATE
--------- ----------- ----------
   100001       20001 01-Jan-99
   100002       20001 02-Jan-99
   100005       20004 28-Aug-99
   100006       20005 28-Aug-99
```

You may combine **AND**s and **OR**s in any **SELECT** statement. When **AND** and **OR** appear in the same **WHERE** clause, all of the **AND**s are performed before all of the **OR**s, because **AND** has a higher priority than **OR**.

Functions

As stated previously, functions modify the value of a column or literal, allowing data to be displayed in a different format from the way it is stored within the database. Functions can be used wherever a column name can be used— i.e., in the **SELECT** clause, the **WHERE** clause, or the **ORDER BY** clause. Functions can be classified into five different types:

- *Character*—Operates on character columns or literal values
- *Number*—Operates on numeric values or numeric literals
- *Date*—Operates on date columns
- *Conversion*—Changes the data type of the column
- *Group*—Groups information together

All functions can be written in notation form. The notation I will use to describe the functions will be as follows:

- *Column*—Any named database column
- *Value*—Any literal, character, numeric, or date value
- |—Represents the **OR** operator
- *i*—Represents a number
- *x*—Represents a string
- *chars*—Represents a number of specified characters
- *date*—Represents a date column

The general makeup of a function is its name followed by the parameters enclosed in parentheses—i.e., **NVL**(*column,value*).

The following sections describe the common functions used within SQL*Plus, along with an example of each one's use.

Character Functions

The character functions covered here are:

- **UPPER** and **LOWER**
- **INITCAP**
- **LPAD** and **RPAD**
- **LENGTH**

- SUBSTR
- INSTR
- DECODE
- **LTRIM** and **RTRIM**

UPPER And LOWER

The **UPPER** function forces any string the function operates on into uppercase. It is written as:

```
UPPER(column|value)
```

Listing 5.22 is an example of this function.

Listing 5.22   The **UPPER** function.

```
SQL> select city from suppliers;

CITY
--------------------
London
London
New York
New York
Hull

SQL> select upper(city) from suppliers;

UPPER(CITY)
--------------------
LONDON
LONDON
NEW YORK
NEW YORK
HULL
```

The **LOWER** function does, as you would expect, the opposite of **UPPER**: It changes any string or column the function operates on into lowercase. The syntax for the **LOWER** function is:

```
LOWER(column|value)
```

For an example, see Listing 5.23.

Listing 5.23   The **LOWER** function.

```
SQL> select lower(city) from suppliers;
```

```
LOWER(CITY)
--------------------
london
london
new york
new york
hull
```

INITCAP

The **INITCAP** function changes the column or text values it operates on by making the initial letter of all words uppercase and the rest of the word lowercase. It is written as:

```
INITCAP(column|value)
```

For an example, see Listing 5.24.

Listing 5.24   The INITCAP function.

```
SQL> select country from suppliers;

COUNTRY
--------------------
England
England
USA
USA
England

SQL> select initcap(country) from suppliers;

INITCAP(COUNTRY)
--------------------
England
England
Usa
Usa
England
```

As you can see in the example, the *USA* records have been changed to *Usa*, but the *England* records have stayed the same, as they were already capitalized.

LPAD And RPAD

The **LPAD** function pads the column or literal from the left to a total width of *i* characters. The leading characters are filled with *x*. If *x* is not specified, the value is padded with spaces.

As you can see in Listing 5.25, I have left-padded the city column with asterisks to 10 characters. The syntax for **LPAD** is:

```
LPAD(column|value,i,'x')
```

Listing 5.25   The LPAD function.

```
SQL> select lpad(city,10,'*') from suppliers;

LPAD(CITY,
----------
****London
****London
**New York
**New York
******Hull
```

The **RPAD** function does exactly the same, except it pads the field to the right instead of the left. Listing 5.26 shows the same example as Listing 5.25, but using **RPAD**. The syntax for **RPAD** is:

```
RPAD(column|value,i,'x')
```

Listing 5.26   The RPAD function.

```
SQL> select rpad(city,10,'*') from suppliers;

RPAD(CITY,
----------
London****
London****
New York**
New York**
Hull******
```

LENGTH

The **LENGTH** function returns the number of characters in the column value or literal specified. The example in Listing 5.27 shows the **Supplier_Name** field and its associated length. Note that spaces are counted if they split up words. The syntax for **LENGTH** is:

```
LENGTH(column|value)
```

Listing 5.27   The *LENGTH* function.

```
SQL> select supplier_name,length(supplier_name)
  2  from suppliers;

SUPPLIER_NAME                           LENGTH(SUPPLIER_NAME)
--------------------------------------- ---------------------
Test Company Ltd                                           16
Training Company Inc                                       20
Widget Design Inc                                          17
JRF Relational Associates Ltd                              29
Hardware Ltd                                               12
```

SUBSTR

SUBSTR is the substring function, used for extracting parts of text from a column. **SUBSTR** extracts a string of i characters, starting at position *pos*, from the column value or literal. If i is omitted, the string is extracted from i to the end of the string. The **SUBSTR** function is written as:

```
SUBSTR(column|value,pos,i)
```

In Listing 5.28, **SUBSTR** is used to extract a string of five characters, starting with Position two, from the **Supplier_Name** column.

Listing 5.28   The *SUBSTR* function.

```
SQL> select substr(supplier_name,2,5) from suppliers;

SUBSTR
------
est C
raini
idget
RF Re
ardwa
```

INSTR

The **INSTR** function finds the character position of the ith occurrence of x in the literal or column value starting from character position *pos*. If *pos* and i are omitted, the function returns the character position of the first occurrence of the string. The example in Listing 5.29 shows the **INSTR** function displaying the character position of the second a in the **Supplier_Name** column. The syntax for **INSTR** is:

```
INSTR(column|value,'x',pos,n)
```

Listing 5.29   The *INSTR* function.

```
SQL> select supplier_name from suppliers;

SUPPLIER_NAME
----------------------------------------
Test Company Ltd
Training Company Inc
Widget Design Inc
JRF Relational Associates Ltd
Hardware Ltd

SQL> select instr(supplier_name,'a',1,2)
  2  from suppliers;

INSTR(SUPPLIER_NAME,'A',1,2)
---------------------------
                          0
                         14
                          0
                         13
                          6
```

DECODE

The **DECODE** function is one of the most widely used and best functions available. It has numerous uses. The **DECODE** function acts as a case of if...then...else construct. Its syntax is:

```
DECODE(column|compareval,testval1,outval1,[testval2,outval2, ...,]defaultval)
```

DECODE is best described with an example, as in Listing 5.30.

Listing 5.30   The *DECODE* function.

```
SQL> select city from suppliers;

CITY
--------------------
London
London
New York
New York
Hull

SQL> select decode(city,'London','Pound',
  2                     'New York','Dollar',
  3                     '???')
  4  from suppliers;
```

```
DECODE
------
Pound
Pound
Dollar
Dollar
???
```

Basically, the example in Listing 5.30 says: Decode the city column of the **SUPPLIERS** table, and if it is London, replace this with Pound, or if it is New York, replace this with Dollar, or if it is anything else, replace it with ???. As I said previously, **DECODE** is a basic **IF** statement.

LTRIM And RTRIM

The **LTRIM** function removes from the left leading occurrences of *x*. **LTRIM** is written as:

```
LTRIM(column|value,'x')
```

For an example, see Listing 5.31.

Listing 5.31   The LTRIM function.

```
SQL> select product_name from products;

PRODUCT_NAME
----------------------------------------
A Nut
B Nut
1cm Screw
1cm Nail
1mm Washer
2mm Washer
2cm Nail
2cm Screw
3cm Screw
C Nut

10 rows selected.

SQL> select ltrim(product_name,'12C') from products;

LTRIM(PRODUCT_NAME,'12C')
----------------------------------------
A Nut
B Nut
cm Screw
cm Nail
mm Washer
```

```
mm Washer
cm Nail
cm Screw
3cm Screw
 Nut

10 rows selected.
```

The example in Listing 5.31 removes characters from the left-hand side of the **Product_Name** column where the characters are either a *1, 2, C,* or all of these.

The **RTRIM** function performs the same as **LTRIM**, except it removes characters from the right. Listing 5.32 shows an example of the use of **RTRIM**. Its syntax is the same as **LTRIM**:

```
RTRIM(column|value,'x')
```

Listing 5.32   The RTRIM function.

```
SQL> select product_name from products;

PRODUCT_NAME
----------------------------------------
A Nut
B Nut
1cm Screw
1cm Nail
1mm Washer
2mm Washer
2cm Nail
2cm Screw
3cm Screw
C Nut

10 rows selected.

SQL> select rtrim(product_name,'wer')
  2  from products;

RTRIM(PRODUCT_NAME,'WER')
----------------------------------------
A Nut
B Nut
1cm Sc
1cm Nail
1mm Wash
2mm Wash
2cm Nail
2cm Sc
```

```
3cm Sc
C Nut

10 rows selected.
```

The text to the right-hand side of the column is trimmed wherever the characters *w*, *e*, or *r* appear. Notice that more than one character has been trimmed in each case, as we specified that the *e* should be trimmed as well.

Number Functions

The number functions covered here are:

- ROUND
- TRUNC
- CEIL and FLOOR
- POWER
- SIGN
- ABS
- MOD

ROUND

The **ROUND** function rounds the column or numeric literal to *i* decimal places. If *i* is omitted, the value or column is rounded to no decimal places. If, however, the value of *i* is negative, the numbers to the left of the decimal point are rounded.

The syntax for **ROUND** is:

```
ROUND(column|value,i)
```

For an example of the **ROUND** function, see Listing 5.33.

Listing 5.33   The ROUND function.

```
SQL> select unit_price/number_ordered
  2  from order_details;

UNIT_PRICE/NUMBER_ORDERED
-------------------------
                       .2
                       .2
```

```
                      1
                     .1
                     .4
              .13333333
                    .16
                     .6
                      1
                     .4
                     .1
                    .12
```

12 rows selected.

```
SQL> select round(unit_price/number_ordered,2)
  2  from order_details;

ROUND(UNIT_PRICE/NUMBER_ORDERED,2)
----------------------------------
                                .2
                                .2
                                 1
                                .1
                                .4
                               .13
                               .16
                                .6
                                 1
                                .4
                                .1
                               .12
```

12 rows selected.

TRUNC

The **TRUNC** command truncates the column or value to *i* decimal places. This is different from the **ROUND** function in that no rounding takes place; the decimal places are just lost.

Syntax for **TRUNC** is:

```
TRUNC(column|value,i)
```

Listing 5.34 is an example of **TRUNC**.

Listing 5.34   *The **TRUNC** function.*

```
SQL> select unit_price/number_ordered
  2  from order_details;
```

```
UNIT_PRICE/NUMBER_ORDERED
-------------------------
                       .2
                       .2
                        1
                       .1
                       .4
                .13333333
                      .16
                       .6
                        1
                       .4
                       .1
                      .12

12 rows selected.

SQL> select trunc(unit_price/number_ordered,3)
  2  from order_details;

TRUNC(UNIT_PRICE/NUMBER_ORDERED,3)
----------------------------------
                               .2
                               .2
                                1
                               .1
                               .4
                             .133
                              .16
                               .6
                                1
                               .4
                               .1
                              .12

12 rows selected.
```

CEIL And FLOOR

The **CEIL** command finds the smallest integer that is greater than or equal to the column or value. This is useful for rounding up all numbers; so, for example, the number 1.1 would become the number 2.

CEIL is written as:

```
CEIL(column|value)
```

The **CEIL** function is shown in Listing 5.35.

Listing 5.35 *The CEIL function.*

```
SQL> select unit_price/number_ordered
  2  from order_details;

UNIT_PRICE/NUMBER_ORDERED
-------------------------
                       .2
                       .2
                        1
                       .1
                       .4
                .13333333
                      .16
                       .6
                        1
                       .4
                       .1
                      .12

12 rows selected.

SQL> select ceil(unit_price/number_ordered)
  2  from order_details;

CEIL(UNIT_PRICE/NUMBER_ORDERED)
-------------------------------
                              1
                              1
                              1
                              1
                              1
                              1
                              1
                              1
                              1
                              1
                              1
                              1

12 rows selected.
```

The **FLOOR** function does the opposite of **CEIL**; it rounds everything down to the largest integer less than or equal to the column or value. The syntax for the **FLOOR** function is:

```
FLOOR(column|value)
```

Listing 5.36 is an example of the **FLOOR** function.

Listing 5.36   *The **FLOOR** function.*

```
SQL> select unit_price/number_ordered
  2  from order_details;

UNIT_PRICE/NUMBER_ORDERED
-------------------------
                       .2
                       .2
                        1
                       .1
                       .4
                .13333333
                      .16
                       .6
                        1
                       .4
                       .1
                      .12

12 rows selected.

SQL> select floor(unit_price/number_ordered)
  2  from order_details;

FLOOR(UNIT_PRICE/NUMBER_ORDERED)
--------------------------------
                               0
                               0
                               1
                               0
                               0
                               0
                               0
                               0
                               1
                               0
                               0
                               0

12 rows selected.
```

POWER

The **POWER** function raises the column or literal value to the ith power.

POWER is written as:

```
POWER(column|value,i)
```

In Listing 5.37, the **Number_Ordered** column is squared.

Listing 5.37   The *POWER* function.

```
SQL> select number_ordered from order_details;

NUMBER_ORDERED
--------------
            20
            10
            10
            20
            10
            15
            25
            10
            10
            10
            20
            50

12 rows selected.

SQL> select power(number_ordered,2) from order_details;

POWER(NUMBER_ORDERED,2)
-----------------------
                    400
                    100
                    100
                    400
                    100
                    225
                    625
                    100
                    100
                    100
                    400
                   2500

12 rows selected.
```

SIGN

The **SIGN** function returns a -1 if the column or value specified is negative, a 1 if positive, and a 0 if the value is 0.

The syntax for **SIGN** is:

```
SIGN(column|value)
```

The **SIGN** function is shown in Listing 5.38.

Listing 5.38   *The **SIGN** function.*

```
SQL> select sign(-99),
  2         sign(99-99),
  3         sign(99)
  4  from dual;

SIGN(-99) SIGN(99-99)  SIGN(99)
--------- ----------- --------
       -1           0        1
```

ABS

The **ABS** function returns the absolute value of the column or value specified. The absolute value is the value with no sign—for example, the value -99 becomes 99. The syntax for **ABS** is:

```
ABS(column|value)
```

Listing 5.39 shows an example of the **ABS** function.

Listing 5.39   *The **ABS** function.*

```
SQL> select abs(-99),
  2         abs(99-99),
  3         abs(99)
  4  from dual;

 ABS(-99) ABS(99-99)   ABS(99)
--------- ----------- --------
       99           0        99
```

MOD

The **MOD** function finds the remainder of the first column or value divided by the second column or value.

MOD is written as:

```
MOD(column1|value1,column2|value2)
```

For an example of the **MOD** function, see Listing 5.40.

Listing 5.40   *The **MOD** function.*

```
SQL> select mod(100,9)
  2  from dual;
```

```
MOD(100,9)
----------
         1
```

Date Functions

One of the many advantages of using Personal Oracle8 is the way it handles dates. Because the Oracle database stores date columns internally as a number, you can perform arithmetic operations on them. The default format for the date is DD-MON-YY (for example, 12-JAN-98). If you don't specify a time when entering the date, Oracle stores the default time of 12:00 a.m.

Personal Oracle8 handles the year 2000 problem by using Julian dates—the number of days from 01-JAN-4712 BC. This gives you a common starting point for all date arithmetic; for example, to add three days onto today's date, you could use the **SYSDATE+3** command in your **SELECT** statement.

The date functions this section looks at are:

- ADD_MONTHS
- NEXT_DAY
- LAST_DAY
- TRUNC
- NEW_TIME

ADD_MONTHS

The **ADD_MONTHS** function adds *i* months to the column or literal date you specify. **ADD_MONTHS** is written as:

```
ADD_MONTHS(date,i)
```

An example is shown in Listing 5.41, which adds three months to the order date in the **ORDERS** table.

Listing 5.41   The ADD_MONTHS function.

```
SQL> select order_date,add_months(order_date,3)
  2  from orders;

ORDER_DAT ADD_MONTH
--------- ---------
01-Jan-99 01-Apr-99
02-Jan-99 02-Apr-99
```

```
01-May-98 01-Aug-98
01-Jun-98 01-Sep-98
28-Aug-99 28-Nov-99
28-Aug-99 28-Nov-99

6 rows selected.
```

NEXT_DAY

The **NEXT_DAY** function returns the date of the next day (**CHAR**), from the specified date (**DATE**). **NEXT_DAY** is written as:

```
NEXT_DAY(date,char)
```

The **CHAR** field can be either the name or number of the day. The days in Oracle start on Monday (1) and end on Sunday (7). For example, Listing 5.42 shows the two different ways to return the same result, the first column showing the Friday and the second column showing day number 5, a Friday.

Listing 5.42   The **NEXT_DAY** function.

```
SQL> select next_day('17-DEC-97','FRIDAY'),
  2         next_day('17-DEC-97',5)
  3  from dual;

NEXT_DAY( NEXT_DAY(
--------- ---------
19-Dec-97 19-Dec-97
```

LAST_DAY

The **LAST_DAY** function returns the date of the last day in the month contained in the date. This takes into account leap years. The syntax for **LAST_DAY** is:

```
LAST_DAY(date)
```

Listing 5.43 shows the last day in the month for three dates.

Listing 5.43   The **LAST_DAY** function.

```
SQL> select last_day('10-FEB-1998'),
  2         last_day('28-APR-1999'),
  3         last_day('01-FEB-2000')
  4  from dual;

LAST_DAY( LAST_DAY( LAST_DAY(
--------- --------- ---------
28-Feb-98 30-Apr-99 29-Feb-00
```

TRUNC

The **TRUNC** function truncates the specified date to the first date of that month if **CHAR** is MONTH; if **CHAR** is YEAR, **TRUNC** returns the first date of the year. **TRUNC** is written as:

```
TRUNC(date,char)
```

The **TRUNC** function is shown in Listing 5.44.

Listing 5.44   The **TRUNC** function.

```
SQL> select * from orders;

 ORDER_ID CUSTOMER_ID ORDER_DAT DISPATCHE ORDER_DUE
--------- ----------- --------- --------- ---------
   100001       20001 01-Jan-99 10-Jan-99 31-Jan-99
   100002       20001 02-Jan-99 11-Jan-99 31-Jan-99
   100003       20002 01-May-98 09-May-98 31-May-98
   100004       20003 01-Jun-98 03-Jun-98 10-Jun-98
   100005       20004 28-Aug-99 29-Aug-99 30-Sep-99
   100006       20005 28-Aug-99 10-Sep-99 31-Aug-99

6 rows selected.

SQL> select trunc(order_date,'MONTH'),
  2          trunc(order_date,'YEAR')
  3  from orders;

TRUNC(ORD TRUNC(ORD
--------- ---------
01-Jan-99 01-Jan-99
01-Jan-99 01-Jan-99
01-May-98 01-Jan-98
01-Jun-98 01-Jan-98
01-Aug-99 01-Jan-99
01-Aug-99 01-Jan-99

6 rows selected.
```

NEW_TIME

The **NEW_TIME** function returns the date and time in *timezone2* when date and time in *timezone1* are specified by date. This sounds fairly complex, but is straightforward when seen in an example (Listing 5.45). The syntax for **NEW_TIME** is:

```
NEW_TIME(date,timezone1,timezone2)
```

Table 5.3 shows the available time zones.

Table 5.3 *Available time-zone information.*

Time Zone	*Description*
AST	Atlantic Standard Time
ADT	Atlantic Daylight Time
BST	Bering Standard Time
BDT	Bering Daylight Time
CST	Central Standard Time
CDT	Central Daylight Time
EST	Eastern Standard Time
EDT	Eastern Daylight Time
GMT	Greenwich Mean Time
HST	Alaska-Hawaii Standard Time
HDT	Alaska-Hawaii Daylight Time
MST	Mountain Standard Time
MDT	Mountain Daylight Time
NST	Newfoundland Standard Time
PST	Pacific Standard Time
PDT	Pacific Daylight Time
YST	Yukon Standard Time
YDT	Yukon Daylight Time

The example in Listing 5.45 introduces a new function, called **TO_CHAR**, which basically changes the format of the date, so you can see the time. The **TO_CHAR** function is explained in greater detail in the next section. For Listing 5.45, you need to know only what it does. The first **SELECT** statement takes today's date and time in GMT and gives the equivalent time in CST.

Listing 5.45   *The **NEW_TIME** function.*

```
SQL> select to_char(new_time(sysdate,'GMT','CST'),'DD-MON-YY HH:MI:SS') from
dual;

TO_CHAR(NEW_TIME(S
------------------
17-DEC-97 04:14:21

SQL> select to_char(sysdate,'dd-MON-YY HH:MI:SS') from dual;

TO_CHAR(SYSDATE,'D
------------------
17-DEC-97 10:14:49
```

Conversion Functions

Conversion functions convert data types—for example, character data types to number data types. The conversion functions this section looks at are:

- TO_NUMBER
- TO_CHAR
- TO_DATE

TO_NUMBER

The **TO_NUMBER** function takes a number stored in character format and converts it into a number. A number stored in character format can be represented by '99'—i.e., a number in single quotes. Remember, the single quotes represent character strings. This function's syntax is:

```
TO_NUMBER(char)
```

Listing 5.46 shows an example of **TO_NUMBER**.

Listing 5.46   The **TO_NUMBER** function.

```
SQL> select to_number('99')
  2  from dual;

TO_NUMBER('99')
---------------
             99
```

The **TO_NUMBER** function is useful primarily when inserting data into a table, making sure it is in a number format.

TO_CHAR

The **TO_CHAR** function converts a number or date into character format specified by format. If format is not specified, the number or date is converted into a string. **TO_CHAR** is written as:

```
TO_CHAR(number|date,[format])
```

For an example, see Listing 5.47.

Listing 5.47   The **TO_CHAR** function.

```
SQL> select to_char(99)
  2  from dual;

TO
--
99
```

TO_CHAR is useful when inserting data into a table that has to be in character format.

The format mentioned in the **TO_CHAR** function is used to change the format of the date displayed. The format value is only for display purposes and is not stored internally as it is displayed. The format values can be split into two groups: number formats and date formats. Tables 5.4 and 5.5 show the available formats for number and date fields.

Table 5.4   Number format models.

Format	Example	Description
9	999	Leading zeros are blank, leading spaces if positive
0	099	Returns as above but with leading zeros
$	$999	Returns value with a leading dollar sign
MI	999MI	Returns a trailing minus sign when value is negative
S	S999	Returns value with a leading plus (+) or minus (-) sign
PR	999PR	Returns a negative in angled brackets—e.g., <678>
D	99D99	Returns a decimal point wherever D is placed
G	9G999	Returns the group separator wherever G is placed
C	C999	Returns the ISO currency symbol wherever C is placed
,	9,999	Returns a comma in the specified position
.	99.99	Returns a dot in the specified position
EEEE	9.9EEEE	Returns a value using scientific notation
RN or rn	RN or rn	Returns a value in roman numerals in uppercase or lowercase
FM	FM99.9	Returns a value with no leading or trailing blanks

Table 5.5   Date format models.

Format	Meaning
"text"	The "text" is reproduced in the result
AD or A.D.	AD indicator
AM or A.M.	Meridian indicator
BC or B.C.	BC indicator
D	Day of week, 1 through 7

(continued)

Table 5.5 *Date format models (continued).*

Format	Meaning
DAY	Name of the day, padded to nine characters
DD	Day of the month
DDD	Day of the year
DY	Abbreviated name of the day
HH	Hour of the day
HH12	Hour of the day using 12-hour clock notation
HH24	Hour of the day using 24-hour clock notation
J	Julian day, based on the Julian calendar; this must be an integer
MI	Minute
MM	Month number
MON	Short name month
MONTH	Name of the month, padded to nine characters
PM or P.M.	Meridian indicator
RM	Roman numeral month—e.g., VII for July
RR	Rounds the century up if year <50 and last two digits of current year are >=50; rounds century down if year >=50 and last two digits of current year are <50
RRRR	Same as RR, but accepts four- and two-digit years
SS	Seconds
SSSSS	Number of seconds past midnight
YEAR	Year spelled out
YYYY	Four-digit year
YYY or YY or Y	Last three, two, or one digit of the year

Listing 5.48 shows an example of **TO_CHAR** using date formats.

Listing 5.48 The TO_CHAR date format.

```
SQL> select sysdate,
  2          to_char(sysdate,'Day DD Month, Year')
  3   from dual;

SYSDATE    TO_CHAR(SYSDATE,'DAYDDMONTH,YEAR')
---------  --------------------------------------------
17-Dec-97  Wednesday 17 December , Nineteen Ninety-Seven
```

In Listing 5.48, notice that the format mask and output are both in mixed case. That means if you capitalize the first letter of the format mask, the first letter of the result will be capitalized.

TO_DATE

The **TO_DATE** function converts the character value supplied into a date value according to the format specified. The format is optional; if not used, the **CHAR** must be in the default date format DD-MON-YY. All of the date formats shown in Table 5.5 can be used, along with some others that are not listed. See your SQL documentation for more information. This function's syntax is:

```
TO_DATE(char,[format])
```

Listing 5.49 shows an example of the **TO_DATE** function.

Listing 5.49   The **TO_DATE** function.

```
SQL> select to_date('1997/12/25','YYYY/MM/DD')
  2  from dual;

TO_DATE('
---------
25-Dec-97
```

Again, the **TO_DATE** function is used primarily when inserting dates into tables where you know the format of the date input.

Nested Functions

All of these functions can be nested, as you saw in Listing 5.45, where the **NEW_TIME** function was nested in the **TO_CHAR** function. Listing 5.50 is another example of a nested function, where the **UPPER** and **LOWER** functions are nested within the **DECODE** function.

Listing 5.50   An example of nested functions.

```
SQL> select decode(city,'London',UPPER(city),
  2                     'New York',LOWER(city),
  3                     city)
  4  from suppliers;

DECODE(CITY,'LONDON'
--------------------
LONDON
LONDON
new york
new york
Hull
```

Group Functions

Group functions are usually used to provide summary information, such as averages, the number of rows in a table, or the maximum value of a column from the database tables. This information is usually seen on reports. The group functions covered here are:

- COUNT
- AVG
- MIN and MAX
- SUM

COUNT

The **COUNT** function returns the number of *exp* that are not null in a table. Using the **DISTINCT** option, it will return the number of distinct rows in the table. You can use an asterisk in the parentheses to signify all rows, if you need to see how many rows are in a table. The syntax for **COUNT** is:

```
COUNT([DISTINCT|ALL]exp)
```

An example is shown in Listing 5.51, where the first **SELECT** statement shows the number of rows in the **SUPPLIERS** table, the second statement shows the number of rows with a not null **Product_Name**, and the third statement returns the number of distinct rows in the **ORDER_DETAILS** table.

Listing 5.51 *Three examples of the **COUNT** function.*

```
SQL> select count(*)
  2  from suppliers;

 COUNT(*)
---------
        5

SQL> select count(product_name)
  2  from products;

COUNT(PRODUCT_NAME)
-------------------
                 10

SQL> select count(distinct order_id)
  2  from order_details;
```

```
COUNT(DISTINCTORDER_ID)
-----------------------
                      6
```

AVG

The **AVG** function returns the average value of *i*, where *i* can be a column. The **DISTINCT** option will give you an average of the distinct values of *i*. **ALL** is the default and does not need to be entered. The syntax for **AVG** is:

```
AVG([DISTINCT|ALL]i)
```

See Listing 5.52 for an example.

Listing 5.52   The AVG function.

```
SQL> select avg(unit_cost_price)
  2  from products;

AVG(UNIT_COST_PRICE)
--------------------
                5.12

SQL> select avg(distinct unit_cost_price)
  2  from products;

AVG(DISTINCTUNIT_COST_PRICE)
----------------------------
                   5.3555556
```

MIN And MAX

The **MIN** function returns the minimum value of the expression. Its syntax is:

```
MIN([DISTINCT|ALL]exp)
```

Listing 5.53 is an example of the **MIN** function.

Listing 5.53   The MIN function.

```
SQL> select min(unit_cost_price)
  2  from products;

MIN(UNIT_COST_PRICE)
--------------------
                  .5
```

The **MAX** function is the opposite of **MIN**. It returns the maximum value of the expression. The syntax is:

```
MAX([DEFAULT|ALL]exp)
```

You can see an example of the **MAX** function in Listing 5.54.

Listing 5.54   The **MAX** function.

```
SQL> select max(unit_cost_price)
  2  from products;

MAX(UNIT_COST_PRICE)
--------------------
                  20
```

SUM

The **SUM** function returns the total value of all values in *exp*. The *exp* must be numeric, and nulls are ignored. The syntax of the **SUM** function is:

```
SUM([DISTINCT|ALL]exp)
```

Listing 5.55 shows an example of the **SUM** function.

Listing 5.55   The **SUM** function.

```
SQL> select sum(unit_cost_price)
  2  from products;

SUM(UNIT_COST_PRICE)
--------------------
                51.2
```

The GROUP BY Clause

Until now, all of the group functions have acted on the table as a whole. The **GROUP BY** clause allows you to group rows within the table depending upon column values. The function then returns summary information for each group of rows. Listing 5.56 gives a good example of this using the **ORDER_DETAILS** table. The first statement shows what data the table contains. The second statement shows the number of items ordered per order.

Listing 5.56   The **GROUP BY** clause.

```
SQL> select * from order_details;
```

```
ORDER_ID PRODUCT_ID NUMBER_ORDERED UNIT_PRICE
-------- ---------- -------------- ----------
  100001      5002             20          4
  100001      5001             10          2
  100001      5003             10         10
  100002      5001             20          2
  100003      5002             10          4
  100004      5001             15          2
  100004      5002             25          4
  100005      5004             10          6
  100005      5003             10         10
  100005      5002             10          4
  100006      5001             20          2
  100003      5004             50          6

12 rows selected.

SQL> select order_id,sum(number_ordered)
  2  from order_details
  3  group by order_id;

ORDER_ID SUM(NUMBER_ORDERED)
-------- -------------------
  100001                  40
  100002                  20
  100003                  60
  100004                  40
  100005                  30
  100006                  20

6 rows selected.
```

You have to keep in mind one major rule when using the **GROUP BY** clause: Any column or expression that appears in the **SELECT** list that is not a group function must also appear in the **GROUP BY** clause.

The HAVING Clause

The **HAVING** clause is used in conjunction with the **GROUP BY** clause to limit which groups you are able to see. The selection is made upon the value of the group function. An example of this clause is seen in Listing 5.57, which uses the previous example to display the number of items in each order. I have limited it just to show all **Order_id**s with more than 40 items.

Listing 5.57   The HAVING clause.

```
SQL> select order_id,sum(number_ordered)
  2  from order_details
```

```
3  group by order_id
4  having sum(number_ordered) > 40;

ORDER_ID SUM(NUMBER_ORDERED)
-------- -------------------
  100003                  60
```

BEYOND THE BASICS

Now that you've learned the basics of the **SELECT** statement, you can move on to more advanced techniques for accessing your data using **SELECT**. You will also learn how to add in, update, and delete your data through SQL*Plus.

ADVANCED SQL*PLUS

The art of getting more meaningful data out of the database by using SQL*Plus in conjunction with the database design.

In the previous chapter, you learned how to use the basic functions of SQL*Plus. This chapter will explore some of the more complex SQL*Plus functions, enabling you to perform more complex queries on the demo database. The topics covered in this chapter range from joining tables together for more flexibility to writing queries within queries.

JOINING TABLES

Typically, the information you need will not be found in just one table in the database, but in two or more. SQL*Plus can combine rows from one table with rows from another, using corresponding column values. This is referred to as a *join*.

To make a join between two tables, you specify the two columns that hold the values the tables are to be joined on, as shown in Listing 6.1.

Listing 6.1   *A join using two tables.*

```
SQL> select supplier_name,product_name
  2  from suppliers,
  3       products
  4  where suppliers.supplier_id = products.supplier_id;


SUPPLIER_NAME                           PRODUCT_NAME
-------------------------------------- --------------
Hardware Ltd                            A Nut
Hardware Ltd                            B Nut
Test Company Ltd                        1cm Screw
Training Company Inc                    1cm Nail
JRF Relational Associates Ltd           1mm Washer
JRF Relational Associates Ltd           2mm Washer
Training Company Inc                    2cm Nail
Test Company Ltd                        2cm Screw
Test Company Ltd                        3cm Screw
Hardware Ltd                            C Nut

10 rows selected.
```

To find suppliers that supply products, you look in the **SUPPLIERS** table to find the supplier name and in the **PRODUCTS** table to find the product name. For each product, you store the supplier's identifier, and then you join the two tables by their supplier identifier. The result of the query puts the supplier name and product name on the same row of the output. Note that:

- All tables accessed are listed in the **FROM** clause, separated by a comma.

- The **WHERE** clause specifies the columns used in the join, and the column names are prefixed with the table names. This avoids ambiguity when joining more than one table with the same column name.

Table Aliases

In certain queries, every column name would need prefixing by its table name, which could result in a long-winded and unreadable statement. Through the **FROM** clause, you can create a temporary label, or *alias*, which can be a shortened version of the table name. This short alias can then be used throughout the **SELECT** statement to reference the table, instead of using the full table name.

This table alias should be short, but it should still bear a resemblance to the original table name so you, and others reading your **SELECT** statement, will easily understand it. A common practice is to make these aliases single characters. You should not make two aliases the same. Listing 6.2 shows the **SELECT** statement from Listing 6.1, using aliases.

Listing 6.2   Using table aliases.

```
SQL> select s.supplier_name,p.product_name
  2  from suppliers s,
  3       products p
  4  where s.supplier_id = p.supplier_id;

SUPPLIER_NAME                            PRODUCT_NAME
-------------------------------------    ------------
Hardware Ltd                             A Nut
Hardware Ltd                             B Nut
Test Company Ltd                         1cm Screw
Training Company Inc                     1cm Nail
JRF Relational Associates Ltd            1mm Washer
JRF Relational Associates Ltd            2mm Washer
Training Company Inc                     2cm Nail
Test Company Ltd                         2cm Screw
Test Company Ltd                         3cm Screw
Hardware Ltd                             C Nut

10 rows selected.
```

The output from the query shown in Listing 6.2 is the same as that of Listing 6.1, but the query is easier to read and a lot shorter. Note that:

- The alias name and the table name are separated by one or more spaces in the **FROM** clause.

- The alias is separated from other table names by a comma.

- The alias is used as a prefix to column names to avoid ambiguity; even when ambiguity is not a problem, this practice will speed up the processing of the **SELECT** statement.

Product Joins

If, when you select from more than one table, the **WHERE** clause has no join condition, the output is a *product join*. A product join links each row of the first table to each row of the second table, producing a large output. This may be necessary when creating new tables, but is easy to overlook when writing large **SELECT** statements. If you receive a lot more output than you expect when executing such a query, look at your statement to check for any product joins. Listing 6.3 shows an example of a product join between the **CUSTOMERS** and **ORDERS** tables.

Listing 6.3   A product join.

```
SQL> select c.customer_name,o.order_id
  2  from customers c,
  3       orders o;
```

```
CUSTOMER_NAME                                ORDER_ID
----------------------------------------     --------
DEF Ltd                                        100001
ABC Ltd                                        100001
GHI Inc                                        100001
JKL Inc                                        100001
MNO Ltd                                        100001
DEF Ltd                                        100002
ABC Ltd                                        100002
GHI Inc                                        100002
JKL Inc                                        100002
MNO Ltd                                        100002
DEF Ltd                                        100003
ABC Ltd                                        100003
GHI Inc                                        100003
JKL Inc                                        100003
MNO Ltd                                        100003
DEF Ltd                                        100004
ABC Ltd                                        100004
GHI Inc                                        100004
JKL Inc                                        100004
MNO Ltd                                        100004
DEF Ltd                                        100005

CUSTOMER_NAME                                ORDER_ID
----------------------------------------     --------
ABC Ltd                                        100005
GHI Inc                                        100005
JKL Inc                                        100005
MNO Ltd                                        100005
DEF Ltd                                        100006
ABC Ltd                                        100006
GHI Inc                                        100006
JKL Inc                                        100006
MNO Ltd                                        100006

30 rows selected.
```

Equi-Joins

In Listing 6.1, the **Supplier_id** columns of the **SUPPLIERS** and **PRODUCTS** tables were used as the join columns. The join condition was where the **Supplier_id** column in the **SUPPLIERS** table was equal to the **Supplier_id** column in the **PRODUCTS** table. This is known as an *equi-join*, where one column equals another.

Non-Equi-Joins

When any condition other than one column equaling another is used to form a join condition, this is known as a *non-equi-join*. Listing 6.4 shows an example of a non-equi-join where the **SELECT** statement shows all product identifiers and where the order **Unit_Price** is within the range specified in the **PRODUCTS** table for cost and retail price for order identifier 100003. This is a non-equi-join, as the join condition operator is **BETWEEN**.

Listing 6.4   A non-equi-join.

```
SQL> select p.product_id, od.order_id
  2  from order_details od,
  3       products p
  4  where od.unit_price between p.unit_cost_price and p.unit_retail_price
  5  and od.order_id = 100003;

PRODUCT_ID  ORDER_ID
----------  --------
      5002    100003
      5003    100003
      5004    100003
      5004    100003
      5007    100003
      5010    100003
      5010    100003

7 rows selected.
```

Inner Joins

If a row does not satisfy the join condition specified, it will not appear in the output of the query. For example, Listing 6.5 shows which supplier supplied which product. Notice that supplier 1003 does not supply any products; therefore, because this does not satisfy the join condition, the information for the supplier is not displayed. This is known as an *inner join*.

Listing 6.5   An inner join.

```
SQL> select s.supplier_id,s.supplier_name,p.product_name
  2  from suppliers s,
  3       products p
  4  where s.supplier_id = p.supplier_id
  5  order by s.supplier_id;

SUPPLIER_ID SUPPLIER_NAME                            PRODUCT_NAME
----------- ---------------------------------------- ------------
       1001 Test Company Ltd                         1cm Screw
       1001 Test Company Ltd                         2cm Screw
```

```
1001 Test Company Ltd                        3cm Screw
1002 Training Company Inc                     1cm Nail
1002 Training Company Inc                     2cm Nail
1004 JRF Relational Associates Ltd           1mm Washer
1004 JRF Relational Associates Ltd           2mm Washer
1005 Hardware Ltd                            A Nut
1005 Hardware Ltd                            C Nut
1005 Hardware Ltd                            B Nut

10 rows selected.
```

Outer Joins

An outer join is the same as an inner join, except that it joins rows with no corresponding row in the other table to the equivalent of a null row. The outer join operator—a plus sign enclosed in parentheses—is associated with the column that may have the null values. Listing 6.6 shows the same example as Listing 6.5, but uses an outer, rather than an inner, join. Notice that the supplier details are displayed for supplier identifier 1003, but no product details are associated with it. This is because the supplier identifier is picked up from the **SUPPLIERS** table and joined to the **PRODUCTS** table; in this case, there is no join, so it is joined to a null row, returning no information from the **PRODUCTS** table.

Listing 6.6 An outer join.

```
SQL> select s.supplier_id,s.supplier_name,p.product_name
  2   from suppliers s,
  3        products p
  4   where s.supplier_id = p.supplier_id (+)
  5   order by s.supplier_id;

SUPPLIER_ID SUPPLIER_NAME                               PRODUCT_NAME
----------- ---------------------------------------    ------------
       1001 Test Company Ltd                           1cm Screw
       1001 Test Company Ltd                           2cm Screw
       1001 Test Company Ltd                           3cm Screw
       1002 Training Company Inc                       1cm Nail
       1002 Training Company Inc                       2cm Nail
       1003 Widget Design Inc
       1004 JRF Relational Associates Ltd              1mm Washer
       1004 JRF Relational Associates Ltd              2mm Washer
       1005 Hardware Ltd                               A Nut
       1005 Hardware Ltd                               C Nut
       1005 Hardware Ltd                               B Nut

11 rows selected.
```

Self Joins

By using table aliases, you can join a table to itself—that is, join a row in a table to another row within the same table. This is often useful with tables that are designed to hold hierarchical information. Consider Listing 6.7, which shows a table holding employee information. This table also stores the identification of each employee's manager—for example, Smith's manager is Connell.

Listing 6.7   A list of all employees.

```
SQL> select * from employees;

   EMP_NO EMP_NAME       SALARY MANAGER_NO
--------- ---------- --------- ----------
      100 SMITH          10000        104
      101 JONES          11000        104
      102 BROWN          12000        104
      103 HUGHES         13000        104
      104 CONNELL        11000
```

This table could be used in a self join—for example, to display all employees who earn more than their managers, as shown in Listing 6.8.

Listing 6.8   A self join.

```
SQL> select staff.emp_name,
  2         staff.salary,
  3         manager.emp_name,
  4         manager.salary
  5  from employees staff,
  6       employees manager
  7  where staff.manager_no = manager.emp_no
  8  and staff.salary > manager.salary;

EMP_NAME       SALARY EMP_NAME       SALARY
----------- --------- ----------- ---------
BROWN          12000 CONNELL        11000
HUGHES         13000 CONNELL        11000
```

Notice in Listing 6.8 that the aliases **staff** and **manager** both refer to the same table, **EMPLOYEES**. The join condition joins the two tables on manager number and employee number. The output from the join condition is then passed to the second condition, which extracts the staff with salaries greater than their managers.

SET OPERATORS

Set operators combine subsets of tables created by **SELECT** statements. As its name suggests, a set operator operates on sets of data, with tables being joined by columns rather than rows. A query may consist of a number of separate **SELECT** statements, the results of which are combined according to the set operator specified, to give one set of data as output. Set operators have one main restriction: You must specify the same number of columns in each separate **SELECT** statement, and each column must be of the same data type as its corresponding columns.

You can use the **ORDER BY** clause with any of the set operators, with the proviso that it is used in only one of the comprising queries. You must place the **ORDER BY** clause at the end of the query. Because the column names can be different in each of the **SELECT** statements, when using the **ORDER BY** clause with set operators, you have to specify the *position* of the column to order by, not the *name* of the column.

The following list summarizes the important rules for using set operators:

- **SELECT** statements must select the same number of columns.

- Corresponding columns must be of the same data type.

- Duplicate rows are automatically eliminated, so you don't need to use the **DISTINCT** operator.

- You should order by column position only.

- The **ORDER BY** clause must appear at the end of the statement.

- The column names from the first **SELECT** statement appear in the output.

- You can use multiple set operators in one statement.

UNION

The **UNION** operator returns all rows retrieved by either of the queries shown in Listing 6.9. This operator automatically returns distinct rows. For example, Listing 6.9 shows a union of two **SELECT** statements—it takes the output from the first **SELECT** statement and combines it with the output from the second, with no duplicates.

Listing 6.9 *The **UNION** operator.*

```
SQL> select supplier_name
  2  from suppliers
  3  union
```

```
     4  select product_name
     5  from products;

SUPPLIER_NAME
----------------------------
1cm Nail
1cm Screw
1mm Washer
2cm Nail
2cm Screw
2mm Washer
3cm Screw
A Nut
B Nut
C Nut
Hardware Ltd
JRF Relational Associates Ltd
Test Company Ltd
Training Company Inc
Widget Design Inc

15 rows selected.
```

As you can see from Listing 6.9, the **UNION** statement goes between the two **SELECT** statements. If there were three **SELECT** statements, you would have two **UNION** operators—one between each set of two **SELECT** statements.

INTERSECT

The **INTERSECT** operator returns all rows retrieved by both of the queries shown in Listing 6.10—the *intersection*. This set operator, again, automatically returns distinct rows. Suppose you want to find all products for which the **Unit_Cost_Price** is less than 5 and the **Supplier_id** is 1004. One way to write this would be with the **INTERSECT** operator, as shown in Listing 6.10. This returns the product name for all products with a cost of less than 5; it also returns the product name for all products supplied by supplier number 1004. Once **INTERSECT** has retrieved the two sets of data, it displays the information that is common to both queries—in this case, a 1mm and a 2mm Washer.

Listing 6.10   The **INTERSECT** operator.

```
SQL> select product_name
  2  from products
  3  where unit_cost_price < 5
  4  intersect
  5  select product_name
  6  from products
```

```
  7  where supplier_id = 1004;

PRODUCT_NAME
- - - - - - - - - - - - -
1mm Washer
2mm Washer
```

MINUS

The **MINUS** operator returns the rows retrieved by the first query that are not retrieved in the second query. Listing 6.11 is an example of the **MINUS** operator.

Listing 6.11   The *MINUS* operator.

```
SQL> select product_name from products
  2  where unit_cost_price < 5
  3  minus
  4  select product_name from products
  5  where supplier_id = 1004;

PRODUCT_NAME
- - - - - - - - - - - - -
1cm Nail
A Nut
B Nut
C Nut
```

SUBQUERIES

A subquery is a **SELECT** statement that appears within another **SELECT** statement. The second **SELECT** can appear in either the **WHERE** clause or the **HAVING** clause. It is sometimes referred to as a *subselect* or *inner select*. The subselect is usually executed first, and the value (or values) it returns is passed to the outer **SELECT** statement to execute. Subqueries are useful when output is determined based on values held within tables, rather than using external values. You usually see subqueries in the **WHERE** clause, where they must be surrounded by parentheses.

Single-Row Subqueries

A single-row subquery returns only one value from the inner **SELECT** statement. It is then used in the outer **SELECT** statement to complete the condition. For example, to find out the name of the product that retails at the lowest price, you could use the subquery in Listing 6.12.

Listing 6.12   A single-row subquery.

```
SQL> select product_name,unit_retail_price
  2  from products
  3  where unit_retail_price = (select min(unit_retail_price)
  4                                    from products);

PRODUCT_NAME    UNIT_RETAIL_PRICE
--------------  ------------------
1mm Washer                       1
```

Listing 6.12 executes in the following steps:

- Uses the **MIN** function to return the minimum **Unit_Retail_Price** from the **PRODUCTS** table.

- Uses the value returned from the **MIN** statement to display the product name and retail price.

A single-row subquery limits you to only one conditional operator, such as =, <, >, or <=.

Multiple-Row Subqueries

You can write subqueries so more than one row is returned to the outer **SELECT** statement. These are known as multiple-row subqueries. To identify each supplier's cheapest product, for example, you could write the **SELECT** statement shown in Listing 6.13.

Listing 6.13   A multiple-row subquery.

```
SQL> select supplier_id,product_name
  2  from products
  3  where (supplier_id,unit_retail_price) in
  4                (select supplier_id,min(unit_retail_price)
  5                 from products
  6                 group by supplier_id);

SUPPLIER_ID PRODUCT_NAME
----------- --------------
       1001 1cm Screw
       1002 1cm Nail
       1004 1mm Washer
       1005 A Nut
```

Through the use of the **MIN** function and the **GROUP BY** clause, the subquery in Listing 6.13 returns a list of values—the **Supplier_id** and minimum **Unit_Retail_Price**—for each supplier. The **WHERE** clause of the outer query checks which rows of the **PRODUCTS** table match with both of the values returned from the subquery. For this subquery, note that:

- You can specify more than one column to match. These columns must be enclosed in parentheses.

- The subquery is fully enclosed in parentheses.

- If the subquery returns no rows, the outer query will return no rows.

ANY And ALL

Oracle has two new operators that you can use with subqueries returning more than one row. They are used in the **WHERE** or **HAVING** clause of the outer query. These new operators— ANY and ALL—are used in conjunction with the other conditional operators.

The **ANY** condition operates similarly to a logical **OR**. It compares a value from the outer query to each value in the list returned from the subquery according to the conditional operator specified. Only one value must meet the condition before the condition is classed as true.

The **ALL** condition operates similarly to a logical **AND**. It compares a value from the outer query to each value in the list returned from the subquery. All must meet the condition before the condition is classed as true.

Consider the **EMPLOYEES** table in Listing 6.14. This table stores the employee information, including departments and job titles.

Listing 6.14   The **EMPLOYEES** table.

```
SQL> select * from employees;

    EMP_NO EMP_NAME      SALARY MANAGER_NO   DEPT_NO JOB_TITLE
--------- ---------- --------- ---------- --------- ----------
       100 SMITH         10000        104         1 MANAGER
       101 JONES         11000        104         2 CLERK
       102 BROWN         12000        104         1 CLERK
       103 HUGHES        13000        104         3 CLERK
       104 CONNELL       11000                    1 CHAIRMAN
```

With the **ANY** operator, you can issue a query to find employees who have a job title that equals a job in department 1, as shown in Listing 6.15.

Listing 6.15   The **ANY** operator.

```
SQL> select emp_name,job_title,dept_no
  2  from employees
  3  where job_title = any (select distinct job_title
  4                         from employees
  5                         where dept_no = 1)
  6  and dept_no != 1;
```

```
EMP_NAME   JOB_TITLE   DEPT_NO
---------- ----------- --------
JONES      CLERK             2
HUGHES     CLERK             3
```

The order of execution for this **SELECT** statement is as follows:

- The subquery is executed first. It returns one column of job titles for all employees in department number 1.

- The job titles are then fed to the outer query, which executes to match any of the list supplied by the subquery to the values in the **EMPLOYEES** table.

- Department number 1's job titles will be returned, but keep in mind that you don't want to see these in the final output. The statement then checks for all rows where **Dept_No** != 1.

You could write a similar statement using the **ALL** operator to display all employees who have job titles that don't appear in department number 2, as shown in Listing 6.16.

Listing 6.16   The ALL operator.

```
SQL> select emp_name,job_title,dept_no
  2  from employees
  3  where job_title != all (select job_title
  4                          from employees
  5                          where dept_no = 2);

EMP_NAME   JOB_TITLE   DEPT_NO
---------- ----------- --------
SMITH      MANAGER           1
CONNELL    CHAIRMAN          1
```

The order of execution for this statement is as follows:

- The subquery is executed first. It returns a list of the job titles within department number 2.

- The job titles are fed into the outer query, which executes to match rows from the employees table where the job title does not match all of the jobs returned by the subquery.

You may have noticed that the **ANY** and **ALL** operators are similar to the **IN** and **NOT IN** operators. In fact, they are interchangeable. It is still worth knowing what the **ANY** and **ALL** operators do, even though **IN** and **NOT IN** are more commonly used.

The HAVING Clause

You can nest subqueries within the **HAVING** clause, as well as within the **WHERE** clause. For example, Listing 6.17 shows all departments that have a higher average salary than department number 1.

Listing 6.17   Nested subquery within the HAVING clause.

```
SQL> select dept_no,avg(salary)
  2  from employees
  3  having avg(salary) > (select avg(salary)
  4                             from employees
  5                             where dept_no = 1)
  6  group by dept_no;

  DEPT_NO AVG(SALARY)
--------- -----------
        3       13000
```

Multiple Subqueries

A subquery, just like any other **SELECT** statement, can be composed of more than one **SELECT** statement, joined by the use of set operators—**UNION**, **MINUS**, and **INTERSECT**—as explained previously. Listing 6.18 shows an example of multiple subqueries, returning the employees whose manager is the same as the manager of Smith or Jones.

Listing 6.18   Multiple subqueries.

```
SQL> select emp_name,job_title
  2  from employees
  3  where manager_no in (select manager_no
  4                             from employees
  5                             where emp_name = 'SMITH'
  6                             union
  7                             select manager_no
  8                             from employees
  9                             where emp_name = 'JONES');

EMP_NAME   JOB_TITLE
---------- ----------
SMITH      MANAGER
JONES      CLERK
BROWN      CLERK
HUGHES     CLERK
```

Notice that the parentheses surround the entire subquery. This example uses the **IN** operator, but could just as easily use the **ANY** operator. This is a good way to write a **SELECT** statement when the values to be supplied by the subquery are held in different tables.

Nested Subqueries

A subquery, just like any other query, can be nested within itself. This subquery within a subquery is shown in Listing 6.19, where a **SELECT** statement is used to show all employees with a salary greater than the maximum salary of department 2.

Listing 6.19   A nested subquery.

```
SQL> select emp_name,job_title
  2  from employees
  3  where salary > (select max(salary)
  4                  from employees
  5                  where dept_no in (select dept_no
  6                                    from employees
  7                                    where dept_no < 2
  8                                    )
  9                  );

EMP_NAME    JOB_TITLE
---------- ----------
HUGHES      CLERK
```

The example in Listing 6.19 could, of course, have been written without the nested subquery. It was written this way to prove the point that nested subqueries are the same as any other queries. Notice the way the parentheses are placed—when using multiple nested subqueries, this placement helps identify where each one starts and finishes.

There are some limits on how far you can nest subqueries, though you are unlikely ever to come anywhere close to these limits of SQL*Plus:

- An outer query can have up to 16 inner queries at level 1 (the first level of nesting).

- Within any level 1 query, you can have up to 255 nested subqueries.

Correlated Subqueries

The statement in a normal subquery is executed once and the resulting rows returned to the outer query, which is then executed. A correlated subquery operates in the reverse: The outer query is executed once and the subquery executed once for each row returned from the outer query. It is called a *correlated subquery*, because each of the rows returned from the outer query is related in value to the subquery. For example, look at the **WHERE** clause of the subquery in Listing 6.20.

Listing 6.20   A correlated subquery.

```
SQL> select emp_no,
  2         salary,
```

```
 3          dept_no
 4   from employees o
 5   where salary > (select avg(salary)
 6                     from employees i
 7                     where i.dept_no = o.dept_no)
 8   order by o.dept_no;

  EMP_NO     SALARY   DEPT_NO
---------  ---------  --------
     102      12000         1
```

In Listing 6.20, the correlated subquery shows all employees who earn more than the average for their respective departments. The table aliases use **i** and **o**, signifying the inner and outer queries. If these aliases were omitted, the query would still produce the required output, as unqualified columns are looked up in the tables of that subquery and then in the tables of the enclosing subquery.

You can see that the inner subquery is joined to the outer query. This is the correlation, which joins the rows from the outer query to those of the inner query.

EXISTS

The **EXISTS** operator is usually used with correlated subqueries. **EXISTS** checks whether a value exists in the subquery. It returns true if the value exists—i.e., the subquery returns at least one row. Try to use this operator as frequently as possible, as it is very efficient and cuts down the number of accesses to the database, therefore speeding up queries. Once the operator has found one record, it stops looking for more because it knows the statement must be true.

To find all employees with at least one person reporting to them, you could issue the query shown in Listing 6.21.

Listing 6.21   The *EXISTS* operator.

```
SQL> select emp_no,
  2         emp_name,
  3         dept_no
  4   from employees o
  5   where exists (select i.emp_no
  6                   from employees i
  7                   where i.manager_no = o.emp_no);

  EMP_NO EMP_NAME      DEPT_NO
--------- ----------   --------
     104 CONNELL             1
```

General Rules For Subqueries

When using subqueries, you must follow a number of rules:

- The subquery must be enclosed in parentheses.

- The subquery must not have an **ORDER BY** clause.

- Any **ORDER BY** clause must come at the end of the outer **SELECT** statement.

- Set operators may be used in the subquery.

- The subquery is always executed from the deepest nested subquery to the outer query, except in the case of the correlated subquery, where the opposite is true.

- You may use logical and SQL operators, as well as the **ANY** and **ALL** operators.

SUBSTITUTION VARIABLES

A substitution variable in a **SELECT** statement enables you to change the value each time it is executed, allowing all-purpose queries to be used. A substitution variable is prefixed with an ampersand symbol (**&**). When the statement is executed, the interpreter sees this symbol and prompts the user for its value. The query is then executed with the new value for the variable. If the query is executed again, the interpreter will once again prompt the user for its new value. In Listing 6.22, a substitution variable queries all employees within a specified department.

Listing 6.22   A substitution variable.

```
SQL> select emp_name,
  2         job_title,
  3         salary
  4  from employees
  5  where dept_no = &department_number;
Enter value for department_number: 1
old   5: where dept_no = &department_number
new   5: where dept_no = 1

EMP_NAME    JOB_TITLE     SALARY
----------  ----------  --------
SMITH       MANAGER        10000
BROWN       CLERK          12000
CONNELL     CHAIRMAN       11000
```

Once the query is executed, you're prompted for the value of the **Department_Number** variable. When you enter the value and press Enter, Personal Oracle8 shows you the old and new values for the substitution variable. In the example in Listing 6.22, because the **Dept_No** field is of type **NUMBER**, you don't need to enclose the substitution variable in single quotes; if, however, the field is of type **CHAR**, **VARCHAR2**, or **DATE**, you will need single quotes. You can use multiple substitution variables within one **SELECT** statement; when you execute the statement, you're asked for the value of each variable in turn.

You can also prompt for a column name at execution time, using substitution variables. This is a way of making general-purpose queries, as shown in Listing 6.23.

Listing 6.23 *Substituting column variables.*

```
SQL> select emp_name,
  2          &column1,
  3          &column2
  4  from employees
  5  where dept_no = &department_number;
Enter value for column1: job_title
old   2:          &column1,
new   2:          job_title,
Enter value for column2: salary
old   3:          &column2
new   3:          salary
Enter value for department_number: 1
old   5: where dept_no = &department_number
new   5: where dept_no = 1

EMP_NAME    JOB_TITLE      SALARY
----------  ----------   --------
SMITH       MANAGER         10000
BROWN       CLERK           12000
CONNELL     CHAIRMAN        11000
```

In Listing 6.23, at execution time, the interpreter asks you for the values for **column1** and **column2**. It then replaces these in the query and asks for the required department. If you wish to default some text into the substitution variable, use a period (.) and the text you wish to default, as shown in Listing 6.24.

Listing 6.24 *Defaulting text using substitution variables.*

```
SQL> select emp_no,
  2          emp_name,
  3          dept_no
  4  from employees
  5  where salary = &enter_salary_in_thousands.000;
Enter value for enter_salary_in_thousands: 11
old   5: where salary = &enter_salary_in_thousands.000
new   5: where salary = 11000
```

```
  EMP_NO EMP_NAME    DEPT_NO
--------- ---------- --------
     101 JONES             2
     104 CONNELL           1
```

With single ampersands, you are prompted for the value of the substitution variable each time the statement is executed. It is not saved, so if the value is used twice in the query, you'll be prompted for it twice.

Double Ampersands (&&)

If a substitution variable is prefixed with double ampersands (**&&**), SQL*Plus will prompt for the value of only the first variable. The next variable of the same name will be defaulted to the same value as the first. Once the value of the variable is defined, it is stored within SQL*Plus for the duration of the SQL*Plus session. Listing 6.25 shows a **SELECT** statement using the same substitution variable twice. Notice that you are prompted for the value of the variable only once and that it saves the values, as the same statement is executed twice.

Listing 6.25 *Substitution variables with double ampersands.*

```
SQL> select emp_no,emp_name
  2    from employees
  3    where dept_no = &&department_number
  4    union
  5    select manager_no,job_title
  6    from employees
  7    where dept_no = &&department_number;
Enter value for department_number: 1
old    3: where dept_no = &&department_number
new    3: where dept_no = 1
old    7: where dept_no = &&department_number
new    7: where dept_no = 1

   EMP_NO EMP_NAME
--------- ----------
      100 SMITH
      102 BROWN
      104 CLERK
      104 CONNELL
      104 MANAGER
          CHAIRMAN

6 rows selected.

SQL> /
old    3: where dept_no = &&department_number
```

```
new     3: where dept_no = 1
old     7: where dept_no = &&department_number
new     7: where dept_no = 1

   EMP_NO EMP_NAME
--------- ----------
      100 SMITH
      102 BROWN
      104 CLERK
      104 CONNELL
      104 MANAGER
          CHAIRMAN

6 rows selected.
```

DEFINE And UNDEFINE Commands

The **DEFINE** command allows you to display the value of all variables set within the current session. You can also use **DEFINE** to create and set new variables. If you just type in "DEFINE" at the SQL prompt, you'll see all of the defined values within your current session. Listing 6.26 shows the output of a **DEFINE** command executed after Listing 6.25.

Listing 6.26   Output from the **DEFINE** command.

```
SQL> define
DEFINE _SQLPLUS_RELEASE = "800030000" (CHAR)
DEFINE _EDITOR         = "Notepad" (CHAR)
DEFINE _O_VERSION      = "Personal Oracle8 Release 8.0.3.0.0 - Production
With the Partitioning option
PL/SQL Release 8.0.3.0.0 - Production" (CHAR)
DEFINE _O_RELEASE      = "800030000" (CHAR)
DEFINE DEPARTMENT_NUMBER = "1" (CHAR)
```

A number of other variables are set within each session. You can change most of these with the **DEFINE** command. To change a variable, just issue the **DEFINE** command as shown:

```
DEFINE variable_name = new_value
```

UNDEFINE, as its name suggests, undefines a variable from within SQL*Plus. To undefine a variable that is already set, issue the following command:

```
UNDEFINE variable_name
```

Both of these commands can be shortened for use within SQL*Plus. You can shorten the **DEFINE** command to **DEF**, and the **UNDEFINE** command to **UNDEF**.

Passing Parameters

Until now, we've been working purely with the SQL buffer—that is, writing a command and then executing it. Within SQL*Plus, you can save the SQL buffer to a file to be stored on your hard disk. To save the contents of the SQL buffer within SQL*Plus, just type in "SAVE", followed by a file name. This will save the SQL buffer to a file. If you specify an extension in the **SAVE** command, the file will be saved to the C:\ORAWIN95\BIN directory; if you just specify a file name, SQL*Plus automatically appends the .SQL extension to the file. Naming all SQL files with a .SQL extension is a good practice.

To execute a saved file, you have to use the **START** command. Thus, you would use the following command to execute a file called jrf:

```
START jrf
```

This will automatically execute the contents of the file name jrf.sql in the C:\ORAWIN95\BIN directory.

You can pass parameters to files executed within SQL*Plus. To do so, use the ampersand operator along with the parameter number. If more than one parameter is used, variable **&1** will be replaced by the first parameter, variable **&2** by the second parameter, and so on. Listing 6.27 shows an example of passing two parameters to a file.

Listing 6.27   Passing parameters to a file.

```
SQL> select emp_no,
  2         emp_name
  3  from employees
  4  where dept_no = &1
  5  and manager_no = &2
  6
SQL> save example1
Created file example1
SQL> start example1 1 104
old   4: where dept_no = &1
new   4: where dept_no = 1
old   5: and manager_no = &2
new   5: and manager_no = 104

   EMP_NO EMP_NAME
--------- ----------
      100 SMITH
      102 BROWN
```

Listing 6.27 shows the following:

- The query is written.
- The query is then saved with the file name example1.
- The file example1 is then executed with two parameters: **Dept_No** and **Manager_No**.
- The output is displayed.

ACCEPT Command

The **ACCEPT** command allows you to define variables from the command line, using user-defined prompts. This allows you to refine your statements so they look more professional. This has advantages over using the **DEFINE** command, as you can specify what the prompt will say, what the data types are, and even hide the output. The syntax for the **ACCEPT** command is

```
ACCEPT variable [NUMBER|CHAR] [NOPROMPT|PROMPT 'text'] [HIDE]
```

where:

- **NUMBER|CHAR** determines the data type of the variable being defined.
- **PROMPT** '*text*' determines how the prompt will read when entered.
- **NOPROMPT** makes **ACCEPT** skip a line and wait for an input from the user, displaying no prompt to the user.
- **HIDE** does not echo the user's response to the prompt. This is useful for entering passwords.

INSERT STATEMENT

The **INSERT** statement is used to insert rows into tables. You can choose from a number of ways to get all of the data into your database, including SQL*Loader and Import. The **INSERT** command is the preferred option when inserting relatively small amounts of information—i.e., fewer than 50 rows. You can combine **INSERT** with a **SELECT** statement to select the data you want to insert into a table. To insert rows into a table, the table must be in your schema and you must have the **INSERT** privilege. If you wish to insert rows into a table outside of your schema, you must have been granted the **INSERT** privilege by the table owner or have the **INSERT ANY TABLE** privilege.

I'll begin with an explanation of the easier options for inserting rows into a table. The syntax for a simple **INSERT** command is as follows:

```
INSERT INTO {tablename|viewname} [(column,column, ...)] VALUES (value,value,...)
```

This syntax is best described with a simple example. Listing 6.28 shows such an example: inserting a row into the **CUSTOMERS** table.

Listing 6.28   *Simple **INSERT** to the **CUSTOMERS** table.*

```
SQL> desc customers
 Name                             Null?     Type
 ------------------------------ --------- ----
 CUSTOMER_ID                      NOT NULL NUMBER(5)
 CUSTOMER_NAME                    NOT NULL VARCHAR2(40)
 ADDRESS_LINE_1                   NOT NULL VARCHAR2(40)
 ADDRESS_LINE_2                            VARCHAR2(40)
 CITY                             NOT NULL VARCHAR2(20)
 COUNTRY                                   VARCHAR2(20)
 TELEPHONE_NUMBER                          NUMBER(20)
 CONTACT_NAME                              VARCHAR2(25)

SQL> insert into customers
  2  (customer_id,customer_name,address_line_1,address_line_2,city)
  3* values
  4  (99999,'ZZZZZZZZZZ','Line 1','Line 2','Anytown');

1 row created.

SQL> select customer_id,address_line_1,city
  2  from customers;

CUSTOMER_ID ADDRESS_LINE_1                           CITY
----------- ---------------------------------------- --------
      20002 2 The Street                             London
      20001 1 The Street                             London
      20003 102W 52nd St                             New York
      20004 105 5th Ave                              New York
      20005 5 The Mall                               Hull
      99999 Line 1                                   Anytown

6 rows selected.
```

In Listing 6.28, I first describe the table I am inserting into, to see which columns are not null (which columns you must populate when a row is inserted). I then execute the simple **IN-SERT** statement, which is made up from the following four lines:

- *Line 1*—Specifies that the rows are to be inserted into the **CUSTOMERS** table.

- *Line 2*—Specifies which columns the data will be inserted into. If you are inserting into every column in the table, you could remove this line; however, it's a good idea to leave it in because table specifications can change over time, and this line makes the SQL statement easier to read.

- *Line 3*—Tells Oracle that the next line contains the values to populate the columns in Line 2 with.

- *Line 4*—Holds the data for the **INSERT** command. Notice that the data in this line corresponds exactly to the columns in Line 2. Each column in Line 2 must have a corresponding entry in this line. Also notice that single quotes are placed around the data items that are defined in the **CUSTOMERS** table as **VARCHAR2**. This also applies to **DATE** data types.

Once the **INSERT** has completed, I select the rows from the **CUSTOMERS** table to check that the **INSERT** has worked as expected. Because this particular **INSERT** statement inserts only five of the eight columns in the **CUSTOMERS** table, the other three columns are populated with null values. You could specify this within the **INSERT** statement, as shown in Listing 6.29.

Listing 6.29 *Specifying null values within the **INSERT** statement.*

```
SQL> insert into customers
  2  (customer_id,customer_name,address_line_1,address_line_2,
  3   city,country,telephone_number,contact_name)
  4  values
  5  (99998,'XXXXXXXXXX','Line 1','Line 2','Anytown',NULL,NULL,NULL);

1 row created.

SQL> select customer_id,address_line_1,city
  2  from customers;

CUSTOMER_ID ADDRESS_LINE_1                           CITY
----------- ---------------------------------------- ----------------
      20002 2 The Street                             London
      20001 1 The Street                             London
      20003 102W 52nd St                             New York
      20004 105 5th Ave                              New York
      20005 5 The Mall                               Hull
      99999 Line 1                                   Anytown
      99998 Line 1                                   Anytown

7 rows selected.
```

When entering **DATE** data types into a table, the default format is DD-MON-YY, the century value defaults to 19 (see Chapter 10 for the National Language Support parameters for the year 2000 problems), and the time defaults to midnight. If you wish to insert a different format for the **DATE** data type—for example, enter a date in the 21st century or enter a specific time—you will need to use the **TO_DATE** function within the **INSERT** statement. (Chapter 5 covers the syntax for the **TO_DATE** function.) Listing 6.30 shows an example of using this function.

Listing 6.30 *Using the **TO_DATE** function within an **INSERT** statement.*

```
SQL> desc orders
 Name                                   Null?    Type
 -------------------------------------  -------- ----
 ORDER_ID                               NOT NULL NUMBER(6)
 CUSTOMER_ID                            NOT NULL NUMBER(5)
 ORDER_DATE                             NOT NULL DATE
 DISPATCHED_DATE                        NOT NULL DATE
 ORDER_DUE_DATE                         NOT NULL DATE

SQL> insert into orders
  2  (order_id,customer_id,order_date,
  3   dispatched_date,order_due_date)
  4  values
  5  (999999,20001,'10-DEC-99','15-DEC-99',
  6   to_date('01/10/2000','MM/DD/YYYY'));

1 row created.

SQL> select * from orders;

  ORDER_ID CUSTOMER_ID ORDER_DAT DISPATCHE ORDER_DUE
 --------- ----------- --------- --------- ---------
    100001       20001 01-Jan-99 10-Jan-99 31-Jan-99
    100002       20001 02-Jan-99 11-Jan-99 31-Jan-99
    100003       20002 01-May-98 09-May-98 31-May-98
    100004       20003 01-Jun-98 03-Jun-98 10-Jun-98
    100005       20004 28-Aug-99 29-Aug-99 30-Sep-99
    100006       20005 28-Aug-99 10-Sep-99 31-Aug-99
    999999       20001 10-Dec-99 15-Dec-99 10-Jan-00

7 rows selected.
```

INSERTs Using SELECT Statements

As previously stated, you can insert data into a table, where the data is retrieved by a **SELECT** statement. For this type of **INSERT**, you remove the **VALUES** clause and replace it with a **SELECT** statement. Note the following points in doing so:

- Always execute the **SELECT** statement prior to including it in the **INSERT**, so you know what data is going to be inserted into your table. This is a safety precaution, as **SELECT** statements sometimes do not return what you expected, and you do not want to fill up your table unnecessarily.

- Always make sure the **SELECT** statement returns the columns in the same order as they are specified in the columns list of the **INSERT** statement.

- Always make sure the data type for each column of data you are returning via the **SELECT** statement is the same for its corresponding column within the column list of the **INSERT** statement.

The syntax for combining the **SELECT** statement within the **INSERT** statement is as follows:

```
INSERT INTO {tablename|viewname}
{column,column,column ...}
SELECT select list
FROM table(s)
```

In Listing 6.31, some details from the **CUSTOMERS** table are inserted into the **SUPPLIERS** table.

***Listing 6.31** Using **SELECT** within an **INSERT** statement.*

```
SQL> desc suppliers
 Name                             Null?    Type
 -------------------------------- -------- ----
 SUPPLIER_ID                      NOT NULL NUMBER(4)
 SUPPLIER_NAME                    NOT NULL VARCHAR2(40)
 ADDRESS_LINE_1                   NOT NULL VARCHAR2(40)
 ADDRESS_LINE_2                            VARCHAR2(40)
 CITY                             NOT NULL VARCHAR2(20)
 COUNTRY                                   VARCHAR2(20)
 TELEPHONE_NUMBER                          NUMBER(20)
 CONTACT_NAME                              VARCHAR2(25)

SQL> insert into suppliers
  2  (supplier_id,supplier_name,address_line_1,
  3   address_line_2,city)
  4  select customer_id-90000,
  5        customer_name,
  6        address_line_1,
  7        address_line_2,
  8        city
  9  from customers
 10  where customer_id > 90000;
```

```
2 rows created.

SQL> select supplier_id,address_line_1,city
  2  from suppliers;

SUPPLIER_ID ADDRESS_LINE_1                                CITY
----------- --------------------------------------------- --------
       1001 1 The Street                                  London
       1002 2 The Street                                  London
       1003 52nd Street                                   New York
       1004 42nd Street                                   New York
       1005 57 The Close                                  Hull
       9998 Line 1                                        Anytown
       9999 Line 1                                        Anytown

7 rows selected.
```

UPDATE STATEMENT

The **UPDATE** statement allows you to alter one or more rows within a table. This means you can change the value of one column in any row without deleting and reinserting the row. The **UPDATE** statement is used fairly frequently and is useful for updating multiple rows at the same time. The syntax for the **UPDATE** statement is as follows:

```
UPDATE {tablename|viewname}
SET column = {expression|subquery} ...
[WHERE condition]
```

In this syntax:

- The **WHERE** clause is shown as optional. If it were omitted, the **UPDATE** would occur for each row of the table; otherwise, the **UPDATE** affects each row returned from the **WHERE** clause.

- For every row that is returned, the columns to the left of the equals sign (=) are set to the values returned by the corresponding expression to the right.

- Alternatively, you can specify the column list and value list in parentheses:

  ```
  (column, column, column ...) = (value, value, value ...)
  ```

For you to be able to update a row within a table, the table must reside within your own schema and you must have update access to it. If you wish to update a table outside of your own schema—i.e., one owned by another user—you must have the **UPDATE ANY TABLE** privilege or have been granted the **UPDATE** privilege by the owner of the table.

Listing 6.32 shows a simple example, where all rows in the **PRODUCTS** table have the **Reorder_Level** increased by 50 percent.

Listing 6.32   A simple *UPDATE* statement.

```
SQL> select product_id,
  2          product_name,
  3          reorder_level
  4  from products;

PRODUCT_ID PRODUCT_NAME                              REORDER_LEVEL
---------- ---------------------------------------- -------------
      5001 A Nut                                              100
      5002 B Nut                                              100
      5003 1cm Screw                                          500
      5004 1cm Nail                                           200
      5005 1mm Washer                                          50
      5006 2mm Washer                                          50
      5007 2cm Nail                                           200
      5008 2cm Screw                                          500
      5009 3cm Screw                                          500
      5010 C Nut                                              100

10 rows selected.

SQL> update products
  2  set reorder_level = reorder_level * 1.5;

10 rows updated.

SQL> select product_id,
  2          product_name,
  3          reorder_level
  4  from products;

PRODUCT_ID PRODUCT_NAME                              REORDER_LEVEL
---------- ---------------------------------------- -------------
      5001 A Nut                                              150
      5002 B Nut                                              150
      5003 1cm Screw                                          750
      5004 1cm Nail                                           300
      5005 1mm Washer                                          75
      5006 2mm Washer                                          75
      5007 2cm Nail                                           300
      5008 2cm Screw                                          750
      5009 3cm Screw                                          750
      5010 C Nut                                              150

10 rows selected.
```

I did not use a **WHERE** clause in Listing 6.32, so all of the rows were updated. If I were now to add a **WHERE** clause to the **UPDATE** statement to update only the **Reorder_Level** for nails, it would look like Listing 6.33.

Listing 6.33   A more complex **UPDATE** statement.

```
SQL> select product_id,
  2          product_name,
  3          reorder_level
  4   from products;

PRODUCT_ID PRODUCT_NAME                              REORDER_LEVEL
---------- ----------------------------------------- -------------
      5001 A Nut                                               150
      5002 B Nut                                               150
      5003 1cm Screw                                           750
      5004 1cm Nail                                            300
      5005 1mm Washer                                           75
      5006 2mm Washer                                           75
      5007 2cm Nail                                            300
      5008 2cm Screw                                           750
      5009 3cm Screw                                           750
      5010 C Nut                                               150

10 rows selected.

SQL> update products
  2   set reorder_level = reorder_level * 1.5
  3   where product_name like '%Nail%';

2 rows updated.

SQL> select product_id,
  2          product_name,
  3          reorder_level
  4   from products;

PRODUCT_ID PRODUCT_NAME                              REORDER_LEVEL
---------- ----------------------------------------- -------------
      5001 A Nut                                               150
      5002 B Nut                                               150
      5003 1cm Screw                                           750
      5004 1cm Nail                                            450
      5005 1mm Washer                                           75
      5006 2mm Washer                                           75
      5007 2cm Nail                                            450
      5008 2cm Screw                                           750
      5009 3cm Screw                                           750
      5010 C Nut                                               150

10 rows selected.
```

You can also specify more than one column to change within the **UPDATE** statement. For example, to increase the **Unit_Cost_Price** by 10 percent and the **Unit_Retail_Price** by 20 percent for all screws in one **UPDATE** statement, you would use the SQL statement shown in Listing 6.34.

Listing 6.34 *Updating more than one column at a time.*

```
SQL> select product_name,
  2          unit_cost_price,
  3          unit_retail_price
  4  from products;

PRODUCT_NAME                          UNIT_COST_PRICE UNIT_RETAIL_PRICE
------------------------------------- --------------- -----------------
A Nut                                               1                 2
B Nut                                               2                 4
1cm Screw                                           5                10
1cm Nail                                            3                 6
1mm Washer                                         .5                 1
2mm Washer                                         .7               1.4
2cm Nail                                            6                12
2cm Screw                                          10                20
3cm Screw                                          20                40
C Nut                                               3                 6

10 rows selected.

SQL> update products
  2  set unit_cost_price = unit_cost_price * 1.1,
  3      unit_retail_price = unit_retail_price * 1.2
  4  where product_name like '%Screw%';

3 rows updated.

SQL> select product_name,
  2          unit_cost_price,
  3          unit_retail_price
  4  from products;

PRODUCT_NAME                          UNIT_COST_PRICE UNIT_RETAIL_PRICE
------------------------------------- --------------- -----------------
A Nut                                               1                 2
B Nut                                               2                 4
1cm Screw                                         5.5                12
1cm Nail                                            3                 6
1mm Washer                                         .5                 1
2mm Washer                                         .7               1.4
2cm Nail                                            6                12
```

2cm Screw	11	24
3cm Screw	22	48
C Nut	3	6

10 rows selected.

One of the most frequent uses for an **UPDATE** statement is with a **SELECT** statement within the **SET** clause. This allows you more flexibility to change rows within a database. Listing 6.35 shows a simple example, setting the **Unit_Retail_Price** for washers equal to the maximum price within the **PRODUCTS** table.

Listing 6.35 *Using a **SELECT** statement within an **UPDATE**.*

```
SQL> select product_name,
  2          unit_retail_price
  3  from products;

PRODUCT_NAME                            UNIT_RETAIL_PRICE
-------------------------------------- -----------------

A Nut                                                  2
B Nut                                                  4
1cm Screw                                            12
1cm Nail                                              6
1mm Washer                                            1
2mm Washer                                          1.4
2cm Nail                                             12
2cm Screw                                            24
3cm Screw                                            48
C Nut                                                 6

10 rows selected.

SQL> update products
  2  set unit_retail_price = (select max(unit_retail_price)
  3                           from products)
  4  where product_name like '%Washer%';

2 rows updated.

SQL> select product_name,
  2          unit_retail_price
  3  from products;

PRODUCT_NAME                            UNIT_RETAIL_PRICE
-------------------------------------- -----------------

A Nut                                                  2
B Nut                                                  4
1cm Screw                                            12
```

```
1cm Nail                                   6
1mm Washer                                48
2mm Washer                                48
2cm Nail                                  12
2cm Screw                                 24
3cm Screw                                 48
C Nut                                      6

10 rows selected.
```

DELETE STATEMENT

The **DELETE** statement, as its name suggests, deletes rows from tables within the database. With one **DELETE** statement, you can delete one or more rows from any table, as long as you have the correct access permissions. The syntax for the **DELETE** statement is as follows:

```
DELETE FROM [tablename|viewname]
[WHERE condition]
```

When used without a **WHERE** clause, the **DELETE** command deletes all rows from the specified table. When used with a **WHERE** clause, it deletes only the rows returned from the **WHERE** clause.

To delete rows from a table, you must have the table within your schema and you must have the **DELETE** privilege on the table. To delete rows from a table outside of your schema, you must either have been granted the **DELETE** privilege or have the **DELETE ANY TABLE** privilege.

Listing 6.36 shows an example of the **DELETE** command deleting rows from the **PRODUCTS** table.

Listing 6.36   Deleting rows from a table.

```
SQL> select product_id,
  2           product_name
  3  from products;

PRODUCT_ID PRODUCT_NAME
---------- --------------------
      5001 A Nut
      5002 B Nut
      5003 1cm Screw
      5004 1cm Nail
```

```
      5005 1mm Washer
      5006 2mm Washer
      5007 2cm Nail
      5008 2cm Screw
      5009 3cm Screw
      5010 C Nut

10 rows selected.

SQL> delete from products
  2  where product_id = 5010;

1 row deleted.

SQL> select product_id,
  2         product_name
  3  from products;

PRODUCT_ID PRODUCT_NAME
---------- --------------------
      5001 A Nut
      5002 B Nut
      5003 1cm Screw
      5004 1cm Nail
      5005 1mm Washer
      5006 2mm Washer
      5007 2cm Nail
      5008 2cm Screw
      5009 3cm Screw

9 rows selected.
```

The example in Listing 6.36 shows the easiest way to delete rows from a table. If you wish to delete all rows from the **PRODUCTS** table, issue the command:

```
DELETE FROM PRODUCTS;
```

This is one way to delete all records from a table, but the **TRUNCATE** command is another, more elegant way to remove all records from a table. The **TRUNCATE** command has the following syntax:

```
TRUNCATE tablename
```

When all rows are removed using **DELETE**, the space the rows occupied is still allocated to the table, whereas when all rows are removed using **TRUNCATE**, the space for the rows is also removed, allowing other objects within the tablespace to access the freed-up space.

COMMIT AND ROLLBACK

Updates to the database are not made permanent until you take one of the following actions:

- You log out of SQL*Plus.
- You issue a **COMMIT** command.
- You issue a **ROLLBACK** command.
- The database crashes.

When entering and amending data within the database, you can always see the changes you make, but other users cannot see the changes you make to any objects until one of these actions is executed. This may sound strange, but it has some good features. For example, if you changed 1,000 rows within a table and then made a mistake, you could roll back the changes you made to the point before you issued the statement. This is done using the **COMMIT** and **ROLLBACK** commands. The **COMMIT** command tells the database to save all of the work you have done, so it cannot be undone again. The **ROLLBACK** command will roll all of your work back until the last **COMMIT**. Listing 6.37 shows an example of inserting a row into the **ORDERS** table, then rolling it back.

Listing 6.37 *Using the **ROLLBACK** command.*

```
SQL> select * from orders;

  ORDER_ID CUSTOMER_ID ORDER_DAT DISPATCHE ORDER_DUE
--------- ----------- --------- --------- ---------
    100001       20001 01-Jan-99 10-Jan-99 31-Jan-99
    100002       20001 02-Jan-99 11-Jan-99 31-Jan-99
    100003       20002 01-May-98 09-May-98 31-May-98
    100004       20003 01-Jun-98 03-Jun-98 10-Jun-98
    100005       20004 28-Aug-99 29-Aug-99 30-Sep-99
    100006       20005 28-Aug-99 10-Sep-99 31-Aug-99
    999999       20001 10-Dec-99 15-Dec-99 10-Jan-00

7 rows selected.

SQL> insert into orders
  2  values
  3  (999998,20001,'01-JAN-98','01-JAN-98','01-JAN-98');

1 row created.

SQL> select * from orders;
```

```
ORDER_ID CUSTOMER_ID ORDER_DAT DISPATCHE ORDER_DUE
--------- ----------- --------- --------- ---------
   100001       20001 01-Jan-99 10-Jan-99 31-Jan-99
   100002       20001 02-Jan-99 11-Jan-99 31-Jan-99
   100003       20002 01-May-98 09-May-98 31-May-98
   100004       20003 01-Jun-98 03-Jun-98 10-Jun-98
   100005       20004 28-Aug-99 29-Aug-99 30-Sep-99
   100006       20005 28-Aug-99 10-Sep-99 31-Aug-99
   999999       20001 10-Dec-99 15-Dec-99 10-Jan-00
   999998       20001 01-Jan-98 01-Jan-98 01-Jan-98

8 rows selected.

SQL> rollback;

Rollback complete.

SQL> select * from orders;

ORDER_ID CUSTOMER_ID ORDER_DAT DISPATCHE ORDER_DUE
--------- ----------- --------- --------- ---------
   100001       20001 01-Jan-99 10-Jan-99 31-Jan-99
   100002       20001 02-Jan-99 11-Jan-99 31-Jan-99
   100003       20002 01-May-98 09-May-98 31-May-98
   100004       20003 01-Jun-98 03-Jun-98 10-Jun-98
   100005       20004 28-Aug-99 29-Aug-99 30-Sep-99
   100006       20005 28-Aug-99 10-Sep-99 31-Aug-99
   999999       20001 10-Dec-99 15-Dec-99 10-Jan-00

7 rows selected.
```

In this listing, I first select everything from the **ORDERS** table, then insert a row into the **ORDERS** table and select all rows again to prove the row is inserted. I then roll the statement back and select all rows again.

The **COMMIT** command can be used as shown in Listing 6.38 to save your work to the database and stop it from being rolled back. The listing shows a row being added to the **ORDERS** table and then the **COMMIT** taking place. I then try to **ROLLBACK** the IN-SERT and redisplay all of the rows. The last query shows that the **ROLLBACK** has no effect.

Listing 6.38   *Using the **COMMIT** command.*

```
SQL> select * from orders;

ORDER_ID CUSTOMER_ID ORDER_DAT DISPATCHE ORDER_DUE
--------- ----------- --------- --------- ---------
   100001       20001 01-Jan-99 10-Jan-99 31-Jan-99
   100002       20001 02-Jan-99 11-Jan-99 31-Jan-99
   100003       20002 01-May-98 09-May-98 31-May-98
```

```
    100004        20003 01-Jun-98 03-Jun-98 10-Jun-98
    100005        20004 28-Aug-99 29-Aug-99 30-Sep-99
    100006        20005 28-Aug-99 10-Sep-99 31-Aug-99
    999999        20001 10-Dec-99 15-Dec-99 10-Jan-00

7 rows selected.

SQL> insert into orders
  2  values
  3  (999998,20001,'01-JAN-99','01-JAN-99','01-JAN-99');

1 row created.

SQL> commit;

Commit complete.

SQL> select * from orders;

  ORDER_ID CUSTOMER_ID ORDER_DAT DISPATCHE ORDER_DUE
--------- ----------- --------- --------- ---------
    100001        20001 01-Jan-99 10-Jan-99 31-Jan-99
    100002        20001 02-Jan-99 11-Jan-99 31-Jan-99
    100003        20002 01-May-98 09-May-98 31-May-98
    100004        20003 01-Jun-98 03-Jun-98 10-Jun-98
    100005        20004 28-Aug-99 29-Aug-99 30-Sep-99
    100006        20005 28-Aug-99 10-Sep-99 31-Aug-99
    999999        20001 10-Dec-99 15-Dec-99 10-Jan-00
    999998        20001 01-Jan-99 01-Jan-99 01-Jan-99

8 rows selected.

SQL> rollback;

Rollback complete.

SQL> select * from orders;

  ORDER_ID CUSTOMER_ID ORDER_DAT DISPATCHE ORDER_DUE
--------- ----------- --------- --------- ---------
    100001        20001 01-Jan-99 10-Jan-99 31-Jan-99
    100002        20001 02-Jan-99 11-Jan-99 31-Jan-99
    100003        20002 01-May-98 09-May-98 31-May-98
    100004        20003 01-Jun-98 03-Jun-98 10-Jun-98
    100005        20004 28-Aug-99 29-Aug-99 30-Sep-99
    100006        20005 28-Aug-99 10-Sep-99 31-Aug-99
    999999        20001 10-Dec-99 15-Dec-99 10-Jan-00
    999998        20001 01-Jan-99 01-Jan-99 01-Jan-99

8 rows selected.
```

KNOWLEDGE TO BUILD ON

In this chapter, you've learned some of the more advanced features of SQL*Plus. You'll need all these techniques to manipulate information when you come to Chapter 12, which discusses PL/SQL. Chapter 7 explains how to use SQL*Loader to input large quantities of data into your database. Personal Oracle8 comes into its own when it handles large amounts of data. If you wish to know more about writing reports, Chapter 8 explains the use of SQL*Plus to create detailed reports.

LOADING DATA INTO YOUR DATABASE

An easy way to get a large amount of data into your database.

In previous chapters, you learned how to create data within a database using the Navigator—a fairly slow process. SQL*Loader allows you to get a great deal of data into your database with relative ease. It also allows you to load data from other systems using common file formats. This chapter will address the use of SQL*Loader. I will include a general discussion about the components of SQL*Loader, showing the syntax and uses of each one. I will then provide several examples of implementing SQL*Loader.

SQL*LOADER

You can put data into your database in a number of ways, depending upon where the data is coming from. If it is from another Oracle database, you can either connect via Open Database Connectivity (ODBC) or use the export and import facility, described in detail in Chapter 14. If, however, the data is coming from another source, such as flat files, you can use SQL*Loader. This has several advantages:

- You can load data from multiple input files of different types.

- You can handle fixed-format, delimited-format, and variable-length records.

- You can manipulate fields with SQL functions before inserting them into the database.

- SQL*Loader supports a range of data types, including **DATE**, **BINARY**, and **PACKED DECIMAL**.

- You can load more than one table at a time.

- You can generate unique values in specified columns.

- You can use the Windows 95 operating system's file or record-management system to access data files.

- SQL*Loader has thorough error reporting, allowing you to adjust files and load all records easily.

- You can use high-performance "direct" loads to load data directly into database files without Oracle processing.

SQL*Loader works by using control files. The control file specifies how and where the data is to be loaded, as well as the format of the data. The control file then processes the data specified, producing a discard file for all records discarded, and a log file for all records added to the database.

SQL*Loader has five main components:

- Control file

- Data file

- Log file

- Discard file

- Bad file

Figure 7.1 shows the main components of SQL*Loader and the data flows within.

As you can see in Figure 7.1, SQL*Loader takes the control and data files as inputs, and outputs the log, discard, and bad files. SQL*Loader writes records to the database as it processes them.

Control File

A SQL*Loader control file is written in SQL*Loader data definition language (DDL). The control file specifies the following items:

- Where to find the data file for loading

- How the data file is delimited, and what the field separators are, if any

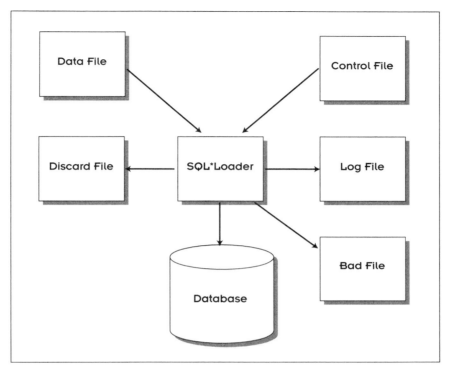

Figure 7.1   *The data flows of SQL*Loader.*

- Column and field specifications

- Which tables the data is to be loaded into

- The data-type specifications

- Specifications for loading the data into the relevant tables

- Specifications for loading column defaults

Listing 7.1 is an example of a simple SQL*Loader control file.

Listing 7.1   *A simple SQL*Loader control file.*

```
LOAD DATA
INFILE 'c:\orawin95\loader\supplier.dat'
APPEND
INTO TABLE SUPPLIERS
FIELDS TERMINATED BY ',' OPTIONALLY ENCLOSED BY '"'
(SUPPLIER_ID,SUPPLIER_NAME,ADDRESS_LINE_1,ADDRESS_LINE_2,
 CITY,COUNTRY,TELEPHONE_NUMBER,CONTACT_NAME)
```

The instruction on Line 1 in Listing 7.1 tells SQL*Loader to load data. Line 2 tells it where the data is by specifying either an operating-system file or the control file itself. Line 3 defines the action to take with the records in the data file; in this case, it will append records to the table named in Line 4. If the **APPEND** line were removed, SQL*Loader would assume the table you are inserting into must be empty; if not, it would return an error.

Line 5 defines the format of the data within the data file. In this case, I have chosen to use comma-separated values (a CSV file); however, defining the data by position is also common practice. (I will discuss loading data by position later in this chapter.) Lines 6 and 7 show the mapping between what appears in the data file and the corresponding column name in the **SUPPLIERS** table. Later in this section, I will explain all of the options available when writing SQL*Loader control files.

Data File

The data file, as its name suggests, is an operating-system file full of data. The file must be of either text or binary format. This chapter deals mainly with text format, but I include a brief discussion on loading binary files. The data within the file can be in one of the following formats:

- *Stream record format (the default)*—Each record in the data file is only as long as needed to store the data—that is, it has no space padding at the end of each record. The record separators are usually carriage returns.

- *Fixed record format*—The records within the data file are all of the same fixed length— that is, there is no space padding within the record. Also, each field within the record has the same fixed length, type, and position.

- *Variable record format*—Each record can be of a different length, but the data type of each field within the record must be constant.

Log File

The log file records all of the transactions made by SQL*Loader for each load. It includes such information as:

- The number of records added.

- The number of records discarded—those that do not fit the criteria supplied by the control file, if any.

- The number of records with errors—those that have Oracle errors in them. An error would occur if, for example, a field in the data file was defined with 10 characters and SQL*Loader tried to insert it into a column allowing only 9 characters.

- The table and data file specifications.

- The action to take upon inserting a record.

- Various session-timing information, such as CPU and execution time.

- Summary information for the SQL*Loader session.

Listing 7.2 shows an example log file for a SQL*Loader session that loads one record into the **SUPPLIERS** table. The control file that produced this log file appears in Listing 7.1.

Listing 7.2 A sample log-file output.

```
SQL*Loader: Release 8.0.3.0.0 - Production on Sun Jan 4 18:22:42 1998

(c) Copyright 1997 Oracle Corporation.  All rights reserved.

Control File:    supplier.ctl
Data File:       supplier.dat
Bad File:        supplier.bad
Discard File:    none specified

 (Allow all discards)

Number to load: ALL
Number to skip: 0
Errors allowed: 50
Bind array:     64 rows, maximum of 65536 bytes
Continuation:   none specified
Path used:      Conventional

Table SUPPLIERS, loaded from every logical record.
Insert option in effect for this table: APPEND

   Column Name                   Position   Len  Term Encl Datatype
------------------------------- ---------- ---- ---- ---- --------------------
SUPPLIER_ID                        FIRST     *   ,   0(") CHARACTER
SUPPLIER_NAME                      NEXT      *   ,   0(") CHARACTER
ADDRESS_LINE_1                     NEXT      *   ,   0(") CHARACTER
ADDRESS_LINE_2                     NEXT      *   ,   0(") CHARACTER
CITY                               NEXT      *   ,   0(") CHARACTER
COUNTRY                            NEXT      *   ,   0(") CHARACTER
TELEPHONE_NUMBER                   NEXT      *   ,   0(") CHARACTER
CONTACT_NAME                       NEXT      *   ,   0(") CHARACTER

Table SUPPLIERS:
  1 Row successfully loaded.
  0 Rows not loaded due to data errors.
  0 Rows not loaded because all WHEN clauses were failed.
  0 Rows not loaded because all fields were null.
```

```
Space allocated for bind array:                46592 bytes(64 rows)
Space allocated for memory besides bind array:     0 bytes

Total logical records skipped:        0
Total logical records read:           1
Total logical records rejected:       0
Total logical records discarded:      0

Run began on Sun Jan 04 18:22:42 1998
Run ended on Sun Jan 04 18:22:43 1998

Elapsed time was:     00:00:01.26
CPU time was:         00:00:00.00
```

Discard File

The discard file holds records SQL*Loader finds that do not match the criteria for loading specified within the control file. The discard file is used only if specified within the control file. If no records are discarded, and you have specified the discard file within the control file, no file will be created.

Within the control file, you can specify the maximum number of discards before terminating the load. SQL*Loader will then process your data file and, upon reaching the maximum number of discarded records, terminate the load. This saves time when loading large amounts of data for the first time, as you may not always get it right the first time. All of the records in the specified discard file appear as they would in the data file. That way, if a problem occurs that you can easily fix, the next time you execute the load, you can use the discard file as your data file.

Bad File

The bad file usually holds records that Oracle rejects. The bad file is written to whenever the database rejects a record that passed the SQL*Loader checks. The main reasons for records being written to the bad file are that they contain the wrong data type or that the field length is greater than that of the column they are being inserted into. Figure 7.2 shows the stages at which each of the discard, bad, and log files are written.

Figure 7.2 mainly shows that the bad file is written only when an insert to the database fails or when the record fails the initial SQL*Loader check. The discard file is written only if records contained within the data file fail the SQL*Loader **WHEN** clause. The next section provides details about the **WHEN** clause.

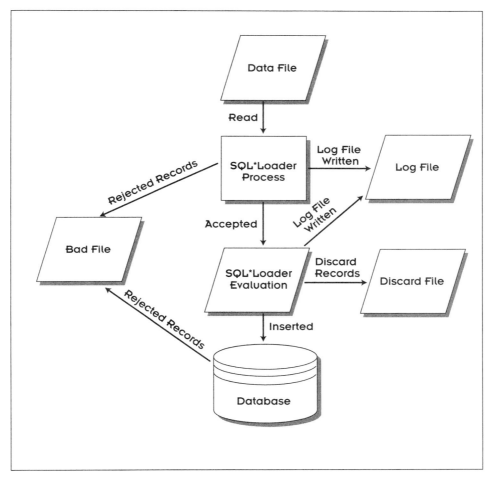

Figure 7.2 *Files written during a SQL*Loader session.*

SQL*LOADER CONTROL FILE REFERENCE

As mentioned before, you write the control file to match the data you wish to load. The control file must have a format that SQL*Loader recognizes. The syntax for the most commonly used control files is shown in this section; for more complex SQL*Loader control files, refer to the Personal Oracle8 documentation. The most commonly used control files, in my experience, are the loads that occur by field position. Listing 7.3 shows a typical control file that allows you to load data by its position within the data file.

Listing 7.3 *An example control file by position.*

```
1   LOAD DATA
2   INFILE 'c:\orawin95\bin\example1.dat'
3   APPEND
4   INTO TABLE SUPPLIERS
5
6   (SUPPLIER_ID       POSITION(01:04) CHAR,
7    SUPPLIER_NAME     POSITION(05:44) CHAR,
8    ADDRESS_LINE_1    POSITION(45:84) CHAR,
9    ADDRESS_LINE_2    POSITION(85:124) CHAR,
10   CITY              POSITION(125:144) CHAR,
11   COUNTRY           POSITION(145:164) CHAR,
12   TELEPHONE_NUMBER  POSITION(165:184) INTEGER EXTERNAL,
13   CONTACT_NAME      POSITION(185:209) CHAR)
```

In Listing 7.3, I numbered the lines to help identify and explain each, but you do not need to insert line numbers. The description for each line of the control file is as follows:

- *Line 1*—Instructs SQL*Loader that the control file contains information for a new load of data. If a load fails partway through, you can use the **CONTINUE_LOAD DATA** command instead of **LOAD DATA** (see the Personal Oracle8 documentation for more details).

- *Line 2*—Tells SQL*Loader where to find the data file containing the data to load. Within the single quotes can be any file name. If no direct path name is given, the file must be in a directory within your path. You can use the asterisk (*) symbol instead of the file name, without single quotes, which signifies that the data you wish to load appears in the control file, after the **BEGINDATA** command. (You can see an example of this in Listing 7.4, Lines 2 and 7.)

- *Line 3*—Allows you to append data to the end of a table. Other values for this parameter are **INSERT**, **REPLACE**, and **TRUNCATE**. The default is **INSERT**. If you use the **INSERT** statement, the table being loaded with data must be empty before the load commences.

- *Line 4*—Defines which table the data will be loaded into. You must have the required privileges to be able to **INSERT** and **UPDATE** data within the table.

- *Line 5*—Left blank for clarity and readability of the control file.

- *Line 6*—Begins position specifications, with the open parenthesis. The first field specified in the control file should match the first field in the data file. This is how SQL*Loader matches up the data in the data file with the correct columns. Line 6 specifies that Positions 1 to 4 of the data file map to the **Supplier_id** column within the **SUPPLIERS** table; also, the characters found there are of the data type **CHAR**.

- *Line 7*—Specifies the next segment of data to be loaded: in this case, **Supplier_Name**, in Positions 5 to 44. This should be of data type **CHAR**.

- *Line 8*—Specifies the next segment of data to be loaded: **Address_Line_1**, in Positions 45 to 84. This should be of data type **CHAR**.

- *Line 9*—Specifies the next segment of data to be loaded: **Address_Line_2**, in Positions 85 to 124. This should be of data type **CHAR**.

- *Line 10*—Specifies the next segment of data to be loaded: **City**, in Positions 125 to 144. This should be of data type **CHAR**.

- *Line 11*—Specifies the next segment of data to be loaded: **Country**, in Positions 145 to 164. This should be of data type **CHAR**.

- *Line 12*—Specifies the next segment of data to be loaded: **Telephone_Number**, in Positions 165 to 184. This should be of data type **INTEGER**.

- *Line 13*—Specifies the next segment of data to be loaded: **Contact_Name**, in Positions 185 to 209. This should be of data type **CHAR**. Remember to close the parentheses at the end of the position specification.

Listing 7.4 shows another common type of control file. It reads data from the control file using delimiters, rather than by position. In this case, the data is contained within the control file, but it could easily have been read in from a data file.

Listing 7.4   *An example control file using field delimiters.*

```
1   LOAD DATA
2   INFILE *
3   INTO TABLE SUPPLIERS
4   FIELDS TERMINATED BY ',' OPTIONALLY ENCLOSED BY '"'
5   (SUPPLIER_ID,SUPPLIER_NAME,ADDRESS_LINE_1,ADDRESS_LINE_2,CITY,
6    COUNTRY,TELEPHONE_NUMBER,CONTACT_NAME)
7   BEGINDATA
8   9999,WIDGETS LTD,"20 BOND ST",,LONDON,UK,12345678,"MR. BOND"
```

The control file in Listing 7.4 allows you to load data by using text delimiters within the data file—in this case, comma-separated values (a CSV file). The description for each line of the control file is as follows:

- *Line 1*—Tells SQL*Loader this is a new load session.

- *Line 2*—Tells SQL*Loader where to find the data file. In this case, as no file name is given and an asterisk used, the data can be found in this control file. This works with a small amount of data, but if you're loading thousands of records, using a separate data file for loading data is a better method.

- *Line 3*—Specifies which table the data is to be loaded into. Notice that in this control file, no **APPEND** is specified, as in Listing 7.3. The default is **INSERT** mode, where the table being loaded with data must be empty. If this is not the case, error messages will be produced and the load will be terminated.

- *Line 4*—Specifies what the field delimiter will be. In this case, I have chosen to use a comma, as this is not a common occurrence in most data files. Be careful what character you choose to be the delimiter. You do not want to use a character or symbol that may appear in your data. The **OPTIONALLY ENCLOSED BY** clause is used to search for any data having commas. The whole field with the comma has to be enclosed in double quotes, indicating to SQL*Loader that this is a piece of data, not a field delimiter.

- *Line 5*—Specifies which fields are contained within the data file. In this case, the list of fields is split into two lines. The specification of the fields within the control file should match the order of the fields within the data file.

- *Line 6*—Second line of the list of fields, begun on Line 5.

- *Line 7*—The **BEGINDATA** command tells SQL*Loader that everything after this line is data. When used in conjunction with the **INFILE** clause in Line 2, you can include the data within your control file.

- *Line 8*—This is the data that will be passed through to SQL*Loader. Notice how some of the fields are enclosed with double quotes; these fields will still be read in as character data types.

METHODS OF LOADING DATA

Within SQL*Loader, there are two methods of loading data into the database:

- *Conventional (the default)*—The conventional-path method uses a standard SQL **INSERT** statement to load the data into the database.

- *Direct*—The direct-path method formats data blocks and writes them directly to the database files, overcoming the overhead of using the Oracle interpreter to translate the data. The direct method usually loads data as fast as the disk will allow, as this load is done at hardware level.

Conventional Method

The conventional method of loading data, which is the default, uses SQL **INSERT** statements to populate tables within the database. When loading via the conventional method, you will not have the database's full attention, as other tasks could be performed by other programs, such as SQL*Plus. The database shares its processing among all connections. Because the conventional method uses **INSERT** statements, this is classed as a connection and, therefore, will be in contention for resources. This can significantly slow the loading process. Although the direct method is faster, you should use the conventional method in the following situations:

- When loading data via SQL*Net, Oracle's networking protocol.

- When loading data while users are accessing the system. The direct method needs exclusive access to tables and indexes.

- When loading data into clustered tables.

- When loading small amounts of data into large indexed tables.

- When you need to apply SQL functions to the data being loaded through the control file.

Direct Method

The direct method of loading data does not use any of the normal Oracle buffers for inserting data. Instead, it formats the data into Oracle data blocks within the database. This bypasses the Oracle processing and allows the writes to be passed quickly to the database. The direct method has a number of advantages:

- Reduces the processing load of the Oracle database.

- Uses only whole blocks of data, which is very efficient.

- Writes data blocks directly to the database.

- Locks all required objects at the start of the load, not once for each statement, as in the conventional method.

- Allows you to presort indexes before creating them.

You should always try to use the direct method to load data into the database. This is especially true when either one of the following applies:

- You need to load a large amount of data in a short amount of time.

- You want to load data in parallel (two or more loads at the same time).

If you wish to use the direct method for loading data into your database, you need to set up your database to allow direct loads. You do so by executing the file C:\ORAWIN95\RDBMS80\ADMIN\catldr.sql through SQL*Plus as the user **SYS**. This creates a number of views within the database to enable the direct-load method. See Example 6 later in this chapter for an example of using the direct-load method.

Parallel Loads

Parallel loads can use either conventional or direct methods of loading data. A parallel load is where two or more SQL*Loader sessions are active at the same time. They can be loading into either the same table or different parts of the database. This type of loading generally speeds up the time taken to create data within the database. You use parallel loading mainly with the direct method. A parallel load allows multiple direct-path load sessions to load the same data segments concurrently into the database. The use of parallel loads has further restrictions—for example, rows can only be appended. For further details of parallel loads, please consult the Personal Oracle8 documentation.

SQL*LOADER EXAMPLES

SQL*Loader on Personal Oracle8 for Windows 95 is a DOS-based program and must be executed through a DOS window, using the command **sqlldr80**. If you execute the command by itself, it shows the syntax you need for executing it, shown in Listing 7.5.

Listing 7.5   Syntax for SQL*Loader.

```
SQL*Loader: Release 8.0.3.0.0 - Production on Tue Jan 6 20:21:5 1998
(c) Copyright 1997 Oracle Corporation.  All rights reserved.

Usage: SQLLOAD keyword=value [,keyword=value,...]

Valid Keywords:

    userid -- ORACLE username/password
   control -- Control file name
       log -- Log file name
       bad -- Bad file name
      data -- Data file name
   discard -- Discard file name
discardmax -- Number of discards to allow       (Default all)
      skip -- Number of logical records to skip  (Default 0)
      load -- Number of logical records to load  (Default all)
    errors -- Number of errors to allow          (Default 50)
      rows -- Number of rows in conventional path bind array or between direct
                path data saves
                 (Default: Conventional path 64, Direct path all)
  bindsize -- Size of conventional path bind array in bytes  (Default 65536)
```

```
     silent -- Suppress messages during run
               (header,feedback,errors,discards,partitions)
     direct -- use direct path                       (Default FALSE)
    parfile -- parameter file: name of file that contains parameter specifica-
               tions
   parallel -- do parallel load                      (Default FALSE)
       file -- File to allocate extents from
skip_unusable_indexes -- disallow/allow unusable indexes or index partitions
                    (Default FALSE)
skip_index_maintenance -- do not maintain indexes, mark affected indexes as
                    unusable  (Default FALSE)
commit_discontinued -- commit loaded rows when load is discontinued  (Default
                    FALSE)
```

PLEASE NOTE: Command-line parameters may be specified either by position or by keywords. An example of the former case is 'sqlload scott/tiger foo'; an example of the latter is 'sqlload control=foo userid=scott/tiger'. One may specify parameters by position before but not after parameters specified by keywords. For example, 'sqlload scott/tiger control=foo logfile=log' is allowed, but 'sqlload scott/tiger control=foo log' is not, even though the position of the parameter 'log' is correct.

To use SQL*Loader, you have to specify a number of parameters to the **sqlldr80** program. A brief explanation of the main parameters follows:

- *userid*—The Personal Oracle8 username and password. For the demo user of our database, the command would be **userid=demo/demo**. The slash (/) command is the separator of the username and password.

- *control*—Specifies the control file to use for this SQL*Loader session. This would look something like:

```
control=c:\orawin95\loader\example1.ctl
```

- *parfile*—Use if you wish all parameters to be read from an operating-system file. For example, you could set up a file to store the control-file name, the username, and password, and then use the command:

```
sqlldr80 parfile=c:\orawin95\loader\your_filename
```

This would read in all of your commands as if the file name, username, and password were specified on the command line.

- *parallel*—Denotes a parallel load. If you wish to use parallel loads, set this parameter to TRUE.

Most of the parameters you can use on the command line can also be used in the control file. I find that using as many parameters as possible in the control file—therefore cutting down the number of parameters on the command line—is a lot easier. For the command line, I usually use just the **userid** and **control** parameters; I put the other parameters in the relevant control file. The keywords do not have to appear in the command line; you can omit them and use just the parameter value, but you must keep them in the order specified by the syntax.

The next sections provide examples of each different loading technique. They are designed to use as much of the SQL*Loader functionality as possible. For this reason, you may not want to take these exact control files and implement them on your system. By all means, test them as they appear here, but if you do use them to import large amounts of data, check the control files to ensure you are not using parts of SQL*Loader you do not need.

Example 1—Loading Fixed-Length Records

This first example shows you the loading of data by its position from an external data file. Listings 7.6, 7.7, and 7.8 show the command line, control file, and data file being used.

Listing 7.6   *Command line for loading by position.*

```
sqlldr80 userid=demo/demo control=example1.ctl
```

Listing 7.7   *Control file for loading by position.*

```
LOAD DATA
INFILE 'c:\orawin95\loader\example1.dat'
APPEND
INTO TABLE ORDERS

(ORDER_ID        POSITION(01:06) INTEGER EXTERNAL,
 CUSTOMER_ID     POSITION(07:11) INTEGER EXTERNAL,
 ORDER_DATE      POSITION(12:20) DATE,
 DISPATCHED_DATE POSITION(21:29) DATE,
 ORDER_DUE_DATE  POSITION(30:38) DATE)
```

Listing 7.8   *Data file for loading by position.*

```
9999901000101-JAN-9901-FEB-9901-FEB-99
9999911000101-FEB-9901-MAR-9901-MAR-99
9999921000101-MAR-9901-APR-9901-APR-99
9999931000101-APR-9901-MAY-9901-MAY-99
9999941000101-MAY-9901-JUN-9901-JUN-99
9999951000101-JUN-9901-JUL-9901-JUL-99
```

```
9999961000101-JUL-99          01-AUG-99
9999971000101-AUG-9901-SEP-9901-SEP-99
9999981000101-SEP-9901-OCT-9901-OCT-99
9999991000101-OCT-9901-NOV-9901-NOV-99
```

Example 2—Loading Variable-Length Records

This second example loads the same data as shown in Listing 7.8, using variable-length records, with the data file included within the control file. Listings 7.9 and 7.10 show the command line and the control file being used. As this control file does not specify the option to use for creating records within the database, the **ORDERS** table must be empty prior to the load taking place.

Listing 7.9   *Command line for variable-length records.*

```
sqlldr80 userid=demo/demo control=example2.ctl
```

Listing 7.10   *Control file for loading variable-length records.*

```
LOAD DATA
INFILE *
INTO TABLE ORDERS
FIELDS TERMINATED BY ',' OPTIONALLY ENCLOSED BY '"'
(ORDER_ID,CUSTOMER_ID,ORDER_DATE,DISPATCHED_DATE,ORDER_DUE_DATE)
BEGINDATA
999990,10001,01-JAN-99,01-FEB-99,01-FEB-99
999991,10001,01-FEB-99,01-MAR-99,01-MAR-99
999992,10001,01-MAR-99,01-APR-99,01-APR-99
999993,10001,01-APR-99,01-MAY-99,01-MAY-99
999994,10001,01-MAY-99,01-JUN-99,01-JUN-99
999995,10001,01-JUN-99,01-JUL-99,01-JUL-99
999996,10001,01-JUL-99,,01-AUG-99
999997,10001,01-AUG-99,01-SEP-99,01-SEP-99
999998,10001,01-SEP-99,01-OCT-99,01-OCT-99
999999,10001,01-OCT-99,01-NOV-99,01-NOV-99
```

Example 3—Loading A Delimited File

This third example loads the same data as shown in Listing 7.8, using delimiters, with the data file included within the control file. Listings 7.11 and 7.12 show the command line and the control file being used. Notice in this control file, I specify the dates as having a different input format. Oracle will interpret these dates and convert them to standard Oracle dates. You can specify other data types within the control file.

Listing 7.11 *Command line for Example 3.*

```
sqlldr80 demo/demo example3.ctl
```

Listing 7.12 *Control file for using delimiters.*

```
LOAD DATA
INFILE *
APPEND
INTO TABLE ORDERS
FIELDS TERMINATED BY "," OPTIONALLY ENCLOSED BY '"'
(ORDER_ID,CUSTOMER_ID,
 ORDER_DATE DATE(20) "DD-Month-YYYY",
 DISPATCHED_DATE DATE(20) "DD-Month-YYYY",
 ORDER_DUE_DATE DATE(20) "DD-Month-YYYY")
BEGINDATA
999990,10001,01-January-1999,01-February-1999,01-February-1999
999991,10001,01-February-1999,01-March-1999,01-March-1999
999992,10001,01-March-1999,01-April-1999,01-April-1999
999993,10001,01-April-1999,01-May-1999,01-May-1999
999994,10001,01-May-1999,01-June-1999,01-June-1999
999995,10001,01-June-1999,01-July-1999,01-July-1999
999996,10001,01-July-1999,,01-August-1999
999997,10001,01-August-1999,01-September-1999,01-September-1999
999998,10001,01-September-1999,01-October-1999,01-October-1999
999999,10001,01-October-1999,01-November-1999,01-November-1999
```

Example 4—Loading Combined Records

This fourth example loads files that could be made up from more than one input file. Listings 7.13, 7.14, and 7.15 show the command line, control file, and data files being used. The control file shown in Listing 7.14 is written to load in only those records whose first character is an exclamation mark (!). Notice in the control file, we use a discard file, set up to allow a maximum of 99 records to be discarded. The records inserted are assumed to be already there, as the **REPLACE** option is used. This will delete all records and insert these new ones. In the data file in Listing 7.15, each record is split into two lines.

Listing 7.13 *Command line for Example 4.*

```
sqlldr80 userid=demo/demo control=example4.ctl
```

Listing 7.14 *Control file for combined file loads.*

```
LOAD DATA
INFILE "example4.dat"
DISCARDFILE "example4.dis"
DISCARDMAX 99
REPLACE
```

```
CONTINUEIF (1) = '!'
INTO TABLE ORDERS
(ORDER_ID         POSITION(01:06) INTEGER EXTERNAL,
 CUSTOMER_ID      POSITION(07:11) INTEGER EXTERNAL,
 ORDER_DATE       POSITION(12:20) DATE,
 DISPATCHED_DATE  POSITION(21:29) DATE,
 ORDER_DUE_DATE   POSITION(30:38) DATE)
```

Listing 7.15 *Data file for Example 4.*

```
9999901000101-JAN-
9901-FEB-9901-FEB-99
9999911000101-FEB-
9901-MAR-9901-MAR-99
9999921000101-MAR-
9901-APR-9901-APR-99
9999931000101-APR-
9901-MAY-9901-MAY-99
9999941000101-MAY-
9901-JUN-9901-JUN-99
9999951000101-JUN-
9901-JUL-9901-JUL-99
9999961000101-JUL-
99        01-AUG-99
9999971000101-AUG-
9901-SEP-9901-SEP-99
9999981000101-SEP-
9901-OCT-9901-OCT-99
9999991000101-OCT-
9901-NOV-9901-NOV-99
```

Example 5—Loading Into Multiple Tables

This example loads files into multiple tables from one data file. Listings 7.16, 7.17, and 7.18 show the command line, control file, and data files being used. In the data file in Listing 7.18, the records for **Order_id**s 999995 and 999999 are larger than the rest. This enables you to pick out the orders and populate the **ORDER_DETAILS** table with information. The control file shown in Listing 7.17 is written to interpret the **Order_id** and insert data into tables based upon the value of the **Order_id**. Notice that the control file specifies a bad file. The records inserted are assumed to be already there. As the **REPLACE** option is used, this will delete all records and insert these new ones.

Listing 7.16 *Command line for Example 5.*

```
sqlldr80 demo/demo example5.ctl
```

Listing 7.17 *Control file for Example 5.*

```
LOAD DATA
INFILE 'example5.dat'
BADFILE 'example5.bad'
DISCARDFILE 'example5.dis'
REPLACE

INTO TABLE ORDERS
(ORDER_ID        POSITION(01:06) INTEGER EXTERNAL,
 CUSTOMER_ID     POSITION(07:11) INTEGER EXTERNAL,
 ORDER_DATE      POSITION(12:20) DATE,
 DISPATCHED_DATE POSITION(21:29) DATE,
 ORDER_DUE_DATE  POSITION(30:38) DATE)

INTO TABLE ORDER_DETAILS
WHEN ORDER_ID = '999995'
  (ORDER_ID        POSITION(01:06) INTEGER EXTERNAL,
   PRODUCT_ID      POSITION(39:42) INTEGER EXTERNAL,
   NUMBER_ORDERED  POSITION(43:48) INTEGER EXTERNAL,
   UNIT_PRICE      POSITION(49:54) DECIMAL)

INTO TABLE ORDER_DETAILS
WHEN ORDER_ID = '999999'
  (ORDER_ID        POSITION(01:06) INTEGER EXTERNAL,
   PRODUCT_ID      POSITION(39:42) INTEGER EXTERNAL,
   NUMBER_ORDERED  POSITION(43:48) INTEGER EXTERNAL,
   UNIT_PRICE      POSITION(49:54) DECIMAL)
```

Listing 7.18 *Data file for Example 5.*

```
9999901000101-JAN-9901-FEB-9901-FEB-99
9999911000101-FEB-9901-MAR-9901-MAR-99
9999921000101-MAR-9901-APR-9901-APR-99
9999931000101-APR-9901-MAY-9901-MAY-99
9999941000101-MAY-9901-JUN-9901-JUN-99
9999951000101-JUN-9901-JUL-9901-JUL-99123410     10
9999961000101-JUL-99          01-AUG-99
9999971000101-AUG-9901-SEP-9901-SEP-99
9999981000101-SEP-9901-OCT-9901-OCT-99
9999991000101-OCT-9901-NOV-9901-NOV-991234100    9
```

Example 6—Loading Using The Direct Path

Example 6 loads files using the direct-path method. Listings 7.19, 7.20, and 7.21 show the command line, control file, and data files being used. Notice in the command-line syntax in Listing 7.19 that the parameter **DIRECT** is set to TRUE, enabling the direct-load method. The control file shown in Listing 7.20 is written as a normal positional load control file.

Listing 7.19 *Command line for Example 6.*

```
sqlldr80 demo/demo example6.ctl direct=true
```

Listing 7.20 *Control file for Example 6.*

```
LOAD DATA
INFILE 'example6.dat'
INSERT
INTO TABLE ORDERS
(ORDER_ID        POSITION(01:06) INTEGER EXTERNAL,
 CUSTOMER_ID     POSITION(07:11) INTEGER EXTERNAL,
 ORDER_DATE      POSITION(12:20) DATE,
 DISPATCHED_DATE POSITION(21:29) DATE,
 ORDER_DUE_DATE  POSITION(30:38) DATE)
```

Listing 7.21 *Data file for Example 6.*

```
9999901000101-JAN-9901-FEB-9901-FEB-99
9999911000101-FEB-9901-MAR-9901-MAR-99
9999921000101-MAR-9901-APR-9901-APR-99
9999931000101-APR-9901-MAY-9901-MAY-99
9999941000101-MAY-9901-JUN-9901-JUN-99
9999951000101-JUN-9901-JUL-9901-JUL-99
9999961000101-JUL-99        01-AUG-99
9999971000101-AUG-9901-SEP-9901-SEP-99
9999981000101-SEP-9901-OCT-9901-OCT-99
9999991000101-OCT-9901-NOV-9901-NOV-99
```

THE NEXT STEP

In this chapter, you learned how to load information into your database using SQL*Loader. As mentioned earlier, another way to load data into your database is to use the import method. This is quicker if your data to be imported is from another Oracle database. In the next chapter, you will learn how to use the report-formatting features of SQL*Plus.

Reporting From Your Database

CHAPTER 8

Using SQL*Plus to write and generate readable reports.

In Chapter 7, I explained how to get a lot of data into your database in a short amount of time. This chapter will show you how to write and generate reports using SQL*Plus. The information provided here will build on the commands used in preceding chapters and will incorporate the report-formatting features of SQL*Plus.

As you've already seen, the **SELECT** statement produces relatively simple output: Column headings are derived from column names, although column aliases can be used. You can use SQL*Plus to enhance the output from your SQL statements. SQL*Plus commands differ from SQL commands in the following ways:

- SQL*Plus commands do not relate to specific **SELECT** statements.

- You can enter SQL*Plus commands on only one line, and you must use a hyphen to split a command across more than one line.

- SQL*Plus commands are not saved in the SQL buffer.

- SQL*Plus commands are effective for the whole session.

SQL*Plus commands set up the environment in which SQL statements are executed. For example, you may set the headings for each **SELECT** statement, or you may use page numbers for the data returned.

SET COMMAND

Within SQL*Plus, you can set parameters during execution. These parameters define the way the output from your SQL statements is displayed. The syntax for setting a parameter is as follows:

```
SET   parameter_name value
```

This syntax for the **SET** command sets ***parameter_name*** to be the ***value*** given. Mostly, the values given are either TRUE or FALSE. Some of the parameters cannot be set from within a SQL*Plus session. If you have certain values that you would like set every time you enter a SQL*Plus session, you can create a file called login.sql and place it in the directory you normally enter SQL*Plus in, or anywhere in the Windows 95 path.

If you would like to save the environment you are currently working under in a SQL*Plus session, you can create a SQL file that will re-create the environment. For example, to create a file called environ.sql, which has the settings for the current environment, at the **SQL>** prompt type:

```
store set environ.sql create
```

This command creates a file in your current directory that contains the commands to re-create your current environment. To re-create your current environment at any time, just execute the environ.sql file by using the **START** or @ command.

A number of different parameters are available to set within any SQL*Plus session. Some of the more useful are listed in the next sections; for a list of all available parameters, check the Oracle documentation.

arraysize

The **arraysize** parameter defines the number of rows that Oracle returns in each batch. When you submit a request to return rows, the database batches these rows before it returns any to the screen. Using **arraysize**, you can specify the size of each batch. **arraysize** can be any value from 1 to 5,000; the default is 15. A large value for this parameter increases the efficiency for queries that return large numbers of rows. Sometimes, when returning rows with a large number of columns, the most efficient course is to set this parameter to 1.

autotrace

The **autotrace** parameter, when set to **ON**, displays the execution plan for the executed SQL statement. This is useful when trying to increase performance. The default value for this parameter is **OFF**. **autotrace** can be enabled only when **PLAN_TABLE** exists. You create this table by executing the utlxplan.sql script in the C:\ORAWIN95\RDBMS80\ ADMIN directory. The values for this parameter are:

- *ON*—Turns **autotrace** on.

- *OFF*—Turns **autotrace** off, which is the default.

- *TRACEONLY*—Specifies that you wish to see only the trace information, not the statistics information.

Listing 8.1 shows an example of **autotrace**.

Listing 8.1   The *autotrace* facility.

```
SQL> set autotrace on
SQL> select * from order_details;

  ORDER_ID PRODUCT_ID NUMBER_ORDERED UNIT_PRICE
---------- ---------- -------------- ----------
    100001       5002             20          4
    100001       5001             10          2
    100001       5003             10         10
    100002       5001             20          2
    100003       5002             10          4
    100004       5001             15          2
    100004       5002             25          4
    100005       5004             10          6
    100005       5003             10         10
    100005       5002             10          4
    100006       5001             20          2
    100003       5004             50          6

12 rows selected.


Execution Plan
----------------------------------------------------
   0      SELECT STATEMENT Optimizer=CHOOSE
   1    0   TABLE ACCESS (FULL) OF 'ORDER_DETAILS'
```

```
Statistics
-----------------------------------------------
        0  recursive calls
        3  db block gets
        2  consistent gets
        0  physical reads
        0  redo size
     1119  bytes sent via SQL*Net to client
      655  bytes received via SQL*Net from client
        4  SQL*Net roundtrips to/from client
        1  sorts (memory)
        0  sorts (disk)
       12  rows processed
```

In the listing, you can see the output from the query, then the execution plan, and, finally, the statistics. The execution plan displays the route that Oracle chose to execute the SQL statement. For more detailed information on the use of tracing SQL statements and other performance improvements, see Chapter 18.

echo

The **echo** parameter, when set to **ON**, echoes each command as it is executed from a command file. The valid values for this parameter are **ON** and **OFF**, the default being **OFF**. This parameter is effective only when executing commands from an operating-system file—i.e., when using the **START** or **@** command.

editfile

Whenever you use the **EDIT** command to edit a SQL statement within the SQL buffer, you create a file called afiedt.buf. This is the default file name for any edited file from within SQL*Plus. You can change it through the use of the **editfile** parameter. You could set **editfile** to create a file in a specific directory by issuing the following command:

```
SET EDITFILE c:\orawin95\bin\temp.buf
```

Then, whenever you type the **EDIT** command, you'll create a file in C:\ORAWIN95\BIN called temp.buf. This is useful if you wish to keep all edited files in one place. If you just give a file name, as in the default, a file will be created in your current directory, and you'll end up with lots of files called afiedt.buf in lots of directories.

feedback

You may have noticed in previous listings in this book, that when a SQL statement is issued, the number of records selected appears after the records are displayed; sometimes, however, this number does not appear. When a SQL statement is issued within SQL*Plus, if the number of rows returned is less than six, it does not display this information. The **feedback** parameter is used to change this default value. Setting this parameter to 0 effectively turns the parameter off. This is useful when writing reports, as you do not always want to see how many records are returned.

heading

The **heading** parameter either displays or suppresses the printing of column headings on queries. The default is **ON**. To turn headings off, set the **heading** parameter to **OFF**. This is another feature that is useful when writing reports. An example is shown in Listing 8.2.

*Listing 8.2 Using the **heading** parameter.*

```
SQL> select * from orders;
ORDER_ID  CUSTOMER_ID ORDER_DAT DISPATCHE ORDER_DUE
--------  ----------- --------- --------- ---------
   100001       20001 01-Jan-99 10-Jan-99 31-Jan-99
   100002       20001 02-Jan-99 11-Jan-99 31-Jan-99
   100003       20002 01-May-98 09-May-98 31-May-98
   100004       20003 01-Jun-98 03-Jun-98 10-Jun-98
   100005       20004 28-Aug-99 29-Aug-99 30-Sep-99
   100006       20005 28-Aug-99 10-Sep-99 31-Aug-99

6 rows selected.

SQL> set heading off
SQL> select * from orders;

   100001       20001 01-Jan-99 10-Jan-99 31-Jan-99
   100002       20001 02-Jan-99 11-Jan-99 31-Jan-99
   100003       20002 01-May-98 09-May-98 31-May-98
   100004       20003 01-Jun-98 03-Jun-98 10-Jun-98
   100005       20004 28-Aug-99 29-Aug-99 30-Sep-99
   100006       20005 28-Aug-99 10-Sep-99 31-Aug-99

6 rows selected.
```

linesize

The **linesize** option sets the maximum number of characters that SQL*Plus displays on one line before displaying a new line. The default value for this parameter is 80, the minimum is 1, and the maximum is system-dependent. This value is also used in conjunction with other parameters—for example, **TTITLE** and **BTITLE**, which use the value of **linesize** to calculate the center of the page. When spooling text to a file, you'll find this parameter useful if you have lines with more than 80 characters; if the value were left at 80, it would insert a carriage return after each 80 characters.

long

The **long** parameter is used for displaying **LONG** data types. As a **LONG** data type can be anything up to 2 gigabytes, displaying this on the screen is not sensible. Setting the **long** parameter to 500, for example, displays the first 500 characters of the column.

newpage

The **newpage** parameter sets the number of blank lines between the top of the new page and the title (adding titles is discussed later in this chapter). The default for this parameter is 1. This parameter has a number of settings:

- *1*—Displays one blank line between the title and the top of the page; this is the default.

- *n*—Displays the number (n) of blank lines between the top of the page and the title. Setting this to 0 will produce a form feed at the beginning of each page and usually clears the screen on most terminals.

- *NONE*—Does not print a blank line or issue a form feed between pages.

Use the **newpage** parameter when formatting output for reports, examples of which you can see later in this chapter.

numformat

The **numformat** parameter sets the format of all numbers displayed within queries. The syntax of the **numformat** parameter is:

```
SET NUMFORMAT text
```

For example,

```
SET NUMFORMAT 999.99
```

would display all numbers with two decimal places.

The section describing the **FORMAT** clause of the **COLUMN** command later in this chapter provides details about *text* as a number format. The example in Listing 8.3 shows the number format set to 999.999. This displays only numbers up to three significant figures, with three decimal places. You will notice that hash marks are displayed when the number overflows the number format. You can also see that, where numbers are displayed, three decimal places are used.

Listing 8.3   The *numformat* parameter.

```
SQL> set numformat 999.999
SQL> select * from order_details;

ORDER_ID PRODUCT_ID NUMBER_ORDERED UNIT_PRICE
-------- ---------- -------------- ----------
######## ########           20.000      4.000
######## ########           10.000      2.000
######## ########           10.000     10.000
######## ########           20.000      2.000
######## ########           10.000      4.000
######## ########           15.000      2.000
######## ########           25.000      4.000
######## ########           10.000      6.000
######## ########           10.000     10.000
######## ########           10.000      4.000
######## ########           20.000      2.000
######## ########           50.000      6.000

12 rows selected.
```

numwidth

The **numwidth** parameter sets the width of displayed numbers. The default is 10—that is, you can display numbers up to 10 characters in width. If you tried to display a number with 11 characters, SQL*Plus would display the field filled with hash marks, as seen in Listing 8.3. This indicates an overflow. To display the required field, you must increase the value of **numwidth**.

pagesize

The **pagesize** parameter sets the number of lines displayed per page. The default is 24, the number of lines on a normal screen. For reports, you may want to set this value to 60 or 66, depending upon the size of the paper you're using. Setting this parameter to 0 suppresses all headings, page breaks, titles, and blank lines on the report.

pause

The **pause** parameter allows you to control, via the keyboard, the scrolling of your terminal. This parameter only pauses the screen; the execution still takes place behind the scenes. **pause** has three values:

- *ON*—Pauses the display at the beginning of each page displayed.

- *OFF*—Does not pause at all; this is the default.

- *text*—The text entered causes that text to be displayed each time the display is paused. If multiple words are to be used, they must be enclosed in single quotes. For example, to display the text "Press Enter to continue..." at each pause, you would issue the command:

```
SET PAUSE 'Press Enter to continue...'
```

For the text to be effective, you have to set the **pause** parameter to **ON** either before or after issuing the command.

The **pause** parameter is invaluable when running large queries that return lots of rows.

showmode

The **showmode** parameter controls whether the old and new values are displayed when setting system parameters using the **SET** command. Listing 8.4 shows an example of the **showmode** parameter. In this listing, the **pagesize** parameter is changed to 10. Notice that with the **showmode** parameter enabled, it also displays the old value. The default setting for the **showmode** parameter is **OFF**.

Listing 8.4   The *showmode* parameter.

```
SQL> set showmode on
new: showmode BOTH
SQL> set pagesize 10
old: pagesize 1
new: pagesize 10
SQL>
SQL> set pagesize 1
old: pagesize 10
new: pagesize 1
```

space

Normally, when SQL statements execute, the output is displayed in columns that are separated from each other by one space. The **space** parameter allows you to space out the columns to a predetermined value. In Listing 8.5, for example, the **space** parameter is changed to 3 from its default of 1, so the output has three spaces instead of one between columns.

Listing 8.5   The *space* parameter.

```
SQL> select * from order_details;
```

```
ORDER_ID PRODUCT_ID NUMBER_ORDERED UNIT_PRICE
--------- ----------- --------------- ----------
   100001      5002             20           4
   100001      5001             10           2
   100001      5003             10          10
   100002      5001             20           2
   100003      5002             10           4
   100004      5001             15           2
   100004      5002             25           4
   100005      5004             10           6
   100005      5003             10          10
   100005      5002             10           4
   100006      5001             20           2
   100003      5004             50           6

12 rows selected.

SQL> set space 3
SQL> select * from order_details;

ORDER_ID    PRODUCT_ID    NUMBER_ORDERED    UNIT_PRICE
---------   ----------    --------------    ----------
   100001        5002                20             4
   100001        5001                10             2
   100001        5003                10            10
   100002        5001                20             2
   100003        5002                10             4
   100004        5001                15             2
   100004        5002                25             4
   100005        5004                10             6
   100005        5003                10            10
   100005        5002                10             4
   100006        5001                20             2
   100003        5004                50             6

12 rows selected.
```

sqlprompt

The **sqlprompt** parameter changes the default prompt you receive when entering SQL commands. Normally, you see the **SQL>** prompt when in SQL*Plus, but you can change it to anything you like using the **sqlprompt** parameter. This is sometimes useful on machines where you have multiple databases. You could set the prompt to be the database name, so you know which database you're working on. Listing 8.6 shows an example of changing the prompt.

Listing 8.6   The **sqlprompt** parameter.

```
SQL> set sqlprompt 'Hello World>'
Hello World>
```

```
Hello World>
Hello World>
Hello World>
```

Notice that to include a space in the prompt, you must specify the prompt between single quotes.

termout

The **termout** parameter controls the display of output while executing commands from an operating-system file. When using this parameter, you should remember that only commands executed through a file are affected; all commands entered interactively, at the **SQL>** prompt, will still display output. This parameter is set to either **ON** or **OFF**. When **ON**, output will be displayed as normal; this is the default. When **OFF**, output will not be seen on the terminal screen. This is useful when executing large reports and spooling them to a file. The spooling of reports to a file is covered in a later section in this chapter.

time

When the **time** parameter is set to **ON**, the current time is displayed before each command prompt. The default for this parameter is **OFF**, which displays no time information. Listing 8.7 shows an example of **time**.

Listing 8.7   The *time* parameter.

```
SQL>set time on
12:28:04 SQL>
12:28:04 SQL>
12:28:04 SQL>
12:28:05 SQL>
12:28:05 SQL>
12:28:05 SQL>
12:28:05 SQL>
12:28:05 SQL>
12:28:05 SQL>
12:28:06 SQL>
12:28:06 SQL>
```

timing

The **timing** parameter is useful when you are performance-tuning SQL statements. After each execution of a SQL statement, **timing** displays the amount of time it took to execute the SQL statement. On a Windows 95 platform, the time displayed is in thousandths of a second. In the example shown in Listing 8.8, the SQL statement is executed in 0.61 seconds realtime.

Listing 8.8   The *timing* parameter.

```
SQL>set timing on
SQL>select * from order_details;

 ORDER_ID PRODUCT_ID NUMBER_ORDERED UNIT_PRICE
--------- ---------- -------------- ----------
   100001       5002             20          4
   100001       5001             10          2
   100001       5003             10         10
   100002       5001             20          2
   100003       5002             10          4
   100004       5001             15          2
   100004       5002             25          4
   100005       5004             10          6
   100005       5003             10         10
   100005       5002             10          4
   100006       5001             20          2
   100003       5004             50          6

12 rows selected.

 real: 610
```

underline

You use the **underline** parameter to change the value of the underline character within SQL*Plus. As you've seen in all earlier examples, a SQL statement is output in the form of columns. Each column has a heading and a line between the heading and the data. With the **underline** parameter, you can change this line to any nonalphanumeric character, excluding a space. This parameter has three clauses:

- *ON*—Turns **underline** on and defaults the underline character to a dash (-).

- *OFF*—Turns **underline** off altogether—i.e., it does not display any underline characters.

- *CHAR*—Sets the underline character to be whatever you set **CHAR** to be. The **CHAR** variable must not be set to any alphanumeric or white-space character.

See Listing 8.9 for an example of the **underline** parameter.

Listing 8.9   The *underline* parameter.

```
SQL>select * from orders;

 ORDER_ID CUSTOMER_ID ORDER_DAT DISPATCHE ORDER_DUE
--------- ----------- --------- --------- ---------
   100001       20001 01-Jan-99 10-Jan-99 31-Jan-99
```

```
     100002          20001 02-Jan-99 11-Jan-99 31-Jan-99
     100003          20002 01-May-98 09-May-98 31-May-98
     100004          20003 01-Jun-98 03-Jun-98 10-Jun-98
     100005          20004 28-Aug-99 29-Aug-99 30-Sep-99
     100006          20005 28-Aug-99 10-Sep-99 31-Aug-99

6 rows selected.

SQL>set underline off
SQL>select * from orders;

  ORDER_ID CUSTOMER_ID ORDER_DAT DISPATCHE ORDER_DUE
     100001          20001 01-Jan-99 10-Jan-99 31-Jan-99
     100002          20001 02-Jan-99 11-Jan-99 31-Jan-99
     100003          20002 01-May-98 09-May-98 31-May-98
     100004          20003 01-Jun-98 03-Jun-98 10-Jun-98
     100005          20004 28-Aug-99 29-Aug-99 30-Sep-99
     100006          20005 28-Aug-99 10-Sep-99 31-Aug-99

6 rows selected.

SQL>set underline *
SQL>select * from orders;

  ORDER_ID CUSTOMER_ID ORDER_DAT DISPATCHE ORDER_DUE
********* *********** ********* ********* *********
     100001          20001 01-Jan-99 10-Jan-99 31-Jan-99
     100002          20001 02-Jan-99 11-Jan-99 31-Jan-99
     100003          20002 01-May-98 09-May-98 31-May-98
     100004          20003 01-Jun-98 03-Jun-98 10-Jun-98
     100005          20004 28-Aug-99 29-Aug-99 30-Sep-99
     100006          20005 28-Aug-99 10-Sep-99 31-Aug-99

6 rows selected.

SQL>set underline on
SQL>select * from orders;

  ORDER_ID CUSTOMER_ID ORDER_DAT DISPATCHE ORDER_DUE
--------- ----------- --------- --------- ---------
     100001          20001 01-Jan-99 10-Jan-99 31-Jan-99
     100002          20001 02-Jan-99 11-Jan-99 31-Jan-99
     100003          20002 01-May-98 09-May-98 31-May-98
     100004          20003 01-Jun-98 03-Jun-98 10-Jun-98
     100005          20004 28-Aug-99 29-Aug-99 30-Sep-99
     100006          20005 28-Aug-99 10-Sep-99 31-Aug-99

6 rows selected.
```

The first part of Listing 8.9 shows a full listing of the **ORDERS** table. Notice how it defaults to the hyphen character. The full listing is then shown in two other ways: first, with the **underline** parameter turned off, and second, with it set to an asterisk. Finally, the **underline** parameter is turned on again and a full listing displayed.

verify

The **verify** parameter, when set, displays the old values for SQL substitution variables, which were introduced in Chapter 6. The default for this parameter is **ON**, which shows the previous value of the substitution variable. Listing 8.10 shows an example of the **verify** command turned **ON** and **OFF**.

Listing 8.10   The* verify *parameter.

```
SQL>select * from orders
  2  where order_id = &order_id;
Enter value for order_id: 100001
old    2: where order_id = &order_id
new    2: where order_id = 100001

 ORDER_ID CUSTOMER_ID ORDER_DAT DISPATCHE ORDER_DUE
--------- ----------- --------- --------- ---------
   100001       20001 01-Jan-99 10-Jan-99 31-Jan-99

SQL>show verify
verify ON
SQL>set verify off
SQL>select * from orders
  2  where order_id = &order_id;
Enter value for order_id: 100001

 ORDER_ID CUSTOMER_ID ORDER_DAT DISPATCHE ORDER_DUE
--------- ----------- --------- --------- ---------
   100001       20001 01-Jan-99 10-Jan-99 31-Jan-99
```

In Listing 8.10, you select all orders using the substitution variable **&Order_id**. Notice that you are asked for the new value, then shown the old value. In the next SQL statement, with the **verify** parameter turned **OFF**, you are not shown the old value. This is useful when writing reports that have some user input. Usually, you don't like to see the old values, because they clutter up the output.

THE COLUMN COMMAND

The **COLUMN** command within SQL*Plus specifies the display attributes for a given column, such as:

- The text for the column heading
- The alignment of the column headings
- The format of the **NUMBER** data types
- The wrapping of columns

The **COLUMN** command also lists the current attributes for all columns. The syntax for the **COLUMN** command is:

```
COLUMN [column|expr] option ...
```

The [*column|expr*] operator means that either a column name or an expression may be used with the **COLUMN** command. When using a column name, which is usually the case, you should make sure the column name is identical to that of the column name you wish to change the attributes for within the **SELECT** statement. For example, if the **SELECT** statement uses a column of a+b, then you cannot use b+a with the **COLUMN** command. It has to match exactly the column used with the **SELECT** statement.

If you select columns with the same name from different tables, a **COLUMN** command for that column name will apply to both columns—that is, a **COLUMN** command for the column **Order_id** applies all columns named **Order_id** that you reference within the session. The **COLUMN** command ignores table name prefixes within the **SELECT** command. To format columns with the same name, give them aliases and format the alias names. Spaces are also ignored unless the name is placed within double quotes.

The *option* must be one of the following:

- *ALIAS aliasname*—Gives an alias to the column specified. The alias can then be used within **BREAK**, **COMPUTE**, and other **COLUMN** commands.

- *CLEAR*—Resets all of the values for the column to their defaults. To reset all columns to their default values, use the **CLEAR COLUMNS** command.

- *FOLD_AFTER*—Inserts a carriage return after the column heading and after each row in the column.

- *FOLD_BEFORE*—Inserts a carriage return before the column heading and before each row of the column.

- *FORMAT format*—Specifies the display format of the column. See the "Column Formats" section in this chapter for more information.

- *HEADING text*—Defines the heading for the specified column. If the heading clause is not used, the heading defaults to the column name in the **SELECT** list. To include a heading on multiple lines, use the **HEADSEP** character (normally the | symbol).

- *JUSTIFY (LEFT\CENTER\CENTER\RIGHT)*—Justifies the heading to the **LEFT**, **RIGHT**, or **CENTER** of the column. If you do not use a **JUSTIFY** clause, headings for **NUMBER** columns default to **RIGHT**, and headings for other column types default to **LEFT**.

- *LIKE (expr\alias)*—Copies the display attributes of another column. For example, to use the **Unit_Price** formats for the **Retail_Price** column, you could use the command:

```
COLUMN RETAIL_PRICE LIKE UNIT_PRICE
```

- *NEWLINE*—Has the same effect as the **FOLD_BEFORE** option.

- *NEW_VALUE variable*—Allows values taken from tables to be stored as SQL*Plus variables. These can then be referenced within the **TTITLE** command.

- *NOPRINT\PRINT*—Controls the printing of the column (the column heading and all the selected values). **NOPRINT** turns the printing of the column off. **PRINT** turns it on.

- *OLD_VALUE variable*—Allows values taken from tables to be stored as SQL*Plus variables. This can then be referenced within the **TTITLE** command.

- *ON\OFF*—Controls the status of display attributes for a column.

- *WRAPPED\WORD_WRAPPED\TRUNCATED*—Specifies how SQL*Plus treats a data type or **DATE** string that is too wide for a column.

The **COLUMN** command used by itself will display all of the column attributes set within SQL*Plus. Listing 8.11 shows an example output from the **COLUMN** command executed with no parameters.

Listing 8.11   *Displaying all column attributes.*

```
SQL>column
column    other_plus_exp ON
format    a44

column    other_tag_plus_exp ON
format    a29

column    object_node_plus_exp ON
format    a8

column    plan_plus_exp ON
format    a60

column    parent_id_plus_exp ON
```

```
heading    'p'
format     990

column     id_plus_exp ON
heading    'i'
format     990

column     ERROR ON
format     A65
word_wrap

column     LINE/COL ON
format     A8

column     ROWLABEL ON
format     A15
```

The example in Listing 8.11 inserts a carriage return before the column heading and before each row of the column. SQL*Plus does not insert an extra carriage return before the first column in the **SELECT** list.

COLUMN FORMATS

The **COLUMN** command specifies how SQL*Plus formats the data and heading when used in SQL*Plus reports. The formats that can be used within a **COLUMN** command are shown in Table 8.1.

Table 8.1 *Column format types.*

Format	Description	Example Format	Output
A*n*	Alphanumeric *n* wide	A3	123
9	Numeric position	999	123
0	Enforce leading zeros	099	012
$	Floating currency symbol	$99	$12
.	Decimal point	99.99	12.12
,	Comma	9,999	1,234
MI	Minus sign	999MI	123-
PR	Parenthesize negative numbers	999PR	<123>
EEEE	Scientific notation	99.999EEE	1.234E+04
V	Raise to the power of V	9999V99	123400
B	Blank zero values	B999.99	

Examples

The listings in this section provide examples of the **COLUMN** command and how it affects the data returned in **SELECT** statements.

Listing 8.12 shows how to make the **Supplier_Name** column 40 characters wide, with the heading on multiple lines.

Listing 8.12   *Using multiple lines in a heading.*

```
SQL>column supplier_name format a40 heading 'Supplier|Name'
SQL>select supplier_name
  2  from suppliers;

Supplier
Name
----------------------------------------
Test Company Ltd
Training Company Inc
Widget Design Inc
JRF Relational Associates Ltd
Hardware Ltd
```

Listing 8.13 shows the **Unit_Price** column with leading zeros and currency sign.

Listing 8.13   *Using leading zeros and currency sign.*

```
SQL>column unit_price format $000999.99 heading 'Unit Price'
SQL>select unit_price
  2  from order_details;

 Unit Price
 ----------
 $000004.00
 $000002.00
 $000010.00
 $000002.00
 $000004.00
 $000002.00
 $000004.00
 $000006.00
 $000010.00
 $000004.00
 $000002.00
 $000006.00

12 rows selected.
```

In Listing 8.14, I show how to create a simple report using a fairly complex SQL statement and some **COLUMN** formatting statements. The first section shows the SQL statement with no formatting; then the **COLUMN** formats are defined and the SQL statement executed again.

Listing 8.14   *Using column values to create reports.*

```
SQL>select c.customer_name,o.order_id,od.product_id,od.number_ordered
  2  from customers c,
  3       orders o,
  4       order_details od
  5  where c.customer_id = o.customer_id
  6  and    o.order_id = od.order_id;


CUSTOMER_NAME                             ORDER_ID PRODUCT_ID NUMBER_ORDERED
---------------------------------------- --------- ---------- ---------------
ABC Ltd                                    100001       5002              20
ABC Ltd                                    100001       5001              10
ABC Ltd                                    100001       5003              10
ABC Ltd                                    100002       5001              20
DEF Ltd                                    100003       5002              10
GHI Inc                                    100004       5001              15
GHI Inc                                    100004       5002              25
JKL Inc                                    100005       5004              10
JKL Inc                                    100005       5003              10
JKL Inc                                    100005       5002              10
MNO Ltd                                    100006       5001              20
DEF Ltd                                    100003       5004              50

12 rows selected.

SQL>column customer_name format a15 heading 'Customer Name'
SQL>column order_id format 99999999 heading 'Order Id'
SQL>column product_id format 9999999 heading 'Product|Id'
SQL>column number_ordered format 9999 heading 'Number|Ordered'
SQL>/

                             Product   Number
Customer Name    Order Id        Id  Ordered
--------------- ---------- -------- -------
ABC Ltd             100001     5002       20
ABC Ltd             100001     5001       10
ABC Ltd             100001     5003       10
ABC Ltd             100002     5001       20
DEF Ltd             100003     5002       10
GHI Inc             100004     5001       15
GHI Inc             100004     5002       25
JKL Inc             100005     5004       10
```

```
JKL Inc              100005      5003      10
JKL Inc              100005      5002      10
MNO Ltd              100006      5001      20
DEF Ltd              100003      5004      50

12 rows selected.
```

REPORT HEADINGS AND FOOTERS

The commands to create report headers and footers are **REPHEADER**, **REPFOOTER**, **TTITLE**, and **BTITLE**. You use these commands to produce top and bottom titles on reports created using SQL*Plus.

REPHEADER And REPFOOTER

If the **REPHEADER** command is used on its own, it will display the current report header defined within SQL*Plus; likewise, the **REPFOOTER** command by itself will display the current report footer. Listing 8.15 shows an example of **REPHEADER**.

Listing 8.15   *Displaying the current **REPHEADER** value.*

```
SQL>repheader
repheader ON and is the following 17 characters:
'Customer Report'
SQL>
```

REPHEADER and **REPFOOTER** commands use the following syntax

```
REPHEADER [PAGE] [printspec [text|variable] ...] | [OFF|ON]
REPFOOTER [PAGE] [printspec [text|variable] ...] | [OFF|ON]
```

where *printspec* is one of the following specifiers used to format the *text:*

- *COL n*—Sets the indent to column number *n* of the current line.

- *SKIP n*—Skips *n* lines before displaying the header or footer.

- *TAB n*—Skips *n* columns before printing the required header text.

- *LEFT*—Aligns to the left all text on the current line.

- *CENTER*—Centers the text on the current line.

- *RIGHT*—Aligns to the right all text on the current line.

- *BOLD*—Instructs SQL*Plus to print the characters on the current line in boldface type. On some terminals, this may appear on three consecutive lines.

- *FORMAT text*—Formats the *text* to any of the column formats mentioned in the previous section.

The **page** parameter begins a new page after printing the report header or footer. The *variable* parameter is used to print a user variable or one of the following system-maintained variables:

- *SQL.LNO*—The current line number
- *SQL.PNO*—The current page number
- *SQL.RELEASE*—The current Oracle release number
- *SQL.SQLCODE*—The current error code
- *SQL.USER*—The username of the current user

The **ON** and **OFF** commands turn the header or footer either on or off. When turned off, the required header or footer is not displayed. Listing 8.16 is an example of using headers and footers.

Listing 8.16   Using the **REPHEADER** and **REPFOOTER** commands.

```
SQL>repheader skip 2 'Customer Report'
SQL>repfooter tab 10 'END OF REPORT'
SQL>select c.customer_name,
  2        o.order_id,
  3        od.product_id,
  4        od.number_ordered
  5  from customers c,
  6        orders o,
  7        order_details od
  8  where c.customer_id = o.customer_id
  9  and   o.order_id = od.order_id;


Customer Report
                         Product  Number
Customer Name   Order Id      Id Ordered
--------------  ---------- -------- -------
ABC Ltd            100001     5002      20
ABC Ltd            100001     5001      10
ABC Ltd            100001     5003      10
ABC Ltd            100002     5001      20
DEF Ltd            100003     5002      10
GHI Inc            100004     5001      15
GHI Inc            100004     5002      25
JKL Inc            100005     5004      10
```

```
JKL Inc              100005      5003      10
JKL Inc              100005      5002      10
MNO Ltd              100006      5001      20
DEF Ltd              100003      5004      50
          END OF REPORT

12 rows selected.
```

TTITLE And BTITLE

The **TTITLE** and **BTITLE** commands are used in a similar way to **REPHEADER** and **REPFOOTER** and have the same syntax:

```
TTITLE [printspec|ON|OFF]
BTITLE [printspec|ON|OFF]
```

The section on **REPHEADER** and **REPFOOTER** provided details about the *printspec* specifier. An example of using **TTITLE** and **BTITLE** is shown in Listing 8.17.

Listing 8.17 *Using the TTITLE and BTITLE commands.*

```
SQL>ttitle left 'Produced By : 'sql.user skip 1 -
>         left 'Customer Report' skip 2
SQL>btitle tab 10 'END OF REPORT'
SQL>select c.customer_name,
  2         o.order_id,
  3         od.product_id,
  4         od.number_ordered
  5  from customers c,
  6         orders o,
  7         order_details od
  8  where c.customer_id = o.customer_id
  9  and    o.order_id = od.order_id;

Produced By : DEMO
Customer Report


                          Product  Number
Customer Name   Order Id       Id Ordered
--------------  ---------  -------- -------
ABC Ltd              100001      5002      20
ABC Ltd              100001      5001      10
ABC Ltd              100001      5003      10
ABC Ltd              100002      5001      20
DEF Ltd              100003      5002      10
GHI Inc              100004      5001      15
GHI Inc              100004      5002      25
JKL Inc              100005      5004      10
```

```
JKL Inc            100005      5003        10
JKL Inc            100005      5002        10
MNO Ltd            100006      5001        20
DEF Ltd            100003      5004        50




        END OF REPORT

12 rows selected.
```

NEW_VALUE VARIABLE

One of the clauses available to the **COLUMN** command is **NEW_VALUE**, which allows you to assign a value to a variable and then use it within your reports. See Listing 8.18 for an example using **NEW_VALUE**.

Listing 8.18 *Using the **NEW_VALUE** parameter.*

```
SQL>column sysdate new_value todays_date
SQL>select sysdate from dual;

SYSDATE
-------
02-Jan-98
SQL>ttitle left 'Date : ' todays_date skip 2 'Customer Report'
SQL>select c.customer_name,
  2         o.order_id,
  3         od.product_id,
  4         od.number_ordered
  5  from customers c,
  6         orders o,
  7         order_details od
  8  where c.customer_id = o.customer_id
  9  and   o.order_id = od.order_id;

Date : 02-Jan-98

Customer Report
                           Product  Number
Customer Name    Order Id       Id Ordered
--------------- --------- -------- -------
ABC Ltd            100001      5002        20
ABC Ltd            100001      5001        10
ABC Ltd            100001      5003        10
ABC Ltd            100002      5001        20
DEF Ltd            100003      5002        10
```

```
GHI Inc            100004    5001    15
GHI Inc            100004    5002    25
JKL Inc            100005    5004    10
JKL Inc            100005    5003    10
JKL Inc            100005    5002    10
MNO Ltd            100006    5001    20
DEF Ltd            100003    5004    50

12 rows selected.
```

In this listing, the **NEW_VALUE** clause sets up a variable called **todays_date**. This is then initialized by selecting the system date. The value is stored in the **todays_date** variable and used within the report's title.

THE BREAK COMMAND

The **BREAK** command allows you to specify break points within a report. Reports are usually broken down into manageable chunks. For example, in Listing 8.18, you might want the customer report to break on **Customer_Name**—that is, you can throw a number of lines or pages between each customer.

Each **BREAK** statement overrides the last **BREAK** statement. For that reason, if you wish to have multiple breaks in your report, they all must be specified within the one **BREAK** statement.

The syntax for **BREAK** is

```
BREAK [ON element [action ...]]
```

where the *element* is one of the following

- *Column Name*—Causes a break when the column value for the column changes
- *User-Defined Expression*—Same as Column Name
- *Row*—Causes the report to break each time the **SELECT** statement returns a row
- *Report*—Causes a break at the end of the report

and where *action* matches the following syntax:

```
[SKIP n|[SKIP] PAGE] [NODUPLICATES|DUPLICATES]
```

In the syntax for the *action* parameter, the variables have the following meanings:

- *SKIP n*—Skips *n* lines on each break in the report.
- *SKIP PAGE*—Skips a page on each break in the report.

- *NODUPLICATES*—Prints blanks on a report when the value of a break column has not changed; this is the default.

- *DUPLICATES*—Prints the value of the break column every time.

Listing 8.19 is an example of using the **BREAK** command.

Listing 8.19 Using the **BREAK** command.

```
SQL>break on customer_name page on order_id skip 1
SQL>select c.customer_name,
  2         o.order_id,
  3         od.product_id,
  4         od.number_ordered
  5  from customers c,
  6         orders o,
  7         order_details od
  8  where c.customer_id = o.customer_id
  9  and   o.order_id = od.order_id
 10  order by 1,2;
```

Customer Name	Order Id	Product Id	Number Ordered
ABC Ltd	100001	5002	20
		5001	10
		5003	10
	100002	5001	20

Customer Name	Order Id	Product Id	Number Ordered
DEF Ltd	100003	5002	10
		5004	50

Customer Name	Order Id	Product Id	Number Ordered
GHI Inc	100004	5001	15
		5002	25

Customer Name	Order Id	Product Id	Number Ordered
JKL Inc	100005	5004	10
		5003	10
		5002	10

```
                          Product  Number
Customer Name    Order Id      Id  Ordered
--------------   ---------  --------  -------
MNO Ltd            100006      5001      20
```

```
12 rows selected.
```

Notice in this listing that the **ORDER BY** clause is added to the SQL statement. This is so the **BREAK** command acts on the columns in the correct order. To display all of the **BREAK** commands currently set, use the **BREAK** command by itself, as shown in Listing 8.20.

Listing 8.20   *Displaying the current break points.*

```
SQL>break
break on customer_name page  nodup
        on order_id skip 1 nodup

SQL>
```

To clear all of the current breaks, issue the command **CLEAR BREAKS**. The **BREAK** command is often used in conjunction with the **COMPUTE** command to create subtotals at break points.

THE COMPUTE COMMAND

The **COMPUTE** command performs actions on breaks created by the **BREAK** command. The syntax for the **COMPUTE** command is

```
COMPUTE function [LABEL text] OF column ON breaks
```

where the variables have the following meanings:

- *LABEL text*—Displays a label in the output.
- *OF*—Specifies the column whose value is to be computed.
- *ON*—Specifies the break at which to evaluate the **COMPUTE** command.

For example, this is a valid **COMPUTE** command:

```
COMPUTE SUM OF NUMBER_ORDERED ON CUSTOMER_NAME
```

As you can see, in the *function* parameter you can use numeric functions, such as **AVG**, **SUM**, **MIN**, and **MAX**. For the **COMPUTE** command to execute, you must meet four conditions:

- The column you specify in the **ON** clause must appear in the **SELECT** statement.

- The column you specify in the **ON** clause must appear in the most recent **BREAK** command.

- If you reference either ROW or REPORT in the **ON** clause, you must also reference it in the **BREAK** command.

- One or more of the columns specified in the **OF** clause must appear in the **SELECT** statement.

When the **COMPUTE** command is used without any clauses, it displays the current settings for all COMPUTEs, as shown in Listing 8.21.

Listing 8.21   Displaying the current settings for the **COMPUTE** command.

```
SQL>compute
COMPUTE sum LABEL 'sum' OF number_ordered ON customer_name
SQL>
```

To clear all values for the **COMPUTE** command, issue the **CLEAR COMPUTES** command at the **SQL>** prompt. Listing 8.22 shows an example of the **COMPUTE** statement from Listing 8.21, issued against the Customer Report, with a break on **Customer_Name**.

Listing 8.22   Using the **COMPUTE** command.

```
SQL>compute sum label 'TOTAL' of number_ordered on customer_name
SQL>break on customer_name skip 1
SQL>select c.customer_name,
  2          o.order_id,
  3          od.product_id,
  4          od.number_ordered
  5   from customers c,
  6          orders o,
  7          order_details od
  8   where c.customer_id = o.customer_id
  9   and    o.order_id = od.order_id
 10   order by 1,2;


                         Product  Number
Customer Name    Order Id      Id Ordered
- - - - - - - - -    - - - - - - -   - - - - - - -  - - - - - -
ABC Ltd            100001     5002      20
                   100001     5001      10
                   100001     5003      10
                   100002     5001      20
***************                        - - - - - - -
TOTAL                                    60
```

```
DEF Ltd              100003    5002      10
                     100003    5004      50
***************                        -------
TOTAL                                     60

GHI Inc              100004    5001      15
                     100004    5002      25
***************                        -------
TOTAL                                     40

JKL Inc              100005    5004      10
                     100005    5003      10
                     100005    5002      10

                              Product  Number
Customer Name    Order Id      Id Ordered
--------------   ---------  -------- -------
***************                        -------
TOTAL                                     30

MNO Ltd              100006    5001      20
***************                        -------
TOTAL                                     20


12 rows selected.
```

THE SPOOL COMMAND

The **SPOOL** command stores the output from queries in operating-system files. The syntax for the **SPOOL** command is:

```
SPOOL [filename.ext]|OFF|OUT
```

To spool the output from a query to a file, use the following steps:

1. Issue the **SPOOL temp.lis** command, where **temp.lis** can be any file name.

2. Execute your query.

3. Once the query has finished executing, type the **SPOOL OFF** command. SQL*Plus will close the file and place it in your current directory, the default being C:\ORAWIN95\BIN, your Oracle home directory.

You can spool directly to a connected printer with the **SPOOL OUT** command. Remember, when spooling output from a command file, use the **set termout off** parameter.

OTHER TOOLS

In this chapter, you learned how to create reports using the power of SQL*Plus. This is a basic tool for creating reports. Other tools are available, such as Oracle*Reports, a graphically oriented reporting tool that is extremely good.

In the next chapter, you will build on knowledge you gained in Chapter 3. Whereas Chapter 3 covered the creation of users at a very basic level, Chapter 9 will show you how to set up and use predefined and user-defined roles.

Users, Roles, And Security

In the previous chapter, I discussed reporting from the demo database. To write reports, you need to hold information within the database. That information is stored by specific users who have a number of roles available to them. The users and roles within a database are extremely important because they provide the required level of security for the data. I'll cover security in more detail later in this chapter. First, let's talk about users.

Users—who needs them? You do!

USERS

Users are Oracle's way of letting the database know who you are and what access permissions you have. Within Personal Oracle8, a user is identified by a username and password. Once connected to the database, users have access to all of the objects they own. Depending upon which roles users have been granted, they can manipulate (create and delete) their objects. Users create all of the objects—tables, views, sequences, indexes, etc.—in the database.

Users are normally created by a database administrator (DBA), who then associates a number of other items with the newly created user:

- A username

- A password

- A default tablespace

- A temporary tablespace

- Which roles the user has access to (for more information on roles, see the following sections)

A *username* should be no more than 30 characters or numbers and should not include any commas, spaces, or special characters (which are usually those you use the Shift key to generate). These same rules apply to the creation of passwords. (More information on passwords is available later in this chapter.)

Tablespaces store objects within any Oracle database (tablespaces will be covered in more detail later in this book). If you do not specify a default or temporary tablespace when creating a user, the SYSTEM tablespace becomes the default. SYSTEM, as will be explained later, is not the ideal tablespace for the default or temporary tablespace, as this will reduce performance. Usually, two other tablespaces exist—normally called USERS and TEMP. The USERS tablespace should be the default, and TEMP the temporary tablespace. The default tablespace defines where all of the objects created by the user should be stored automatically. This is the case when the user does not define where the object should be stored. The temporary tablespace is the location Oracle uses to create any temporary objects or sorts (within SQL statements) for the user.

Creating Users

At present, you can create a user within Personal Oracle8 three different ways: through the Navigator, as shown in Chapter 3; through SQL*Plus; or through Server Manager (covered in Chapter 17). SQL*Plus is usually the fastest method, though you may find it easier, at first, to use the Navigator.

Creating A User Through SQL*Plus

To create a user through SQL*Plus, you first have to log in to the database as a user with the required privileges. Whenever you come into contact with an Oracle database, you will always find at least two users: **SYSTEM** and **SYS**. When creating users, you should always try to use the **SYSTEM** user, which has privileges to do almost anything it likes. For this reason,

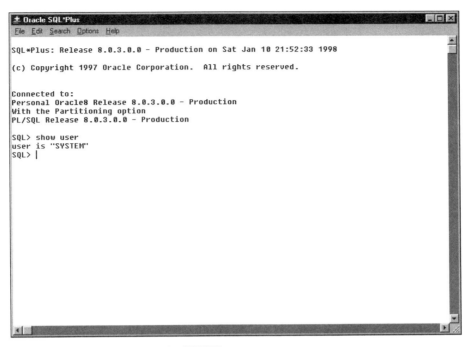

Figure 9.1 *Logging in to SQL*Plus as the **SYSTEM** user.*

you have to be careful when using **SYSTEM**. Figure 9.1 shows an example of a user logged in as the **SYSTEM** user.

Whenever a database is created from scratch, the **CREATE DATABASE** statement automatically creates **SYSTEM** and **SYS** users. The passwords are always set to be MANAGER for the **SYSTEM** user and CHANGE_ON_INSTALL for the **SYS** user. Table 9.1 lists all users and their passwords that appear on a standard installation from the Personal Oracle8 CD-ROM.

Now that you are logged in as the **SYSTEM** user, you must perform a couple of checks before you can create a user. First, you must make sure that the user does not already exist. To do so,

Table 9.1 *Default usernames and passwords.*

USERNAME	PASSWORD
INTERNAL	ORACLE
SCOTT	TIGER
SYSTEM	MANAGER
SYS	CHANGE_ON_INSTALL
DEMO	DEMO
PO8	PO8

access the **DBA_USERS** view. (A view can be used in the same way as a table, but is usually made up of data from more than one table; see Chapter 11 to learn more about views.) This view stores all of the information about users. Listing 9.1 shows the view's format.

Listing 9.1   DBA_USERS *view structure.*

```
SQL> desc dba_users
 Name                            Null?     Type
 ------------------------------- --------  ----
 USERNAME                        NOT NULL  VARCHAR2(30)
 USER_ID                         NOT NULL  NUMBER
 PASSWORD                                  VARCHAR2(30)
 ACCOUNT_STATUS                  NOT NULL  VARCHAR2(32)
 LOCK_DATE                                 DATE
 EXPIRY_DATE                               DATE
 DEFAULT_TABLESPACE              NOT NULL  VARCHAR2(30)
 TEMPORARY_TABLESPACE            NOT NULL  VARCHAR2(30)
 CREATED                         NOT NULL  DATE
 PROFILE                         NOT NULL  VARCHAR2(30)
 EXTERNAL_NAME                             VARCHAR2(4000)
```

This listing shows details of the **DBA_USERS** view within the **SYSTEM** user. Notice that the view contains a column that stores the password in an encrypted format. To use this view to check details about existing users, you can issue the command in Listing 9.2, which shows the details of the required parameters for the **CREATE USER** command.

Listing 9.2   *User details from the* **DBA_USERS** *view.*

```
SQL> select username,default_tablespace,temporary_tablespace
  2  from dba_users;

USERNAME                        DEFAULT_TABLESPACE              TEMPORARY_TABLESPACE
------------------------------- ------------------------------- --------------------
SYS                             SYSTEM                          SYSTEM
SYSTEM                          USER_DATA                       TEMPORARY_DATA
DBSNMP                          SYSTEM                          SYSTEM
SCOTT                           USER_DATA                       TEMPORARY_DATA
P08                             SYSTEM                          SYSTEM
EXPLORER                        USER_DATA                       TEMPORARY_DATA
DEMO                            USER_DATA                       TEMPORARY_DATA

7 rows selected.
```

Once you have checked that the user you are creating does not already exist, you must check which tablespaces are available. For this, look at the **DBA_TABLESPACES** view within the **SYSTEM** user, which shows all tablespaces allocated to the current database. Listing 9.3 shows the structure of the **DBA_TABLESPACES** view.

*Listing 9.3   The **DBA_TABLESPACES** view structure.*

```
SQL> desc dba_tablespaces
 Name                           Null?    Type
 ------------------------------ -------- ----
 TABLESPACE_NAME                NOT NULL VARCHAR2(30)
 INITIAL_EXTENT                          NUMBER
 NEXT_EXTENT                             NUMBER
 MIN_EXTENTS                    NOT NULL NUMBER
 MAX_EXTENTS                    NOT NULL NUMBER
 PCT_INCREASE                   NOT NULL NUMBER
 MIN_EXTLEN                              NUMBER
 STATUS                                  VARCHAR2(9)
 CONTENTS                                VARCHAR2(9)
 LOGGING                                 VARCHAR2(9)
```

The **DBA_TABLESPACES** view contains information for the sizing of the tablespace. The only columns you are interested in are **Tablespace_Name** and **Status**. This gives you the tablespace information you'll need to create your user. To use this view for checking details about existing tablespaces, you can issue the command shown in Listing 9.4, which again shows the details of the required parameters for the **CREATE USER** command.

*Listing 9.4   Tablespace information from the **DBA_TABLESPACES** view.*

```
SQL> select tablespace_name,status
  2  from dba_tablespaces;

 TABLESPACE_NAME                STATUS
 ------------------------------ --------
 SYSTEM                         ONLINE
 USER_DATA                      ONLINE
 ROLLBACK_DATA                  ONLINE
 TEMPORARY_DATA                 ONLINE
```

The **Status** column shows the status of each tablespace. You should not use a tablespace that is offline for any of your users, unless you know the reason it is offline. You can now use this information to make up your **CREATE USER** command. The command is fairly simple to use. It has a few options you should be aware of, but may not use. These options give you the ability to:

- Limit the amount of disk space the user is allowed to use in each tablespace. These are usually called *tablespace quotas*.

- Lock a user account—i.e., don't give access to anyone.

- Unlock user accounts.

- Allocate profiles to users. A *profile* is a set of limits on database resources, such as **PASSWORD_LOCK_TIME** and **FAILED_LOGIN_ATTEMPTS**. (See the section on profiles in this chapter for more information.)

The syntax for the most common **CREATE USER** command is as follows:

```
CREATE USER username IDENTIFIED BY password
DEFAULT TABLESPACE default_tablespace_name
TEMPORARY TABLESPACE temporary_tablespace_name
QUOTA size ON tablespace_name...
PROFILE profile_name
PASSWORD EXPIRE
ACCOUNT LOCK|UNLOCK
;
```

Listing 9.5 is an example of a simple **CREATE USER** command, where a user called **RICHARDF** is created with the password and username the same. Listing 9.5 also shows the default and temporary tablespaces being set.

Listing 9.5   A simple **CREATE USER** command.

```
SQL> create user richardf identified by richardf
  2   default tablespace user_data
  3   temporary tablespace temporary_data;

User created.

SQL>
```

The following sections explain other features of the **CREATE USER** command.

QUOTA

The **QUOTA** option of the **CREATE USER** command allows you, as the database administrator, to specify how much space the user is allowed within the specified tablespaces. Listing 9.6 shows a typical example of this option.

Listing 9.6   Defining user quotas.

```
SQL> create user richardf identified by richardf
  2   default tablespace user_data
  3   temporary tablespace temporary_data
  4   quota 1M on user_data
  5   quota 500K on temporary_data;

User created.
```

To check this, you would use the **DBA_TS_QUOTAS** view, which shows all of the quotas defined for the users. Listing 9.7 is an example of this view.

Listing 9.7 *Displaying users and their quotas.*

```
SQL> select tablespace_name,
  2          username,
  3          bytes,
  4          max_bytes
  5  from dba_ts_quotas;

TABLESPACE_NAME                 USERNAME                        BYTES MAX_BYTES
------------------------------- ------------------------------- -------- ---------
TEMPORARY_DATA                  EXPLORER                             0        -1
USER_DATA                       EXPLORER                             0        -1
TEMPORARY_DATA                  DEMO                                 0        -1
USER_DATA                       DEMO                            133120        -1
TEMPORARY_DATA                  RICHARDF                             0    512000
USER_DATA                       RICHARDF                             0   1048576

6 rows selected.
```

This listing shows that the user **RICHARDF** has 500K of available space in the TEMPORARY_DATA tablespace and 1MB available in the USER_DATA tablespace. The **Bytes** column shows how much space the user has used. A negative value in the **Max_Bytes** column means that the user has unlimited space usage within the tablespace.

PASSWORD EXPIRE

The **PASSWORD EXPIRE** option allows you to make the user's password expire upon logging in for the first time. This means you can give the user an initial password, but, after logging in, the user will have to change it immediately. Listing 9.8 shows an example of a user being created and then logging in with the **CONNECT** command. If the user tries to enter the same password again when prompted to change it, Personal Oracle8 will disconnect the session.

Listing 9.8 *Using the **PASSWORD EXPIRE** option.*

```
SQL> create user richardf identified by richardf
  2  default tablespace user_data
  3  temporary tablespace temporary_data
  4  password expire;

User created.
```

```
SQL> connect
Enter user-name: richardf
Enter password: ********
ERROR:
ORA-28001: the account has expired


Changing password for richardf
Old password: ********
New password: *******
Retype new password: *******
Connected.
SQL>
```

ACCOUNT LOCK/UNLOCK

You can also lock and unlock user accounts using the **CREATE USER** command. Once a user account is locked, no one can use it again until it is unlocked. Listing 9.9 shows a session where the **SYSTEM** user creates a locked account, then tries to log in to that account. An error message is displayed saying the account is locked. The account is then unlocked using the **ALTER USER** command, and the account entered.

Listing 9.9 *Locking and unlocking user accounts.*

```
SQL> create user richardf identified by richardf
  2   default tablespace user_data
  3   temporary tablespace temporary_data
  4   account lock;

User created.

SQL> grant connect to richardf;

Grant succeeded.
SQL> connect
Enter user-name: richardf
Enter password: ********
ERROR:
ORA-28000: the account is locked


Warning: You are no longer connected to ORACLE.
SQL> connect
Enter user-name: system
Enter password: *******
```

```
Connected.
SQL> alter user richardf account unlock;

User altered.

SQL> connect
Enter user-name: richardf
Enter password: ********
Connected.
SQL>
```

In Listing 9.9, I used a command that grants **CONNECT** access to the user before the account is entered. This privilege, which is required before the user can connect to the database, and another privilege, **RESOURCE**, allow users to connect and create objects within the database. The descriptions of both roles are as follows:

- *CONNECT*—Allows the user to connect to the database and query tables he or she has access to.

- *RESOURCE*—Allows the user to create objects within the schema—tables, indexes, and views.

Navigator automatically assigns the role **CONNECT** to a newly created user. This does not happen when you create the user through SQL*Plus.

PASSWORDS

Passwords are Oracle's way of imposing security on the database. A password is usually needed to gain access to any database user. In older versions of Oracle, passwords did not have a lot of functionality—they were either set or not set. In Personal Oracle8, passwords have greater functionality. When used in conjunction with profiles (discussed later in this chapter), passwords become more powerful.

Lifetime And Expiration

Password lifetime and expiration let you set appropriate life spans for passwords. This is especially useful for systems where passwords need to be changed on a regular basis. The *lifetime* of a password is the time it is valid. Once the lifetime is over, the password will expire, the account will be unusable, and a new password will have to be set.

Grace periods are a new Oracle feature. Once the lifetime of a password is over, the grace period kicks in, allowing the user to access the database with the old password for a predetermined time. The user is expected to change the password within this grace period. If the password is not changed, the user's account is locked. Warning messages that appear each time the user connects to the database within the grace period ask for a change of password. You can create the user with an expired password from the start. Then the user enters the grace period, if any, on the first connection to the database.

Password Complexity

Password complexity ensures that each password is not easy to guess by people who want to gain access illegally. Oracle implements password complexity by using the following default rules:

- A password must be a minimum of four characters in length.

- A password must not match any word on an internal list of simple words, such as *welcome.*

- A password must differ from the previous password by at least three characters.

Password History

Oracle can check passwords that have previously been used by the same user. Sometimes users alternate passwords, using one until it expires, then using another, then switching back to the previous one, and so on. The password history option checks each password the user enters and stores it within the database. The database won't allow the user to enter a previously used password as the new password. This option implements user profiles. These profiles, discussed later in this chapter, decide the rules for password history—for example, how far back to go.

ORACLE'S SPECIAL USERS

Oracle has a number of users created for specific reasons when the database is created. This section explains what each user is, and when and where it should be used.

SYSTEM

The **SYSTEM** user is created automatically when the database is created. This user is granted all system privileges for the database. The default password is MANAGER; it is a good idea to change this password once the database is installed. The username has access to additional and internal database objects that display administrative information. You should avoid creating any objects by the **SYSTEM** user, unless they are for the whole of the database; for example, do not create tables for individual use, but creating tables that monitor the database would be acceptable. The DBA usually has access to all of the **SYSTEM** objects. Creating a separate user for the DBA, with the same privileges as the **SYSTEM** user, is a good idea.

SYS

The **SYS** user is, again, automatically created with the database. This user is granted the **DBA** role (roles are discussed later in this chapter). The default password for the **SYS** user is CHANGE_ON_INSTALL, which indicates that changing the password once the database is installed is a good idea.

All of the base tables are owned by the **SYS** user. The objects you can see through the **SYS-TEM** user are based on these tables owned by **SYS**. They are internal Oracle tables; the database cannot run without them. Do not delete any of the objects owned by the **SYS** user. Again, do not create any objects as the **SYS** user. You should not use this user, unless instructed to do so by a member of Oracle support.

INTERNAL

The **INTERNAL** user is used only with Server Manager, which is a special program for performing DBA-type duties against the database. These include:

- Starting the database

- Stopping the database

- Recovering the database

- Setting database options, such as archive logging

The **INTERNAL** user is available in Personal Oracle8 as a backward-compatibility step. The new way of using the **INTERNAL** password is to use the roles **SYSOPER** and **SYSDBA**. Server Manager is discussed in detail in Chapter 17.

PUBLIC

PUBLIC is accessible to all logged-in users. This user gives everybody access to objects within the database. For example, suppose you have created a table within your user; instead of giving access to each user individually, you can give access to your table to the **PUBLIC** user, making it available to every user. You will usually find the **PUBLIC** user used within **GRANT** and **REVOKE** statements, discussed later in this chapter.

SCHEMAS

A *schema* is a collection of objects associated with a specific user. When a database user is created, the database engine automatically creates a schema with the same name as the user. In this context, the words *schema* and *user* are interchangeable, and are often used to mean the same thing.

PROFILES

A *profile* is a set of specific resource limits that can be assigned to an Oracle username. Profiles give the DBA an easy and efficient way to manage resource usage within the database. When a user logs in to the database, a profile is assigned. This profile may be the default, where the user can do nearly anything, or a predefined profile created by the DBA. Some of the resources that can be limited are:

- Number of concurrent sessions the user can establish (not relevant here)
- Amount of CPU time available to the user's session
- Amount of CPU time available to a single call to Oracle
- Amount of logical I/O available to the user's session
- Amount of logical I/O available to a single call to Oracle
- Amount of idle time the user's session is allowed
- Amount of connect time the user's session is allowed
- Account locking after unsuccessful log-in attempts
- Password expiration
- Password grace period
- Password reuse and complexity restrictions

You can create and assign different profiles to different users, thus giving some users a higher level of access than others. You should only use profiles if the security policy of your site requires resource limiting. This does not really apply to the world of the PC and Personal Oracle8. Nonetheless, some of the available profile options can be legitimately used within a Personal Oracle8 database:

- *FAILED_LOGIN_ATTEMPTS*—Specifies the maximum number of failed log-in attempts until the user account is locked.

- *PASSWORD_LIFE_TIME*—Specifies the maximum number of days a password can be used without being changed. If the password is not changed within that lifetime, further connections are disallowed.

- *PASSWORD_REUSE_TIME*—Specifies the minimum number of days before a password can be used again. If the **PASSWORD_REUSE_MAX** value is set to an integer, this value must be set to UNLIMITED.

- *PASSWORD_REUSE_MAX*—Specifies the minimum number of password changes before the password can be used again.

- *PASSWORD_LOCK_TIME*—Specifies the number of days the account will be locked if the required number of failed log-ins has occurred.

- *PASSWORD_GRACE_TIME*—Specifies the number of days the grace period covers. This will generate a warning message each time the user logs in to the database during the grace period.

An example of creating a user profile and then checking what has been created is shown in Listings 9.10 through 9.14.

Listing 9.10 *Creating a user profile.*

```
SQL> create profile demo_user limit
  2     failed_login_attempts 3
  3     password_life_time 30
  4     password_lock_time 1
  5     password_grace_time 5;

Profile created.
```

Listing 9.11 *Assigning a user profile.*

```
SQL> create user demouser identified by guest
  2    temporary tablespace temporary_data
  3    default tablespace user_data
  4    profile demo_user;

User created.
SQL> grant connect to demouser;

Grant succeeded.
```

Listing 9.12 *Checking the user profile.*

```
SQL> select * from dba_profiles
  2   order by profile;
```

```
PROFILE      RESOURCE_NAME                        RESOURCE LIMIT
----------   ----------------------------------   -------- --------------
DEFAULT      COMPOSITE_LIMIT                       KERNEL   UNLIMITED
DEFAULT      FAILED_LOGIN_ATTEMPTS                 PASSWORD UNLIMITED
DEFAULT      PASSWORD_LIFE_TIME                    PASSWORD UNLIMITED
DEFAULT      PASSWORD_REUSE_TIME                   PASSWORD UNLIMITED
DEFAULT      PASSWORD_REUSE_MAX                    PASSWORD UNLIMITED
DEFAULT      PASSWORD_VERIFY_FUNCTION              PASSWORD UNLIMITED
DEFAULT      PASSWORD_LOCK_TIME                    PASSWORD UNLIMITED
DEFAULT      PASSWORD_GRACE_TIME                   PASSWORD UNLIMITED
DEFAULT      PRIVATE_SGA                           KERNEL   UNLIMITED
DEFAULT      CONNECT_TIME                          KERNEL   UNLIMITED
DEFAULT      IDLE_TIME                             KERNEL   UNLIMITED
DEFAULT      LOGICAL_READS_PER_CALL                KERNEL   UNLIMITED
DEFAULT      LOGICAL_READS_PER_SESSION             KERNEL   UNLIMITED
DEFAULT      CPU_PER_CALL                          KERNEL   UNLIMITED
DEFAULT      CPU_PER_SESSION                       KERNEL   UNLIMITED
DEFAULT      SESSIONS_PER_USER                     KERNEL   UNLIMITED
DEMO_USER    COMPOSITE_LIMIT                       KERNEL   DEFAULT
DEMO_USER    PRIVATE_SGA                           KERNEL   DEFAULT
DEMO_USER    CONNECT_TIME                          KERNEL   DEFAULT
DEMO_USER    PASSWORD_GRACE_TIME                   PASSWORD 5
DEMO_USER    IDLE_TIME                             KERNEL   DEFAULT
DEMO_USER    PASSWORD_LOCK_TIME                    PASSWORD 1
DEMO_USER    LOGICAL_READS_PER_CALL                KERNEL   DEFAULT
DEMO_USER    PASSWORD_VERIFY_FUNCTION              PASSWORD DEFAULT
DEMO_USER    LOGICAL_READS_PER_SESSION             KERNEL   DEFAULT
DEMO_USER    FAILED_LOGIN_ATTEMPTS                 PASSWORD 3
DEMO_USER    PASSWORD_LIFE_TIME                    PASSWORD 30
DEMO_USER    PASSWORD_REUSE_TIME                   PASSWORD DEFAULT
DEMO_USER    PASSWORD_REUSE_MAX                    PASSWORD DEFAULT
DEMO_USER    CPU_PER_CALL                          KERNEL   DEFAULT
DEMO_USER    CPU_PER_SESSION                       KERNEL   DEFAULT
DEMO_USER    SESSIONS_PER_USER                     KERNEL   DEFAULT

32 rows selected.
```

Listing 9.13   *Checking profile default values.*

```
SQL> connect
Enter user-name: demouser
Enter password: *****
Connected.
SQL> select * from user_password_limits;

RESOURCE_NAME                      LIMIT
---------------------------------- --------------
FAILED_LOGIN_ATTEMPTS              3
PASSWORD_LIFE_TIME                 30
```

```
PASSWORD_REUSE_TIME                 UNLIMITED
PASSWORD_REUSE_MAX                  UNLIMITED
PASSWORD_VERIFY_FUNCTION            UNLIMITED
PASSWORD_LOCK_TIME                  1
PASSWORD_GRACE_TIME                 5

7 rows selected.
```

Listing 9.14 *Displaying all users defined.*

```
SQL> connect
Enter user-name: system
Enter password: *******
Connected.
SQL> select username,
  2          account_status,
  3          default_tablespace,
  4          temporary_tablespace,
  5          profile
  6  from dba_users;
```

USERNAME	ACCOUNT_STATUS	DEFAULT_TABLESPACE	TEMPORARY_TABLESPACE	PROFILE
SYS	OPEN	SYSTEM	SYSTEM	DEFAULT
SYSTEM	OPEN	USER_DATA	TEMPORARY_DATA	DEFAULT
DBSNMP	OPEN	SYSTEM	SYSTEM	DEFAULT
SCOTT	OPEN	USER_DATA	TEMPORARY_DATA	DEFAULT
DEMO	OPEN	USER_DATA	TEMPORARY_DATA	DEFAULT
RICHARDF	EXPIRED	USER_DATA	TEMPORARY_DATA	DEFAULT
EXPLORER	OPEN	USER_DATA	TEMPORARY_DATA	DEFAULT
PO8	OPEN	SYSTEM	SYSTEM	DEFAULT
DEMOUSER	OPEN	USER_DATA	TEMPORARY_DATA	DEMO_USER

```
9 rows selected.
```

ROLES

Roles facilitate management of the privileges within a Personal Oracle8 database. A *role* is a named group of privileges granted to a user or another role. The following list gives some indication of why using roles is easy:

- *The number of grants are reduced*—Rather than granting each privilege individually to every user, you can group privileges together and then issue one grant.

- *Dynamic management*—When you need to alter a privilege, you need only change the privilege within the role. This then propagates the change through to the user, as the user is assigned only a role and not the contents of that role.

- *Selective availability*—Roles granted to users can be enabled or disabled selectively. This allows control of a user's privileges in any situation.

DBAs usually create roles for applications. This is the way most applications handle security. If you create a number of roles with varying privileges, a user can have access to a specific role and have more or less access to the data within the application. You can also create a role with a password to prevent unauthorized use.

Managing Roles Within SQL*Plus

A number of predefined roles are available when Personal Oracle8 installs a database for you. To view these roles through SQL*Plus, once you log in as the **SYSTEM** user, you can query the **DBA_ROLES** view, as shown in Listing 9.15.

Listing 9.15 *Viewing available roles.*

```
SQL> select * from dba_roles;

ROLE                            PASSWORD
------------------------------- --------
CONNECT                         NO
RESOURCE                        NO
DBA                             NO
SNMPAGENT                       NO
SELECT_CATALOG_ROLE             NO
EXECUTE_CATALOG_ROLE            NO
DELETE_CATALOG_ROLE             NO
AQ_USER_ROLE                    NO
IMP_FULL_DATABASE               NO
EXP_FULL_DATABASE               NO
RECOVERY_CATALOG_OWNER          NO
AQ_ADMINISTRATOR_ROLE           NO
DEMO_ROLE                       NO

13 rows selected.
```

To view the privileges assigned to each role, use the **DBA_ROLE_PRIVS** view, as shown in Listing 9.16.

Listing 9.16 *Viewing privileges assigned to roles.*

```
SQL> select grantee,
  2         granted_role
  3  from dba_role_privs
  4  order by grantee;
```

```
GRANTEE                               GRANTED_ROLE
------------------------------------  --------------------------
DBA                                   DELETE_CATALOG_ROLE
DBA                                   EXECUTE_CATALOG_ROLE
DBA                                   EXP_FULL_DATABASE
DBA                                   IMP_FULL_DATABASE
DBA                                   SELECT_CATALOG_ROLE
DBSNMP                                CONNECT
DBSNMP                                RESOURCE
DBSNMP                                SNMPAGENT
DEMO                                  CONNECT
DEMO                                  DBA
DEMOUSER                              CONNECT
DEMO_ROLE                             CONNECT
DEMO_ROLE                             DBA
DEMO_ROLE                             EXP_FULL_DATABASE
DEMO_ROLE                             IMP_FULL_DATABASE
DEMO_ROLE                             RESOURCE
EXPLORER                              CONNECT
EXP_FULL_DATABASE                     EXECUTE_CATALOG_ROLE
EXP_FULL_DATABASE                     SELECT_CATALOG_ROLE
IMP_FULL_DATABASE                     EXECUTE_CATALOG_ROLE
IMP_FULL_DATABASE                     SELECT_CATALOG_ROLE
P08                                   DBA
P08                                   DEMO_ROLE
RICHARDF                              CONNECT
SCOTT                                 CONNECT
SCOTT                                 RESOURCE
SYS                                   AQ_ADMINISTRATOR_ROLE
SYS                                   AQ_USER_ROLE
SYS                                   CONNECT
SYS                                   DBA
SYS                                   DELETE_CATALOG_ROLE
SYS                                   EXECUTE_CATALOG_ROLE
SYS                                   EXP_FULL_DATABASE
SYS                                   IMP_FULL_DATABASE
SYS                                   RECOVERY_CATALOG_OWNER
SYS                                   RESOURCE
SYS                                   SELECT_CATALOG_ROLE
SYS                                   SNMPAGENT
SYSTEM                                DBA

39 rows selected.
```

The **CREATE ROLE** command creates a role within SQL*Plus. The **GRANT** command assigns privileges to roles and access to the required privileges. Listing 9.17 shows how to create a role and assign privileges to it.

Listing 9.17   *Creating a role through SQL*Plus.*

```
SQL> create role jrf;

Role created.

SQL> grant dba to jrf;

Grant succeeded.

SQL> grant alter any table to jrf;

Grant succeeded.

SQL> grant create any index to jrf;

Grant succeeded.

SQL> grant jrf to demo;

Grant succeeded.
```

This listing can be described in the following steps:

1. First, create an empty role called **JRF**.

2. Grant the role **DBA** to **JRF**.

3. Grant the **ALTER ANY TABLE** privilege to **JRF**.

4. Grant the **CREATE ANY INDEX** privilege to the role.

5. You now have a role containing permissions. The last statement grants the new role **JRF** to the user **DEMO**.

6. The user **DEMO** now has all of the privileges set up through the new role **JRF**. Remember, the new role also contains a role (**DBA**), so the user **DEMO** also has all of the **DBA** privileges.

The **REVOKE** command removes permissions from either a role or a user. The syntax is:

```
REVOKE privilege FROM [user|role]
```

Listing 9.18 shows an example of the **DBA** role being removed from the **DEMO_ROLE** role. The listing shows the role in place, the role being revoked, and, finally, the listing from **DBA_ROLE_PRIVS** to prove the role has been removed.

Listing 9.18   The *REVOKE* command.

```
SQL> select * from dba_role_privs
  2  where grantee = 'DEMO_ROLE';

GRANTEE                          GRANTED_ROLE                    ADM DEF
-------------------------------- ------------------------------- --- ---
DEMO_ROLE                        CONNECT                         NO  YES
DEMO_ROLE                        DBA                             NO  YES
DEMO_ROLE                        EXP_FULL_DATABASE               NO  YES
DEMO_ROLE                        IMP_FULL_DATABASE               NO  YES
DEMO_ROLE                        RESOURCE                        NO  YES

SQL> revoke dba from demo_role;

Revoke succeeded.

SQL> select * from dba_role_privs
  2  where grantee = 'DEMO_ROLE';

GRANTEE                          GRANTED_ROLE                    ADM DEF
-------------------------------- ------------------------------- --- ---
DEMO_ROLE                        CONNECT                         NO  YES
DEMO_ROLE                        EXP_FULL_DATABASE               NO  YES
DEMO_ROLE                        IMP_FULL_DATABASE               NO  YES
DEMO_ROLE                        RESOURCE                        NO  YES
```

Managing Roles Within The Navigator

It is sometimes easier for the beginner to use the Navigator to create and use roles and privileges. This is a good option for the novice user, as it allows point-and-click access to all of the available options for configuring roles.

To enter the Navigator, use the following path: Start|Programs|Personal Oracle8 For Windows95|Oracle8 Navigator. Once in the Navigator, double-click on the Personal Oracle8 folder. It will expand to show the folders below it. Then double-click on the Projects folder, which will show all of the projects available. Right-click on the project you wish to set the role up in, then click on New and Role... (as shown in Figure 9.2). This will enable you to create a role.

At this point, you need to enter a name for the new role. In my example, I call the new role **DEMO_ROLE**. This is also the point where you decide if you need to password-protect your role. This means the user would need to give a password before using the specified role. This safeguard is necessary only when designing roles to act as security for in-house applications. Figure 9.3 shows the window for creating the role name.

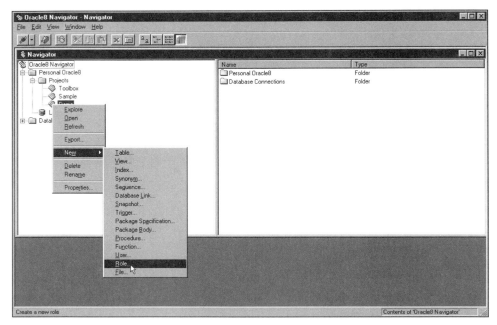

Figure 9.2 *Creating a role.*

Figure 9.3 *New Role Properties window.*

Once you've entered the name (and password, if required), you need to click on the Role/ Privilege tab at the top of the window. This allows you to assign roles and privileges to your new role. Figure 9.4 is an example of the Role/Privilege window.

Figure 9.4 *Displaying by role.*

As soon as you enter this window, it displays all of the roles available for assigning to your new role. You can also display all of the privileges available for your role by clicking on the Privileges radio button, as shown in Figure 9.5.

In my example, I chose to assign roles to the new role first. I chose the following roles:

- CONNECT
- DBA
- EXP_FULL_DATABASE

Figure 9.5 *Displaying by privilege.*

- IMP_FULL_DATABASE
- RESOURCE

Figure 9.6 shows the assignment of these roles. They were chosen from the right-hand window by clicking on the < button.

The next job is to assign the required privileges, if any, to the new role. Click on the Privileges radio button to display the Privileges screen. The privileges I decided to use are as follows:

- **CREATE ANY INDEX**
- **CREATE ANY TABLE**
- **CREATE SEQUENCE**
- **CREATE SYNONYM**

Figure 9.7 shows the assignment of these privileges. Again, they were chosen from the right-hand window by clicking on the < button.

Once this is complete, the only job remaining is to click on the OK button to send the information to the database. You will be left with a Navigator screen like that shown in Figure 9.8.

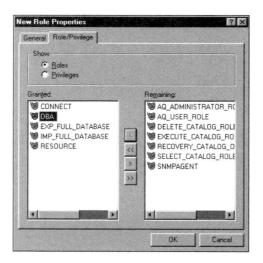

Figure 9.6   *Assigning roles to the new role.*

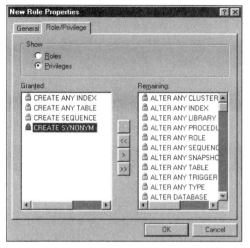

Figure 9.7   *Assigning privileges to the new role.*

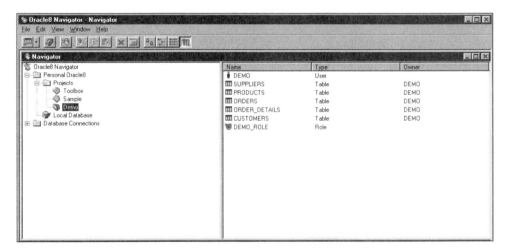

Figure 9.8   *Navigator with role created.*

BEYOND THE BASICS

This chapter has taught you the basics of security with users, profiles, and roles. This really only scratches the surface of security measures within an Oracle8 database. Chapter 15 will delve deeper into other security issues, such as auditing, backups, and restoration of data.

The next chapter deals with a topic I have touched on in earlier chapters: data types. It will give you a thorough insight into the different data types available with Oracle8.

Oracle Data Types

In the previous chapter, I discussed the concept and use of users, roles, and security. In this chapter, I delve deeper into the subject of data types, which was briefly covered in Chapter 4. Most of the data types discussed here are available in all flavors of Oracle8, although a few are not included in Personal Oracle8; where this is the case, I will give reasons why and suggestions of other data types to use.

What type of data do you have? Do you need any more?

Data types are, as the name suggests, types of data. Data within a database can be grouped into different types—for example, numeric and character. You use data types when creating tables to specify which type of data each column can hold. A number of different data types are available within an Oracle database. Most are Oracle-specific, but other types are included to comply with SQL databases. The following sections explain each data type in detail, giving examples and suggestions for using each.

VARCHAR AND VARCHAR2

VARCHAR and **VARCHAR2** are character data types, meaning they can store alphanumeric data (either characters or numbers, or both). **VARCHAR** and **VARCHAR2** store variable-length data. When you create a table using a **VARCHAR** or **VARCHAR2** data type, you specify the maximum size of the data to be held within a column. Remember, the size you specify is in *bytes*, not *characters*. This makes a difference in the number of characters you can store within a column if you are using a multibyte character set. (I will describe character sets in more detail later in this chapter.)

If, for example, you create a table with a column defined with a **VARCHAR2** data type to be 100 bytes in length, meaning you can store up to 100 characters within this column, if you are using a single-byte character set. If you insert into this column some data that is 50 bytes in length, then only those 50 bytes are stored within the database. Some other data types would store the whole column size within the database—in this case, 100 bytes—which would be a waste of space. For this reason, using **VARCHAR2** data types is better when the data is most likely to be of a variable length. Figure 10.1 shows an example using an eight-byte **VARCHAR2** column.

The definition for a **VARCHAR2** data type can vary from 1 to 4,000. Avoid using **VARCHAR** data types, because these may be used to store different types of variable-length data in future versions of Oracle. The best option is always to use **VARCHAR2** data types when specifying variable-length columns. Listing 10.1 shows an example of creating a small table with two columns, both of which are **VARCHAR2** data types.

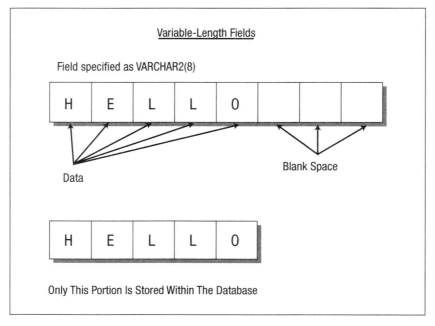

Figure 10.1   *Example of storing a **VARCHAR2** data type within a database.*

Listing 10.1 VARCHAR2 example.

```
SQL> create table varchar2_demo
  2  (full_name varchar2(100),
  3   address   varchar2(500));

Table created.
SQL> insert into varchar2_demo
  2  values ('Richard Fieldhouse','12345 asdfghjkl Street, anytown, anywhere');

1 row created.

SQL> select * from varchar2_demo;

FULL_NAME            ADDRESS
-----------------    ----------------------------------------
Richard Fieldhouse   12345 asdfghjkl Street, anytown, anywhere
```

CHAR

The **CHAR** data type stores fixed-length character strings. As in **VARCHAR** and **VARCHAR2**, **CHAR** stores alphanumeric data. When you create a table using the **CHAR** data type, you specify the maximum length of the data—again, with the number of bytes, not characters. The definition for a **CHAR** data type can be any number from 1 to 2,000 (the default is 1). When Oracle stores data within a fixed data type, it can guarantee:

- When data is inserted into the column, it will have a fixed length.

- If you give a longer value than the column size with trailing blanks, the blanks are trimmed off to the fixed-length size.

- If a shorter value than the maximum size is stored within a **CHAR** data type, the value is space-padded to the fixed length, as shown in Figure 10.2.

- If the value given is too large to fit into the fixed-length size, an error will be returned.

Figure 10.2 shows a simple 8-byte **CHAR** column being inserted into a database. With fixed-length columns, all spaces are stored within the database. The field is padded to the maximum length of the field with spaces. Using the **CHAR** data type is a good idea when specifying fields you know are of a specific length. A column that holds ZIP codes (or postal codes) lends itself to **CHAR** data types, because these codes are of a finite length, and 99 percent of the data inserted into such a column will be the same length.

Listing 10.2 shows an example of a simple table being created with two columns, both of which are defined as being of data type **CHAR**. The listing also shows data being inserted and the results displayed.

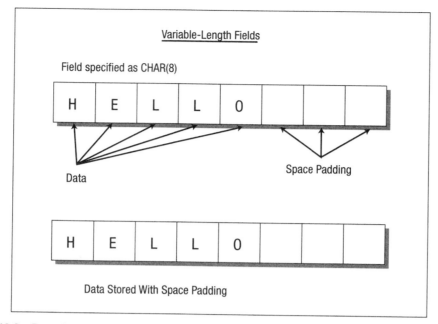

Figure 10.2 *Example of storing a **CHAR** data type within a database.*

Listing 10.2   *CHAR example.*

```
SQL> create table char_demo
  2  (State    char(2),
  3   zip_code char(8));

Table created.

SQL> insert into char_demo
  2  values ('NJ','ABC12345');

1 row created.

SQL> select * from char_demo;

ST ZIP_CODE
-- --------
NJ ABC12345
```

NUMBER

The **NUMBER** data type stores fixed and floating-point numbers. This data type is purely for numeric data and does not allow you to store any non-numeric characters within it.

Virtually any type of number can be stored within a **NUMBER** column, such as:

- Positive numbers (from 1×10^{-130} to $9.99...9 \times 10^{125}$, with up to 38 significant digits)

- Negative numbers (from -1×10^{-130} to $9.99...99 \times 10^{125}$, with up to 38 significant digits)

- Zero values

- Positive and negative infinite values

When specifying the **NUMBER** data type within a table, you do not have to define the size of the variable. The number column can store values in different forms, such as normal notation (1800) and scientific notation (1.8E3). You can, however, define the *precision* (size of the number) and *scale* (number of decimal places) of the number by enclosing them in parentheses after the data type. For example,

```
NUMBER(precision,scale)
```

or

```
NUMBER(7,2)
```

would allow all numbers less than or equal to seven digits and would store them with two decimal places.

If the precision is not supplied within the **NUMBER** data type, the column will store any numeric values. If no scale is specified, the scale defaults to zero—that is, no decimal places. To specify a number with no precision, but with a scale, you would use the following definition:

```
NUMBER(*,2)
```

This provides no limit to the number, but will always store it with two decimal places.

Using precision and scale to define **NUMBER** data types is always a good idea, because this allows Oracle to do some checking when the data is input. Table 10.1 shows some examples of outputs from different settings of precision and scale.

Line by line, Table 10.1, shows the following:

- *Line 1*—This is the default **NUMBER** data type, with no precision or scale specified. The number remains unchanged.

Table 10.1 *Example of **NUMBER** precision and scale.*

Line Number	Original Number	NUMBER Format	Resultant Number
1	1,234,567.79	NUMBER	1234567.79
2	1,234,567.79	NUMBER(*,1)	1234567.8
3	1,234,567.79	NUMBER(9)	1234568
4	1,234,567.79	NUMBER(9,2)	1234567.79
5	1,234,567.79	NUMBER(9,1)	1234567.8
6	1,234,567.79	NUMBER(6)	Error In Precision
7	1,234,567.79	NUMBER(7,-2)	1234500

- *Line 2*—This specifies a scale of 1, with no precision, identified by the asterisk (*) symbol. The digits to the left of the decimal point stay unchanged, whereas the digits to the right of the decimal point are rounded to one decimal place.

- *Line 3*—This specifies 9 as the precision.

- *Line 4*—This is an example of how a number is usually specified, with a precision and a scale. The original number is unchanged.

- *Line 5*—This is an example of a number with two decimal places being passed to a format with one decimal place, with a scale of 1. The number is rounded to the nearest decimal place.

- *Line 6*—This is an error. The number being passed to the number format has seven digits to the left of the decimal point. Oracle cannot store the number in a six-digit format.

- *Line 7*—When a negative scale is specified, Oracle rounds the data to the left of the decimal point. In this example, the scale is -2, meaning round to two places to the left of the decimal point—that is, round down to the nearest hundred.

Oracle stores numeric data in a variable-length format. Each numeric value is stored in scientific notation. The leading or trailing zeros of numbers entered are not stored within the database.

DATE

The **DATE** data type stores dates. As one of the most flexible data types Oracle provides, **DATE** allows you to store a date in a single format, yet display it in many different formats. The **DATE** data type stores a four-digit year, a two-digit month, a two-digit day, the hours, the minutes, and the seconds for any given date. The Julian date range (explained later in this section) for which Oracle can store dates is 1-January-4712 BC through 31-December-4712.

A date stored in an Oracle database is in its own fixed-length internal format. The standard date format is DD-MON-YY (e.g., 19-JAN-98). The problem with dates stored by default is that they have only two digits for the year, which causes a problem when you need to store dates outside of the twentieth century. The default assumes the two-digit year to be in the twentieth century. For more details, read the section in this chapter on the year 2000 issues.

Time is stored within a **DATE** data type in a 24-hour format. The default is HH:MI:SS (hours:minutes:seconds). Whenever a date is entered into a **DATE** data type, Oracle always stores a time, whether or not one is entered. If a time is not entered, it defaults to 00:00:00, or midnight. If you wish to enter only a time and not a date, it will default to the first day of the current month. To enter a time into the database, use the **TO_DATE** function, discussed in Chapter 5.

Julian Dates

Julian dates allow Oracle to define any date as a number, calculated as the number of days from 01-January-4712 BC. This gives a number somewhere around 2.4 million for dates in the late twentieth century. Any date stored in the database is first converted into the Julian date and then stored as a number. This is why Oracle has extremely good built-in date handling. To view dates in their Julian format, you use the 'J' format mask of the **TO_CHAR** command, as shown in Listing 10.3.

Listing 10.3   Displaying Julian dates.

```
SQL> select order_id,
  2         to_char(order_date,'J'),
  3         to_char(dispatched_date,'J'),
  4         to_char(order_due_date,'J')
  5  from orders;

 ORDER_ID TO_CHAR TO_CHAR TO_CHAR
--------- ------- ------- -------
   100001 2451180 2451189 2451210
   100002 2451181 2451190 2451210
   100003 2450935 2450943 2450965
   100004 2450966 2450968 2450975
   100005 2451419 2451420 2451452
   100006 2451419 2451432 2451422

6 rows selected.
```

Remember, the number returned when using the Julian date is not a true number. Before any calculations can be performed with the date, you have to use the **TO_NUMBER** function.

Some of Oracle's date-handling features allow you to manipulate dates by using arithmetic—that is, you can add and subtract numbers to and from dates. In doing so, Oracle takes into account all of the different calendars used throughout the world. Listing 10.4 shows an example of Oracle's date arithmetic.

Listing 10.4 Date arithmetic.

```
SQL> select sysdate + 10
  2  from dual;

SYSDATE+1
--------
29-Jan-98

SQL> select sysdate - 10
  2  from dual;

SYSDATE-1
--------
09-Jan-98
```

In Listing 10.4, the first **SQL>** statement adds 10 to the current date. This chapter is being written on 19-Jan-1998, so the output from the system date plus 10 days is 29-Jan-1998. The same applies to subtraction. Listing 10.5 is an interesting example of Oracle's date-handling skills, showing the switch from the Gregorian to the Julian calendar, in which 10 days are lost. Oracle takes this into account and alters your arithmetic accordingly.

Listing 10.5 An interesting date example.

```
SQL> select to_date('01-OCT-1582') + 1 "Date"
  2  from dual;

Date
--------
02-Oct-82

SQL> select to_date('02-OCT-1582') + 1 "Date"
  2  from dual;

Date
--------
03-Oct-82
```

```
SQL> select to_date('03-OCT-1582') + 1 "Date"
  2  from dual;

Date
--------
04-Oct-82

SQL> select to_date('04-OCT-1582') + 1 "Date"
  2  from dual;

Date
--------
15-Oct-82
```

The Year 2000

As previously noted, Oracle stores all date information in the Julian format. Because of that, the year is always stored with four digits—for example, 1998 or 2001. All of Oracle's utilities handle four-digit years.

A problem occurs when just a two-digit year is entered into the database. Oracle assumes the date to be within this century. Therefore, all years should be entered in a four-digit format when dealing with the next, or other, centuries. The **RR** format mask of the **TO_CHAR** function also deals with dates in different centuries, as discussed in Chapter 5.

NCHAR AND NVARCHAR2

The **NCHAR** and **NVARCHAR2** data types are used to store National Language Support (NLS) data. NLS is a way of storing different character sets within a database.

The **NCHAR** data type is the same as the **CHAR** data type, except that it is used primarily for storing fixed-length character strings that correspond to a fixed-length national character set. Likewise, the **NVARCHAR2** data type is similar to **VARCHAR2**, but is used for storing variable-length character strings that correspond to variable-length character sets.

When specifying tables with columns made up of **NCHAR** and **NVARCHAR2** columns, you must be sure to allow enough space for the characters to be stored, because you need to allow for the type of character set you are using—for example, multibyte character sets. A column defined as being of type **NCHAR** can store characters up to a maximum length of 2,000 bytes, or the number of characters you can store in 2,000 bytes. The maximum length of a column defined as a **NVARCHAR2** data type is 4,000 bytes, or as many characters as you can store within 4,000 bytes.

LONG

The **LONG** data type, which is from a previous release of Oracle, appears in Oracle8 only for compatibility with previous releases. It can store variable-length character strings of up to 2GB (or 2,000MB) in length. **LONG** was originally used for storing large amounts of text within a database. Oracle now suggests restricting the use of **LONG** data types and instead using **CLOB** or **NCLOB** data types (described later in this chapter) for storing large amounts of character data.

Oracle still uses **LONG** data types in the data dictionary to store the definitions of views. **LONG** has many restrictions associated with it, including:

- Only one **LONG** data type is allowed in any one table.

- **LONG** and **LONG RAW** data types cannot be replicated.

- SQL functions cannot reference **LONG** data types.

- **LONG** data types cannot appear in constraints.

- **LONG** data types cannot be used in **WHERE**, **GROUP BY**, or **ORDER BY** clauses or with the **DISTINCT** operator in **SELECT** statements.

- **LONG** data types cannot be indexed.

- **LONG** data types cannot be used in the **SELECT** list of a subquery.

- **LONG** and **LONG RAW** data types cannot be used in distributed SQL statements.

These are only a few reasons you shouldn't use **LONG** data types within your applications. Oracle now provides other data types for you to use.

RAW AND LONGRAW

Like the **LONG** data type, the **RAW** and **LONGRAW** data types are holdovers from previous Oracle releases. (Oracle8 provides new data types, **BLOB** and **BFILE**, as explained in the next sections, for storing large amounts of binary data.) **RAW** and **LONGRAW** are used for storing raw data—i.e., binary data. This binary data is usually used for storing picture files or sound effects within the database. The maximum size is 2GB for a **LONGRAW** data type and 2K for a **RAW** data type. One advantage of the **RAW** data type is that Oracle does not interpret its contents; it is left to the application to do that—i.e., play the sound or show the picture. Also, the **RAW** data type, unlike the **LONGRAW**, can be indexed (see Chapter 17 for more about indexing).

BLOB, CLOB, AND NCLOB

With version 8, Oracle now supports large objects (**LOB**s), which are used to store such information as pictures and sound. As databases become more common, their content becomes more varied; for example, people may wish to store sound, movie footage, and all sorts of other information within a database. The use of large objects enables that sort of data to be stored. Usually, the maximum size of a **LOB** is 4GB. The three different **LOB** data types are:

- *BLOB*—Stores unstructured binary data, often referred to as raw data.

- *CLOB*—Stores fixed-length single-byte character data.

- *NCLOB*—Stores fixed-length multibyte character data.

Some differences exist between the **LOB** data types and the **LONG** and **RAW** data types:

- **LOB**s can appear as a part of a user-defined data type, whereas **LONG** and **RAW** data types cannot. User-defined data types are discussed later in this chapter.

- The maximum size of a **LOB** data type is 4GB, whereas a **LONG** data type can store a maximum of only 2GB.

- You can use a **LOB** data type to gain access to data randomly, whereas a **LONG** data type gives you only sequential access to its data.

Oracle lets you manage the storage of each **LOB** individually. All **LOB** data types can be stored within either a table or a tablespace. Oracle also provides an option to store **LOB** data types externally from the database. This type of **LOB**, known as a **BFILE** data type, is discussed in the next section. All **LOB** data types participate fully within transactions; they can be committed and rolled back for any transaction.

BFILE

The **BFILE** data type is another one of Oracle's new large objects. It is sometimes referred to as an *external large object*, because it is stored separately from the database, usually as a file within the operating system. The file can reside on any normal media that operating systems use, such as CD-ROMs and optical disks. One limitation is that a **BFILE** cannot span devices—that is, you cannot have a **BFILE** data type of which 500MB is stored on one CD-ROM and 500MB on another CD-ROM. **BFILE** data types cannot participate in database transactions—they cannot be committed or rolled back. They are just there and used by the application that calls them. Special routines allow access to these **LOB** data types, enabling you to store and retrieve the information.

The **BFILE** data type stores unstructured raw binary data. The column within the database that is defined as type **BFILE** stores a pointer to the operating-system file. Remember that BFILEs are read-only data types.

DATA TYPE CONVERSIONS

When Oracle is manipulating data that the user has given it, it sometimes receives the wrong format. Usually the user's fault, this problem normally occurs when Oracle is expecting a number and receives a character field populated with numbers. In this case, Oracle allows the processing to take place as it converts the character data to numeric data. This is known as data type conversion. As discussed in Chapter 5, you can use a number of functions to convert data:

- CHARTOROWID
- HEXTORAW
- RAWTOHEX
- ROWIDTOCHAR
- TO_CHAR
- TO_DATE
- TO_NUMBER

Under a number of conditions, Oracle can automatically convert the data type. Data type conversion occurs mainly where the data type is used in an expression—for example, the equals expression within the **WHERE** clause of a **SELECT** statement. Oracle can convert from one data type to another, as shown in Table 10.2.

Table 10.2 *Data type conversion for expressions.*

FROM	TO
VARCHAR2 or CHAR	NUMBER
NUMBER	VARCHAR2
VARCHAR2 or CHAR	DATE
DATE	VARCHAR2
VARCHAR2 or CHAR	ROWID
ROWID	VARCHAR2
MLSLABEL	VARCHAR2
VARCHAR2 or CHAR	HEX
HEX	VARCHAR2

In each case shown in Table 10.2, Oracle will perform the data type conversion only if the value stored in the FROM column is of the data type in the TO column. As an example of this, Listing 10.6 shows a table being created with two columns—one with a data type of **VARCHAR2** and one with **NUMBER**. Both columns are populated with numeric data. A **SELECT** statement is issued, comparing the columns. Then the data type conversion is done, without the user knowing, and a result is displayed.

Listing 10.6 *Data type conversion example.*

```
SQL> create table conversion_test
  2  ( character_column varchar2(10),
  3    number_column number );

Table created.
SQL> insert into conversion_test
  2  values ('12345',12345);

1 row created.

SQL> insert into conversion_test
  2  values ('12345',67890);

1 row created.

SQL> select * from conversion_test;

CHARACTER_ NUMBER_COLUMN
---------- ------------
12345             12345
12345             67890

SQL> select * from conversion_test
  2  where character_column = number_column;

CHARACTER_ NUMBER_COLUMN
---------- ------------
12345             12345
```

In this listing, I populated the table with two rows—one where the same value was stored in differing formats and one where different values were stored. When the **SELECT** statement is issued to find all rows where the **Character_Column** and **Number_Column** values are identical, Oracle performs a data type conversion. In this case, Oracle converted the **VARCHAR2** data type to a **NUMBER** data type and then completed the **SELECT** statement.

CHARACTER SETS

The character set of the database can be any valid set you wish. The character set is generated when the database is first created and can never be changed while the database is running. The only way to change it is to delete the database and re-create a new one with a different character set. Many character sets are available for use. The standard sets are US7ASCII and EBCDIC. Oracle supports multibyte character sets, in which a character is stored in more than one byte. The following list names all character sets that may be used. Refer to your Oracle documentation for which one you should use.

- AL24UTFFSS
- AR8ADOS710, AR8ADOS710T, AR8ADOS720, AR8ADOS720T
- AR8APTEC715, AR8APTEC715T
- AR8ARABICMAC, AR8ARABICMACS, AR8ARABICMACT
- AR8ASMO708PLUS, AR8ASMO8X
- AR8EBCDICX
- AR8HPARABIC8T, AR8ISO8859P6
- AR8MSAWIN, AR8MSWIN1256
- AR8MUSSAD768, AR8MUSSAD768T
- AR8NAFITHA711, AR8NAFITHA711T, AR8NAFITHA721, AR8NAFITHA721T
- AR8SAKHR706, AR8SAKHR707, AR8SAKHR707T
- AR8XBASIC
- BG8MSWIN
- BG8PC437S
- BLT8CP921, BLT8EBCDIC1112, BLT8MSWIN1257, BLT8PC775
- BN8BSCII
- CDN8PC863
- CH7DEC
- CL8BS2000, CL8EBCDIC1025, CL8EBCDIC1025X, CL8ISO8859P5, CL8KOI8R
- CL8MACCYRILLIC, CL8MACCYRILLICS, CL8MSWIN1251
- D7DEC

- D7SIEMENS9780X, DK7SIEMENS9780X

- D8BS2000, D8EBCDIC273

- DK8BS2000, DK8EBCDIC277

- E7DEC

- E7SIEMENS9780X

- E8BS2000

- EE8EBCDIC870, EE8ISO8859P2, EE8MACCE, EE8MACCES

- EE8MACCROATIAN, EE8MACCROATIANS, EE8MSWIN1250, EE8PC852

- EEC8EUROASCI, EEC8EUROPA3

- EL8DEC, EL8EBCDIC875, EL8GCOS7, EL8ISO8859P7

- EL8MACGREEK, EL8MACGREEKS, EL8MSWIN1253

- EL8PC437S, EL8PC737, EL8PC851, EL8PC869

- ET8MSWIN923

- F7DEC

- F7SIEMENS9780X

- F8BS2000, F8EBCDIC297

- HU8ABMOD, HU8CWI2

- I7DEC, I7SIEMENS9780X

- I8EBCDIC280

- IN8ISCII

- IS8MACICELANDIC, IS8MACICELANDICS, IS8PC861

- IW7IS960

- IW8EBCDIC1086, IW8EBCDIC424, IW8ISO8859P8

- IW8MACHEBREW, IW8MACHEBREWS, IW8MSWIN1255, IW8PC1507

- JA16DBCS, JA16DBCSFIXED, JA16EBCDIC930, JA16EUC, JA16EUCFIXED

- JA16EUCYEN, JA16MACSJIS, JA16SJIS, JA16SJISFIXED, JA16SJISYEN

- JA16TSTSET, JA16TSTSET2, JA16VMS

- KO16DBCS, KO16KSC5601, KO16KSCCS

- LA8ISO6937, LA8PASSPORT

- LT8MSWIN921, LT8PC772, LT8PC774

- LV8PC1117, LV8PC8LR, LV8RST104090

- N7SIEMENS9780X

- N8PC865

- NDK7DEC

- NE8ISO8859P10, NEE8ISO8859P4

- NL7DEC

- RU8BESTA, RU8PC855, RU8PC866

- S7DEC, S7SIEMENS9780X, S8BS2000, S8EBCDIC278, SE8ISO8859P3

- SF7ASCII, SF7DEC

- TH8MACTHAI, TH8MACTHAIS, TH8TISASCII, TH8TISEBCDIC

- TR7DEC, TR8DEC, TR8EBCDIC1026, TR8MACTURKISH, TR8MACTURKISHS

- TR8MSWIN1254, TR8PC857

- US16TSTFIXED

- US7ASCII

- US8BS2000, US8ICL, US8NOOP, US8PC437

- UTF8

- VN8VN3

- WE8BS2000, WE8BS2000L5, WE8DEC, WE8DG

- WE8EBCDIC284, WE8EBCDIC285, WE8EBCDIC37, WE8EBCDIC37C

- WE8EBCDIC500, WE8EBCDIC500C, WE8EBCDIC871, WE8GCOS7

- WE8HP, WE8ICL, WE8ISO8859P1, WE8ISO8859P9

- WE8ISOICLUK, WE8MACROMAN8, WE8MACROMAN8S

- WE8MSWIN1252, WE8NCR4970, WE8NEXTSTEP, WE8PC850, WE8PC860

- WE8ROMAN8
- YUG7ASCII
- ZHS16CGB231280, ZHS16DBCS, ZHS16GBK, ZHS16MACCGB231280
- ZHT16BIG5, ZHT16CCDC, ZHT16DBCS, ZHT16DBT, ZHT32EUC
- ZHT32SOPS, ZHT32TRIS, ZHT32TRISFIXED

THE USE OF ROWIDS

Through **ROWID**s, Oracle can uniquely identify every row within the database. The **ROWID** for each row is stored when the data is inserted into the database. Oracle8 uses extended **ROWID**s. Older versions used restricted **ROWID**s. Oracle's new extended **ROWID**s cater to the object side of the database. They allow Oracle to uniquely identify rows within different objects, such as partitioned and nested tables. Extended **ROWID**s are made up of four pieces of information and are stored in hexadecimal format. The **ROWID** is displayed as one large **HEX** number, which can be split into four parts—A, B, C, and D, as shown here:

AAAAAABBBCCCCCCDDD

The values for the **ROWID** are made up of four parts, as follows:

- *AAAAAA*—The segment number of the object. You can have more than one object with the same object number if both are held within the same schema.
- *BBB*—The number of the data file where the object is stored. When a database is created, all data files are given a unique number.
- *CCCCCC*—The block number that contains the row. All block numbers are relative to the data file in which they are contained.
- *DDD*—The row number within the data block.

With this information, Oracle can uniquely identify all rows within a database. Listing 10.7 shows an example of the **ROWID**s within the **PRODUCTS** table. Bear in mind that the **ROWID** is relative to the machine the database is stored on. If the database is re-created, the **ROWID**s may be different.

Listing 10.7   *A list of **ROWID**s within the **PRODUCTS** table.*

```
SQL> select rowid,
  2          product_id
  3  from products;
```

```
ROWID                PRODUCT_ID
-----------------    ----------
AAAAePAACAAAAHeAAA         5001
AAAAePAACAAAAHeAAB         5002
AAAAePAACAAAAHeAAC         5003
AAAAePAACAAAAHeAAD         5004
AAAAePAACAAAAHeAAE         5005
AAAAePAACAAAAHeAAF         5006
AAAAePAACAAAAHeAAG         5007
AAAAePAACAAAAHeAAH         5008
AAAAePAACAAAAHeAAI         5009
AAAAePAACAAAAHeAAJ         5010
```

10 rows selected.

As you can see from this example, I selected the **Rowid** and **Product_id** columns from the **PRODUCTS** table. The **Rowid** column is known as a *pseudo column*, which is one that always exists. It does not have to appear in the table to be selected. Listing 10.8 shows the ROWID broken down into its parts, using the **SUBSTR** function.

Listing 10.8 *ROWIDs and their component parts.*

```
SQL> select substr(rowid,1,6) "Object",
  2         substr(rowid,7,3) "File",
  3         substr(rowid,10,6) "Block",
  4         substr(rowid,16,3) "Row"
  5  from products;

Object File Block  Row
------ ---- ------ --
AAAAeP AAC  AAAAHe AAA
AAAAeP AAC  AAAAHe AAB
AAAAeP AAC  AAAAHe AAC
AAAAeP AAC  AAAAHe AAD
AAAAeP AAC  AAAAHe AAE
AAAAeP AAC  AAAAHe AAF
AAAAeP AAC  AAAAHe AAG
AAAAeP AAC  AAAAHe AAH
AAAAeP AAC  AAAAHe AAI
AAAAeP AAC  AAAAHe AAJ
```

10 rows selected.

ROWIDs can be extremely useful to the budding Oracle developer, but not too many people are well versed in their use. **ROWIDs** can help the developer in many ways:

- They are the quickest way to access any row within the database.

- They are a unique identifier to every row within the database. This is useful when trying to delete duplicate rows.

- In larger implementations of Oracle8, they can show how your data is laid out across disks. You can see which file your data is in by accessing the File portion of the **ROWID**. This is useful when working with *striped* data files (those spread across more than one disk).

SUMMING UP

In this chapter, you learned about the different data types available, and which ones should be used for which type of data. The information within this chapter can be applied to any Oracle8 database. The next chapter discusses some more concepts of storing data: views. The next chapter also covers Oracle's sequencing objects and synonyms.

Views, Sequences, and Synonyms

In this chapter, I will introduce three concepts: views, sequences, and synonyms. These are all used in conjuction with each other to form some of the data security of an Oracle database. For more about security, please refer to Chapter 15. You can use the topics introduced in this chapter to restrict access to the underlying data of tables.

Making it easier for users to see and use the data.

VIEWS

A view is similar to a table because it contains rows and columns of data. It differs, however, in that a table contains data associated only with the table, whereas a view can contain data from more than one table, as its contents are based upon a **SELECT** statement. The rows returned from the **SELECT** statement make up the data for the view; the columns of the view are made up from the columns supplied within the **SELECT** statement. Once created, a view can be treated just like a table. The data stored within a view can change whenever you access it, because the data just consists of the rows returned from the **SELECT** statement that the view is based on.

The advantages of using views are as follows:

- *Views give added security*—The user can see only the data predefined by the creator of the view. An example is the **ORDERS** table. You may not want everyone to see the column **Dispatched_Date**, so you could create a view that selects all of the other columns. Therefore, the users who have access only to the view would never get to see the **Dispatched_Date** column.

- *Views make queries easier*—If you have a query that you access regularly—for example, joining the **ORDERS** table to the **ORDER_DETAILS** table—you could create a view of this information, then give access to this view only to the people who need it. This makes the programmers' job easier, because they do not even need to know that the information is derived from more than one table. It also makes the novice users' job easier because they may not know how to join two tables.

- *Views make information easier to display*—The view can contain just a subset of the columns in the actual table. This makes the information easier to see, because no extraneous data is associated with the SQL statement. For example, using views is a good way to rename columns within tables to make the information more readable.

- *Views can make applications run more smoothly*—If a view of a base table (one of the tables the view is based on) is used to form part of an application, the application can still function normally if it is upgraded or changed and the base table has columns added to it.

- *Views can improve performance*—A database administrator can use partitioned tables (one table split into several smaller tables) within an Oracle8 database. If partitioned views are also used, users can query a smaller chunk of the table, rather than one large table.

A view is always created from a **SELECT** statement. The tables the **SELECT** statement uses to generate the data for the view are known as the *base tables*. A base table can be another view—for example, a view based upon the **V$** views contained within the **SYSTEM** user account (for more information on the **V$** views, see Chapter 18).

A view on its own does not store any data—it is just a SQL statement. When the view is accessed, the SQL statement is executed, and the rows returned are treated as rows returned from a table.

Views can be treated just as you would treat any other table within an Oracle database—that is, you can insert rows into them, update them, and delete rows from them. Restrictions on these operations are discussed later in this section. All of the operations performed on the view, such as deleting rows from it, directly change the base tables of the view.

Another type of view exists within Personal Oracle8: the object view. I have included a discussion of the object view in Chapter 13, along with the other features of Personal Oracle8 objects.

Prerequisites For Creating Views

Before you can create a view, you must comply with the following:

- You will need the privilege **CREATE VIEW** to create a view within your own schema; to create a view elsewhere, you will need the **CREATE ANY VIEW** privilege.

- The owner of the view (the username you use to create the view) must have access to all of the base tables referenced within the view. This access must be given to the user explicitly—i.e., via the **GRANT** privilege command, not through a role.

Because a view is an object that gathers its data when executed and is based on other tables, it is possible for the view to be created one day, and one of the tables the view is based on to be deleted the next day. What happens to the view? When the view is created, it is stored (that is, the statement to retrieve the data is stored) within the data dictionary. The data dictionary is where Oracle looks up information about all of the objects created within the database. Therefore, the definition for the view always exists, even if the tables it is based on are not present. Whenever a base table is dropped or renamed, this causes a problem, and the view is marked by Oracle as being invalid. Now whenever you try to access that view, Oracle will try to recompile it. If it recompiles successfully, the query will go ahead as normal, and the user will not even know that the view was invalid. If, however, the view is still invalid, it is reported to the user, who will then have to diagnose and fix the problem. For a view to be valid, all tables referenced by the view must exist.

How To Create Views

You are now ready to create some views in the demonstration database, either through the Navigator or SQL*Plus. In this section, I will show you how to create simple views using both methods.

The Navigator Method

To create a view within the demo project, you will need to start the Navigator in the usual way. This will automatically start the database if it's not already started. I am going to create a simple view based on two columns of the **CUSTOMERS** table. Figure 11.1 shows the easiest way to create a view: Right-click on the demo project, then click on New, followed by View.

This gives you the window for naming and defining the view you are about to create, shown in Figure 11.2. The figure shows the name of the new view, **DEMO_VIEW1**, and the username who owns it, **DEMO**.

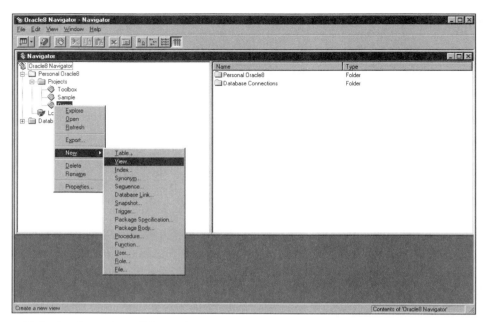

Figure 11.1 *Creating a view within a project.*

Figure 11.2 *Naming the view.*

Once you have chosen a name and owner for your view, click the Design tab to reveal how to create and apply tables to your view. The first field to enter is the database field, which allows you to choose the database you wish to create the view in. In larger systems that do not use Personal Oracle8, you may have a choice of more than one database. For this example, just choose the default. Once you have selected which database to use, you will be prompted with a password box, where you should enter the password for the owner of the view (the password for the username you entered in the previous screen). Once this has been entered and accepted, you are shown which tables and views you have access to. Remember, a view can be based upon another view. Figure 11.3 shows the window defining the tables and views available to you.

Double-clicking on the **CUSTOMERS** table will open it up and show you the columns contained within it, as you can see in Figure 11.4. Double-clicking on the column name you wish to include in the view will enter that column in the lower section of this window. For the example, I used the **Customer_Name** and **City** columns.

Figure 11.3   _Choosing the base table for the view._

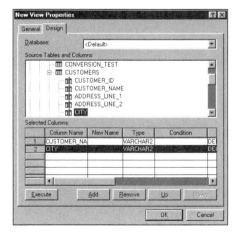

Figure 11.4   _Choosing the columns for the view._

Once the columns are chosen, you'll see that the button marked Execute is activated. If you click on this button, Personal Oracle8 will show you the output of the view being defined, as seen in Figure 11.5.

Once you're sure you picked up the correct columns, close the Execute window and click on the OK button. This creates the view you just defined and returns you to the Navigator. You'll find that the view you just created is available to your project, as shown in Figure 11.6.

The SQL*Plus Method

I find that the easiest way to create views is through SQL*Plus. It allows you more flexibility, because you can more easily create views with joins (more on join views later in this chapter). In this section, I'll show you how to create a view that is exactly the same as the one created in the previous section. Then, you can compare the two methods and choose the best one for you.

The SQL*Plus method of creating a view uses the **CREATE VIEW** statement, just as the Navigator method does, but it puts a fancy front end onto it. I'll use a simple form of **CREATE VIEW** for this initial example; other features of **CREATE VIEW** will be discussed later in this chapter. The syntax for a simple **CREATE VIEW** statement is:

```
CREATE VIEW viewname AS subquery
```

In the listings that follow, a simple view is created and checked from within SQL*Plus. Listing 11.1 shows the view being designed. The best way to design the view is with a **SELECT**

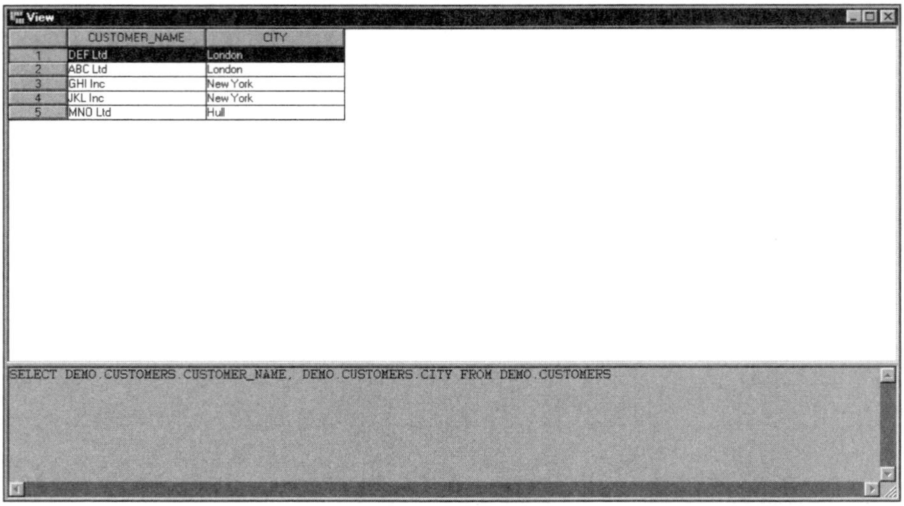

Figure 11.5 *Checking that the view is defined correctly.*

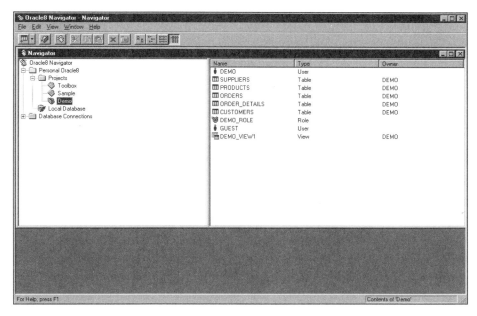

Figure 11.6 *Checking that the view is available in the Projects window.*

statement. That way, you will see exactly what the results are when the view is created. In this case, you select two columns (**Customer_Name** and **City**) from the **CUSTOMERS** table.

Listing 11.1 *Designing the view.*

```
SQL> select customer_name, city from customers;

CUSTOMER_NAME                               CITY
----------------------------------------    ----------------
DEF Ltd                                     London
ABC Ltd                                     London
GHI Inc                                     New York
JKL Inc                                     New York
MNO Ltd                                     Hull
```

Listing 11.2 shows the view being created. All you need to do is use the SQL statement created in Listing 11.1 with the **CREATE VIEW** statement.

Listing 11.2 *Creating the view.*

```
SQL> create view Demo_view2 as
  2  select customer_name, city from customers;

View created.
```

Once the view is created, you can check it by describing its format. At this point, you can't tell that the object you are describing is a view; to any other users, it will be exactly as if they are accessing a table. Once you are happy with the makeup of the view, you can use it in a **SELECT** statement to check that the data is what you expect. All of this is shown in Listing 11.3.

Listing 11.3   Checking the view.

```
SQL> desc demo_view2
 Name                                  Null?     Type
 ------------------------------------  --------  ----
 CUSTOMER_NAME                         NOT NULL  VARCHAR2(40)
 CITY                                  NOT NULL  VARCHAR2(20)


SQL> select * from demo_view2;

CUSTOMER_NAME                              CITY
----------------------------------------  ----------------
DEF Ltd                                   London
ABC Ltd                                   London
GHI Inc                                   New York
JKL Inc                                   New York
MNO Ltd                                   Hull
```

Other View Options

In the previous examples, I showed you a very simple view, based on one table that has no limits. I will now show you some of the other options you can use when creating views.

CHECK OPTION

Using **CHECK OPTION** when you create views allows you to limit their functionality. The **DEMO_VIEW1** and **DEMO_VIEW2** views created in the previous examples are both updatable. This means they can be used to update through, because the user **DEMO** owns the table as well as the view. When this is the case, you can use **CHECK OPTION** to limit the amount of updatable data to only the data the view can see. For example, Listing 11.4 creates a view that shows only the data from the **ORDER_DETAILS** table that is relevant to order number 100001.

Listing 11.4   The order details for order 100001.

```
SQL> create view order_100001_view as
  2  select order_id,
  3         product_id,
  4         number_ordered,
  5         unit_price
```

```
6  from order_details
7  where order_id = 100001
8  with check option constraint order_100001;

View created.

SQL> select * from order_100001_view;


 ORDER_ID PRODUCT_ID NUMBER_ORDERED UNIT_PRICE
 -------- ---------- -------------- ----------
   100001       5002             10          4
   100001       5001             10          2
   100001       5003             10         10
```

This view can see the details for order 100001 only. With **CHECK OPTION** created, this allows you to change only the details the view can see—i.e., anything to do with order number 100001. Listing 11.5 shows an example of updating the value **Number_Ordered** from 20 to 10 for **Product_id** 5002.

Listing 11.5   *Updating the **Number_Ordered** column.*

```
SQL> update order_100001_view
  2  set number_ordered = 10
  3  where product_id = 5002;

1 row updated.

SQL> select * from order_100001_view;


 ORDER_ID PRODUCT_ID NUMBER_ORDERED UNIT_PRICE
 -------- ---------- -------------- ----------
   100001       5002             10          4
   100001       5001             10          2
   100001       5003             10         10
```

If, for example, you try to update a value the view cannot see, you'll receive an error message, as shown in Listing 11.6.

Listing 11.6   *Updating a column the view cannot see.*

```
SQL> insert into order_100001_view
  2  values (100002,5001,999,10);
insert into order_100001_view
            *
ERROR at line 1:
ORA-01402: view WITH CHECK OPTION where-clause violation
```

Listing 11.6 shows that an error is returned when a row is inserted via the view, which does not conform to the view's **CHECK OPTION**.

FORCE Option

As mentioned earlier, it is possible to create a view that later may be invalid. By using the **FORCE** option, you can create a view that has errors immediately. This can be useful if you want to preempt a table from being created. You can create a view on a table that does not exist yet; when the table exists, the view will automatically become valid. An invalid view can be created if the view's definition has no syntax errors. Listing 11.7 shows an example of the **FORCE** option to create a view for a table that does not exist.

Listing 11.7 *Using the **FORCE** option in the **CREATE VIEW** statement.*

```
SQL> create force view invalid_view_demo as
  2  select * from asdfghjkl;

Warning: View created with compilation errors.

SQL> select * from invalid_view_demo;
select * from invalid_view_demo
              *
ERROR at line 1:
ORA-04063: view "DEMO.INVALID_VIEW_DEMO" has errors
```

In this example, the view has been created, but it remains invalid because the base table does not exist. This is proved when I try to display the contents of the view.

To compile the view manually, you would use the **ALTER VIEW** command:

```
ALTER VIEW viewname COMPILE
```

This statement will compile the view and make it valid if all of the base tables exist and the definition of the view has no syntax errors.

REPLACE Option

The **REPLACE** option is used to replace a view of the same name that already exists. For example, suppose you wish to remove a column from a view that already exists. Normally, you would have to drop the view and re-create it. You can, however, replace the view by using the **REPLACE** command, as shown in Listing 11.8.

Listing 11.8 *Using the **REPLACE** option.*

```
SQL> create or replace view order_100001_view as
  2  select order_id,
```

```
3            product_id,
4            number_ordered
5  from order_details
6  where order_id = 100001
7  with check option constraint order_100001;

View created.

SQL> select * from order_100001_view;


  ORDER_ID PRODUCT_ID NUMBER_ORDERED
  -------- ---------- --------------
    100001       5002             10
    100001       5001             10
    100001       5003             10
```

In my experience, the **REPLACE** option is always advisable when creating views. It overcomes a lot of hurdles when upgrading existing software.

Join Views

A join view is made up from more than one table or view. In other words, you have to use a **SELECT** statement with a join in it to create the view. A join view cannot be made up from a **SELECT** statement that includes any of the following functions:

- **DISTINCT**

- **GROUP BY**

- **ORDER BY**

- Any pseudo column, such as **Rownum**

- Any aggregate functions, such as **SUM, MIN, MAX**, etc.

- Any set operators, such as **UNION, MINUS, INTERSECT**, etc.

You can use join views to update values through. Such views are known as *updatable views*, defined as being views where **INSERT**, **UPDATE**, and **DELETE** operations are permitted. To see if a specific view is updatable, you can look at the **USER_UPDATABLE_COLUMNS** view showing which columns are updatable for any object. Listing 11.9 is an example of this view being used with **DEMO_VIEW1**.

Listing 11.9 Is the view updatable?

```
SQL> desc user_updatable_columns
 Name                               Null?    Type
 ---------------------------------- -------- ----
 OWNER                              NOT NULL VARCHAR2(30)
 TABLE_NAME                         NOT NULL VARCHAR2(30)
 COLUMN_NAME                        NOT NULL VARCHAR2(30)
 UPDATABLE                                   VARCHAR2(3)
 INSERTABLE                                  VARCHAR2(3)
 DELETABLE                                   VARCHAR2(3)

SQL> select column_name,updatable,insertable,deletable
  2  from user_updatable_columns
  3  where table_name = 'DEMO_VIEW1';


COLUMN_NAME                  UPD INS DEL
---------------------------- --- --- ---
CUSTOMER_NAME                YES YES YES
CITY                         YES YES YES
```

You can see that **DEMO_VIEW1** is updatable on all columns. You can then create a join view of the order information, as shown in Listing 11.10.

Listing 11.10 Creating a join view.

```
SQL> select o.order_id,
  2         c.customer_name,
  3         p.product_name,
  4         od.number_ordered
  5  from orders o,
  6       customers c,
  7       products p,
  8       order_details od
  9  where c.customer_id = o.customer_id
 10  and   o.order_id = od.order_id
 11  and   od.product_id = p.product_id

ORDER_ID CUSTOMER_NAME   PRODUCT_NAME    NUMBER_ORDERED
-------- --------------- --------------- ---------------
  100001 ABC Ltd         B Nut                       20
  100001 ABC Ltd         A Nut                       10
  100001 ABC Ltd         1cm Screw                   10
  100002 ABC Ltd         A Nut                       20
  100003 DEF Ltd         B Nut                       10
  100004 GHI Inc         A Nut                       15
  100004 GHI Inc         B Nut                       25
```

```
    100005 JKL Inc        1cm Nail              10
    100005 JKL Inc        1cm Screw             10
    100005 JKL Inc        B Nut                 10
    100006 MNO Ltd        A Nut                 20
    100003 DEF Ltd        1cm Nail              50

12 rows selected.

SQL> create view order_view as
  2  select o.order_id,
  3         c.customer_name,
  4         p.product_name,
  5         od.number_ordered
  6  from orders o,
  7       customers c,
  8       products p,
  9       order_details od
 10  where c.customer_id = o.customer_id
 11  and   o.order_id = od.order_id
 12  and   od.product_id = p.product_id;

View created.

SQL> select * from order_view;


ORDER_ID CUSTOMER_NAME    PRODUCT_NAME    NUMBER_ORDERED
-------- ---------------  --------------- ---------------
  100001 ABC Ltd          B Nut                       20
  100001 ABC Ltd          A Nut                       10
  100001 ABC Ltd          1cm Screw                   10
  100002 ABC Ltd          A Nut                       20
  100003 DEF Ltd          B Nut                       10
  100004 GHI Inc          A Nut                       15
  100004 GHI Inc          B Nut                       25
  100005 JKL Inc          1cm Nail                    10
  100005 JKL Inc          1cm Screw                   10
  100005 JKL Inc          B Nut                       10
  100006 MNO Ltd          A Nut                       20
  100003 DEF Ltd          1cm Nail                    50

12 rows selected.
```

In this listing, I have created a join view that is based on a join of four tables: **CUSTOMERS**, **ORDERS**, **ORDER_DETAILS**, and **PRODUCTS**. This join view shows, at a glance, the number of products ordered by each customer.

Restrictions When Using Join Views

Before you can update data through views, you must be aware of this rule: Any **UPDATE**, **DELETE**, or **INSERT** statement performed on a join view can update only one of the base tables.

Partitioned Views

Partitioned views are used independently of partitioned tables (see Chapter 13 for details about partitioned tables). The concept of partitioned views came into being with version 7.3 of Oracle's database. A partitioned view is made up of more than one table. The structures for all the tables within the view are the same.

Suppose you create three address tables to store customer information. In the first table, you store all surnames between *A* and *H*; in the second, all surnames between *I* and *Q*; and in the third, all surnames between *R* and *Z*. You can use a partitioned view to view all of the tables as a whole—i.e., add all three tables back together again—or to view all of the data. The partitioned view can specify what the partitions are and, when queried, use only the specified partition. These views can improve performance and availability of the data.

You have two options available when creating partitioned views: You can specify check constraints or specify a **WHERE** clause within the view. Both options have their advantages. This section will explain both options, using the example in the previous paragraph.

Using Check Constraints

The three tables would be created as shown in Listing 11.11.

Listing 11.11 Creating the base tables.

```
SQL> create table surname_a_h
  2 (surname    varchar2(20),
  3* city       varchar2(20));

Table created.

SQL> create table surname_i_q
  2 as select * from surname_a_h;

Table created.

SQL> create table surname_r_z
  2 as select * from surname_a_h;

Table created.
```

Once these tables are created, you can add check constraints to enforce the integrity of the data, as shown in Listing 11.12.

Listing 11.12   Creating check constraints.

```
SQL> alter table surname_a_h
  2* add constraint con1 check(upper(substr(surname,1,1)) between 'A' and 'H');

Table altered.

SQL> alter table surname_i_q
  2  add constraint con2 check(upper(substr(surname,1,1)) between 'I' and 'Q');

Table altered.

SQL> alter table surname_r_z
  2  add constraint con3 check(upper(substr(surname,1,1)) between 'R' and 'Z');

Table altered.
```

With check constraints in place, you can create the view, as shown in Listing 11.13.

Listing 11.13   Creating a partitioned view.

```
SQL> create view surname as
  2  select * from surname_a_h
  3  union all
  4  select * from surname_i_q
  5  union all
  6  select * from surname_r_z;

View created.
```

With the view now in place, all three tables can be queried using the one view. If a query selects only surnames that begin with the letter *B*, then Oracle accesses only one of the tables within the view, thus improving performance, because the whole view does not have to be searched.

Using A WHERE Clause

Instead of using the check constraint option, you can use the **WHERE** clause. The **WHERE** clause is inserted as a part of the definition of the view. Listing 11.14 shows an example of the **WHERE** clause option, used against the tables created for the check constraint option.

*Listing 11.14   Creating a partitioned view using the **WHERE** clause.*

```
SQL> create view surname2 as
  2  select * from surname_a_h
  3  where initcap(substr(surname,1,1)) between 'A' and 'H'
```

```
4  union all
5  select * from surname_i_q
6  where initcap(substr(surname,1,1)) between 'I' and 'Q'
7  union all
8  select * from surname_r_z
9  where initcap(substr(surname,1,1)) between 'R' and 'Z';

View created.
```

This type of view has some disadvantages:

- Because there are no constraints on the base tables, a row inserted into the wrong table—i.e., someone with the surname of Adams inserted in the **SURNAME_I_Q** table—would be lost from the view.

- Reviewing the partitioning information using Oracle's data dictionary is difficult, because the criteria for this is held within the view definition.

Benefits Of Partitioned Views

Partitioned views have a number of benefits:

- *Increased data availability*—With a partitioned view, you can drop one of the base tables and re-create it or import a large amount of data into it. While this is taking place, the view will still operate, as it does not depend upon the table being there. This is possible because all parts of the view are independent of each other.

- *The Oracle database automatically knows about partitioned views and can optimize your query accordingly*—For example, if the query is accessing the **SURNAME_A_H** table, only the database knows that the other two tables are not going to be used, so it does not access them at all. This is known as *partition elimination*.

- *Partitioned views are increasingly common within data warehouses*—This is true because of the way they handle large amounts of data and because the optimization methods are provided as standard.

Deleting Views

Once you have created any type of view, you may wish to remove it from your database. You can do so by using the **DROP VIEW** command. You are, by default, allowed to drop any view you create within your own schema. If you need to drop a view that exists in another user's schema, you'll need the **DROP ANY VIEW** privilege. To drop a view, all you have to do is use the **DROP VIEW** command. Its syntax is:

```
DROP VIEW viewname
```

For example, Listing 11.15 shows the view **SURNAME2** being dropped.

Listing 11.15   Dropping a view.

```
SQL> drop view surname2;

View dropped.
```

SEQUENCES

Sequences are used within Oracle to provide sequential numbers. They are Oracle's way of implementing sequential-number generation. Sequential numbers are most often used to insert unique values into tables and provide primary keys for tables. Suppose two users want to insert a row into the **CUSTOMERS** table. Using sequences, you could automatically generate the **Customer_id** whenever a customer is entered. This would mean the user would not have to input the customer's identification number. When two users insert to the table at the same time, using sequences, Oracle handles the locking of the sequence and ensures that no duplicate entries are made to the table.

Sequential numbers are completely independent of tables and views. A sequential number exists as an object in its own right. One single sequence can be used in more than one table. Once created, the sequence can be accessed by all users who are given the correct privileges.

Sequences come into their own in a multiuser environment—which Personal Oracle8 is not—because they cut down the time you have to wait for locks within the database. Sequences can, and should, be used in your Personal Oracle8 database. If your database is implemented on a larger system, sequences will ensure the integrity of the data. A sequential number can be up to 38 numbers long and can increment in any step you wish; the default increment is 1.

To use a sequential number, you include a call to it in the SQL statement. You have two options when accessing sequential numbers: You can either generate a new one—i.e., the next in the sequence—or you can look at the current value of the sequential number. When selecting a sequential number, you are the only user with access to that specific number. To look at the current number of a sequence, you must have already selected a value from the sequence within the current session.

Creating Sequences

When creating sequences, you must make the sequence name identifiable. This is normally done by adding _S after the name to denote it is a sequence. For example, if you have a table called **PRODUCTS**, then a sequence that is going to be used to provide the **Product_id** would be named **PRODUCTS_S**. If you keep this naming strategy in mind when creating objects, they will be easier to identify later, when you may have hundreds of objects. If you are going to create a sequence within your own schema, you must have the **CREATE SE-QUENCE** privilege. If you need to create a sequence within another user's schema, you must have the **CREATE ANY SEQUENCE** privilege. You create a sequence with the **CREATE SEQUENCE** command. The syntax is as follows:

```
CREATE SEQUENCE sequencename INCREMENT BY n
START WITH n
MAXVALUE n|NOMAXVALUE
MINVALUE n|NOMINVALUE
CYCLE|NOCYCLE (default)
CACHE n|NOCACHE
ORDER|NOORDER
```

Listing 11.6 is an example of creating sequences to use with the demonstration database.

Listing 11.16   Creating sequences via SQL*Plus.

```
SQL> create sequence customers_s
  2   increment by 1
  3   start with 1000
  4   maxvalue 9999
  5   minvalue 1000;

Sequence created.

SQL> create sequence orders_s
  2   increment by 1
  3   start with 10000
  4   maxvalue 99999
  5   minvalue 10000;

Sequence created.

SQL> create sequence order_details_s
  2   increment by 1
  3   start with 1000
  4   maxvalue 9999
  5   minvalue 1000;

Sequence created.

SQL> create sequence products_s
  2   increment by 1
  3   start with 1000
  4   maxvalue 9999
  5   minvalue 1000;

Sequence created.
```

```
SQL> create sequence suppliers_s
  2   increment by 1
  3   start with 10000
  4   maxvalue 99999
  5   minvalue 10000;

Sequence created.
```

These sequences have been created with the following properties:

- They increment in ascending order by 1.

- The values start at 1000 or 10000.

- The maximum value allowed in these sequences is 9999 or 99999.

- The minimum value allowed in these sequences is 1000.

When a sequence is created, the definition is stored as a row in a table within the SYSTEM tablespace. This ensures that sequences are always available to all users, as the SYSTEM tablespace is always accessible to every user.

A full description of each part of the **CREATE SEQUENCE** syntax is included later in this chapter.

INCREMENT BY

The **INCREMENT BY** option tells Oracle what to increment the sequential number by. The value can be either positive or negative. If positive, the increments are in ascending order; if negative, the increments are in descending order, or decrements. The default value for this option is 1.

START WITH

This option tells Oracle which number to start at for the sequential-number generation. It can be any number. As you can see in Listing 11.16, I start the sequential number at the value 1000 or 10000.

MAXVALUE

This option defines the largest value allowed for the sequential number—in Listing 11.16, it is set to 9999 or 99999. For sequences that are ascending, the default value for the **MAXVALUE** option is 10e27−1. For descending sequences, this value defaults to 1.

MINVALUE

This option is similar to the **MAXVALUE** option, but it defines the lowest number allowed within the sequence. For sequences that are ascending, the default value for **MINVALUE** is 1, and the default value for descending values is 10e27–1.

CYCLE

The **CYCLE** option tells Oracle to cycle the number to **MINVALUE** when **MAXVALUE** is reached for ascending sequences, and cycle **MINVALUE** to **MAXVALUE** for descending sequences. The default for this option is **NOCYCLE**, where no cycling will take place. Once the end of a sequence is reached, no more numbers will be generated.

CACHE

The **CACHE** option tells Oracle to cache the number of values given for the sequence into memory at database startup or sequence creation. Once the set of numbers in the cache has been used, Oracle reads in another set of numbers. This speeds up access to the sequential numbers. The only drawback is that when the database is shut down, all sequential numbers still held in memory are lost. The default for this option is **NOCACHE**. When the **CACHE** option is used, the default is for 20 sequences to be cached into memory. The maximum number of numbers that can be cached into memory is calculated from the following formula: **MAXVALUE – MINVALUE**. One problem with caching numbers within mem-ory is that Oracle can skip sequential numbers, as some may be lost when the database is brought down.

ORDER

The **ORDER** option for the **CREATE SEQUENCE** command causes the sequences to be output in the order they are requested. This option is not often used, as sequential numbers are usually output in order anyway.

Creating Sequences Through The Navigator

To create a sequence through the Navigator, you first start the Navigator. Click on Projects and right-click on the project you wish to create the sequence for. Then select New and Sequence, as shown in Figure 11.7.

Once you select the sequence, you see a window, as shown in Figure 11.8, which you need to fill in with the details for creating the sequence.

Once you enter the details, click on the OK button to create your sequence. The database creates the sequence and returns you to the Navigator, where you will see your sequence in place. See Figure 11.9 for an example.

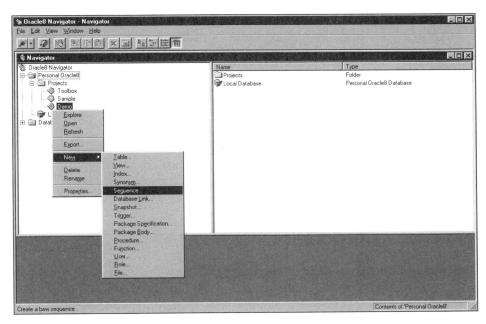

Figure 11.7   Creating a sequence in your project.

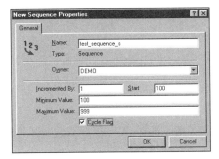

Figure 11.8   Specifying the details for a sequence.

Altering Sequences

You may sometimes need to alter sequences once they have been created. For example, you may wish to change the **MAXVALUE** or **INCREMENT**. This is possible through SQL*Plus. If you wish to alter a sequence in your own schema, you won't need any special privileges, because you own it. If, however, you wish to alter a sequence within another user's schema, you'll need the **ALTER ANY SEQUENCE** privilege.

The only option you cannot change about a sequence is the **START WITH** value. To change this value, you must drop the sequence and re-create it. To alter a sequence, you need to use the **ALTER SEQUENCE** command. This command has the same syntax as the **CREATE**

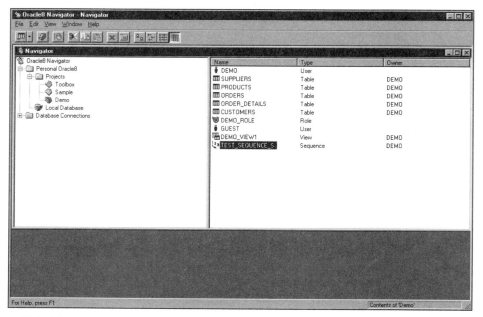

Figure 11.9 *The sequence has now been created.*

SEQUENCE command, with the exception of the **START WITH** clause. Listing 11.17 shows the **PRODUCTS_S** sequence being altered.

Listing 11.17 *Altering a sequence.*

```
SQL> alter sequence products_s
  2   increment by 10
  3   maxvalue 1000000
  4   minvalue 1;

Sequence altered.
```

init.ora Parameters And Sequences

Oracle reads the init.ora parameters, supplied by a file, when it starts up any database. These parameters control how specific parts of the database work. One of the options within the init.ora file is **sequence_cache_entries**. This sets the maximum number of sequences that can be cached within memory at any one time. Always try to overestimate this value; allowing too few sequences within memory can cause problems with sequences missing values.

For details of setting **init.ora** parameters, refer to Chapter 17.

Dropping Sequences

When you need to remove a sequence from the database, you can do so in two ways:

- Through the Navigator, by right-clicking on the sequence you wish to drop and then clicking on Delete.

- Through SQL*Plus, by using the **DROP SEQUENCE** statement.

You'll always be able to drop any sequence you own, but if you need to drop a sequence within another user's schema, you will need the **DROP ANY SEQUENCE** privilege. Listing 11.18 shows an example of the **DROP SEQUENCE** statement being used on the **TEST_SEQUENCE_S** sequence just created.

Listing 11.18   Dropping a sequence.

```
SQL> drop sequence test_sequence_s;

Sequence dropped.
```

Using Sequences

Sequences are used by including references to them within your **SELECT** statement. You can reference two values: the next value in the sequence (**NEXTVAL**) and the current value of the sequence (**CURRVAL**). Listing 11.19 shows the uses of sequences.

Listing 11.19   Using sequences.

```
SQL> select sequence_name from user_sequences;

SEQUENCE_NAME
------------------------------
CUSTOMERS_S
ORDERS_S
ORDER_DETAILS_S
PRODUCTS_S
SUPPLIERS_S

SQL> select customers_s.nextval from dual;

  NEXTVAL
--------
    1000

SQL> select customers_s.nextval from dual;

  NEXTVAL
--------
    1001
```

```
SQL> select customers_s.currval from dual;

  CURRVAL
---------
     1001
```

In this example, I followed these steps:

1. I checked which sequences I have access to by querying the **USER_SEQUENCES** view.

2. Then I selected the next value from the **CUSTOMERS_S** sequence. Notice that this is the number 1000 (the value for **START WITH**). Also notice the way the sequence is selected. I used the sequence name, then a dot, and then the operation I wished to perform on the sequence. The **SELECT** statement is taken from the **DUAL** table, which is just one column wide and has only one row in it. By selecting from this table, I know I will return only one row.

3. I selected the next value again. Notice the number retrieved is the next number within the sequence.

4. I then selected the current value. This is the same value as the previous **SELECT** statement. Remember, I said that the sequential number has to be initiated within your session before you can select the current value. Selecting the next value from the sequential number initiates it within your session. Listing 11.20 shows what happens when the sequential number is not initiated within the session and you select the current value.

Listing 11.20 *Selecting the current value of an uninitialized sequential number.*

```
SQL> select products_s.currval from dual;
select products_s.currval from dual
                *
ERROR at line 1:
ORA-08002: sequence PRODUCTS_S.CURRVAL is not yet defined in this session
```

SYNONYMS

Synonyms are alias names for tables, views, sequences, or packages. Virtually any object that can be referenced through a **SELECT** statement can use synonyms. Synonyms do not store data; they are just pointers that send you in the correct direction for obtaining the information they want. The most common use for synonyms is security. With synonyms, you can:

- Hide the name of the object owner.

- Hide the whereabouts of the object.

- Make SQL statements easier to write for end users.

Synonyms are useful for designing applications because they hide the location, name, and owner of the object they point to. If the applications access all of the tables through synonyms, only the synonyms need to be changed if a table or view name changes. That means you do not have to grant individual access to everybody again and again. You can also use synonyms to simplify SQL statements. For example, if you have a table where the name is very large, you can use a synonym to shorten the name and reference the synonym within the **SELECT** statement.

The two types of synonyms available for use are public and private, described in the next sections.

Public Synonyms

Public synonyms are owned by the **PUBLIC** user (remember, this user is accessible to everyone). If you create a public synonym, every user of the database will be able to access your object through the public synonym. To create a public synonym, you must have the **CREATE PUBLIC SYNONYM** privilege.

Private Synonyms

Private synonyms are stored within the schema of the user who creates them. These synonyms can then be granted to individual users for tighter security. To create a private synonym within your own schema, you must have the **CREATE SYNONYM** privilege; to create a private synonym in another user's schema, you must have the **CREATE ANY SYNONYM** privilege.

Uses Of Synonyms

The best way to describe the uses of synonyms is to use an example. Suppose the demo database is created by the user **DEMO**, and all of the tables are under the **DEMO** schema. Suppose another user, **FRED**, wants to gain access to the data in the **DEMO** schema. To do so, he would have to use the schema prefix to all of the tables he requires access to. Listing 11.21 shows **FRED** selecting all information from the **ORDER_DETAILS** table.

Listing 11.21   Selecting details from the **ORDER_DETAILS** table.

```
SQL> select * from order_details;
select * from order_details
              *
ERROR at line 1:
ORA-00942: table or view does not exist


SQL> select * from demo.order_details;

  ORDER_ID PRODUCT_ID NUMBER_ORDERED UNIT_PRICE
  -------- ---------- -------------- ----------
    100001       5002             10          4
    100001       5001             10          2
    100001       5003             10         10
    100002       5001             20          2
    100003       5002             10          4
    100004       5001             15          2
    100004       5002             25          4
    100005       5004             10          6
    100005       5003             10         10
    100005       5002             10          4
    100006       5001             20          2
    100003       5004             50          6

12 rows selected.
```

FRED first tries to select all information from a table called **ORDER_DETAILS**. This fails, because the table specified is not within **FRED**'s schema. Not until **FRED** prefixes the table name with the owner of the table will he have access to the table—assuming that **FRED** has been granted access to the table in the first place. Now, suppose **FRED** created a private synonym for the **ORDER_DETAILS** table, as shown in Listing 11.22.

Listing 11.22   Creating a private synonym.

```
SQL> create synonym order_details for demo.order_details;

Synonym created.

SQL> select * from order_details;

  ORDER_ID PRODUCT_ID NUMBER_ORDERED UNIT_PRICE
  -------- ---------- -------------- ----------
    100001       5002             10          4
    100001       5001             10          2
    100001       5003             10         10
    100002       5001             20          2
```

100003	5002	10	4
100004	5001	15	2
100004	5002	25	4
100005	5004	10	6
100005	5003	10	10
100005	5002	10	4
100006	5001	20	2
100003	5004	50	6

```
12 rows selected.
```

Once he has created the private synonym, **FRED** can call the table **ORDER_DETAILS** and access the data. This is okay for the user **FRED**, but you cannot expect all users to create their own synonyms. This is where public synonyms come into play. With public synonyms, you can create one that is accessible to all users. They will still need to be granted access to the table for any data to be seen. Listing 11.23 shows the creation of a public synonym. Remember, to create public synonyms, you must have the required privileges, best done by a DBA account, such as **SYSTEM**.

Listing 11.23 *Creating a public synonym.*

```
SQL> connect
Enter user-name: system
Enter password: *******
Connected.
SQL> create public synonym order_details for demo.order_details;

Synonym created.

SQL> connect
Enter user-name: susan
Enter password: *****
Connected.
SQL> select * from order_details;

  ORDER_ID PRODUCT_ID NUMBER_ORDERED UNIT_PRICE
  -------- ---------- -------------- ----------
    100001       5002             10          4
    100001       5001             10          2
    100001       5003             10         10
    100002       5001             20          2
    100003       5002             10          4
    100004       5001             15          2
    100004       5002             25          4
    100005       5004             10          6
    100005       5003             10         10
    100005       5002             10          4
```

```
100006      5001         20       2
100003      5004         50       6
```

12 rows selected.

Notice that the user **SUSAN** can now see the data in the **ORDER_DETAILS** table. Because of the use of synonyms, the user **SUSAN** does not know where the **ORDER_DETAILS** table is or who owns it.

Dropping Synonyms

To drop any private synonyms that you own, you must have the **DROP ANY SYNONYM** privilege. To drop a public synonym, you must have the **DROP PUBLIC SYNONYM** privilege.

Listing 11.24 shows an example of dropping a private synonym.

Listing 11.24   Dropping a private synonym.

```
SQL> connect
Enter user-name: fred
Enter password: ****
Connected.
SQL> drop synonym order_details;

Synonym dropped.
```

This example shows a user logging in as **FRED** and dropping the private synonym **ORDER_DETAILS**. Notice that you do not have to specify that it is a private synonym. If you use **DROP SYNONYM**, Oracle automatically knows it is a private one.

Listing 11.25 shows an example of dropping a public synonym.

Listing 11.25   Dropping a public synonym.

```
SQL> connect
Enter user-name: system
Enter password: *******
Connected.
SQL> drop public synonym order_details;

Synonym dropped.
```

This example shows the user logging in as the **SYSTEM** user (a DBA) and dropping the **ORDER_DETAILS** public synonym. Notice that the word **PUBLIC** is specified. If not, Oracle would try to drop a private synonym by the same name.

WHAT HAVE YOU LEARNED?

In this chapter, I have guided you through the maze of sequences and synonyms, and given a thorough explanation of the uses of views within Personal Oracle8. The next chapter explains PL/SQL, a procedural add-on to SQL*Plus. SQL*Plus has a number of limitations—for example, you cannot loop within a statement. PL/SQL allows you to do this and gives the programmer a more structured language.

PL/SQL

In previous chapters, you gathered the skills to write simple queries and more complex joins using SQL*Plus. This chapter takes that knowledge and introduces another dimension: the procedure. This chapter will explain the basics of PL/SQL and introduce you to its uses, including stored procedures, packages, and database triggers. Using the knowledge gained from this chapter, you will be able to enhance all of your database applications.

PL/SQL, from the beginning.

PL/SQL—THE BEGINNINGS

PL/SQL is the procedural language (PL) extension to Structured Query Language (SQL). This allows you to add loops and other normal programming constructs to your database applications. PL/SQL uses named or unnamed blocks of code, known as *PL/SQL blocks,* to store statements. An unnamed block of PL/SQL is an *anonymous block.* The format for PL/SQL statements is similar to that of C, so if you already have some knowledge of C programming, you have a head start. PL/SQL is used to implement database objects, such as:

- *Stored procedures (functions)*—User-defined database functions that can be accessed through triggers or user programs.

- *Packages*—Sets of PL/SQL procedures that can be used within all database applications.

- *Database triggers*—A piece of PL/SQL that can be fired off with a SQL command—for example, to insert a row into a table.

A PL/SQL program can contain PL/SQL functions, procedures, and anonymous blocks.

Basic PL/SQL

PL/SQL is written in blocks. Normally, three blocks are associated with any PL/SQL program:

- *Declaration*—Declares all of the variables and constants used within the PL/SQL program.

- *Executable*—Defines the code that is executed when the PL/SQL block is executed.

- *Exception*—This optional block handles any error conditions that arise from executing the executable block. This will be discussed later in this chapter.

The best way to write a block of PL/SQL is to use an editor, such as Notepad, on your PC. Writing your PL/SQL block within an editor is easier than writing directly into the SQL*Plus buffer. You can then execute your PL/SQL within SQL*Plus by using the @ or **START** command.

The best way to understand a PL/SQL block is to get right in and start looking at a sample piece of PL/SQL. The examples in Listings 12.1 and 12.2 show a piece of PL/SQL that decreases the **Units_In_Stock** for **Product_id** 5001 by 1. If this value is 0 or less, a message is written to the **MESSAGES** table (specifically created for this purpose) stating that the product is out of stock. Listing 12.2 shows the **MESSAGES** table being accessed to check the execution of the PL/SQL block.

Listing 12.1 An example PL/SQL block.

```
DECLARE
   quantity NUMBER(5);
BEGIN
   SELECT units_in_stock
     INTO quantity
     FROM products
     WHERE product_id = 5001
     FOR UPDATE OF units_in_stock;
   IF quantity > 0 THEN
```

```
      UPDATE products
      SET units_in_stock = units_in_stock - 1
      WHERE product_id = 5001;
      INSERT INTO messages VALUES (1,'Product ID 5001 decreased by 1');
   ELSE
      INSERT INTO messages VALUES (2,'Product ID 5001 OUT OF STOCK');
   END IF;
   COMMIT;
END;
/
```

Listing 12.2 *Checking the output from the PL/SQL block.*

```
SQL> @c:\plsql\example1.sql

PL/SQL procedure successfully completed.

SQL> select * from messages
  2  ;

MESSAGE_ID MESSAGE_TEXT
---------- ----------------------------------------
         1 Product ID 5001 decreased by 1

SQL> update products
  2   set units_in_stock = 0
  3   where product_id = 5001;

1 row updated.

SQL> @c:\plsql\example1.sql

PL/SQL procedure successfully completed.

SQL> select * from messages;

MESSAGE_ID MESSAGE_TEXT
---------- ----------------------------------------
         1 Product ID 5001 decreased by 1
         2 Product ID 5001 OUT OF STOCK
```

The PL/SQL block shown in Listing 12.1 has an **IF..THEN..ELSE** construct. This gives you an added dimension with your SQL statements. You can now write procedures that react to the data within your database. The PL/SQL block in Listing 12.1 is an anonymous block, as it is not named.

To help you understand how this block of PL/SQL works, I will split it into sections and explain what is being done in each one.

Section 1

Section 1 is the declaration section, which consists of only two lines. Only one variable—**quantity**—is declared. The declaration section is:

```
DECLARE
   quantity NUMBER(5);
```

Within a PL/SQL block, the declaration section is optional. If you wish to define any variables within the block, however, you must declare them in this section. The declaration section always begins with the word **DECLARE**. This is followed on the next line by the variables you are declaring, along with their types and default values, if any. All of these statements end with a semicolon, which is true for all PL/SQL statements. In the example, I declare a variable called **quantity**, being of type **NUMBER**, with space for five digits. Here are some more examples of declarations of variables:

```
DECLARE
Telephone_Number    NUMBER(15);
Country             VARCHAR2(20)  := 'United Kingdom';
Amount              NUMBER(8,2)  := 99.99;
```

Notice that in these declarations, some of the variables declared are assigned initial values. These can be thought of as constants, or default values. Notice they are assigned a value with the := operator (this is the assignment operator, not the equals operator). All declarations are local to the block—that is, if a variable is declared in one block, it can be used only within the same block without being declared again.

Section 2

Section 2 is the executable section of the PL/SQL block. This is the most important section of the PL/SQL block and is mandatory. This section always begins with the word **BEGIN**. This is followed by any number of statements to make up the remainder of the block. The section then ends with the word **END**. In this case, the executable section contains the following:

```
BEGIN
   SELECT units_in_stock
     INTO quantity
     FROM products
     WHERE product_id = 5001
     FOR UPDATE OF units_in_stock;
   IF quantity > 0 THEN
     UPDATE products
     SET units_in_stock = units_in_stock - 1
```

```
      WHERE product_id = 5001;
      INSERT INTO messages VALUES (1,'Product ID 5001 decreased by 1');
   ELSE
      INSERT INTO messages VALUES (2,'Product ID 5001 OUT OF STOCK');
   END IF;
   COMMIT;
END;
```

This example has five SQL statements and five PL/SQL operators. This section is best explained in steps:

1. *BEGIN*—This tells PL/SQL that this is the start of the executable section (PL/SQL operator).

2. *SELECT*—This takes the value for **Units_In_Stock** from the **PRODUCTS** table, where the **Product_id** is 5001, and puts the value in the **quantity** variable, which was assigned in the declaration section. The **FOR UPDATE** line locks the row, so that no other process can access this record to change the value while you are using it (SQL statement).

3. *IF quantity > 0*—This line is the start of the **IF..THEN..ELSE** construct. It will execute code depending upon the value of the **quantity** variable (PL/SQL operator).

4. *UPDATE*—This statement is executed only if the value of **quantity** is greater than 0. It decrements the value of **Units_In_Stock** by 1 (SQL statement).

5. *INSERT*—This line is executed only if the value of the **quantity** variable is greater than 0. The **INSERT** statement creates a message in the **MESSAGES** table defining the outcome of the **UPDATE** statement (SQL statement).

6. *ELSE*—This line is the corresponding operator for the **IF..THEN** statement. All lines, up until **END IF**, are executed if the criteria in the **IF** statement fails (PL/SQL operator).

7. *INSERT*—This line is executed only if the quantity variable is less than or equal to 0, in which case a message is produced in the **MESSAGES** table (SQL operator).

8. *END IF*—This line defines the end of the **IF..THEN..ELSE** construct. All lines following this are executed in turn (PL/SQL operator).

9. *COMMIT*—This commits all changes to the database and unlocks the row reserved for **UPDATE**. This line is executed no matter what the value of the **quantity** variable is.

10. *END*—This defines the end of the PL/SQL block. It is usually followed by a / operator, which tells SQL*Plus to execute the PL/SQL block.

As shown in the example, PL/SQL allows you to use SQL statements to assign values and use the PL/SQL operators to change the flow of the PL/SQL block. Using PL/SQL, you can define procedures and functions within the database. These can then be accessed and used to manipulate data within the database. As PL/SQL is a block-structured language, each block normally solves a specific problem, and as blocks can be used within blocks, you get a very structured approach to problem solving.

Reserved Words

As with all programming languages, you cannot use certain words within your PL/SQL programs. A list of all known reserved words follows:

- ABORT, ACCEPT, ACCESS, ADD, ALL, ALTER, AND, ANY, ARRAY, ARRAYLEN, AS, ASC, ASSERT, ASSIGN, AT, AUDIT, AUTHORIZATION, AVG

- BASE_TABLE, BEGIN, BETWEEN, BINARY_INTEGER, BODY, BOOLEAN, BY

- CASE, CHAR, CHAR_BASE, CHECK, CLOSE, CLUSTER, CLUSTERS, COLAUTH, COLUMN, COMMENT, COMMIT, COMPRESS, CONNECT, CONSTANT, CRASH, CREATE, CURRENT, CURRVAL, CURSOR

- DATABASE, DATA_BASE, DATE, DBA, DEBUGOFF, DEBUGON, DECLARE, DECIMAL, DEFAULT, DEFINTION, DELAY, DELETE, DESC, DIGITS, DISPOSE, DISTINCT, DO, DROP

- ELSE, ELSIF, END, ENTRY, EXCEPTION, EXCEPTION_INIT, EXCLUSIVE, EXISTS, EXIT

- FALSE, FETCH, FILE, FLOAT, FOR, FORM, FROM, FUNCTION

- GENERIC, GOTO, GRANT, GROUP

- HAVING

- IDENTIFIED, IF, IMMEDIATE, IN, INCREMENT, INDEX, INDEXES, INDICATOR, INITIAL, INSERT, INTEGER, INTERFACE, INTERSECT, INTO, IS

- LEVEL, LIKE, LIMITED, LOCK, LONG, LOOP
- MAX, MAXEXTENTS, MIN, MINUS, MLSLABEL, MOD, MODE
- NATURAL, NATURALN, NEW, NEXTVAL, NOAUDIT, NOCOMPRESS, NOT, NOWAIT, NULL, NUMBER, NUMBER_BASE
- OF, OFFLINE, ON, ONLINE, OPEN, OPTION, OR, ORDER, OTHERS, OUT
- PACKAGE, PARTITION, PCTFREE, PLS_INTEGER, POSITIVE, POSITIVEN, PRAGMA, PRIOR, PRIVATE, PRIVILEGES, PROCEDURE, PUBLIC
- RAISE, RANGE, RAW, REAL, RECORD, REF, RELEASE, REMR, RENAME, RESOURCE, RETURN, REVERSE, REVOKE ROLLBACK, ROW, ROWID, ROWLABEL, ROWNUM, ROWS, ROWTYPE, RUN
- SAVEPOINT, SCHEMA, SELECT, SEPARATE, SESSION, SET, SHARE, SMALLINT, SPACE, SQL, SQLCODE, SQLERRM, START, STATE, STATEMENT, STDDEV, SUBTYPE, SUCCESSFUL, SUM, SYNONYM, SYSDATE
- TABAUTH, TABLE, TABLES, TASK, TERMINATE, THEN, TO, TRIGGER, TRUE, TYPE
- UID, UNION, UNIQUE, UPDATE, USE, USER
- VALIDATE, VALUES, VARCHAR, VARCHAR2, VARIANCE, VIEW, VIEWS
- WHEN, WHENEVER, WHERE, WHILE, WITH, WORK, WRITE
- XOR

When creating variables for programs, I always try to create words that have meaning. For example, the variable **12345** doesn't mean anything to anybody, whereas **my_phone_no** does.

The Use Of Variables And Data Types

The procedural option allows you to define variables and constants that can be used within a PL/SQL block. All variables and constants must be declared within the block in which they appear. These variables can be defined as any data type you can use within Personal Oracle8. For example, to declare a variable to store the current date, you could specify it as follows:

```
TODAYS_DATE DATE;
```

You can also assign values to the variables you define. These can be defined in two different ways: either by using the assignment operator (:=) or by selecting values from the database into the variable. Examples of both declarations are shown here:

```
VAT := unit_price * 0.175;
FULL_PRICE := unit_price * 1.175;

SELECT unit_price * 0.175 INTO VAT FROM PRODUCTS WHERE PRODUCT_ID = 5001;
```

Constants

A constant is a variable that keeps its value at all times. Constants are useful for declaring such variables as sales tax, which usually remains the same at all times in a particular region. Constants are defined the same as variables, except the word **CONSTANT** is added to the declaration. The value must then be assigned to the constant immediately, after which you cannot change it. For example, the current rate of sales tax in the United Kingdom is 17.5 percent; this could be defined as:

```
sales_tax CONSTANT NUMBER(2,2) := 17.50;
```

Attributes

All PL/SQL variables have attributes, which allow you to reference the different attributes for any column or row within the database. They are useful when you do not know the data type of the variable you wish to use. They also have the advantage that if the data type of the column changes, you do not have to recode all of your PL/SQL.

A good example of an attribute associated with each column is **%TYPE**. You would use this attribute to assign your variable to the same data type as the database column referenced in the declaration statement. For example, if you have a variable called **product_reference** and wish to declare the variable as having the same data type as the **Product_id** column of the **PRODUCTS** table, you would issue the following declaration statement:

```
PRODUCT_REFERENCE PRODUCTS.PRODUCT_ID%TYPE;
```

Another attribute you may wish to use is **%ROWTYPE**. You can use PL/SQL to group records together; groups of records are known as *cursors*. The **%ROWTYPE** attribute allows you to specify data types to match the field returned by the cursor. (Cursors are explained in the next section.) In the following example

```
DECLARE
CUST_REC CUSTOMERS%ROWTYPE;
CUST_NAME := CUST_REC.CUSTOMER_NAME;
CUST_ADD_1 := CUST_REC.ADDRESS_LINE_1;
```

the variable **cust_rec** is defined as having the data types of the columns for the **CUSTOMERS** table. The next line declares the variable **cust_name**, which is given the same data type as the **Customer_Name** column within the **CUSTOMERS** table, as the **cust_rec** variable is defined in the line with the **%ROWTYPE** attribute.

Suppose you had a cursor that brought back the **Customer_Name**, **Address_Line_1**, and **Address_Line_2** columns from the **CUSTOMERS** table. The **%ROWTYPE** attribute could be used to assign the data types for these columns to variables, in the following way:

```
DECLARE
CURSOR c1 IS SELECT customer_name,address_line_1,address_line_2 FROM CUSTOMERS;
cust_rec c1%ROWTYPE;
```

To read the values into the cursor, you would use the **FETCH** statement, which would set the attributes to the data types of the returned columns.

Cursors

Cursors are used as named work areas for PL/SQL. Once a cursor is defined, the values it holds can be referenced by using the name of the cursor. Two types of cursors may be defined: implicit and explicit.

Implicit Cursors

Personal Oracle8 automatically assigns implicit cursors. They are used mainly for statements that return one row. Because implicit cursors are automatically assigned, you don't need to worry too much about them; you just need to know they exist.

Explicit Cursors

An explicit cursor is defined when you name a specific cursor. For example, the following example defines an explicit cursor:

```
DECLARE
CURSOR c1 IS SELECT customer_name,address_line_1,address_line_2 FROM CUSTOMERS;
```

An explicit cursor can return more than one row. In this example, the cursor will return all of the rows contained within the **CUSTOMERS** table. The rows returned are called the *result set*. The cursor points to the first record of those returned. This is similar to working with files—i.e., open the file, process the records, and then close the file. You can use the following statements to manipulate cursors:

- *OPEN cursor*—Executes the cursor named and stores the rows returned within the cursor, with the cursor pointing to the first record of the result set.

- *FETCH cursor*—Retrieves the row the cursor is pointing to and advances the cursor to point to the next row.

- *CLOSE cursor*—Closes the cursor.

Cursors are used mainly with loop constructs. This way, the result set from the cursor can be processed. The construct to use is the cursor **FOR** loop. Using this type of loop means that you do not need to use the **OPEN**, **FETCH**, and **CLOSE** statements, as these are implicitly done through the **FOR** loop. Listing 12.3 is an example.

Listing 12.3   A cursor FOR loop.

```
DECLARE
   CURSOR c1 IS
      SELECT product_name, unit_price FROM products;
BEGIN
   FOR prod_rec IN c1 LOOP
      price_total :=  price_total + emp_rec.unit_price;
   END LOOP;
```

This listing shows a PL/SQL block that adds up all of the **Unit_Price**s within the **PRODUCTS** table and stores the results in a variable called **price_total**. As you can see, the cursor is not opened nor a **FETCH** statement used. This is implicitly done, as is the defining of **prod_rec** using the %**ROWTYPE** attribute. The loop construct opens the cursor, executes it, fetches each value for the **Unit_Price**, and calculates the **price_total**. Once all rows have been fetched, the cursor is closed.

Loops

One of the major advantages to using PL/SQL is the use of loop constructs. A number of different types of loop constructs are available:

- IF..THEN..ELSE
- FOR..LOOP

- WHILE..LOOP
- EXIT..WHEN
- GOTO

IF..THEN..ELSE

You use the **IF..THEN..ELSE** construct when a decision has to be made depending upon the value of a database column or variable. For example, you may want to add sales tax to an item if the **Unit_Price** is greater than a predefined value, as shown in Listing 12.4. The **IF** clause checks the value of the expression. If the expression is evaluated to be true, the statements following the **THEN** clause are executed; if the expression is evaluated to be false, the statements following the **ELSE** clause are executed. The **ENDIF** statement ends the **IF..THEN..ELSE** construct.

Listing 12.4 *An example **IF..THEN..ELSE** construct.*

```
DECLARE
 price NUMBER(7,2);
 sales_tax_1 CONSTANT NUMBER(2,2) := 30.00;
 sales_tax_2 CONSTANT NUMBER(2,2) := 10.00;
BEGIN
 SELECT unit_price INTO price FROM products
   FOR UPDATE OF unit_price;
 IF price > 30 THEN
   UPDATE products
     SET unit_price = ((unit_price * sales_tax_1 / 100) + unit_price)
     WHERE unit_price = price;
 ELSE
   UPDATE products
     SET unit_price = ((unit_price * sales_tax_2 / 100) + unit_price)
     WHERE unit_price = price;
 ENDIF;
 COMMIT;
END;
```

This example shows that all **Unit_Price**s greater than 30 have the **Sales_Tax_1** percentage added to them. All **Unit_Price**s less than or equal to 30 have the **Sales_Tax_2** percentage added to them.

FOR..LOOP

The **FOR..LOOP** construct allows you to loop a specific number of times. For example, you could loop once for each product within the **PRODUCTS** table. This statement is useful when updating a lot of information that is dependent upon other information within the database. Listing 12.5 is an example of the **FOR..LOOP**, which simply echoes a line to the screen for each of the iterations.

Listing 12.5   An example *FOR..LOOP*.

```
FOR I IN 1..50 LOOP
 dbms_output('I is equal to '||I);
END LOOP;
```

The **FOR..LOOP** can also be used by specifying the number of times the loop should be executed using a variable, as follows:

```
FOR I IN 1..max_loop LOOP
 dbms_output('I is equal to '||I);
END LOOP;
```

In this example, the loop would run to the value of the **max_loop** variable, which must be defined before the **FOR..LOOP** construct is executed.

WHILE..LOOP

The **WHILE..LOOP** construct is similar to **FOR..LOOP**, except in the way it is processed. With the **WHILE..LOOP** statement, the expression associated with the **WHILE** clause is evaluated each time the construct loops. For each time the expression is true, the statements contained within **WHILE..LOOP** are executed. Once the expression becomes either false or null, the loop is exited. You can think of this construct in the following way: While the statement is true, do the following.... A typical example of the **WHILE..LOOP** statement is shown in Listing 12.6, where records are inserted into a table until a counter reaches a specific value. This type of statement is often used when creating test data for systems.

Listing 12.6   An example *WHILE..LOOP*.

```
DECLARE
 I NUMBER := 1;
BEGIN
 WHILE I <= 100 LOOP
  I := I + 1;
  INSERT INTO TEST VALUES (I);
 END LOOP;
 COMMIT;
END;
```

EXIT WHEN

You can use the **EXIT WHEN** statement within a loop to exit, once a desired condition is met. Listing 12.7 shows a simple loop that exits once a variable is set to the desired value.

When the statement is executed, it checks the value of the **WHEN** clause, and if it is true, it exits the loop; if the condition is false, the loop is executed again, until the condition is true.

Listing 12.7   An example *EXIT WHEN* statement.

```
LOOP
  ...
  I := I + J;
  EXIT WHEN I > 1000;
END LOOP
```

This is an example of an infinite loop—i.e., the loop will continue forever, or until the **EXIT** statement is met. Using the **LOOP** command initiates an infinite loop.

GOTO

Before I explain the **GOTO** statement, I would like to issue a warning about using it. The **GOTO** statement is an unconditional branch, meaning that the processing of your PL/SQL block will be transferred to wherever the **GOTO** statement points. The use of **GOTO** is considered to be a sign of bad programming. Other statements should be used to write the PL/SQL block another way. In other words, avoid using the **GOTO** statement at all costs.

As I mentioned, the **GOTO** statement is an unconditional branch. For the branch to work, you have to give it a place to branch to. This is called a *label*. Labels within PL/SQL are defined by enclosing the label name between << and >>. In your block, you can say **GOTO my_label**, and the processing will continue from the label marked **<<my_label>>**. Listing 12.8 shows an example of this.

Listing 12.8   An example *GOTO* statement.

```
DECLARE
  max_loop CONSTANT NUMBER := 100;
  I NUMBER;
BEGIN
  dbms_output('Processing is here');
  GOTO my_label;
  dbms_output('Now processing is here');

<<my_label>>
  dbms_output('After the GOTO statement');
END;
```

This example always misses the line that echoes "Now processing is here" to the screen, as the **GOTO** statement is used to skip that line of code.

Procedures And Functions

One of the advantages to using Personal Oracle8 is the modular programming available within PL/SQL. Modular programming is accomplished through procedures and functions. Nearly all business processes can be broken down into component parts. These parts can then be coded in PL/SQL as either procedures or functions, called *program units* or *subprograms*. These subprograms can be invoked from other PL/SQL routines and can have parameters passed to them.

Procedures

Up until now, all of the PL/SQL examples in this chapter have used anonymous blocks. Procedures allow you to name a piece of PL/SQL within an anonymous block. This procedure is available to the database only at the time the PL/SQL block is executed—i.e., it is not stored within the database at all. You can pass parameters to the procedure. You must define the parameters with the procedure using either the **IN** or **OUT** operator, which tells PL/SQL which way the parameter is passed. The syntax for creating a procedure is as follows:

```
PROCEDURE procedure_name [(argument1 ...)] IS
local_variable_declarations
BEGIN
executable_section
END procedure_name;
```

For example, a procedure could be written like this:

```
PROCEDURE proc1 (ID VARCHAR2) IS
I NUMBER(7,2);
BEGIN
 I := I + 1;
 ID := I
END proc1
```

Functions

Functions and procedures are similar. The only difference is that a function returns a value, and a procedure does not have to. A function has a similar syntax to that of a procedure:

```
FUNCTION function_name [(argument1 ...)]
RETURN function_datatype IS
local_variable_declarations
BEGIN
executable_section
RETURN function_value
END function_name;
```

In the following example, a function returns the minimum price of a specified product within the **PRODUCTS** table:

```
FUNCTION min_price (price OUT NUMBER)
RETURN NUMBER IS
BEGIN
 select min(unit_price)
  into price
  from products;
END min_price;
```

With both procedures and functions, you can specify whether the variables they pass are used as input or output variables. The types are as follows:

- *IN*—The parameter is used only as an input value; no value is returned. These values cannot be reset within the procedure or function.

- *OUT*—The parameter is used only as an output value. This value cannot be referenced within the procedure or function; it can only be set and returned.

- *IN OUT*—The parameter is used as both an input and output parameter. The value for this type of parameter can be changed at any time.

Stored Procedures And Functions

The previous sections described the creation of procedures and functions as a part of a PL/SQL block. Once the block has finished executing, the procedures and functions are not available again. You can store procedures and functions within the database, however, making them available to all users all of the time. This is done with stored procedures and functions.

Stored Procedures

A stored procedure is the same as a procedure within a PL/SQL block, except that it is available all of the time. You create the procedure from the SQL*Plus command line or through a file, using the **CREATE PROCEDURE** command. The creation of a stored procedure is best done by writing the procedure within an editor, such as Notepad, and then executing the file from within SQL*Plus using the @ command. The syntax for the **CREATE PROCEDURE** command is as follows:

```
CREATE [OR REPLACE] PROCEDURE procedure_name
[argument1 ...] IS
local_variable_declarations
BEGIN
```

```
executable_section
END procedure_name;
```

The main difference between this and any other definition for a procedure is the use of the **OR REPLACE** clause. If a procedure already exists, this clause replaces it and the **CREATE PROCEDURE** command does not fail. Listing 12.9 shows an example of a stored procedure that takes as its input the customer's identification number, then deletes the customer's details from the **CUSTOMERS** table.

Listing 12.9   An example stored procedure.

```
SQL> CREATE OR REPLACE PROCEDURE delete_customer_records (cust_id NUMBER) IS
  2  BEGIN
  3  delete from customers
  4  where customer_id = cust_id;
  5* END delete_customer_records;
SQL> /

Procedure created.
```

The stored procedure created in Listing 12.9 can now be executed within SQL*Plus. All you have to do is call it from the SQL*Plus command line with the **EXECUTE** command, using **Customer_id** as the input to the procedure, as shown in Listing 12.10.

Listing 12.10   Using a stored procedure.

```
SQL> select customer_id,customer_name
  2  from customers;

CUSTOMER_ID CUSTOMER_NAME
----------- ------------------------
      20002 DEF Ltd
      20001 ABC Ltd
      20003 GHI Inc
      20004 JKL Inc
      20005 MNO Ltd
      99999 ZZZZZZZZZZ
      99998 XXXXXXXXXX

7 rows selected.
SQL> execute delete_customer_records(99999);

PL/SQL procedure successfully completed.

SQL> select customer_id,customer_name
  2  from customers;
```

```
CUSTOMER_ID CUSTOMER_NAME
----------- --------------------------------
      20002 DEF Ltd
      20001 ABC Ltd
      20003 GHI Inc
      20004 JKL Inc
      20005 MNO Ltd
      99998 XXXXXXXXXX

6 rows selected.
```

To remove a procedure you no longer need, just use the **DROP PROCEDURE** command followed by the procedure name you wish to drop. If you own the procedure, it will be removed from Personal Oracle8.

Stored Functions

A stored function is, again, similar to a function within a PL/SQL block, with the exception that it is available all of the time. The function is created from the SQL*Plus command line or through a file by using the **CREATE FUNCTION** command. The syntax for that command is as follows:

```
CREATE [OR REPLACE] FUNCTION function_name
[argument1 ...]
RETURN function_datatype IS
local_variable_declarations
BEGIN
executable_section
RETURN function_value
END function_name;
```

The main difference between this and any other definition for a function is, as is the case with stored procedures, the **OR REPLACE** clause (see the previous section on stored procedures for an explanation). Listing 12.11 is an example of a stored function that takes as its input the customer's identification number and returns the number of orders the customer has placed.

Listing 12.11   An example stored function.

```
SQL> CREATE OR REPLACE FUNCTION no_of_orders (cust_id NUMBER) RETURN NUMBER IS
  2    amount NUMBER;
  3    BEGIN
  4    select count(*)
  5    into amount
  6    from orders
  7    where customer_id = cust_id;
  8    RETURN amount;
```

```
  9* END no_of_orders;
 10  /

Function created.
```

This stored function can now be used within SQL*Plus, just as any other function. All you have to do is call it within a **SELECT** statement, using **Customer_id** as the input to the function, as shown in Listing 12.12.

Listing 12.12   Using a stored function.

```
SQL> select * from orders;

 ORDER_ID CUSTOMER_ID ORDER_DAT DISPATCHE ORDER_DUE
 -------- ----------- --------- --------- ---------
   100001       20001 01-Jan-99 10-Jan-99 31-Jan-99
   100002       20001 02-Jan-99 11-Jan-99 31-Jan-99
   100003       20002 01-May-98 09-May-98 31-May-98
   100004       20003 01-Jun-98 03-Jun-98 10-Jun-98
   100005       20004 28-Aug-99 29-Aug-99 30-Sep-99
   100006       20005 28-Aug-99 10-Sep-99 31-Aug-99
   999999       20001 10-Dec-99 15-Dec-99 10-Jan-00
   999998       20001 01-Jan-99 01-Jan-99 01-Jan-99

8 rows selected.

SQL> select no_of_orders(20001)
  2  from dual;

NO_OF_ORDERS(20001)
-------------------
                  4
```

To remove a function you no longer need, just use the **DROP FUNCTION** command followed by the function name you wish to drop. If you own the function, it will be removed from Personal Oracle8.

Dealing With Errors

What happens if you create stored procedures and functions with errors in them? Personal Oracle8 will tell you that the procedure or function was created with compilation errors, as shown in Listing 12.13. This listing creates the same stored function as in Listing 12.11, but with an error in it.

Listing 12.13   Creating a function with errors.

```
SQL> CREATE OR REPLACE FUNCTION no_of_orders (cust_id NUMBER) RETURN NUMBER IS
  2  amount NUMBER;
```

```
  3  BEGIN
  4  select count(*)
  5  into amount
  6  from orders
  7  where customer_id = cust_ids;
  8  RETURN amount;
  9* END no_of_orders;
SQL> /
```

Warning: Function created with compilation errors.

The problem with the stored function occurs in Line 7. The function is still stored within the database, but it is marked as invalid, so no one can use it. To check where the database thinks the problem with your code is, you have to issue the **SHOW ERRORS** command, which will display the reason the database will not compile your PL/SQL block. Listing 12.14 shows an example of this. When the error in Line 7 is corrected, the function compiles with no errors.

Listing 12.14   *Correcting compilation errors.*

```
SQL> show errors
Errors for FUNCTION NO_OF_ORDERS:

LINE/COL ERROR
-------- ----------------------------------------------------------------
4/1      PL/SQL: SQL Statement ignored
7/21     PLS-00201: identifier 'CUST_IDS' must be declared

SQL> CREATE OR REPLACE FUNCTION no_of_orders (cust_id NUMBER) RETURN NUMBER IS
  2  amount NUMBER;
  3  BEGIN
  4  select count(*)
  5  into amount
  6  from orders
  7  where customer_id = cust_ids;
  8  RETURN amount;
  9* END no_of_orders;
SQL> 7
  7* where customer_id = cust_ids;
SQL> c/cust_ids/cust_id
  7* where customer_id = cust_id;
SQL> l
  1  CREATE OR REPLACE FUNCTION no_of_orders (cust_id NUMBER) RETURN NUMBER IS
  2  amount NUMBER;
  3  BEGIN
  4  select count(*)
  5  into amount
  6  from orders
  7  where customer_id = cust_id;
```

```
 8  RETURN amount;
 9* END no_of_orders;
SQL> /

Function created.
```

Reviewing Procedures And Functions

In most cases, once a stored procedure or function has been created, it needs to be updated at some point. To do this, you will need to look at the code that makes up the procedure or function. All of the code for stored procedures and functions is kept within the database. This is accessible to the owner through the use of the view **USER_SOURCE**. This view contains four columns:

- *NAME*—The name of the stored object.

- *TYPE*—The type of stored object—for example, **PACKAGE BODY** or **FUNCTION**.

- *LINE*—The line number.

- *TEXT*—The text for the specified line.

Listing 12.15 shows the user displaying the text for the function and procedures created previously.

Listing 12.15   *Displaying stored procedures and functions code.*

```
SQL> desc sys.user_source
 Name                                Null?    Type
 ----------------------------------- -------- ----
 NAME                                NOT NULL VARCHAR2(30)
 TYPE                                         VARCHAR2(12)
 LINE                                NOT NULL NUMBER
 TEXT                                         VARCHAR2(4000)

SQL> select line,text
  2  from sys.user_source
  3  where name = 'NO_OF_ORDERS'
  4  order by line;

 LINE TEXT
 ---- -------------------------------------------------------
    1 FUNCTION no_of_orders (cust_id NUMBER) RETURN NUMBER IS
    2 amount NUMBER;
    3 BEGIN
    4 select count(*)
    5 into amount
    6 from orders
```

```
  7 where customer_id = cust_id;
  8 RETURN amount;
  9 END no_of_orders;

9 rows selected.
SQL> select line,text
  2  from sys.user_source
  3  where name = 'DELETE_CUSTOMER_RECORDS'
  4  order by line;

 LINE TEXT
 ---- ---------------------------------------------------------
    1 PROCEDURE delete_customer_records (cust_id NUMBER) IS
    2 BEGIN
    3 delete from customers
    4 where customer_id = cust_id;
    5 END;
```

As you can see, the user **SYS** owns the view **USER_SOURCE**. You can execute a script, called *catdbsyn.sql*, that resides, in a normal installation, in C:\ORAWIN95\RDBMS80\ADMIN. This file will create all of the synonyms required for your user. You can run this script from any account. It also gives you access to the DBA views mentioned in Chapter 17.

Packages

Packages let you collect related procedures and functions and bundle them under one name—for example, a package called **ORDERS_PKG** would contain all procedures and functions related to orders. All packages within PL/SQL are made up of two parts: a package header or specification and a package body. Using packages within your applications has several advantages:

- *Modularity*—All related procedures and functions can be stored within one package, so you always know where they are stored.

- *Better performance*—Using packages results in better performance. The first time the package is used, it is loaded into memory. That means the next time the package is accessed, no disk I/O will take place, because the code is resident within memory.

- *Security*—You can hide package information, if desired. For example, you may have a package that contains two functions and a procedure; if only the two functions are made public, then the package will not be seen by other users.

- *Easier design*—Applications can be designed in a more modular fashion with packages.

Package Headers

The package header, or the specification of the package, is created using the **CREATE PACK-AGE** statement. The package header specifies and defines what appears within the package itself—for example, it would define all of the functions and procedures the package body uses. The syntax for creating a simple package header or specification is as follows:

```
CREATE [OR REPLACE] PACKAGE package_name IS
[[function_declarations...][procedure_declarations ...]]
END package_name;
```

Listing 12.16 is an example of a simple package header, where the package contains the previously defined procedure and function.

Listing 12.16   *Defining a simple package.*

```
SQL> CREATE OR REPLACE PACKAGE chapter12_pkg IS
  2   function no_of_orders (cust_id NUMBER) RETURN NUMBER;
  3   procedure delete_customer_records (cust_id NUMBER);
  4* END chapter12_pkg;
  5   /

Package created.
```

Package Bodies

The package body is where the functions and procedures defined in the package header are actually created. The package body can contain public and private objects. A *public object* is a function or procedure that can be seen and used by all users; a *private object* is a function or procedure that can be seen or used by only the owner of the package. The syntax for creating a package body is:

```
CREATE [OR REPLACE] PACKAGE BODY package_name IS
declaration_section
function_body ...
package_body ...
initialization
END package_name;
```

This specification for a simple package would have a package body specified, as shown in Listing 12.17.

Listing 12.17   *Defining a simple package body.*

```
SQL>CREATE OR REPLACE PACKAGE BODY chapter12_pkg IS
  2   function no_of_orders (cust_id NUMBER) RETURN NUMBER IS
  3    amount NUMBER;
```

```
 4  BEGIN
 5    select count(*)
 6    into amount
 7    from orders
 8    where customer_id = cust_id;
 9    RETURN amount;
10  END no_of_orders;
11  procedure delete_customer_records (cust_id NUMBER) IS
12  BEGIN
13    delete from customers
14    where customer_id = cust_id;
15  END delete_customer_records;
16* END chapter12_pkg;
17  /
```

```
Package body created.
```

As you can see, the package body contains all of the code for the stored procedure and stored function defined previously. If you look at the syntax for creating a package body, you will see that there is an initialization section. This is optional; I do not use it in the example. The initialization section is executed only once—the first time the package is used. This is useful for adding auditing commands to enter rows in tables.

A number of packages that you may find useful come with Personal Oracle8. The following sections describe some of them, along with several suggested uses.

DBMS_STANDARD

The **DBMS_STANDARD** package lets you interact with Personal Oracle8. Its main use is to let you raise unhandled exceptions and pass error messages and codes back to your applications. This is explained further in a later section.

DBMS_OUTPUT

The **DBMS_OUTPUT** package lets you echo text to a SQL*Plus session. This is done by using the **put_line** procedure, which echoes a line of text to the screen. To view the text, you first have to set the **SERVEROUTPUT** parameter to **ON** within SQL*Plus. This package is useful for debugging PL/SQL blocks to echo values of variables.

DBMS_PIPE

Oracle can use a feature called *Named Pipes*, which provides a way of sending information through a pipe to another session. This feature is used mainly in multiuser environments. The **DBMS_PIPE** package allows you to send and receive messages through Named Pipes. For more information on Named Pipes, refer to your Oracle documentation.

UTL_FILE

The **UTL_FILE** package allows Personal Oracle8 to read and write operating-system text files. To open a file within your operating system, you would issue the **FOPEN** command. Then, for instance, you could issue a **put_line** procedure to create a line of text within the file or the **get_line** procedure to read a line from a file.

UTL_HTTP

The **UTL_HTTP** package allows Personal Oracle8 to interact with the Hypertext Transfer Protocol (HTTP) to retrieve information from the Internet or make calls to Oracle WebServer. You can call different Uniform Resource Locators (URLs) and retrieve data, usually in Hypertext Markup Language (HTML).

DBMS_SQL

DBMS_SQL allows PL/SQL to issue SQL statements dynamically at runtime.

DBMS_ALERT

DBMS_ALERT allows you to use database triggers (explained in the next section) to alert you to specific predefined problems. For example, in a stock-control system, you could use this package to check the stock level; if it dropped below a specified level, it would raise an alert to let you know to order more stock.

DBMS_JOB

The **DBMS_JOB** package is a way of executing a statement at predefined times. This acts very much like cron in a Unix system. **DBMS_JOB** acts as a scheduler for executing tasks. The package has a number of procedures, including:

- *submit*—Submits a job to the queue.
- *remove*—Removes a job from the queue.
- *change*—Changes details of a job within the queue.
- *interval*—Changes the interval in which the job executes.
- *run*—Runs the specified job now.

When using **DBMS_JOB**, you can query the view **DBA_JOBS** to find which jobs are in the queue and the view **DBA_JOBS_RUNNING** to find which jobs are running.

These packages are just a few of those supplied by Oracle. To find more information on the other available packages, you can look in the files beginning with DBMS in the C:\ORAWIN95\RDBMS80\ADMIN directory.

Database Triggers

A database trigger is a procedure that is associated with a table. It is an action triggered once a predefined threshold has been met. For example, you could have a database trigger that inserts an audit record in an audit table whenever a record is inserted into the **CUSTOMERS** table. You can fire a trigger on any of the following actions:

- BEFORE INSERT
- AFTER INSERT
- BEFORE UPDATE
- AFTER UPDATE
- BEFORE DELETE
- AFTER DELETE

The main use for database triggers is to provide audit information. The trigger shown in Listing 12.18 creates an audit record in the **MESSAGES** table when a record is inserted into the **CUSTOMERS** table.

Listing 12.18   *An example of an audit database trigger.*

```
SQL> create or replace trigger customers_audit
  2    after insert on customers
  3    for each row
  4  begin
  5    insert into messages
  6      select sysdate,'Row Inserted into CUSTOMERS table.' from dual;
  7* end;
SQL> /

Trigger created.

SQL> select * from messages;

no rows selected

SQL> insert into customers values
  2* (99997,'AAAAA','AAAAA','AAAAA','AAAAA','AAAAA',12345,'AAAAA')
SQL> /

1 row created.

SQL> select * from messages;

MESSAGE_D MESSAGE_TEXT
--------- -----------------------------------------------------------
06-Feb-98 Row Inserted into CUSTOMERS table.
```

Error Handling And Exceptions

In PL/SQL, errors can occur when reading and looping finding records. For example, what happens when you reach the end of the records returned? This is where the exception- and error-handling functionality comes into play. As I stated at the beginning of this chapter, a PL/SQL block has an optional section for exceptions. An exception is defined within your PL/SQL block. When you encounter an error that you may have been expecting, you can raise the exception and exit your PL/SQL block gracefully.

Listing 12.19 shows an example of an exception being defined and raised through a PL/SQL block.

Listing 12.19 *Using exceptions within PL/SQL blocks.*

```
DECLARE
    tel_no_missing EXCEPTION;  -- declares the exception
BEGIN
    IF telephone_number IS NULL THEN
        RAISE tel_no_missing;  -- raises the exception
    ELSE
        DBMS_OUTPUT.PUT_LINE(...)
    END IF;
EXCEPTION
    WHEN tel_no_missing THEN
        -- issue an error message
```

In this example, you can see that in the declaration section, I specifically assign an exception called **tel_no_missing**. This exception is not given any data-type declaration. In the executable section of the PL/SQL block, I test if the telephone number exists; if it does not, then I raise the exception declared previously. Processing then stops in the executable section and is transferred to the exception section, where the action to issue an error message is taken. Notice that I have used comments within the listing. A comment in PL/SQL is prefixed with a double dash (--), which tells the interpreter to ignore anything following on the same line.

WHAT HAVE YOU LEARNED?

In this chapter, I have given you a brief overview of what is involved with PL/SQL. The scope of this book does not cover PL/SQL programming in great detail, as numerous good books have already been written on the subject. This chapter, however, should give you a taste for what is involved and what you can achieve by using the procedural option in the best way. The next chapter will introduce you to the various object-oriented features available for use within Oracle8.

Advanced Database Design And Programming

Learn more about Oracle8's object-oriented features.

In Chapter 11, I discussed the use of views, sequences, and synonyms, which are some of the basic objects Oracle uses to view and handle your data. This chapter will introduce you to the object-oriented features of Oracle8. I say Oracle8 here and not Personal Oracle8, because not all object features are available within Personal Oracle8 in the current release (V8.0.3). Later releases will have more object functionality. This chapter describes the progression of the Oracle database from a purely relational database to the object-relational database.

BACK TO BASICS

I'll start with a short history lesson on the roots of this object-relational database. The Oracle version 6 database, which was released many moons ago, was one of the first relational databases (as we now know them). This was followed closely, in about 1994, by the release of Oracle7, which was, and still is, one of the best databases to use for large-scale applications. Oracle7 was a purely relational database.

With the release of Oracle8, we now have an object-relational database, which is a relational database with objects added on as an option. There has been some debate within the industry whether future databases should be purely object-oriented or object-relational in nature. Oracle has taken the approach that the object-relational database has the best chance to succeed in the database market. The company reached this decision, I believe, because of the following reasons:

- The migration path for an existing user (with Oracle7) is far easier. Because the underlying layer of the database is still relational—the objects option is just another layer of the database—relational databases will still function better in Oracle8. Also, once the existing database is migrated to Oracle8, you can enhance it by adding more object features, thereby leaving the path open for Oracle to create a pure object-oriented database for Oracle9.

- Ad-hoc queries are not generally supported on existing object-oriented databases. One of the big advantages Oracle7 and 8 have is their ability to use SQL to query the database. Most companies could not survive if this feature were taken away.

- Oracle's existing design tools would have to be rewritten to embrace the object technology. This is a major task, because Oracle has some of the best design tools around at the moment.

- End users have more power at their fingertips if the best parts of the object technology are paired with one of the best relational databases. This gives you the best of both worlds.

Objects And Behavior

Objects are talked about a lot; some people talk about them without really knowing what they are. An *object* is simply the representation, in software, of a way of doing tasks. For example, an object could be the creation of an order in a bookstore; it could be the customer who is buying the book. In a relational database, the process of the customer placing an order at the bookstore would involve about six or seven different tables and all of the associated links. If the process for the order changed, the programmer would have to change some or all of the tables. With the object, properties are expected to change, and the object copes with the change automatically. Objects with similar properties and behaviors can be grouped together in a *class*. Classes are usually described as templates for objects.

DEFINING OBJECT ORIENTATION

For an item to be part of the object-oriented model, it must support these five methods:

- Polymorphism
- Encapsulation
- Extensibility
- Inheritance
- Aggregate objects

These are the ground rules for any object-oriented database. These methods are defined within Oracle8, to a varying degree, and are described in more detail in the following sections.

Polymorphism

Polymorphism is the ability of multiple objects to react differently to the same message. To put it in a real-world context, consider two people lying in the sun on a beach: One gets a tan, but the other burns. That is polymorphism.

Oracle8 provides a method of polymorphism by using procedures or functions. For example, you can create a procedure that reacts differently depending on the parameters that are passed to it. If two numeric parameters were passed to a procedure, it could add them together, whereas if two date parameters were passed to the procedure, it could give you the number of days between the two dates. This allows for a standard interface to a related group of objects—in this case, either the addition of two numbers or the subtraction of two dates.

Encapsulation

One of the basic methods for object-orientation is encapsulation—the ability of an object to have a well-defined interface and distinct borders with other objects. You can think of this as a procedure having local variables that can be accessed only within that procedure. Encapsulation has the added advantage of security, as other procedures cannot access any of the variables within another procedure. Think of objects as collections of code grouped together to do a specific job. Encapsulation could be implemented using database triggers, but this is not really practical because you would have to use too many triggers, which would reduce the performance of the database.

Encapsulation declares that an object can be accessed only through its methods. For example, to add an item to an order, you would call the relevant procedure, which in turn would check the available stock, and if enough were available, add the line to the order. With SQL, you can add the line to the order without checking the stock details. You can say that encapsulation cannot be implemented within a relational database. This is a "feature" of Oracle8. (A "feature" is something that Oracle has not yet implemented.)

Extensibility

Extensibility is the ability of a database to be extended using objects, without affecting any other existing objects within the database. This means all objects must be independent of each other. This makes a database very powerful, because you can add new objects without affecting other objects. Extensibility is used with class hierarchies, which are not implemented with Oracle8 until version 8.2.

Inheritance

Inheritance can be thought of as the sharing of code. For example, you could create an object that uses inherited features for another object definition. This is like a hierarchy where you have an object at the top, and all objects below are based, to some extent, upon the features of the top object. Two different types of inheritance exist:

- *Data inheritance*—Where data can inherit attributes from other data within the same class.

- *Function-object inheritance*—Where objects or functions can inherit attributes from other objects or functions within the same class.

Using inheritance, you can take advantage of other objects that have been created with similar behavior to the one being created. Inheritance is not due to be introduced to the Oracle8 database until version 8.2.

Aggregate Objects

You can define aggregate objects with Oracle8. An *aggregate object* is made up from object IDs that can quickly be retrieved from the database at runtime, resulting in better performance from the Oracle8 database. Aggregate objects are similar to views, in that they are made up at execution time. These aggregate objects can also be preassembled and stored within the database, ready to use.

Data And Behavior

Within Oracle8, new constructs allow you to couple data and behavior. For example, say you have a customer who wants to buy a car. Once the customer has chosen the car, he or she elects to use a credit card to pay for it. In this instance, a package could be set up as follows:

```
CUSTOMER.credit_card(123-456-7890,30000)
```

This statement would instruct the database to check the credit card details, so the customer could see if he or she could afford the car. Notice that no SQL is used. The access to the data is done through the use of a procedure—in this case, the **customer** procedure and the **credit_card** subprogram. Eventually, all applications can be coded like this, using objects to access and retrieve information from the database. Listing 13.1 is an example of the process of buying a car.

Listing 13.1 *Example process of buying a car.*

```
BEGIN

CAR.make_and_model('Ford Mustang');
CUSTOMER.details(xxx,yyy,zzz);
CUSTOMER.payment_method;

IF credit_card THEN
 CUSTOMER.credit_card(123-456-7890,30000);
 IF credit_check = 'BAD'
   EXIT 1
 FI
 CAR.price;
ELSE IF cash THEN
 CAR.price - 20%;
FI

END
```

ABSTRACT DATA TYPES

Oracle7 limited the number of data types you were allowed to use. Oracle8 has no such limits, because you can make up your own data types, known as abstract data types or user-defined types. You can create these user-defined types using existing data types or other user-defined types. For example, in a college records system, you could create an address as a data type. Listing 13.2 is an example of a user-defined data type for addresses.

Listing 13.2 *Creating a user-defined data type for addresses.*

```
CREATE TYPE address
(Address_Line_1 varchar2(20),
 Address_Line_2 varchar2(20),
 City           varchar(20),
 State          char(2),
 Zip_Code       char(5));
```

Once the user-defined data type **ADDRESS** is created, you can create other objects that have a data type of **ADDRESS**. For example, Listing 13.3 shows the college records system **REPORT_CARD_HEADER** table, using the **ADDRESS** data type.

Listing 13.3 *The college records REPORT_CARD_HEADER table.*

```
CREATE TABLE report_card_header
(SURNAME       varchar2(20) NOT NULL,
 FORENAME      varchar2(20),
 HOME_ADDRESS address);
```

User-defined types have certain advantages when handling multimedia objects such as sound and video clips. Oracle8 allows you to implement data types that fit into more categories than just **NUMBER** or **CHAR**.

Object types are the different processes found in real life—for example, the issuing of a purchase order could be described as an object type. All object types have three components:

- *Name*—Identifies the object type within the user's schema.

- *Attribute*—The built-in types and definitions of the object type.

- *Methods*—The actual code and functions that perform the associated tasks of the object type. These are usually written in PL/SQL, C, or C++. Methods actually do what the object type describes.

The example in Listing 13.4 shows how you may define the relevant objects with user-defined data types and objects.

Listing 13.4 *Defining data types in the customer/order example.*

```
CREATE TYPE customer AS OBJECT (
  cname         VARCHAR2(20),
  phone         VARCHAR2(10)) ;

CREATE TYPE order_item AS OBJECT (
  item_name    VARCHAR2(30),
  quantity     NUMBER,
  price        NUMBER(8,2)) ;
```

```
CREATE TYPE order_item_table AS TABLE OF order_item ;

CREATE TYPE order AS OBJECT (
   id              NUMBER,
   contact         customer,
   order_items     order_item_table,
   MEMBER FUNCTION
   check_stock     RETURN NUMBER ) ;
```

OBJECT TABLES

Object tables are special tables used to store objects, which can be viewed through the relational structure of a database. For example, to create an object table called **CUSTOMER_DETAILS**, you could issue the following statement:

```
CREATE TABLE customer_details OF customer;
```

In Listing 13.4, I created an object type named **CUSTOMER**. This has been used here to create a table that stores customer details (in this case, names and telephone numbers from the definition of the type **CUSTOMER**). Once the table is created, you can view it in two different ways: either as a single-column table or by looking at the customer name and telephone number in different columns—i.e., you can access the object as one piece of information or by the fields it contains.

Listing 13.5 first inserts a row into the table (notice it uses two columns; it is inserting data into the table as if it has two distinctly different columns) and then selects the details just inserted, using one query column.

Listing 13.5   Using object tables.

```
INSERT INTO customer_details VALUES ("Richard Fieldhouse","1234567890");

SELECT value(c)
FROM customer_details c
WHERE c.cname="Richard Fieldhouse";
```

Row Objects And Column Objects

Rows that are inserted into object tables are known as *row objects*; objects that appear in the columns of object tables are called *column objects*. Each row object receives a unique object identifier (OID); these identifiers are not documented. OIDs allow other objects to reference objects from within tables. The data type used to reference OIDs is **REF**. The **REF** data type references row objects of specific object types. Accessing objects using the **REF** data type is called *de-referencing the REF*, or **DEREF**. You can obtain the **REF** by selecting it from the object, as in Listing 13.6.

Listing 13.6   Obtaining the REF.

```
DECLARE order_ref REF to orders;

SELECT ref(o)
INTO order_ref
FROM orders o
WHERE o.order_id = 10001;
```

Variable Arrays

An array is an ordered set of data elements, all with the same data types. Each element is allocated an index number as to its position within the array. The number of elements inserted into the array defines its size. An array is a beneficial way of storing data. It is a common construct within other programming languages, such as C++.

A variable array is an array of a variable size. Within Oracle, a variable array is known as a **VARRAY**. When specifying a variable array, you always have to specify its maximum size. Listing 13.7 shows the definition of a **VARRAY** called **product_prices**. It will allow a maximum of 50 entries, all of which are of the data type **NUMBER(8,2)**. Data can then be inserted into the **VARRAY**.

Listing 13.7   Defining a VARRAY.

```
CREATE TYPE product_prices AS VARRAY(50) OF NUMBER(8,2);
```

Once the **VARRAY** has been created, no data storage is defined, because the **VARRAY** is defined within the database as a data type. You can use this data type in any of the following ways:

- Object type attribute
- A variable within PL/SQL
- A data type within a table
- A parameter to a function or procedure

The **VARRAY** can also be thought of as the way to implement repeating groups. You can implement repeating groups two ways within Oracle8: either with repeating groups of data items or with OIDs.

Pointers To Tables

A pointer to a table can be thought of as a cell within a table pointing to another table; this scenario is also called *nesting tables*. These pointers have to be unique; therefore, you may use the **ROWID** found within a table, because the **ROWID** points to a row uniquely. The only problem with using a **ROWID** is that it points to a specific physical location—i.e., a file and block number. This piece of information could be moved, thereby giving it a different **ROWID**.

Oracle gets around this problem by giving each row an object ID. This OID stays with the object at all times; therefore, you can access the object with the same OID every time, no matter where the object is placed within the database. Also, if the data is deleted, the OID is also deleted and will never be used again, making it impossible to reference another object accidentally.

OBJECT VIEWS

In Chapter 11, I discussed the concept of the Oracle view as a virtual table made up at execution time. An *object view* is the same, except it is a virtual object table. Object views allow you to manipulate data as in a relational database, but through the concept of object types, as discussed previously. Object views can contain other object data types, such as **VARRAY** and **REF**. By using object views, you can create virtual object tables from data held within object types. Just as in normal views, object views allow you to restrict access to the data held within a number of object tables. Object views allow you to:

- Use relational data within object-oriented applications

- Prototype object-oriented programs without altering relational structures

- Seamlessly convert existing relational models

- Use existing systems with object-oriented add-ons

Using object views has a number of advantages:

- Increased performance

- Easy mapping to existing programming languages, such as C++

- Easy migration path for existing applications

- Ability of existing applications to use object-oriented design

Listing 13.8 is an example of creating an object view.

Listing 13.8 Creating an object view.

```
CREATE TABLE orders
(order_id   NUMBER(3),
 order_name VARCHAR2(20),
 order_date DATE);

CREATE TYPE order_t
(order_id   NUMBER(3),
 order_name VARCHAR2(20),
 order_date DATE);

CREATE VIEW order_view OF order_t
WITH OBJECT OID (order_id) AS
SELECT o.order_id,o.order_name,o.order_date
FROM orders o
WHERE order_date > '01-JAN-1990';
```

In this listing, the object view looks, to the user, like an object table (based on the type **order_t**), with each row having a unique OID. Referencing the object view is done as with any other view—i.e., through a **SELECT** statement. Object views can also be defined from other object views, just as a view can be defined from another view.

Inserting and updating data in an object view are no different than in a normal view. You simply use a SQL statement to update the data, and the base objects are updated, assuming there is no ambiguous data. A view is not updatable if it contains any of the following:

- Joins
- Set operators
- **GROUP BY**
- Group functions
- **DISTINCT**
- Any pseudo columns, such as **RowNum**

If any of these are found within the object view, it is deemed nonupdatable. The way around this is through a special type of trigger (triggers are defined later in this chapter), known as an **INSTEAD OF** trigger. It is so named because *instead of* using the SQL statement to update the object view, it executes the body of the trigger, which can update one of the tables directly. This is the best implementation of updating the object view, because the user has no idea what is happening behind the scenes.

NESTED TABLES

A *nested table* is a set of data of the same data type. It has a single column whose type is either built-in or an object type. As discussed previously, if the nested table has a data type of object type, you can view the columns individually.

PARTITIONED TABLES

Partitioned tables are used independently of partitioned views (see Chapter 11 for details about partitioned views). They came into being with version 7.3 of Oracle's database. A *partitioned table* is made up of multiple tables, all of which have the same structure. Suppose you created three address tables to store customer information. In the first table, you stored all surnames between *A* and *H*; in the second, all surnames between *I* and *Q*; and in the third, all surnames between *R* and *Z*. You could use a partitioned view to view all of the tables as a whole (see Chapter 11). Listing 13.9 is an example of creating a partitioned view.

Listing 13.9 *Creating the base tables for a partitioned view.*

```
SQL> create table surname_a_h
  2  (surname    varchar2(20),
  3* city       varchar2(20));

Table created.

SQL> create table surname_i_q
  2  as select * from surname_a_h;

Table created.

SQL> create table surname_r_z
  2  as select * from surname_a_h;

Table created.

SQL> alter table surname_a_h
  2* add constraint con1 check(upper(substr(surname,1,1)) between 'A' and 'H');

Table altered.

SQL> alter table surname_i_q
  2  add constraint con2 check(upper(substr(surname,1,1)) between 'I' and 'Q');

Table altered.
```

```
SQL> alter table surname_r_z
  2  add constraint con3 check(upper(substr(surname,1,1)) between 'R' and 'Z');

Table altered.

SQL> create view surname as
  2  select * from surname_a_h
  3  union all
  4  select * from surname_i_q
  5  union all
  6  select * from surname_r_z;

View created.
```

In the example, three tables hold surname information; this can be broken down into one table with three partitions—one for each group of surnames. Listing 13.10 shows an example of this table being created.

Listing 13.10   Creating the **SURNAME_PART** partitioned table.

```
SQL> create table surname_part
  2  ( surname varchar(15),
  3    city    varchar(20))
  4  partition by range (surname)
  5  (partition surname_a_h values less than ('H'),
  6   partition surname_i_q values less than ('Q'),
  7   partition surname_r_z values less than ('Z'),
  8*  partition other values less than (maxvalue))
SQL> /

Table created.
```

Listing 13.11 is a different example of a table that collects information for sales analysis.

Listing 13.11   Creating the **SALES_INFO** table.

```
SQL> create table sales_info
  2  ( account_number    number(3),
  3    sales_month       number(2),
  4    total_sales       number(9,2))
  5  partition by range (sales_month)
  6  (partition sales_month1 values less than (2),
  7   partition sales_month2 values less than (3),
  8   partition sales_month3 values less than (4),
  9   partition sales_month4 values less than (5),
 10   partition sales_month5 values less than (6),
 11   partition sales_month6 values less than (7),
 12   partition sales_month7 values less than (8),
 13   partition sales_month8 values less than (9),
```

```
14    partition sales_month9 values less than (10),
15    partition sales_month10 values less than (11),
16    partition sales_month11 values less than (12),
17    partition sales_month12 values less than (13)
18*   partition other values less than (maxvalue))
SQL> /

Table created.
```

With this table, you can see how partitioned tables come into their own. Normally, all of the data would have to be stored in a single table. By using partitions, you can store different parts of the data in different places—i.e., different tablespaces. Partitioning has these advantages:

- Reduces the possibility of data corruption, because the data is spread over many partitions. This also indirectly decreases the amount of downtime for the database.

- Increases performance, because different partitions can be spread over different disk drives, evening out the load.

- Permits independent backup and recovery of partitions.

- Allows the database to support large tables.

- Allows you to support highly intensive queries against your data.

CLUSTERS

Clusters are another method used to store data within tables. A *cluster* is a group of tables that have common columns and are often used together within queries. In the example database, the **SUPPLIERS** and **PRODUCTS** tables have a common column, **Supplier_id**. This could be used to cluster the two tables together. When clustering two tables, Oracle stores the rows for each corresponding row within the same data block in the tablespace. Because the data is stored close together, using clusters has a number of advantages:

- *Reduction in disk I/O*—The disk movement is reduced, so the join times for queries are less.

- *Reduction in the amount of data stored*—When creating a cluster, you have to specify the cluster key—in the example, it would be **Supplier_id**. When the cluster is created, the cluster key is stored only once, whereas, normally, it would be stored twice: once in the **SUPPLIERS** table and once in the **PRODUCTS** table.

Clusters are used mainly when performance is an issue. Clusters can reduce the performance of **INSERT** statements, so use clusters only in high-query databases. Implementing clusters properly is important, because not all tables with common columns are ideal candidates for clustering. The best way to identify tables that could be clustered is to look for those that are referenced within referential integrity constraints and those that are regularly accessed via a join. If you cluster tables that are joined regularly, you cut down on the number of blocks Oracle has to search for the data, therefore improving the performance of the database. If the cluster key is updated regularly, the data has to be moved from block to block. Because this is the key everything is clustered upon, this would decrease performance.

Clusters are similar to indexes (see Chapter 17), in that they alter the way that Oracle accesses the data in the database, but not the data itself. Users do not know they are using a cluster, because all of the processing is transparent.

Cluster Keys

The cluster key is the column(s) that the tables have in common. You specify the cluster key when creating the cluster. You specify the cluster key again when adding tables to the cluster. The maximum number of columns allowable within the cluster key is 16. For each column specified within the cluster key, when a table is entered into the cluster, this key must exist within the table; otherwise, an error occurs.

Cluster Indexes

Once you have created the cluster, you have to create an index on the cluster key. This is known as a *cluster index*. It must exist on the table before any SQL statement can be executed upon the cluster. Oracle uses the cluster index to locate the block where the data is stored. You should create the cluster index in a different tablespace from that of the cluster, because this will also increase performance. Cluster indexes differ from normal indexes in the following ways:

- Even null keys have an entry in the index.
- Cluster indexes contain one entry per cluster key.
- Clusters cannot be accessed if the cluster index is not present.

If the cluster index is accidentally dropped, the data remains within the table, but the users will have no access to it until the cluster index is reinstated.

Hash Clusters

Hash clusters are another way of storing data within a table. They increase the performance of decision support systems (DSSs), which have a high number of queries executed against them. Hash clusters are similar to normal clusters. You create a hashed cluster and add tables to the hashed cluster in the normal fashion. This hashing function generates a spread of numbers (called *hash values*) that are based on cluster-key values. A hash cluster key can either be single or multiple columns. For Oracle to find any given row, it reads the hash cluster key and applies the hash function to it. This gives the data block that the row is stored in, and Oracle reads that block to retrieve the row.

Within a hash cluster, data is stored within the same block where the rows are related (based upon their hash value). This is different from the normal cluster, where rows are stored in relation to the cluster key.

DATABASE TRIGGERS

Database *triggers* are procedures that are executed when a specific action is performed. The action fires the trigger, and the trigger executes a piece of code (a stored procedure), which then does *x*. For example, you can fire a trigger when data is inserted into the **ORDERS** table, stating who performed the update and when it took place.

As discussed here, triggers are similar to stored procedures, explained in detail in Chapter 12. Procedures and triggers differ only in the way they are executed. A procedure is specifically executed by an application or a user, whereas a trigger is executed upon the modification of data. The actions that fires the trigger can be one of the following:

- **INSERT**
- **UPDATE**
- **DELETE**

Triggers can be defined against tables only, not views. If a trigger is defined against the base table of the view and an update to the table takes place, the trigger will fire on the base table. The trigger information is stored separately from the table information. Triggers are used in a number of different ways within an Oracle8 database. Some of their main uses are as follows:

- Generating column values
- Maintaining table access data

- Providing table replication

- Providing the capability to audit specific events

- Enforcing referential integrity

- Enforcing your security policy

- Preventing invalid data entry

For example, you could define a trigger to create an auditing row in the **ORDER_AUDIT** table of the **DEMO** user whenever a new row is inserted into the **ORDERS** table. This can be seen in Listing 13.12.

Listing 13.12 *A database trigger to enforce auditing.*

```
SQL> create or replace trigger order_audit_trg
  2   after insert on orders
  3   for each row
  4   BEGIN
  5     INSERT INTO order_audit values ('This is an audit');
  6* END;
SQL> /

Trigger created.

SQL> select * from order_audit;

no rows selected

SQL> desc orders
 Name                             Null?    Type
 ------------------------------   -------- ----
 ORDER_ID                         NOT NULL NUMBER(6)
 CUSTOMER_ID                      NOT NULL NUMBER(5)
 ORDER_DATE                       NOT NULL DATE
 DISPATCHED_DATE                  NOT NULL DATE
 ORDER_DUE_DATE                   NOT NULL DATE

SQL> insert into orders values
  2   (123456,10002,'30-JAN-99','01-FEB-99','28-FEB-99');

1 row created.

SQL> select * from order_audit;

AUDIT_COMMENT
--------------------
This is an audit
```

The trigger I have defined fires after the row has been inserted into the **ORDERS** table. If, for some reason, the trigger fires and fails to complete, the insert is rolled back and does not take place. The syntax for the **CREATE TRIGGER** command is:

```
CREATE [OR REPLACE] TRIGGER   trigger_name
{BEFORE|AFTER|INSTEAD OF}
{DELETE|INSERT|UPDATE [OF column_name ...]}
ON table_name
```

As you can see from this syntax, a trigger is made up of three distinct parts:

- *An event*—The SQL statement that causes the trigger to fire in the first place. This can be either **INSERT**, **UPDATE**, or **DELETE**. In Listing 13.12, the event is **AFTER INSERT ON ORDERS**.

- *A restriction*—Specifies the expression that must be true for the trigger to fire; in this case, the **FOR EACH ROW** expression is used, which is always true.

- *An action*—The procedure that is executed once the trigger is fired. In this case, it is the **INSERT** statement to the **ORDER_AUDIT** table.

Types Of Triggers

Triggers come in a number of different types:

- *Row triggers*—Fired for each row that is affected by the event.

- *Statement triggers*—Fired once for the statement being executed.

- *BEFORE triggers*—Fired before the action takes place.

- *AFTER triggers*—Fired after the event takes place; these are usually used for auditing.

- *INSTEAD OF triggers*—Provide a way of modifying an object view that cannot be modified directly. With these types of triggers, Oracle executes the trigger instead of executing the trigger statement.

Triggers can be in one of two modes: either enabled or disabled. If a trigger is disabled when the action takes place, the trigger will not fire; if it is enabled, it will fire.

WHAT DO YOU KNOW ABOUT OBJECTS?

In this chapter, I have delved more deeply into the objects layer of Oracle8. I have given you an overview of what is involved in creating and maintaining the many different types of objects. If you need more clarification regarding objects, Oracle's documentation provides many examples. In the next chapter, I discuss how to upgrade an existing Personal Oracle7 database to Personal Oracle8.

Converting A PO7 Database To PO8

This chapter explains the various ways of upgrading to Personal Oracle8 from a Personal Oracle7 database. There are a number of ways to bring a new version of the database onto your PC; this chapter will help you determine which way is the best for you. The chapter covers all of the options available and explains, in detail, the steps involved.

Want to use objects? Upgrade to Personal Oracle8.

OVERVIEW

With the release of Personal Oracle8, Oracle Corporation has provided a new database for users to upgrade to. This database has lots of new features, explained in previous chapters. The main objective of upgrading any database is to ensure a smooth transition from one version to another without losing any data or changing the structure of the database. You can ensure a smooth upgrade to Personal Oracle8 in one of two ways: either by using Oracle's migration utility or by copying the data manually (known as an export and import). This chapter will explain both methods, with hints and tips for using both. You'll want to read through this chapter before deciding upon the strategy for migrating your database.

ORACLE'S MIGRATION UTILITY

Prerequisites

To use Oracle's migration utility, you must ensure that the Personal Oracle7 database on your Windows 95 PC meets the following criteria:

- *The minimum database release is Personal Oracle7 version 7.2.2.1.0*—If the database you have is an earlier version than this, you must either upgrade the database to version 7.3 or use the export and import method.

- *SQL*Net Add-on version 2.0 or above is installed*—If not, install the add-on from the Personal Oracle7 CD-ROM using Oracle Installer.

Once you have a database that meets these minimum requirements, you are ready to use the migration utility to upgrade to Personal Oracle8.

How To Upgrade

Before using the migration utility, you must close down all applications running on your system, including all Personal Oracle7 applications. Make sure the Personal Oracle7 database is closed down. The migration utility needs to start up and reset parameters within the database.

Step 1

As a precautionary step, back up all of your work. If you have the capability to back up the full PC, then do so. You will not need to restore any data back to your PC when the migration utility has finished, but if you find anything wrong with the upgrade, you can start again by restoring the PC to its original state. I cannot stress this enough, as this way of upgrading has caused some problems in the past. After completing the backup, you should read it back into your PC to make sure that it worked. There is nothing worse than having a backup tape or disk fail when you need to restore some information. Most people learn the hard way, like myself, but once you have lost something, you will always make backups of whatever you do.

Step 2

Insert the Personal Oracle8 CD-ROM into the drive. This will automatically invoke the Autorun window, as seen in Figure 1.1 in Chapter 1. From this screen, choose the Begin Installation icon. This will start Oracle Installer, which will ask you for your choice of language. Unless Personal Oracle7 was installed in a different language, the language choice defaults to English (as shown in Figure 1.2 in Chapter 1). Choose the desired language and click on the OK button.

Step 3

This takes you to the Oracle Installation Settings window, where you choose the company name to register the software under and the Oracle home directory you wish to use (refer to Figure 1.3 in Chapter 1). Because you have a previous installation on Windows 95, you will not need to change the Oracle home directory and you shouldn't need to change the company name information. Click on the OK button to continue. The first part of the upgrade is similar to the installation procedure for Personal Oracle8.

Step 4

The Installations Options screen asks which type of installation you will require once the upgrade is complete (see Figure 1.4 in Chapter 1). (The products provided by each of the options are discussed in Chapter 2.) If you need to have the full application available to you, choose the Application Developer option, which installs everything onto your PC. If you wish to remove any part of it, you can use Oracle Installer to do so later. Once you have selected an option, click on the OK button.

Step 5

Oracle Installer now checks your PC to see if any other Oracle products are already installed—in this case, Personal Oracle7 version 7.2 or above. The Installer will prompt you with a message that it has found an earlier version of the database, as shown in Figure 14.1.

In this window, click on the Help button if you want an explanation of the message within the window. Otherwise, click on one of the following buttons for the required action:

- *Yes*—Continue with the automatic migration utility.

- *No*—Continue and perform a manual upgrade once the installation has finished.

- *Cancel*—Abort the upgrade process.

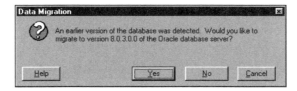

Figure 14.1   *Using the Installer to upgrade from Personal Oracle7.*

If you choose the No button, Oracle Installer will install Personal Oracle8, overwriting everything previously installed. (If you wish to do so, see the section on export and import later in this chapter.) If you choose the Cancel option, Oracle Installer will exit and return you to the Windows 95 desktop. If, however, you choose the Yes option, the automatic migration utility will continue and Oracle Installer will analyze which Oracle products are installed on your PC; this will be indicated on the Oracle Installer screen.

Step 6

A short time after choosing how to proceed with the upgrade, you'll see the Oracle8 Documentation window, shown in Figure 1.6 of Chapter 1. This is where you choose how to have the documentation installed. The answer here will depend on how much free disk space you have. You can install the documentation locally on your hard disk, but if space is at a premium, you may want to select the CD-ROM option. This choice requires that you load the CD-ROM every time you need to access the documentation. Once you have chosen your documentation option, the installer will carry on, analyzing the dependencies, and a progress indication bar will appear on your screen. Personal Oracle8 is now being installed.

Step 7

While the installer is installing the Personal Oracle8 programs to your hard disk, it is checking what you already have installed. In most cases, the SQL*Net Add-on patch will need to be installed. Oracle Installer will automatically do this as part of the migration utility. A message will appear on the screen to indicate this, as shown in Figure 14.2.

Click on the OK button to continue with the migration. This may take a few minutes, depending upon your PC.

Step 8

Once the new Personal Oracle8 programs are installed, you will be presented with a window telling you that the database migration will begin (see Figure 14.3).

Click on the OK button to continue with the migration.

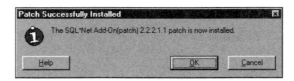

Figure 14.2 *Applying the SQL*Net Add-on patch.*

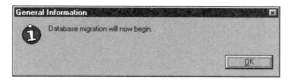

Figure 14.3 *Notification of the migration.*

Step 9

Oracle Installer now starts the Oracle Data Migration Assistant, which will help you with the migration (see Figure 14.4).

This screen displays three active buttons:

- *Cancel*—Aborts the Data Migration Assistant.
- *Help*—Displays information on the Data Migration Assistant.
- *Next*—Navigates to the next screen.

The other buttons are grayed out, but will be available in later screens. Click on the Next button to continue with the migration.

Step 10

The second screen of the Data Migration Assistant is where you choose which database to migrate. In this example, there is only one, shown in Figure 14.5.

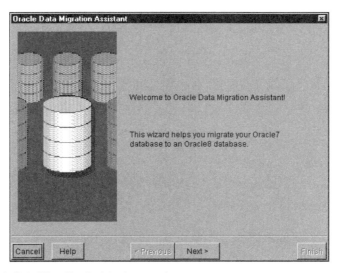

Figure 14.4 *Oracle Data Migration Assistant screen 1.*

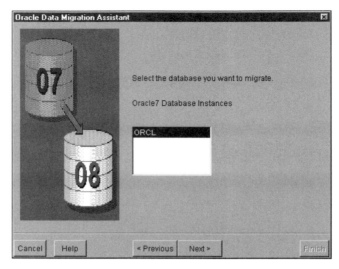

Figure 14.5 *Choose the database to migrate.*

This is the Personal Oracle7 database previously installed, called *ORCL* if you have installed the default Personal Oracle7 database from the CD-ROM. If you have created your own database, you will see the ORACLE_SID for your database, which should already be selected (highlighted in blue). Again, a number of buttons will appear. These are used primarily to navigate from screen to screen. If you have made a mistake and wish to correct it, you can click on the Previous button to go through the previous screens. Once you have selected the correct database, click on the Next button to take you to the next screen.

Step 11

The third screen of the Data Migration Assistant is where you enter the information for the assistant to make changes to your existing database, as shown in Figure 14.6.

The pieces of information required are:

- Database password
- init.ora file name

These two parameters are essential. Without them, the Migration Assistant cannot make any changes to your existing configuration. The database password requires you to give the internal password you set up for the database. init.ora contains the parameters that Oracle uses while starting your database. This file can usually be found in the C:\ORAWIN95\database directory on default installations of Personal Oracle. If yours is not a default installation, use the Browse button to find the init.ora file. It will be called init*database_name*.ora. Once this information is filled in, you may click on the OK button to continue to the next screen.

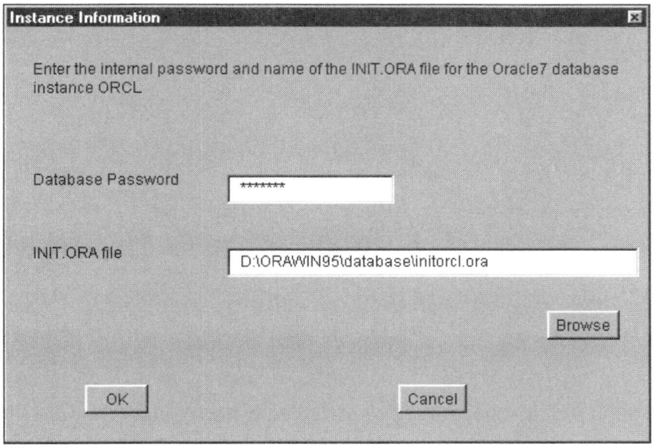

Figure 14.6   *Giving your instance information.*

Step 12

The fourth screen is where the Data Migration Assistant checks to see if you have backed up your database and other files, as shown in Figure 14.7.

On this screen are two boxes. The first is a checkbox; if you leave this box checked, the Data Migration Assistant will make a backup copy of all Oracle files to the directory named in the second box. If you uncheck the box, the Migration Assistant will not do any backup. It is always better to leave the box checked and to provide a directory name for a backup to be

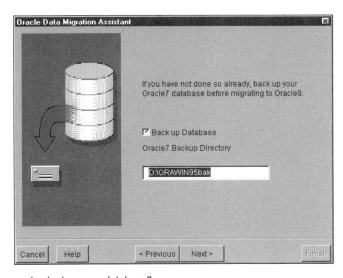

Figure 14.7   *Have you backed up your database?*

done. This should be a supplement to your original backup. Once this is done, click on the Next button to continue.

Step 13

The fifth screen of the Data Migration Assistant is where you may choose an additional national character set for your migrated Personal Oracle8 database, as shown in Figure 14.8.

You don't need to choose an additional national character set for your Personal Oracle8 database. The database character set will automatically be migrated to Personal Oracle8. The national character set, however, is used to display data stored within **NCHAR**, **NVARCHAR2**, and **NCLOB** data types. If you will be viewing information stored within these data types, then you should select the character set required. To do so, simply check the box titled Add National Character Set and select the required set from the list box below. Then click on the Next button to continue to the next screen.

Step 14

When the migration utility starts to migrate your database, it will change lots of database settings. These changes can be stored in a log file for you to review when the migration utility has completed. If you wish to keep a log of the activities of the Data Migration Assistant while it is migrating your database, check the box (see Figure 14.9).

Logging all actions taken by the Data Migration Assistant is always a good idea. This enables you to check if the migration completed without any errors. Take note of the directory it is

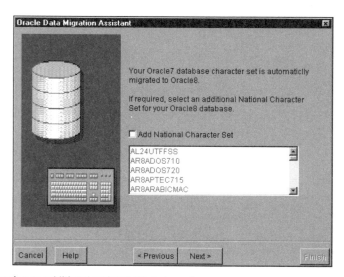

Figure 14.8 *Choosing an additional national character set.*

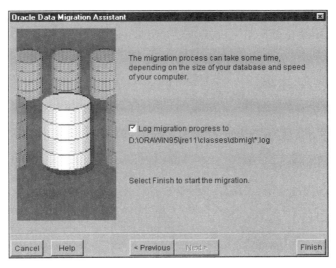

Figure 14.9　*Keeping a log of the activities.*

creating the log file in, usually C:\ORAWIN95\jre11\classes\dbmig in default installations of Personal Oracle8. To complete your migration, click on the Finish button (notice the Next button is grayed out).

While the migration is running, you are presented with a screen that charts its progress, as shown in Figure 14.10.

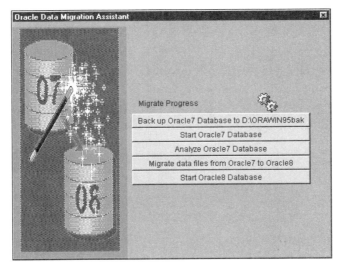

Figure 14.10　*Migrate Progress screen.*

This screen has five blue boxes indicating the actions the Data Migration Assistant must take to migrate your database. The five boxes are as follows:

- Back up Oracle7 Database to *directory_name*

- Start Oracle7 Database

- Analyze Oracle7 Database

- Migrate data files from Oracle7 to Oracle8

- Start Oracle8 Database

These boxes will be grayed out once the Migration Assistant completes each job. This may take some time, as a lot of work is involved in migrating to a different database version. Once in a while, a separate window, called Wait, will appear. This is an application fired up by the migration utility. It requires no action by the user, so you should just wait for it to disappear, usually within a couple of minutes.

Step 15

Once all of the boxes on the Migrate Progress screen are grayed out, the migration is over, and you will see the screen shown in Figure 14.11.

Click on the OK button and the Data Migration Assistant will close, leaving you with the Oracle Installer screen. Again, click on the OK button to tell Oracle Installer that you have finished the session. You will end up at the Windows 95 desktop.

Step 16

At this point, you should check all of the files in the log-file directory, usually C:\ ORAWIN95\jre11\classes\dbmig. All files created on today's date should be checked for errors. Do not be alarmed if you find errors in these files. Some of them may merely report that an object does not exist when it is trying to delete it. You can ignore these types of errors. If all of the files are OK, you can start up your Personal Oracle8 database.

Figure 14.11 *Migration Done window.*

Conclusion

Migrating your database through the Data Migration Assistant, in my experience, is not easy. You will receive lots of errors in the log files, if the migration works at all. I have always found that the easiest way to migrate a database is to use the export and import method. The migration utility has known problems, so I usually recommend using the export and import method, as it is tried and tested. I have found, however, that migrating a purely standard database (one that is a default installation from the Personal Oracle7 CD-ROM) through the migration utility works nine times out of ten.

EXPORT AND IMPORT METHOD

Prerequisites

There are no prerequisites for using the export and import method to migrate a database to Personal Oracle8. You need only to have on your PC the export and import utilities that are part of the standard Personal Oracle7 installation.

How To Upgrade

These utilities are among the most useful backup and restore facilities to use with an Oracle database. They work on databases that are up and running; therefore, you must start up your Personal Oracle7 database before running the utilities. I have included brief descriptions of the function of most parameters where necessary in this chapter, but for full descriptions and examples of the export and import utilities, see Chapter 15, which covers their use and all associated parameters.

To migrate using the export and import method, follow these steps:

Step 1

Check that you have enough existing disk space in which to fit the export file you are about to create. To check how much space the data in your system is using, try one of the following procedures.

- Using the Navigator in Personal Oracle7, right-click on the Local Database icon, then click on Properties. Click on the Tablespace tab to show the space usage for all tablespaces. Look at all of the tablespaces within your database, except the SYSTEM tablespace, and take note of the space-used figure. The sum of these tablespaces is the amount of space needed to create the export file.

• Log in to SQL*Plus and issue the query shown in Listing 14.1. This will show the amount of space—in bytes—used for each tablespace.

Listing 14.1   Determining the amount of space used.

```
SQL> select dfs.tablespace_name,
  2         ddf.bytes - dfs.bytes "Space Used"
  3  from dba_data_files ddf,
  4       dba_free_space dfs
  5  where ddf.file_id = dfs.file_id
  6* and dfs.tablespace_name != 'SYSTEM';


TABLESPACE_NAME                 Space Used
------------------------------- ----------
USER_DATA                           401408
ROLLBACK_DATA                      1640448
TEMPORARY_DATA                        2048
```

Step 2

Next, you need to determine whether your database is set up to use the export and import utilities. You can easily check this by logging in to the database using SQL*Plus and issuing the query shown in Listing 14.2.

Listing 14.2   Checking if your database is set up to run the export and import utilities.

```
SQL> select count(*)
  2  from all_objects
  3  where object_type = 'VIEW'
  4  and object_name like 'EXU7%';


COUNT(*)
--------
     103
```

If the query returns a number similar to the one in the listing, the database is already set up to run the utilities. If Oracle Installer installed the database, the export and import utilities will be automatically set up. If the query returns no records, you will have to set up the import and export routines manually. To do this, you need to run a file called catexp.sql, which is usually located in the C:\ORAWIN95\rdbms72\admin directory. The example I chose uses version 7.2 of Personal Oracle7, which is why the rdbms directory is called rdbms72. Substitute your own version number for this number. To run this file, log in to SQL*Plus as the **SYS** user (it is important you run this file as the **SYS** user). From there, issue the command:

```
@C:\orawin95\rdbms72\admin\catexp.sql
```

This will start to create the necessary views and roles needed for exporting and importing data from your database. Don't worry if, when running the script, you receive errors when Oracle tries to drop an object that does not exist; this is normal. Listing 14.3 is an example of creating the objects.

Listing 14.3   *Creating the export and import objects by hand.*

```
@c:\orawin95\rdbms72\admin\catexp.sql
SQL> grant select any table to exp_full_database;

Grant succeeded.

SQL> grant backup any table to exp_full_database;

Grant succeeded.

SQL> GRANT insert,update,delete
  2    ON sys.incexp
  3    TO exp_full_database;

Grant succeeded.

SQL> GRANT insert,update,delete
  2    ON sys.incvid
  3    TO exp_full_database;

Grant succeeded.

SQL> GRANT insert,update,delete
  2    ON sys.incfil
  3    TO exp_full_database;

Grant succeeded.

SQL> grant exp_full_database to dba;

Grant succeeded.
SQL>
SQL> Rem
SQL> Rem  **************************************************
SQL> Rem  Section 1: Views required by BOTH export and import
SQL> Rem  **************************************************
SQL> Rem
SQL> rem block size
SQL> CREATE OR REPLACE view exu7bsz(blocksize) AS
  2      SELECT ts$.blocksize
  3      FROM   sys.ts$ ts$
  4    /
```

```
View created.

SQL> grant select on exu7bsz to public;

Grant succeeded.

SQL>
SQL> rem all users
SQL> CREATE OR REPLACE view exu7usr
  2       (name, userid, passwd, defrole, datats, tempts, profile#,
  3        profname) AS
  4       SELECT u.name, u.user#, DECODE(u.password, 'N', '', u.password),
  5       DECODE(u.defrole, 0, 'N', 1, 'A', 'L'), ts1.name, ts2.name,
  6       u.resource$, p.name
  7       FROM sys.user$ u, sys.ts$ ts1, sys.ts$ ts2, sys.profname$ p
  8       WHERE u.datats# = ts1.ts# and u.tempts# = ts2.ts# and u.type = 1 and
  9        u.resource$ = p.profile#
 10  /

View created.
```

Step 3

Now you are ready to export all of your data from the Personal Oracle7 database to an export file. This copies all of the tables, indexes, data, etc., from your existing Personal Oracle7 database and creates a file that can be used by the import utility to re-create the objects in a different Oracle database. To do the export, you will need to use a file called exp in the C:\ORAWIN95\bin directory. To execute this file with the required parameters, you will need to open a DOS window and use the **cd** command to change to the C:\ORAWIN95\bin directory. Then, type in the following:

```
c:\orawin95\bin>exp system/manager file=c:\fulldb.dmp full=y log=c:\fulldb.log
```

This tells Oracle to use the export utility (**exp**), with the following parameters:

- *system/manager*—The username and password for the **SYSTEM** user. This is the user for exporting an entire database. You should substitute your password for the **SYSTEM** user.

- *file=c:\fulldb.dmp*—Indicates to Oracle what the file created by the export utility should be called. This file will then be used with the import utility to restore the data to the Personal Oracle8 database. The .dmp extension is commonly used for all export files produced from an Oracle database.

- *full=y*—Tells Oracle that the type of export required is that of a full database. Others, such as incremental, are available.

- *log=c:\fulldb.log*—Logs all of the output to the file named. This is useful for reviewing exactly what was exported.

Listing 14.4 shows the output from an example export. This was from the default install from a Personal Oracle7 database.

Listing 14.4   *Example output from the export utility.*

```
About to export the entire database ...
. exporting tablespace definitions
. exporting profiles
. exporting user definitions
. exporting roles
. exporting resource costs
. exporting rollback segment definitions
. exporting database links
. exporting sequence numbers
. exporting job queues
. exporting refresh groups and children
. exporting cluster definitions
. about to export SYSTEM's tables ...
. . exporting table              DEF$_CALL          0 rows exported
. . exporting table          DEF$_CALLDEST          0 rows exported
. . exporting table       DEF$_DEFAULTDEST          0 rows exported
. . exporting table       DEF$_DESTINATION          0 rows exported
. . exporting table             DEF$_ERROR          0 rows exported
. . exporting table        PRODUCT_PROFILE          0 rows exported
. . exporting table           USER_PROFILE          0 rows exported
. about to export SCOTT's tables ...
. . exporting table                  BONUS          0 rows exported
. . exporting table                   DEPT          4 rows exported
. . exporting table                    EMP         14 rows exported
. . exporting table               SALGRADE          5 rows exported
. about to export DEMO's tables ...
. . exporting table               CUSTOMER         33 rows exported
. . exporting table             DEPARTMENT         11 rows exported
. . exporting table               EMPLOYEE         32 rows exported
. . exporting table                   ITEM        271 rows exported
. . exporting table                    JOB          6 rows exported
. . exporting table               LOCATION          4 rows exported
. . exporting table                  PRICE         58 rows exported
. . exporting table                PRODUCT         31 rows exported
. . exporting table           SALARY_GRADE          5 rows exported
. . exporting table            SALES_ORDER        100 rows exported
. about to export P07's tables ...
. exporting referential integrity constraints
. exporting posttables actions
. exporting synonyms
. exporting views
```

```
. exporting stored procedures
. exporting triggers
. exporting default and system auditing options
Export terminated successfully without warnings.
```

You now have a copy of the data within your Personal Oracle7 database. Keep this file in a safe place, out of the way of the Oracle directories.

Step 4

The next step in the process is to remove all of your Personal Oracle7 software. If the only Oracle product you are using on your PC is Personal Oracle7, then you can just delete the C:\ORAWIN95 directory. Make sure that your export file is not in the ORAWIN95 directory; this will ensure a fresh install of Personal Oracle8. When deleting the ORAWIN95 directory, also remember to remove the oracle.ini and other associated files from the Windows directory. Otherwise, the best way to remove products is through Oracle Installer, which you will usually find in the C:\ORAWIN95\BIN directory under the name of *orainst*. Just highlight what you want to remove in the right-hand window, then click on the Remove button. Remove the following products:

- Online Help

- Oracle Call Interface

- Personal Oracle7

- SQL*Net Add-on

- SQL*Net Client

- SQL*Plus

When Oracle Installer asks if you wish to remove the database already created, click on the OK button. Oracle will then warn you that Oracle Installer will not remove any database files added after the original database. If you have modified the original database in any way, you must remove these files after the installer has finished removing your selected products. Remember that any modified tablespaces must be replaced in the Personal Oracle8 database before you start the import procedure. When asked if you wish to remove SQL*Net configuration files, answer Yes and click on the OK button. Oracle Installer will remove all of your selected products, then return you to the original Installer screen. You will notice that the required products are no longer installed. Click on the Exit button to finish uninstalling Personal Oracle7.

Step 5

Now the time has come to install Personal Oracle8. Insert the CD-ROM into your drive. You will be prompted with the Autorun screen, from which you should click on the Begin

Installation icon. You will now perform a standard installation of Personal Oracle8 to your PC. For full details on how to perform this installation, see Chapter 1, which guides you through the installation process. Make sure that when installing Personal Oracle8, you choose a database to be created automatically. Usually, the best course is to choose the Application Developer installation.

Step 6

You should now have a Personal Oracle8 database and software installed. All that is left is for you to transfer all of your information from Personal Oracle7 into the new database. Remember that if you modified your Personal Oracle7 database in any way—i.e., added extra tablespaces—then you now must create these tablespaces within Personal Oracle8, before the import process begins. You can get your Personal Oracle7 data into your new Personal Oracle8 database in one of two ways:

- Use the **IMP80** command from the DOS prompt
- Use the Oracle8 Navigator

If you wish to use the **IMP80** method, see Step 7.1; if you plan to use the Navigator, see Step 7.2.

Step 7.1

To use the **IMP80** method, you need to start the Personal Oracle8 database, then open a DOS window from Windows 95. Move to the C:\ORAWIN95\bin directory and issue the **IMP80** command as follows (I am assuming you are using a file called fulldb.dmp as the file to import from):

```
IMP80 system/manager file=c:\fulldb.dmp commit=y full=y log=c:\fulldb.log
```

This statement will start a session importing all of the data from your Personal Oracle7 database into the new Personal Oracle8 database. The output will look similar to that of Listing 14.5. Don't worry if a lot of messages are generated saying an object was not created, as it already existed. If you are unsure about the import, look in the log file that was generated.

Listing 14.5 *A sample import session output.*

```
Connected to: Personal Oracle8 Release 8.0.3.0.0 - Production
With the Partitioning option
PL/SQL Release 8.0.3.0.0 - Production

Export file created by EXPORT:V07.02.02 via conventional path
```

```
. . importing table                    "DEF$_CALL"              0 rows imported
. . importing table                    "DEF$_CALLDEST"          0 rows imported
. . importing table                    "DEF$_DEFAULTDEST"       0 rows imported
. . importing table                    "DEF$_DESTINATION"       0 rows imported
. . importing table                    "DEF$_ERROR"             0 rows imported
. . importing table                    "PRODUCT_PROFILE"        0 rows imported
. . importing table                    "USER_PROFILE"           0 rows imported
. importing SCOTT's objects into SCOTT
. . importing table                         "BONUS"             0 rows imported
. . importing table                          "DEPT"             4 rows imported
. . importing table                           "EMP"            14 rows imported
. . importing table                      "SALGRADE"             5 rows imported
. importing DEMO's objects into DEMO
. . importing table                      "CUSTOMER"            33 rows imported
. . importing table                    "DEPARTMENT"            11 rows imported
. . importing table                      "EMPLOYEE"            32 rows imported
. . importing table                          "ITEM"           271 rows imported
. . importing table                           "JOB"             6 rows imported
. . importing table                      "LOCATION"             4 rows imported
. . importing table                         "PRICE"            58 rows imported
. . importing table                       "PRODUCT"            31 rows imported
. . importing table                  "SALARY_GRADE"             5 rows imported
. . importing table                   "SALES_ORDER"           100 rows imported
. importing SYSTEM's objects into SYSTEM
. importing SCOTT's objects into SCOTT
. importing DEMO's objects into DEMO
. importing SYSTEM's objects into SYSTEM
. importing DEMO's objects into DEMO
. importing SYSTEM's objects into SYSTEM
Import terminated successfully.
```

Step 7.2

To use the Navigator to import your data, start the Personal Oracle8 database, then the Navigator. Once you are in the Navigator's main screen, double-click on the Personal Oracle8 folder. This will open up and show two objects: Projects and Local Database. If you click once on the Local Database icon, you will be automatically connected to the new Personal Oracle8 database. If you then right-click on the Local Database icon, a list will appear. From this list, click the Import... option, as shown in Figure 14.12.

You will see a window where you must choose which data file to import to your new database. The window will look like Figure 14.13.

Once you have chosen the file to import and clicked on the Open button, the import utility will execute in a DOS window, exactly the same as the **IMP80** command. When finished, you will be left in the Navigator screen. You should now have a fully working Personal Oracle8 database, populated with your Personal Oracle7 data.

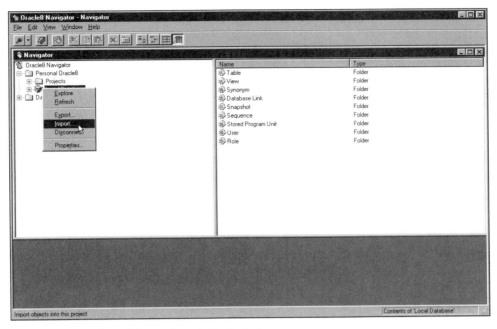

Figure 14.12 *Importing a database through the Navigator.*

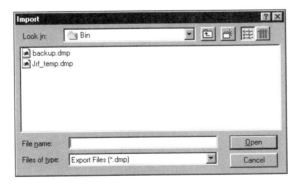

Figure 14.13 *Choosing the file to import.*

POST-INSTALL STEPS

Because you have just created the Oracle8 database, you will need to create some of the objects required for Personal Oracle8. The database you have just imported will not have some of the Oracle8 users.

To create a user, start the Oracle Server Manager by entering a DOS window and typing "svrmgr30" at the prompt. Once inside Server Manager, you will need to issue the following commands:

- connect system/manager

- create user po8 identified by po8;

- grant dba to po8;

- exit

Once you enter these commands, you should see a screen similar to Listing 14.6.

Listing 14.6   Post-install steps.

```
C:\WINDOWS>svrmgr30

Oracle Server Manager Release 3.0.3.0.0 - Production

(c) Copyright 1997, Oracle Corporation.  All Rights Reserved.

Personal Oracle8 Release 8.0.3.0.0 - Production
With the Partitioning option
PL/SQL Release 8.0.3.0.0 - Production

SVRMGR> connect system/manager
Connected.
SVRMGR> create user po8 identified by po8;
Statement processed.
SVRMGR> grant dba to po8;
Statement processed.
SVRMGR> exit
Server Manager complete.
```

ANOTHER TASK MASTERED

In this chapter, you learned how to get data from a Personal Oracle7 database into a Personal Oracle8 database. You can do so in a number of ways, and you will nearly always have some sort of problem. The best way to approach these upgrades is to expect some problems and stay calm when they appear. After all, if you have backed up the data, then you know you have not lost anything (except time). Whichever method you choose for your migration, if you follow the steps outlined in this chapter, you should minimize your problems. The next chapter covers security issues, backups, and restores. It expands on the import and export utilities and introduces the different backup techniques used. The next chapter also covers auditing of database actions for all of you security-conscious people out there.

SECURITY, BACKUP, AND RECOVERY

CHAPTER 15

How to keep your data safe and sound.

Having secure data is an important consideration when using a database system. This chapter addresses the topic of security, providing examples of the types of security you can impose on a Personal Oracle8 database. The chapter also goes into more detail about using the import and export utilities, explained briefly in the previous chapter. I will discuss the way they should be used, along with suggested backup and recovery procedures.

SECURITY

When using Personal Oracle8 on your PC, security may not be the most prominent issue on your mind. Indeed, if the database you are using contains no important information, there may be no point in wrapping it in security. Once you lose something, however, you will think otherwise.

Preventing unauthorized access to your database is the main reason for securing Personal Oracle8. Keep in mind that a database is only as secure as the operating system it is running on. For example, a database running on Windows 95 could easily be deleted unless the operating system is made secure.

This section on security is aimed at the larger implementation of Oracle. Where security is a concern, you should always try, to a varying degree, to use the following safeguards:

- Controlling users

- Controlling passwords

- Checking user privileges

- Using auditing, for checking on who changed what and when

- Protecting data integrity

- Watching for misuse of data

- Securing the operating system and hardware

- Enforcing a usable backup and recovery strategy

Controlling Usernames

When creating and altering users within Oracle, you need to watch three key areas:

- Default tablespace

- Temporary tablespace

- Resource settings

These areas are important for security reasons, because you need to be aware of all users being created. For example, if a user's default tablespace is not set, Personal Oracle8 will default to the SYSTEM tablespace, as shown in Listing 15.1.

Listing 15.1   Checking a user's default tablespace.

```
SQL> select username,
  2         default_tablespace
  3  from dba_users
  4  where username not in ('SYS','SYSTEM');


USERNAME                         DEFAULT_TABLESPACE
-------------------------------  -------------------
DBSNMP                           SYSTEM
SCOTT                            USER_DATA
EXPLORER                         USER_DATA
P07                              SYSTEM
P08                              SYSTEM
RICHARDF                         USER_DATA
DEMO                             USER_DATA
```

```
SUSAN                          SYSTEM
FRED                           SYSTEM
DEMOUSER                       USER_DATA

10 rows selected.
```

Creating user information within the SYSTEM tablespace is not a good idea. Similarly, if the temporary tablespace (where temporary items are stored—for example, when sorting data) is not set, Personal Oracle8 will default to SYSTEM, as shown in Listing 15.2. This is, again, a bad idea—you do not want temporary objects and data dictionary information in the same tablespace. Usually, a tablespace is specifically created for temporary objects.

Listing 15.2   *Checking a user's temporary tablespace.*

```
SQL> select username,
  2          temporary_tablespace
  3  from dba_users
  4  where username not in ('SYS','SYSTEM');

USERNAME                       TEMPORARY_TABLESPACE
------------------------------ --------------------
DBSNMP                         SYSTEM
SCOTT                          TEMPORARY_DATA
EXPLORER                       TEMPORARY_DATA
PO7                            SYSTEM
PO8                            SYSTEM
RICHARDF                       TEMPORARY_DATA
DEMO                           TEMPORARY_DATA
SUSAN                          SYSTEM
FRED                           SYSTEM
DEMOUSER                       TEMPORARY_DATA

10 rows selected.
```

You need resource limits to keep users within their allotted space and processor usage. You implement resource limits with user profiles, as discussed in Chapter 9. To use resource limits within your database, you must first turn them on, by setting the initialization parameter **resource_limit** to TRUE within the init.ora file for the database. Listing 15.3 shows you how to check which user has which profiles set.

Listing 15.3   *Checking user profile resource settings.*

```
SQL> select username,
  2          profile
  3  from dba_users
  4  where username not in ('SYS','SYSTEM');
```

```
USERNAME                        PROFILE
------------------------------  -----------
DBSNMP                          DEFAULT
SCOTT                           DEFAULT
EXPLORER                        DEFAULT
PO7                             DEFAULT
PO8                             DEFAULT
RICHARDF                        DEFAULT
DEMO                            DEFAULT
SUSAN                           DEFAULT
FRED                            DEFAULT
DEMOUSER                        DEMO_USER

10 rows selected.

SQL> select resource_name,
  2          resource_type,
  3            limit
  4   from dba_profiles
  5* where profile = 'DEMO_USER';

RESOURCE_NAME                   RESOURCE LIMIT
------------------------------  -------- ----------
COMPOSITE_LIMIT                 KERNEL   DEFAULT
SESSIONS_PER_USER               KERNEL   DEFAULT
CPU_PER_SESSION                 KERNEL   DEFAULT
CPU_PER_CALL                    KERNEL   DEFAULT
LOGICAL_READS_PER_SESSION       KERNEL   DEFAULT
LOGICAL_READS_PER_CALL          KERNEL   DEFAULT
IDLE_TIME                       KERNEL   DEFAULT
CONNECT_TIME                    KERNEL   DEFAULT
PRIVATE_SGA                     KERNEL   DEFAULT
FAILED_LOGIN_ATTEMPTS           PASSWORD 3
PASSWORD_LIFE_TIME              PASSWORD 30
PASSWORD_REUSE_TIME             PASSWORD DEFAULT
PASSWORD_REUSE_MAX              PASSWORD DEFAULT
PASSWORD_VERIFY_FUNCTION        PASSWORD DEFAULT
PASSWORD_LOCK_TIME              PASSWORD 1
PASSWORD_GRACE_TIME             PASSWORD 5

16 rows selected.
```

Listing 15.3 shows all of the users and their profile options. Only one user has a profile called **DEMO_USER**, which is then checked by using the **DBA_PROFILES** table. Remember, to use profile options, you must set the **resource_limit** parameter to TRUE. Listing 15.4 shows how you can check this parameter by interrogating a system table.

Listing 15.4   *Checking if the **resource_limit** parameter is set.*

```
SQL> select name,
  2         value
  3  from v_$parameter
  4  where name = 'resource_limit';

NAME                 VALUE
-------------------- ----------
resource_limit       FALSE
```

The example shows that resource limiting is not set.

Controlling Passwords

Passwords have become a part of everyday life. Many of us use at least one every day. Passwords are used to protect users against unauthorized access to their data. Most sites have rules for managing passwords—minimum length, frequency of change, and so on. Try to make your passwords difficult to guess, although the more difficult you make them, the harder they are to remember.

Checking User Privileges

After being created within the database, a user is given a password and default and temporary tablespaces. The user now exists within the database, but cannot do anything. Without privileges, a user cannot even log in. The next step, therefore, is to give the user access rights and privileges. This can be done using privileges or roles, as discussed in Chapter 9. Check the privileges assigned to your users. All system privileges should be assigned only to administrative users.

Always try to administer privileges by using roles. This eases the task, because you can have some roles that allow administration duties and others that allow access rights. You should also make the administration roles password protected. To see which roles are associated with which user, use a SQL statement similar to that shown in Listing 15.5.

Listing 15.5   *Checking users and associated roles.*

```
SQL> select * from dba_role_privs;
```

GRANTEE	GRANTED_ROLE	ADM	DEF
DBA	DELETE_CATALOG_ROLE	YES	YES
DBA	EXECUTE_CATALOG_ROLE	YES	YES
DBA	EXP_FULL_DATABASE	NO	YES
DBA	IMP_FULL_DATABASE	NO	YES
DBA	SELECT_CATALOG_ROLE	YES	YES

DBSNMP	CONNECT	NO	YES
DBSNMP	RESOURCE	NO	YES
DBSNMP	SNMPAGENT	NO	YES
DEMO	CONNECT	NO	YES
DEMO	DBA	NO	YES
DEMO	JRF	NO	YES
DEMO	RESOURCE	NO	YES
DEMOUSER	CONNECT	NO	YES
DEMO_ROLE	CONNECT	NO	YES
DEMO_ROLE	EXP_FULL_DATABASE	NO	YES
DEMO_ROLE	IMP_FULL_DATABASE	NO	YES
DEMO_ROLE	RESOURCE	NO	YES
EXPLORER	CONNECT	NO	YES
EXP_FULL_DATABASE	EXECUTE_CATALOG_ROLE	NO	YES
EXP_FULL_DATABASE	SELECT_CATALOG_ROLE	NO	YES
FRED	CONNECT	NO	YES

GRANTEE	GRANTED_ROLE	ADM	DEF
IMP_FULL_DATABASE	EXECUTE_CATALOG_ROLE	NO	YES
IMP_FULL_DATABASE	SELECT_CATALOG_ROLE	NO	YES
JRF	DBA	NO	YES
PO7	DBA	NO	YES
PO8	DBA	NO	YES
PO8	DEMO_ROLE	YES	YES
RICHARDF	CONNECT	NO	YES
RICHARDF	JRF	NO	YES
SCOTT	CONNECT	NO	YES
SCOTT	RESOURCE	NO	YES
SUSAN	CONNECT	NO	YES
SYS	AQ_ADMINISTRATOR_ROLE	YES	YES
SYS	AQ_USER_ROLE	YES	YES
SYS	CONNECT	YES	YES
SYS	DBA	YES	YES
SYS	DELETE_CATALOG_ROLE	YES	YES
SYS	EXECUTE_CATALOG_ROLE	YES	YES
SYS	EXP_FULL_DATABASE	YES	YES
SYS	IMP_FULL_DATABASE	YES	YES
SYS	RECOVERY_CATALOG_OWNER	YES	YES
SYS	RESOURCE	YES	YES

GRANTEE	GRANTED_ROLE	ADM	DEF
SYS	SELECT_CATALOG_ROLE	YES	YES
SYS	SNMPAGENT	YES	YES
SYSTEM	DBA	YES	YES
SYSTEM	JRF	YES	YES

46 rows selected.

In Listing 15.5, the **Grantee** column shows the username or role name, and the **Granted_Role** column shows either the role name or the privilege name granted to the username or role name. For example:

- The user **SUSAN** has a privilege of **CONNECT**.

- The user **RICHARDF** has one role, **JRF**, and one privilege, **CONNECT**. By looking farther up the listing, you can see that the **JRF** role contains a role of **DBA**. If you look still farther up, you will see that the role **DBA** contains other roles and privileges.

In managing your users and roles in this way, you can set up predefined roles and privileges. Then, when the time comes, you have to give access to only a minimal set of roles to give a user the required access rights.

Securing Access Through Tools

Most users access the database one of two ways: through a form that you (or a third party) have created, or through SQL*Plus. When creating forms, you must always make sure users can access only the data they are authorized to see. With SQL*Plus, there are a lot of ways around security; therefore, securing the tool as much as possible is always advisable.

SQL*Plus has a feature, known as the product profile table, that can help you guard against users issuing unauthorized commands, such as **GRANT**. By populating the product profile table with usernames and commands, you can stop users from issuing certain commands. You can use this feature to create user-level security within any Oracle product.

To create the product profile table, you must execute the script v8pup.sql, usually found in the C:\ORAWIN95\DBS directory. This script must be executed from within SQL*Plus as the **SYSTEM** user. Once the table has been created, you can then implement user-level security by inserting rows into the **PRODUCT_USER_PROFILE** table, shown in Listing 15.6.

Listing 15.6   The PRODUCT_USER_PROFILE table.

```
SQL> desc product_user_profile
 Name                            Null?    Type
 ------------------------------- -------- ----
 PRODUCT                         NOT NULL VARCHAR2(30)
 USERID                                   VARCHAR2(30)
 ATTRIBUTE                                VARCHAR2(240)
 SCOPE                                    VARCHAR2(240)
 NUMERIC_VALUE                            NUMBER(15,2)
 CHAR_VALUE                               VARCHAR2(240)
 DATE_VALUE                               DATE
 LONG_VALUE                               LONG
```

For example, to disable a user with the **SELECT** command, you would insert a row into the **PRODUCT_USER_PROFILE** table, as shown in Listing 15.7.

Listing 15.7 *Disabling the **SELECT** statement.*

```
SQL> insert into product_user_profile
  2  values ('SQL*Plus','DEMO','SELECT',null,null,'DISABLED',null,null);

1 row created.

SQL> connect demo/demo
Connected.
SQL> select * from dual;
invalid command: select
```

To reenable the use of the command by the user, you would simply delete the row from the table. Putting a % in the **Userid** column of the table would disable the use of the command for all users. You can disable the following commands:

- **ALTER**
- **ANALYZE**
- **AUDIT**
- **CONNECT**
- **CREATE**
- **DELETE**
- **DROP**
- **EDIT**
- **EXECUTE**
- **EXIT**
- **GET**
- **GRANT**
- **HOST**
- **INSERT**
- **LOCK**
- **NOAUDIT**
- **QUIT**

- RENAME
- REVOKE
- RUN
- SAVE
- SELECT
- SET
- SET ROLE
- SET TRANSACTION
- SPOOL
- START
- TRUNCATE
- UPDATE

You should always restrict access to the **PRODUCT_USER_PROFILE** table by disallowing inserts and updates to all but the database administrator.

Auditing

Auditing allows you to see who changed a piece of data and when. This is invaluable information in a multiuser environment. The Personal Oracle8 database can audit all transactions carried out against the database. To enable auditing, you use the **AUDIT** command, and to turn auditing off, the **NOAUDIT** command.

To enable auditing on your database, you would use the parameter in the init.ora file called **audit_trail**. It can be set to either **OS** or **DB**—that is, either operating system (where all auditing is logged to an operating-system file) or database (where all auditing is logged to a table within the database). If you choose database storage, you should create a tablespace specifically for the audit table, because this can grow to be very large. To issue auditing commands, the user must have the **AUDIT_ANY** privilege.

The three classes of auditing are:

- Access
- Object
- Database

Access

You can audit all successful and unsuccessful accesses to the database—i.e., valid and invalid login attempts. To audit sessions, you need to use the **AUDIT SESSION** statement. When you start auditing, all actions are stored in a central table. If you choose to set **audit_trail** equal to **DB**, this table is called **AUD$** and is held in the **SYS** schema. You would access it by using the table name **SYS.AUD$**. This table has the format shown in Listing 15.8.

*Listing 15.8   The *SYS.AUD$* table.*

```
SQL> desc sys.aud$
 Name                             Null?     Type
 -------------------------------- --------  ----
 SESSIONID                        NOT NULL  NUMBER
 ENTRYID                          NOT NULL  NUMBER
 STATEMENT                        NOT NULL  NUMBER
 TIMESTAMP#                       NOT NULL  DATE
 USERID                                     VARCHAR2(30)
 USERHOST                                   VARCHAR2(128)
 TERMINAL                                   VARCHAR2(255)
 ACTION#                          NOT NULL  NUMBER
 RETURNCODE                       NOT NULL  NUMBER
 OBJ$CREATOR                                VARCHAR2(30)
 OBJ$NAME                                   VARCHAR2(128)
 AUTH$PRIVILEGES                            VARCHAR2(16)
 AUTH$GRANTEE                               VARCHAR2(30)
 NEW$OWNER                                  VARCHAR2(30)
 NEW$NAME                                   VARCHAR2(128)
 SES$ACTIONS                                VARCHAR2(19)
 SES$TID                                    NUMBER
 LOGOFF$LREAD                               NUMBER
 LOGOFF$PREAD                               NUMBER
 LOGOFF$LWRITE                              NUMBER
 LOGOFF$DEAD                                NUMBER
 LOGOFF$TIME                                DATE
 COMMENT$TEXT                               VARCHAR2(4000)
 SPARE1                                     VARCHAR2(255)
 SPARE2                                     NUMBER
 OBJ$LABEL                                  RAW(255)
 SES$LABEL                                  RAW(255)
 PRIV$USED                                  NUMBER
```

The columns you are most interested in for auditing connections to the database are **Userid**, **Timestamp#**, and **Logoff$time**. Listing 15.9 shows an example of turning the session auditing on and the report that can be generated.

Listing 15.9 *Reporting on session auditing.*

```
SQL> audit session;

Audit succeeded.

SQL> connect demo/demo
Connected.
SQL> connect po8/po8
Connected.
SQL> connect system
Enter password: *******
Connected.
SQL> connect sys/change_on_install
Connected.
SQL> connect system/manager
Connected.
SQL> select userid,
  2        to_char(timestamp#,'DD/MM/YY HH:MI:SS') time_on,
  3        to_char(logoff$time,'DD/MM/YY HH:MI:SS') time_off
  4  from sys.aud$;

USERID                        TIME_ON          TIME_OFF
----------------------------- ---------------- ----------------
SYSTEM                        18/02/98 11:08:53 18/02/98 11:17:49
DEMO                          18/02/98 11:17:50 18/02/98 11:17:59
PO8                           18/02/98 11:17:59 18/02/98 11:18:05
SYSTEM                        18/02/98 11:18:05 18/02/98 11:18:13
DEMO                          18/02/98 11:08:47 18/02/98 11:08:52
SYS                           18/02/98 11:18:13 18/02/98 11:18:18
SYSTEM                        18/02/98 11:18:19

7 rows selected.
```

This statement audits all successful and unsuccessful attempts to enter the database. To confine your audit just to unsuccessful attempts, you would issue the **AUDIT SESSION WHENEVER NOT SUCCESSFUL** command. To audit successful attempts only, you would issue the **AUDIT SESSION WHENEVER SUCCESSFUL** command.

Object

You can use another form of the **AUDIT** command to audit objects. This command has the following syntax:

```
AUDIT option ON schema.object_name
BY SESSION/ACCESS
[WHENEVER [NOT] SUCCESSFUL]
```

For example, you can audit inserts, updates, and deletes to a specific table, as shown in Listing 15.10. You can also audit all actions on an object by using **AUDIT ALL**, instead of **AUDIT INSERT,UPDATE,DELETE**.

Listing 15.10 *Example of object auditing.*

```
SQL> conn system/manager
Connected.
SQL> audit insert,update,delete on demo.orders;

Audit succeeded.

SQL> connect demo/demo
Connected.
SQL> select * from orders;

 ORDER_ID CUSTOMER_ID ORDER_DAT DISPATCHE ORDER_DUE
 -------- ----------- --------- --------- ---------
   100001       20001 01-Jan-99 10-Jan-99 31-Jan-99
   100002       20001 02-Jan-99 11-Jan-99 31-Jan-99
   100003       20002 01-May-98 09-May-98 31-May-98
   100004       20003 01-Jun-98 03-Jun-98 10-Jun-98
   100005       20004 28-Aug-99 29-Aug-99 30-Sep-99
   100006       20005 28-Aug-99 10-Sep-99 31-Aug-99
   999999       20001 10-Dec-99 15-Dec-99 10-Jan-00
   999998       20001 01-Jan-99 01-Jan-99 01-Jan-99

8 rows selected.

SQL> insert into orders
  2  values (999997,20002,'01-JAN-1998','01-JAN-1998','01-JAN-1998');

1 row created.

SQL> select * from orders;

 ORDER_ID CUSTOMER_ID ORDER_DAT DISPATCHE ORDER_DUE
 -------- ----------- --------- --------- ---------
   100001       20001 01-Jan-99 10-Jan-99 31-Jan-99
   100002       20001 02-Jan-99 11-Jan-99 31-Jan-99
   100003       20002 01-May-98 09-May-98 31-May-98
   100004       20003 01-Jun-98 03-Jun-98 10-Jun-98
   100005       20004 28-Aug-99 29-Aug-99 30-Sep-99
   100006       20005 28-Aug-99 10-Sep-99 31-Aug-99
   999999       20001 10-Dec-99 15-Dec-99 10-Jan-00
   999998       20001 01-Jan-99 01-Jan-99 01-Jan-99
   999997       20002 01-Jan-98 01-Jan-98 01-Jan-98

9 rows selected.
```

```
SQL> connect system/manager
Connected.

SQL> select username,
  2         obj_name,
  3         owner
  4  from dba_audit_object;

USERNAME              OBJ_NAME              OWNER
--------------------  --------------------  ------------
DEMO                  ORDERS                DEMO
```

Database

Database auditing allows you to audit a set of actions. For example, you can audit all **ROLE** actions by database auditing the **ROLE** command, which would audit the following commands:

- **CREATE ROLE**
- **ALTER ROLE**
- **SET ROLE**
- **DROP ROLE**

By using the **AUDIT ROLE** command, you can audit more than one thing at a time. You can audit most system privileges by specifying the privilege name after the audit command itself. The results of the audit on privileges are viewed in the same way as other audits, using the contents of the following tables:

- **SYS.AUD$**
- **DBA_AUDIT_TRAIL**
- **DBA_AUDIT_TABLE**
- **SYS.DBA_STMT_AUDIT_OPTS**

Guidelines For Auditing

When auditing any database, you must always be careful about the amount of space used by the audit tables, because they can grow very rapidly. The best advice is to report from these tables on a daily basis and clear them (after making a backup of them) periodically. You should always restrict access to the **SYS.AUD$** table, because this can be used to remove audit information. It is also a good idea to audit the audit table itself, which can be done using the following statement:

```
AUDIT INSERT, UPDATE, DELETE, SELECT
ON sys.aud$
BY ACCESS;
```

Always audit selectively. Auditing everything would give you too much information to digest and could cause added processing overhead on your database.

BACKUP

Making backups is a necessary task to be performed at regular intervals. It provides a way of saving your data if the unthinkable happens—and the unthinkable does happen. You can back up data from your Personal Oracle8 database in many different ways. In the following sections, I will show you the two most common ways to back up a small Personal Oracle8 database: the Backup Manager and the export utility (mentioned in Chapter 14). The method you choose depends upon your situation, but, as I will explain later, I suggest using a mixture of the two.

Backup Manager

You access the Backup Manager from your Windows 95 Start button, under the heading Personal Oracle8 for Windows 95. Once you select the Backup Manager, you will see a window appear similar to that shown in Figure 15.1.

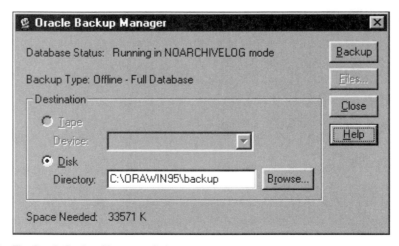

Figure 15.1   The Oracle Backup Manager window.

The Backup Manager window has several sections:

- *Database Status*—Shows the current status of your database—that is, whether it is running and in which mode.

- *Backup Type*—Shows the type of backup that will take place if you click on the Backup button.

- *Destination*—Shows where the backup will store the files. In the example shown, they will be backed up to the C:\ORAWIN95\BACKUP directory. If you have a tape drive, you can select it by choosing the Tape Device radio button. Backups to tape are not supported for Windows 95, but they are supported for Windows NT.

- *Space Needed*—Shows the amount of space needed on your hard disk for the backup to take place.

- *Backup button*—Starts the backup.

- *Files button*—Grayed out when you do not have Archivelog mode (explained later in this section) enabled; when Archivelog mode is enabled, you use this button to choose which files you wish to back up.

- *Close button*—Cancels the backup session.

- *Help button*—Provides help on the Backup Manager window.

While the backup is running, you may be prompted for your database password. When this occurs, just enter your password and click on the OK button.

You can use the Backup Manager to back up your Personal Oracle8 database in one of three ways:

- Archivelog mode with database running

- Noarchivelog mode with database running

- Database not running

In any of the three modes, you do not have to decide which type of backup is required. The Backup Manager will identify the best method automatically. All you have to do is decide where to back up your database to.

In Archivelog mode, you back up your database while it is running. You must switch on archive logging, which is done by uncommenting a line within the init.ora file. This parameter is **log_archive_start**, which is commented in the init.ora file by default. Listing 15.11 shows an example of the Archivelog section of the init.ora file.

Listing 15.11   The Archivelog section of init.ora.

```
# Uncommenting the line below will cause automatic archiving if archiving has
# been enabled using ALTER DATABASE ARCHIVELOG.
# log_archive_start = true
# log_archive_dest = %ORACLE_HOME%\database\archive
# log_archive_format = "%%ORACLE_SID%%T%TS%S.ARC"
```

Now, to start archiving, you must restart the database and issue the **ALTER DATABASE ARCHIVELOG** command. This enables Archivelog mode.

A Noarchivelog backup is where archive logging is switched off and the database is running. This will be the normal backup if your database is running. Again, all you have to do is decide which directory to keep your backups in and click on the Backup button. When performing a restore on this type of backup, you have to restore the whole database.

A database-not-running backup is often referred to as a *cold backup*. It is one of the best backups to perform at regular intervals. Again, with this type of backup, when a restore is needed, you have to restore the whole database.

Export

Export is a utility that extracts data and object definitions from your database. These can then be transferred to another database and imported—copying the data and all definitions to another database. Export creates a binary file that stores the makeup of your database along with all data stored. It creates a file containing the statements to create your objects again. This file cannot be edited, because it is a binary file, and should be used only with the import utility, explained later in this chapter. This is a good way of creating backups of your information, because you can export all of your database or just the bits you are interested in. Once the data is exported, you can selectively import parts to your database.

Navigator Method

Export can be initiated in two ways: either through the Personal Oracle8 Navigator or from the DOS command line. I find that initiating an export session from the command line is more flexible. To export data from your database through the Personal Oracle8 Navigator, start the Navigator, click on the Projects icon, then click on the Database icon to make a connection. Finally, right-click on the Database icon and select Export, as illustrated in Figure 15.2.

This brings up the Export - Save As window, which asks where you would like to store your export file. Type in your file name and location and click on the Save button, as illustrated in Figure 15.3.

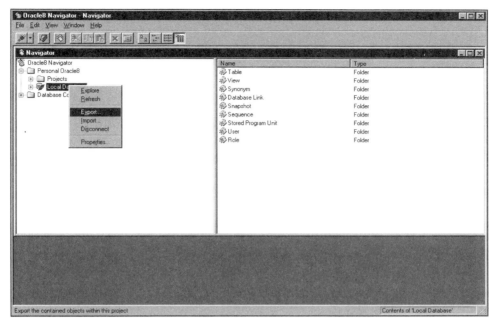

Figure 15.2   *Exporting data through the Navigator.*

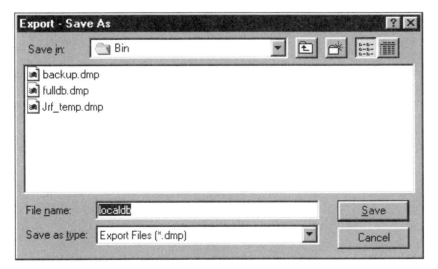

Figure 15.3   *Decide on a file name.*

This then initiates a DOS session in the background that exports all of your data to the specified file. You do not get a choice of which data to export (from the command line, you do). Once the export has finished, you are asked if you wish to view the log file. I suggest you always do so to make sure the export worked properly. If an error occurred during the export, you will see a message displayed to indicate this. Listing 15.12 is an example export log, showing all of the tables and other objects being exported, including the number of rows per table.

Listing 15.12   An example export log file.

```
Connected to: Personal Oracle8 Release 8.0.3.0.0 - Production
With the Partitioning option
PL/SQL Release 8.0.3.0.0 - Production
Export done in WE8ISO8859P1 character set and WE8ISO8859P1 NCHAR character set

About to export the entire database ...
. exporting tablespace definitions
. exporting profiles
. exporting user definitions
. exporting roles
. exporting resource costs
. exporting rollback segment definitions
. exporting database links
. exporting sequence numbers
. exporting directory aliases
. exporting foreign function library names
. exporting object type definitions
. exporting cluster definitions
. about to export SYSTEM's tables via Conventional Path ...
. . exporting table                      DEF$_AQCALL          0 rows exported
. . exporting table                      DEF$_AQERROR         0 rows exported
. . exporting table                        DEF$_CALL          0 rows exported
. . exporting table                    DEF$_CALLDEST          0 rows exported
. . exporting table                 DEF$_DEFAULTDEST          0 rows exported
. . exporting table                 DEF$_DESTINATION          0 rows exported
. . exporting table                       DEF$_ERROR          0 rows exported
. . exporting table                         DEF$_LOB          0 rows exported
. . exporting table                      DEF$_ORIGIN          0 rows exported
. . exporting table                  DEF$_PROPAGATOR          0 rows exported
. . exporting table                    DEF$_TEMP$LOB          0 rows exported
. . exporting table            SQLPLUS_PRODUCT_PROFILE         0 rows exported
. . exporting table                     USER_PROFILE          0 rows exported
. about to export DBSNMP's tables via Conventional Path ...
. about to export SCOTT's tables via Conventional Path ...
. . exporting table                            BONUS          0 rows exported
. . exporting table                             DEPT          4 rows exported
. . exporting table                              EMP         14 rows exported
. . exporting table                         SALGRADE          5 rows exported
. about to export EXPLORER's tables via Conventional Path ...
. about to export DEMO's tables via Conventional Path ...
. . exporting table                        CHAR_DEMO          1 rows exported
```

```
. . exporting table                 CONVERSION_TEST           2 rows exported
. . exporting table                        CUSTOMER          33 rows exported
. . exporting table                       CUSTOMERS           7 rows exported
. . exporting table                      DEPARTMENT          11 rows exported
. . exporting table                        EMPLOYEE          32 rows exported
. . exporting table                       EMPLOYEES           5 rows exported
. . exporting table                            ITEM         271 rows exported
. . exporting table                             JOB           6 rows exported
. . exporting table                             JRF           3 rows exported
. . exporting table                        JRF_TEMP           0 rows exported
. . exporting table                        LOCATION           4 rows exported
. . exporting table                        MESSAGES           1 rows exported
. . exporting table                          ORDERS           9 rows exported
. . exporting table                   ORDER_DETAILS          12 rows exported
. . exporting table                      PLAN_TABLE           0 rows exported
. . exporting table                             POI           1 rows exported
. . exporting table                           PRICE          58 rows exported
. . exporting table                         PRODUCT          31 rows exported
. . exporting table                        PRODUCTS          10 rows exported
. . exporting table                     SALARY_GRADE          5 rows exported
. . exporting table                       SALES_FIGS
. . exporting partition               SALES_MONTH1            0 rows exported
. . exporting partition               SALES_MONTH2            0 rows exported
. . exporting partition               SALES_MONTH3            0 rows exported
. . exporting partition               SALES_MONTH4            0 rows exported
. . exporting partition               SALES_MONTH5            0 rows exported
. . exporting partition               SALES_MONTH6            0 rows exported
. . exporting partition               SALES_MONTH7            0 rows exported
. . exporting partition               SALES_MONTH8            0 rows exported
. . exporting partition               SALES_MONTH9            0 rows exported
. . exporting partition               SALES_MONTH10           0 rows exported
. . exporting partition               SALES_MONTH11           0 rows exported
. . exporting partition               SALES_MONTH12           0 rows exported
. . exporting partition                      OTHER            0 rows exported
. . exporting table                      SALES_ORDER        100 rows exported
. . exporting table                        SUPPLIERS          7 rows exported
. . exporting table                       SURNAME_A_H         0 rows exported
. . exporting table                       SURNAME_I_Q         0 rows exported
. . exporting table                       SURNAME_R_Z         0 rows exported
. . exporting table                      VARCHAR2_DEMO        1 rows exported
. about to export RICHARDF's tables via Conventional Path ...
. about to export DEMOUSER's tables via Conventional Path ...
. about to export FRED's tables via Conventional Path ...
```

Command-Line Method

The command-line method of the export utility is by far the most flexible way to export data from your Personal Oracle8 database. It allows you several options, including:

- Exporting a single user

- Exporting a single table

- Performing an incremental export

- Exporting indexes only

- Exporting the full database

To start the export utility from the command line, you first need to bring up a DOS window. Once the window is active, the command to initiate an export is **EXP80**. Before trying this, take some time to read the rest of this section, which explains the parameters used with the export utility. To see the parameters available for use with the **EXP80** command, type:

```
EXP80 help=y
```

This displays a screen similar to Listing 15.13, showing all of the parameters and their default values.

Listing 15.13 *Displaying export help information.*

```
Keyword   Description (Default)      Keyword       Description (Default)
-----------------------------------------------------------------------
USERID    username/password          FULL          export entire file (N)
BUFFER    size of data buffer        OWNER         list of owner usernames
FILE      output file (EXPDAT.DMP)   TABLES        list of table names
COMPRESS  import into one extent (Y) RECORDLENGTH  length of IO record
GRANTS    export grants (Y)          INCTYPE       incremental export type
INDEXES   export indexes (Y)         RECORD        track incr. export (Y)
ROWS      export data rows (Y)       PARFILE       parameter filename
CONSTRAINTS export constraints (Y)   CONSISTENT    cross-table consistency
LOG       log file of screen output  STATISTICS    analyze objects (ESTIMATE)
DIRECT    direct path (N)
FEEDBACK  display progress every x rows (0)
POINT_IN_TIME_RECOVER    Tablespace Point-in-time Recovery (N)
RECOVERY_TABLESPACES     List of tablespace names to recover
```

You can export data from your Personal Oracle8 database in the following modes:

- *Table mode*—Exports all table information for the table(s) specified. Administrative users can export tables owned by other users; normally, you will be able to export only a table you own—i.e., in your own schema.

- *User mode*—Exports all user objects, such as tables, indexes, and views. This works on a per-user basis—i.e., you tell it which user to export. Administrative users can export the objects for any user.

- *Full database mode*—Exports all of the database information for all users. This also exports all of the system definitions, including tablespaces, with the exception of any objects owned by **SYS**. Only administrative users can export in full database mode. Exporting in this mode also allows you to perform incremental and cumulative backups.

Each of these modes is selected by using different parameters from the command line. If you pass no parameters when invoking the **EXP80** command, it will start up in interactive mode. This is not the best mode to run in, but can be used when you need a quick export.

When using the command-line method, first specify the **EXP80** command and then the relevant parameters required. For example

```
EXP80 system/manager FILE=fulldb.dmp FULL=Y
```

would perform a full database export as the user **SYSTEM** to a file called *fulldb.dmp* in the current directory. The parameters you can use with the export utility are described below.

buffer

The **buffer** parameter specifies the size of the buffer used to retrieve rows from the database. If you are exporting lots of rows from a database, then you want to set this parameter to a high figure—e.g., 1,048,576, which is 1MB. The **buffer** parameter is a figure in bytes. If the buffer is set to zero, the export will retrieve rows one at a time. Any table with a column specified as **ROWID**, **BLOB**, **LOB**, or **LONG** will be exported one row at a time, regardless of the **buffer** parameter.

compress

Use the **compress** parameter to tell the export utility how to handle extents within the database (for a discussion on extent sizing, see Chapter 17). If you set this parameter to Y, all extents will be compressed and your data will be exported in a defragmented state (which is very desirable). If this parameter is set to N, the data will be exported in its original state. The default for this parameter is Y.

consistent

The **consistent** parameter makes the export you produce consistent to a point in time. For example, you could export a database while someone else is using it; thus, some of the data may change while you are exporting it. Setting the **consistent** parameter to Y allows the export utility to see a copy of the data at the time the export begins, so no data changes are backed up. This parameter defaults to N. You cannot set this parameter to Y when doing an incremental backup.

constraints

The **constraints** parameter specifies whether the export utility exports table constraints along with the tables. The default for this is Y. Exporting constraints is always a good idea.

direct

The **direct** parameter tells the export utility whether to use the direct or conventional path for exporting data (for a discussion on the direct method, see Chapter 7). The default for this parameter is N. Using the direct-path method is usually faster than the conventional method, because it reads the data directly rather than through the SQL processor.

feedback

When the **feedback** parameter is set, you get feedback on the number of rows exported. For example, when this parameter is set to 50, a dot will appear on the screen after every 50 rows are exported. The default for this parameter is zero—i.e., no dots are displayed.

file

This required parameter is the name of the file you are exporting the data into. The default file name for **file** is *expdat.dmp*, but never use this name for an export file; you will not know what is contained within it, and a file with this name can easily be overwritten. Always give your export files meaningful names and use the .dmp extension.

full

When set to Y, the **full** parameter performs a full database export. To do so, however, you will need to have been given the **EXP_FULL_DATABASE** role. The default for this parameter is N.

grants

Exporting data without any grants is possible if you set the **grants** parameter to N. The default for this parameter is Y. When set to Y, all grants that are defined within the database against objects you own are exported—unless you are an administrator, in which case all grants defined within the database are exported.

help

The **help** parameter displays the help information, which includes all of the parameters with their default values. If the **help** parameter is set to Y, any other parameter on the command line is ignored. The default for this parameter is N.

inctype

Use the **inctype** parameter when performing incremental or cumulative exports. The options are **INCREMENTAL** (export all objects that have changed since the last incremental export), **CUMULATIVE** (export all objects that have changed since the last cumulative export), or **COMPLETE** (export all objects and then set the cumulative and incremental dates).

indexes

When set, the **indexes** parameter exports indexes, along with the tables. The default for this parameter is Y. Exporting indexes along with the other objects is always a good idea.

log

The **log** parameter tells the export utility which file name and directory to log the output to. This parameter has no default, because the export utility does not usually log any of its output. Set this parameter whenever you do an export, because you should always check that the export was successful.

owner

When set to a username, **owner** indicates to the export utility that the export is to be performed in user mode. This parameter can be supplied as a comma-separated list if more than one user is to be exported.

parfile

When using the export utility, you can use only as many parameters as will fit onto the command line. This may hinder you if you can fit only 80 characters on your command line. By giving **parfile** the name of a parameter file, you can create a file that contains the parameters you require, therefore bypassing the limit on the command-line size.

record

The **record** parameter, when set to Y, records that a cumulative or incremental export was taken. It tells the export utility to set the date and time flag for the incremental and cumulative export.

rows

With the export utility, you can export the definitions of objects and not the data. For example, you can export the table structure without the rows. When set to N, the **rows** parameter does not export any rows from the database. The default for this parameter is Y.

statistics

The **statistics** parameter defines which type of optimizer statistics to gather when the database is reimported. The values for this parameter are **ESTIMATE** (the default), **COMPUTE**, and **NONE**.

tables

Use the **tables** parameter to export specific tables from the database. It indicates to the export utility that the export is to be done in table mode. This parameter can be followed by a list of tables in parentheses and separated by commas. You can see examples later in this chapter.

userid

The **userid** parameter specifies which user is to perform the export. If you need to do a full database export, you could use the **SYSTEM** username and password. You do not need to specify the parameter name if this parameter appears immediately after the **EXP80** command.

Tips On Performing Exports

Because some of these parameters cannot work in conjunction with one another, you have to be careful which ones you use. For example, you should not use the **owner** parameter with the **full** parameter, because a full database export would export all owners. Similarly, specifying the **owner** and **tables** parameters in the same export command can cause an error in the export utility.

Examples Of Different Exports

In this section, I will present three examples of different exports. Listing 15.14 shows part of a full export. Listing 15.15 shows part of an export of the **DEMO** user, and Listing 15.16 shows an example of exporting tables from the **DEMO** user.

Listing 15.14   A full database export.

```
EXP80 system/manager file=fulldb.dmp full=y log=fulldb.log

Connected to: Personal Oracle8 Release 8.0.3.0.0 - Production
With the Partitioning option
PL/SQL Release 8.0.3.0.0 - Production
Export done in WE8ISO8859P1 character set and WE8ISO8859P1 NCHAR character set

About to export the entire database ...
. exporting tablespace definitions
. exporting profiles
. exporting user definitions
. exporting roles
. exporting resource costs
. exporting rollback segment definitions
. exporting database links
. exporting sequence numbers
. exporting directory aliases
. exporting foreign function library names
. exporting object type definitions
. exporting cluster definitions
. about to export SYSTEM's tables via Conventional Path ...
. . exporting table                    DEF$_AQCALL              0 rows exported
. . exporting table                    DEF$_AQERROR             0 rows exported
. . exporting table                     DEF$_CALL               0 rows exported
```

```
. . exporting table                   DEF$_CALLDEST              0 rows exported
. . exporting table                DEF$_DEFAULTDEST              0 rows exported
. . exporting table                DEF$_DESTINATION              0 rows exported
. . exporting table                      DEF$_ERROR              0 rows exported
. . exporting table                        DEF$_LOB              0 rows exported
. . exporting table                     DEF$_ORIGIN              0 rows exported
. . exporting table                 DEF$_PROPAGATOR              0 rows exported
. . exporting table                  DEF$_TEMP$LOB              0 rows exported
. . exporting table          SQLPLUS_PRODUCT_PROFILE              0 rows exported
. . exporting table                    USER_PROFILE              0 rows exported
. about to export DBSNMP's tables via Conventional Path ...
. about to export SCOTT's tables via Conventional Path ...
. . exporting table                           BONUS              0 rows exported
. . exporting table                            DEPT              4 rows exported
. . exporting table                             EMP             14 rows exported
. . exporting table                        SALGRADE              5 rows exported
. about to export EXPLORER's tables via Conventional Path ...
. about to export DEMO's tables via Conventional Path ...
. . exporting table                       CHAR_DEMO              1 rows exported
. . exporting table                 CONVERSION_TEST              2 rows exported
. . exporting table                        CUSTOMER             33 rows exported
```

Listing 15.15   A user export.

```
EXP80 system/manager file=user.dmp owner=demo log=user.log

Connected to: Personal Oracle8 Release 8.0.3.0.0 - Production
With the Partitioning option
PL/SQL Release 8.0.3.0.0 - Production
Export done in WE8IS08859P1 character set and WE8IS08859P1 NCHAR character set

About to export specified users ...
. exporting foreign function library names for user DEMO
. exporting object type definitions for user DEMO
About to export DEMO's objects ...
. exporting database links
. exporting sequence numbers
. exporting cluster definitions
. about to export DEMO's tables via Conventional Path ...
. . exporting table                       CHAR_DEMO              1 rows exported
. . exporting table                 CONVERSION_TEST              2 rows exported
. . exporting table                        CUSTOMER             33 rows exported
. . exporting table                       CUSTOMERS              7 rows exported
. . exporting table                      DEPARTMENT             11 rows exported
. . exporting table                        EMPLOYEE             32 rows exported
. . exporting table                       EMPLOYEES              5 rows exported
. . exporting table                            ITEM            271 rows exported
. . exporting table                             JOB              6 rows exported
. . exporting table                             JRF              3 rows exported
. . exporting table                        JRF_TEMP              0 rows exported
```

```
. . exporting table            LOCATION         4 rows exported
. . exporting table            MESSAGES         1 rows exported
. . exporting table             ORDERS          9 rows exported
. . exporting table        ORDER_DETAILS       12 rows exported
. . exporting table         PLAN_TABLE          0 rows exported
. . exporting table              POI            1 rows exported
. . exporting table             PRICE          58 rows exported
. . exporting table            PRODUCT         31 rows exported
. . exporting table           PRODUCTS         10 rows exported
. . exporting table        SALARY_GRADE         5 rows exported
. . exporting table          SALES_FIGS
. . exporting partition      SALES_MONTH1             0 rows exported
. . exporting partition      SALES_MONTH2             0 rows exported
. . exporting partition      SALES_MONTH3             0 rows exported
. . exporting partition      SALES_MONTH4             0 rows exported
. . exporting partition      SALES_MONTH5             0 rows exported
. . exporting partition      SALES_MONTH6             0 rows exported
. . exporting partition      SALES_MONTH7             0 rows exported
. . exporting partition      SALES_MONTH8             0 rows exported
. . exporting partition      SALES_MONTH9             0 rows exported
. . exporting partition      SALES_MONTH10            0 rows exported
. . exporting partition      SALES_MONTH11            0 rows exported
. . exporting partition      SALES_MONTH12            0 rows exported
. . exporting partition          OTHER               0 rows exported
. . exporting table          SALES_ORDER    100 rows exported
. . exporting table           SUPPLIERS       7 rows exported
. . exporting table          SURNAME_A_H      0 rows exported
. . exporting table          SURNAME_I_Q      0 rows exported
. . exporting table          SURNAME_R_Z      0 rows exported
. . exporting table         VARCHAR2_DEMO      1 rows exported
. exporting synonyms
. exporting views
. exporting stored procedures
. exporting referential integrity constraints
. exporting triggers
. exporting posttables actions
. exporting snapshots
. exporting snapshot logs
. exporting job queues
. exporting refresh groups and children
Export terminated successfully without warnings.
```

Listing 15.16   A table export.

```
EXP80 system/manager file=tables.dmp tables=(demo.products,demo.orders)
 log=tables.log

Connected to: Personal Oracle8 Release 8.0.3.0.0 - Production
With the Partitioning option
```

```
PL/SQL Release 8.0.3.0.0 - Production
Export done in WE8ISO8859P1 character set and WE8ISO8859P1 NCHAR character set

About to export specified tables via Conventional Path ...
Current user changed to DEMO
. . exporting table                        PRODUCTS          10 rows exported
. . exporting table                          ORDERS           9 rows exported
Export terminated successfully without warnings.
```

RECOVERY

Recoveries are usually performed after a database has crashed or become corrupted. I describe two recovery methods here: the Recovery Manager and the import utility. This section describes in some detail the two main ways to recover your Personal Oracle8 database.

Recovery Manager

You can access Oracle Recovery Manager from your Windows 95 Start button, under the heading of Personal Oracle8 for Windows 95. After you select the Recovery Manager, a window will appear, similar to that in Figure 15.4.

When you use the Recovery Manager to recover a Personal Oracle8 database, the type of recovery you can perform depends upon the backup. If you did a full backup of the database in Noarchivelog mode, your only option for recovering the database is to pick Restore From Full Database Backup. If you performed a backup in Archivelog mode, you have all of the

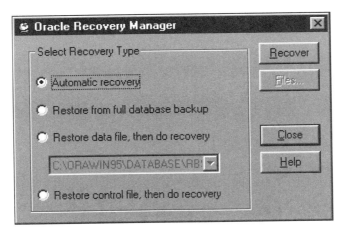

Figure 15.4   *The Oracle Recovery Manager window.*

other options available to you. The windows displayed under Recovery Manager contain various fields, along with the actions you must take to recover your database:

- *Automatic Recovery*—Performs an automatic recovery from the information held within the database regarding the state of the archive logs. This option can be performed only if the database is running in Archivelog mode.

- *Restore From Full Database Backup*—The only route to take if your database was backed up offline or if a backup was taken with no archive logging enabled.

- *Restore Data File, Then Do Recovery*—Restores the selected data file from the list box and then performs an automatic recovery on the database.

- *Restore Control File, Then Do Recovery*—Restores the control file and then performs an automatic recovery on the database.

- *Recover button*—Initiates the recovery process.

- *Files button*—Chooses which archive log files to restore.

- *Close button*—Closes the Recovery Manager window.

- *Help button*—Provides help on the Recovery Manager window.

Import

Import is a utility that uses a previously created export file to load data and object definitions back into the database. This is one of the ways to restore data to your database. With this method, you can selectively import parts of the export to your database. When importing, as exporting, you can use one of two methods: the Navigator or the DOS command line.

Navigator Method

To import data to your database through the Personal Oracle8 Navigator, start the Navigator, click on the Projects icon, then on the Database icon to make a connection, and, finally, right-click on the Database icon and select Import, as shown in Figure 15.5.

This brings up a window asking you where the file to import is. Type in your file name and location, then click on the Open button, shown in Figure 15.6.

This initiates a DOS session in the background, importing all of your data to the database. You do not get a choice of which data to import (from the command line, you do). Once the import has finished, you have the option of viewing the log file. I suggest you always do so to make sure the import worked properly. If an error occurred during the import, a message will be displayed to indicate this.

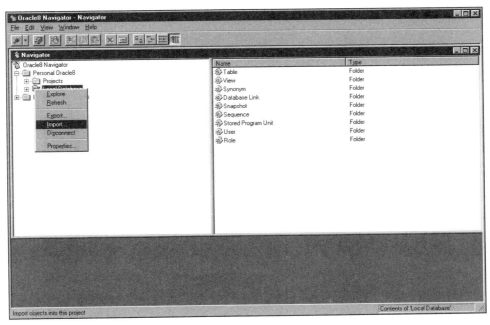

Figure 15.5 *Importing data through the Navigator.*

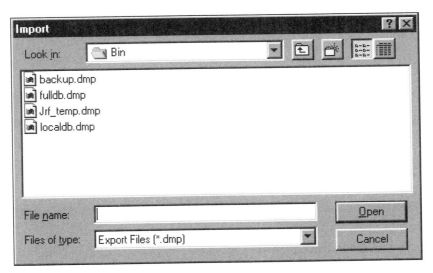

Figure 15.6 *Choose the import file to use.*

I do not suggest you use the import option from the Navigator. The command-line method gives you more functionality.

Command-Line Method

The command-line method of the import utility is by far the most flexible method for importing data to your Personal Oracle8 database. It allows you several options, including:

- Importing a single user

- Importing a single table

- Importing the full database

To start the import utility from the command line, you first need to bring up a DOS window. Once the window is active, you can initiate an import with the **IMP80** command. Before trying this, take some time to read the rest of this section, which explains the parameters used with the import utility. To see the parameters available for use with the **IMP80** command, type:

```
IMP80 help=y
```

This displays a screen similar to Listing 15.17, showing all of the parameters and their default values.

Listing 15.17 Displaying import help information.

```
Keyword   Description (Default)        Keyword      Description (Default)
------------------------------------------------------------------------
USERID    username/password            FULL         import entire file (N)
BUFFER    size of data buffer          FROMUSER     list of owner usernames
FILE      output file (EXPDAT.DMP)     TOUSER       list of usernames
SHOW      just list file contents (N)  TABLES       list of table names
IGNORE    ignore create errors (N)     RECORDLENGTH length of IO record
GRANTS    import grants (Y)            INCTYPE      incremental import type
INDEXES   import indexes (Y)           COMMIT       commit array insert (N)
ROWS      import data rows (Y)         PARFILE      parameter filename
LOG       log file of screen output
DESTROY   overwrite tablespace data file (N)
INDEXFILE write table/index info to specified file
CHARSET   character set of export file (NLS_LANG)
POINT_IN_TIME_RECOVER  Tablespace Point-in-time Recovery (N)
SKIP_UNUSABLE_INDEXES  skip maintenance of unusable indexes (N)
ANALYZE   execute ANALYZE statements in dump file (Y)
FEEDBACK display progress every x rows(0)
```

You can import data to your Personal Oracle8 database in the following modes:

- *Table mode*—Imports all table information for the table(s) specified.

- *User mode*—Imports all user objects, such as tables, indexes, and views. This works on a per-user basis—i.e., you tell it which user to import. Administrative users can import the objects for any user.

- *Full database mode*—Imports all of the database information for all users. This also imports all of the system definitions, including tablespaces, which were exported from the database using the export utility.

Each of these modes is selected by using different parameters from the command line. If you pass no parameters when invoking the **IMP80** command, it will start up in interactive mode. This is not the best mode to run in, but can be used when you need a quick import.

The import utility processes the data in a specific way each time. First, the specified table is created, then the rows are populated to the table, and, finally, indexes are built for the data. This sequence is important because it prevents the referential integrity of the database from being compromised.

When using the command-line method, first specify the **IMP80** command and then the relevant parameters required, just as you would with the export utility. For example

```
IMP80 system/manager FILE=fulldb.dmp FULL=Y
```

would perform a full database import as the user **SYSTEM** to your local database. The parameters you can use with the import utility are described below.

analyze
The **analyze** parameter tells the import utility whether to issue any of the **ANALYZE** commands found in the export file when importing the data. The **ANALYZE** command tells the optimizer the best way to execute a SQL statement. This parameter defaults to Y.

buffer
The **buffer** parameter specifies the size of the buffer used to insert rows into the database. If you are importing lots of rows to a database, then you want to set this parameter to a high figure—e.g., 1,048,576, which is 1MB. The **buffer** parameter is a figure in bytes. If the buffer is set to zero, the import will insert rows one at a time. Any table with a column specified as **ROWID**, **BLOB**, **LOB**, or **LONG** will be imported one row at a time, regardless of the **buffer** parameter.

charset
Use the **charset** parameter only when you are importing an export file generated from an Oracle version 6 database. You would not normally set this parameter; it is included only for backward compatibility.

commit

One of the most useful import parameters is **commit**, which tells the import utility whether a COMMIT should be issued after each array insert. The import utility usually issues a COMMIT after loading each table. If you are loading a large table, you would need large rollback segments to handle all of the data being stored. Using this parameter, you can COMMIT at each array insert, therefore reducing the size of the rollback segments and increasing the performance of large imports. This parameter defaults to N, but setting it to Y is always a good idea.

destroy

Be cautious when using the **destroy** parameter with the import command. As its name suggests, **destroy** will destroy existing database files and reuse them on import. This can be useful when you are creating a new database and wish to overwrite an existing one. The default for this parameter is N.

feedback

The **feedback** parameter, when set, gives you feedback on the number of rows imported. For example, when this parameter is set to 50, a dot will appear on the screen after every 50 rows are imported. The default for this parameter is zero—i.e., no dots are displayed.

file

This required parameter is the name of the file you are importing the data from. The default file name for **file** is *expdat.dmp*. This should be the file name you gave to the export file.

fromuser

The **fromuser** parameter tells the import utility to perform an import in user mode. If you give the parameter a list of usernames, they will be imported from the export file. If the users do not exist, all of their objects will be imported to the user who performed the import.

full

When set to Y, the **full** parameter performs a full database import. To do so, however, you will need to have been given the **IMP_FULL_DATABASE** role. The default for this parameter is N.

grants

Importing data without any grants is possible if you set the **grants** parameter to N. When set to Y, which is the default, all grants defined within the database against objects you own are imported—unless you are an administrator, in which case all grants defined within the database are imported.

help

The **help** parameter displays the help information, which includes all of the parameters with their default values. If the **help** parameter is set to Y, any other parameter on the command line is ignored. The default for this parameter is N.

ignore

The **ignore** parameter specifies how errors received by the import utility are to be handled. Sometimes, when you are importing data into a database, you will see error messages saying that objects already exist. If this is okay and you already know that errors will be produced, set this parameter to Y. Then, the creation of the table will be skipped, but the rows will still be imported. When the parameter is set to N (the default), if you are importing a table and it already exists, an error message will be produced and the table skipped.

inctype

Use the **inctype** parameter when importing an incremental backup. The options for this parameter are **SYSTEM** and **RESTORE**. When set to **SYSTEM**, the most recent versions of the system objects are imported. When set to **RESTORE**, all database objects within the file are imported.

index

When set, the **index** parameter imports indexes along with the tables. The default for this parameter is Y. Importing indexes along with the other objects is always a good idea. If you wish no indexes to be created during the import session, set this parameter to N. This could be desirable when importing into existing tables, because when each row is inserted, the index is maintained. The best option here would be to drop the index from the table, perform an import with no indexes, and then re-create the index.

indexfile

During an import session, all index creation commands can be stored in a file. This file can then be executed at a later stage to re-create the indexes. If the **indexfile** parameter is set, no indexes, tables, or other objects are created within the database through the import session. To set this parameter, you must give it a file name and directory.

log

The **log** parameter tells the import utility which file name and directory to log the output to. This parameter has no default, as the import utility does not usually log any of its output. Set this parameter whenever you do an import, because you need to check that the import was successful.

parfile

When using the import utility, you can use only as many parameters as will fit onto the command line. This may hinder you if you can fit only 80 characters on your command line. By giving the **parfile** parameter the name of a parameter file, you can create a file containing the parameters you require, therefore bypassing the limit on the command-line size.

rows

The import utility allows you to import the definitions of objects and not the data. For example, you can import the table structure without the rows. When set to N, the **row** parameter does not import any rows from the database. The default for this parameter is Y.

show

When specified, the **show** parameter will display the contents of the file to be imported. This does not alter your database at all—the file is just displayed and not executed. The default for this parameter is N.

tables

Use the **tables** parameter to import specific tables from the database. It indicates to the import utility that the import is to be done in table mode. This parameter can be followed by a list of tables in parentheses and separated by commas. To import tables from another user, you have to use this parameter in conjunction with the **fromuser** parameter—i.e., to tell the import utility which user owns the tables you wish to import.

touser

The **touser** parameter is used when importing data from an export file to a different user—i.e., when copying a user's data. It should be used in conjunction with the **fromuser** parameter. For example, specifying **fromuser=demo** and **touser=po8** would import the objects owned by **DEMO** to the user **PO8**.

userid

The **userid** parameter specifies which user is to perform the import. If you need to do a full database import, you should use the **SYSTEM** username and password. You do not need to specify the parameter name if this parameter appears immediately after the **IMP80** command.

REVIEW

In this chapter, I showed you some of the ways to back up and restore your data. For more information, see your Personal Oracle8 documentation, which explains backup and restore in more detail. Within this chapter, I mentioned rollback segments and extents, which are objects that Personal Oracle8 uses internally. The next chapter discusses the internal architecture of Personal Oracle8, to give you an understanding of what goes on behind the scenes.

ORACLE8 ARCHITECTURE AND INTERNALS

What goes on behind the scenes of an Oracle8 database.

The previous chapter addressed security and auditing issues surrounding the Personal Oracle8 database. In this chapter, I discuss the makeup of the Personal Oracle8 database, or what exactly makes it tick. I explain the internal mechanisms, associated objects, and their functions. The chapter deals mainly with the generic Oracle8 database and its component parts. This is the same as the Personal Oracle8 implementation you have on your PC, with some slight differences—e.g., where multiple users are concerned. This approach is intended to give you an overall perspective of what Oracle is all about. It will also prepare you for the next chapter, on performance tuning and administration.

THE ORACLE DATABASE

Databases are just repositories for information—that is, they enable you to store and retrieve information in a variety of ways. Oracle's database is a new dimension of relational database, called an *object-relational database*, discussed in Chapter 13. The database is made up of the Oracle database itself and the Oracle instance. The database and the instance are two different entities—although many people refer to them as the same thing—with interactions between the two. In this section, I explain the difference between the two.

The Parts Of The Database

The database can be divided into two parts: physical and logical.

The Physical Database

The physical database is the actual files you see on your hard disk when using the Explorer. These files contain all of the information entered into your database. They consist of the following:

- *Data files (i.e., tablespaces)*—A database can have one or more data files.

- *Redo log files*—A database must have a minimum of two redo log files.

- *Control files*—A database must have a minimum of one control file.

Each of these files is discussed in more detail later in this chapter. For now, the most important are the data files, where all of your data is stored. Every Oracle8 database has one or more physical data files (a file on your hard disk) associated with it. All of the logical database information is stored within the physical data files. All data files have the following properties:

- Each one can be associated with only one database.

- Tablespaces can use one or more data files.

- Data files can be created to react to the data inserted into them.

As mentioned previously, the data files store all of your data. When a database is in operation, data is read from the data files and stored within memory. If, for example, a user wishes to access the data within the **PRODUCTS** table, and if the data is not already in memory, Oracle will read the data from the relevant data file and store this within memory. The opposite happens when you write information to the database. For example, if you insert a row into a table, this data is not automatically written to the physical data file; it is stored within memory (it is not written immediately because this would decrease performance), in a cache, because writing a lot of data all at once is more efficient than doing little bits all of the time. Writing data to the data files is done by the database writer (DBWR) process, explained later in this chapter.

At any given time, the database could be in one of many different modes. The usual modes are open and closed. When a database is open, any user can connect to it and perform queries. When a database is in closed mode, however, no connections can be made and the data is not accessible. Databases in this state are *shut down.* Databases are normally shut down in order to perform administrative work and backups.

The Logical Database

The logical structure for a database is determined in part by the physical database layout. The logical database defines how the physical database space is to be used. The logical database elements include:

- Tablespaces

- Tables

- Extents

- Segments

- Schemas

- Views

- Sequences

- Indexes

- Synonyms

All of these elements define how the space provided by the physical database files is to be used. The relationships between these objects define the design for the database—i.e., the relational database.

You use the tablespace to store related logical items. For example, all of the tables owned by the user **DEMO** could be stored within one tablespace, and other users may have their own tablespaces. Any given tablespace maps directly onto one or more physical data files. Tablespaces can be used to store any number of different objects. A tablespace can be in one of two states: ONLINE or OFFLINE. When in an OFFLINE state, the tablespace cannot be accessed from the database, which makes administrative tasks, such as backups, much easier to perform.

The logical database contains a number of schemas. As mentioned in Chapter 9, a *schema* is just a collection of objects. A correlation exists between schemas and tablespaces, because a schema can contain objects that are stored within any number of tablespaces.

Within a tablespace, any stored data must tell the tablespace how to store itself. For example, when you create a table, you could tell the database to store it in the USER_DATA tablespace using 5 blocks of space, and the maximum amount of space that could be used is 10 blocks.

These blocks are the lowest level of storage within an Oracle database. One block corresponds to a set number of bytes on the physical disk within your PC.

Each tablespace is divided into a number of blocks, so you can tell the database exactly where to store the data you are creating. The size of the blocks within Oracle is determined when you create the database. In the previous example, I told the database to create a table that is initially 5 blocks in size, with a maximum size of 10 blocks. These blocks are also known as *extents*. An extent can be thought of as a preallocated block. So, in the example, the table I created would have an initial extent of 5 and a maximum extent of 10.

The next section introduces the Oracle instance and describes the differences between it and the database. It is important to understand this fully, because this is the fundamental concept behind the Oracle database.

The Oracle Instance

As I discussed earlier in this chapter, when a query is executed, all of the required information is retrieved from the database and put into memory, if it is not already there, before the user sees it on screen. Oracle reserves and uses a piece of memory for all database transactions. This piece of memory, along with some *processes* (programs that run in memory), is known as the *Oracle instance*. Whenever a database is started, the system global area (SGA) is reserved purely for the Oracle instance. Also at startup time, some background processes are initiated to handle the interaction between the SGA and the database.

Each Oracle instance has two different types of processes associated with it:

- *User processes*—Started whenever a user connects to the database. They handle the interaction between the user and the SGA.

- *Oracle processes*—Automatically started whenever the database is started up. These processes handle the interaction between the SGA and the database (see the "Memory Structures" section later in this chapter for more details).

You can have more than one Oracle instance acting against one database (this is where understanding the differences between an instance and a database is important, and it is a concept that most people do not fully understand). To do so, you must have two machines (this is not relevant to the PC user, because this is implemented only on high-end Unix boxes) and a shared disk array accessible by both machines—i.e., you must have one database that can be accessed by two machines. This way, you can have one instance running on one machine and a second instance running on the other, both accessing the same database structure, as shown in Figure 16.1. This increases resilience, because both machines must fail before the database is inaccessible. It also increases performance in some cases. This configuration is known as *parallel server*, an option for Oracle8 on some higher-specification machines.

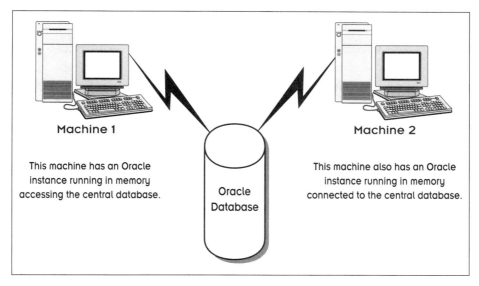

Machine 1

This machine has an Oracle
instance running in memory
accessing the central database.

Oracle
Database

Machine 2

This machine also has an Oracle
instance running in memory
connected to the central database.

Figure 16.1 *An example of an Oracle parallel server.*

MEMORY STRUCTURES

As mentioned in the previous section, the Oracle instance is made up of a memory structure and background processes. This section explains how memory works and the components of the SGA. These memory structures allow Oracle8 to support multiple users on a high-performance database. Oracle uses them to provide access to the underlying database. Whenever I refer to memory structures, I am referring to the RAM on your PC. Therefore, the more RAM available on your PC, the bigger the memory structure can be, allowing more data to be stored within the SGA. The background processes work in conjunction with the memory structure by passing messages between it and the database.

Caching Data

Oracle uses the available memory for storing the SGA. The SGA is really used to cache information into. The act of caching information into memory is really just moving information into an area where it can be read more quickly. Reading anything from memory is infinitely quicker than reading from the hard disk. Within Oracle, most of the tuning available is by altering what is stored within the SGA. The SGA controls the execution of all Oracle statements, including where to read them from. All you have to remember is that caching is the quickest way to access information.

System Global Area (SGA)

As previously mentioned, the SGA is a structure, held within memory, which controls the access and execution of statements against the database. You can have only one SGA per instance. In larger systems with multiple connections to the database at the same time, each connection has access to the SGA. This is known as *sharing* the data within the SGA. For this reason, the SGA is sometimes known as the shared global area. Any user is able to read from the SGA, and a number of background processes write to it. The SGA is split into a number of different areas:

- Database buffer cache
- Redo log buffer
- Shared pool
- Dictionary cache
- Other smaller areas

The SGA is created when the instance is started. It can be created to a predefined size, specified by the user, via the init.ora file. When an instance is shut down, the SGA is deallocated from memory. If the size of the SGA is larger than the available memory, the performance of the database will decrease. Remember, reading from memory is faster than from disk; having an SGA larger than available memory effectively uses part of the hard disk as memory, defeating the purpose of the SGA.

The size of the SGA is determined by the following parameters, found within the init.ora file:

- *db_block_size*—Determines the block size of the database. The value of this parameter is usually set to one of the following: 2,048 (2K), 4,096 (4K), or 8,192 (8K), where the number is in bytes.

- *db_block_buffers*—Defines the number of database buffers within the SGA.

- *log_buffer*—Defines the size of the redo log buffer in bytes (more about redo logs later in this chapter).

- *shared_pool_size*—Defines the amount of space allocated, in bytes, for shared SQL and PL/SQL within the SGA. This is the area where all shared data is stored within the SGA; obviously, the bigger this parameter, the more information you can store within the SGA.

To calculate the size of the buffer cache within the SGA, simply multiply **db_block_size** by **db_block_buffers**. This gives you the size of the buffer cache in bytes. When an instance is started through the Server Manager, the memory structure is displayed, as shown in Listing 16.1.

Listing 16.1   *Starting an Oracle instance through the Server Manager.*

```
Oracle Server Manager Release 3.0.3.0.0 - Production

(c) Copyright 1997, Oracle Corporation.  All Rights Reserved.

Personal Oracle8 Release 8.0.3.0.0 - Production
With the Partitioning option
PL/SQL Release 8.0.3.0.0 - Production

SVRMGR> connect internal
Connected.
SVRMGR> startup
ORACLE instance started.
Total System Global Area         5508612 bytes
Fixed Size                         45584 bytes
Variable Size                    4529140 bytes
Database Buffers                  409600 bytes
Redo Buffers                      524288 bytes
Database mounted.
Database opened.
SVRMGR>
```

The listing shows the components of the SGA. Its overall size is 5,508,612 bytes, consisting of a fixed size of 45,584, a variable size of 4,529,140, database buffers of 409,600, and redo buffers of 524,288. The part of the SGA that holds information on the status of the database and the instance is called the *fixed area*. No data is stored within the fixed area. The following sections describe each of the components of the SGA. (The main components are shown in Figure 16.2.)

Database Buffer Cache

The *database buffer cache* stores the most recently changed blocks from the database. The buffer cache contains both modified and unmodified blocks. Because the most recently used data blocks are stored within memory, this cuts down on the amount of disk accesses needed against the database and, therefore, increases performance. All connections to the database share access to the buffer cache.

All buffers within the buffer cache are divided into two separate areas: the dirty list and the least recently used (LRU) list. The *dirty list* stores information on all dirty buffers, defined as those that have been modified but not yet applied to the database (remember, Oracle does not write all information to the database right away; it is cached in the SGA and written in

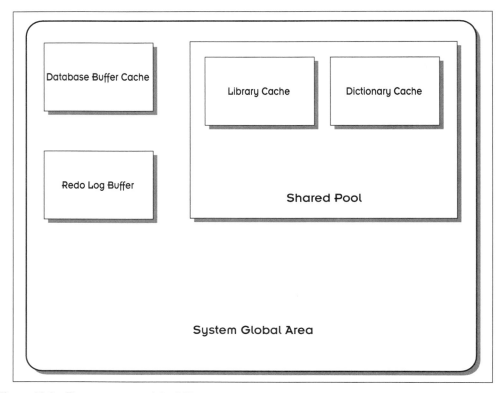

Figure 16.2   The components of the SGA.

one action). The LRU list stores information on all buffers that have not yet been moved to the dirty list. These buffers could be in one of three modes:

- *Free*—Those that have not yet been modified; they are free to be used.
- *Pinned*—Buffers currently in use.
- *Dirty*—Those that have been modified, but are not yet on the dirty list.

The LRU list is in time order of modified buffers. When you use a new buffer, it is added to the top of the list (the most recently used), and all other contents are moved down the list. When you need information from the database that is not already in the buffer cache, a process reads the block of data from the database and adds it to the buffer cache. If the buffer cache has free buffers, the data is read into them. If the buffer cache has no free buffers, the LRU list is read until a free buffer is found or a predefined threshold is encountered. Once this occurs, all dirty buffers move to the dirty buffer list and are written to the database (using the DBWR process, explained later in this chapter). This then frees up some buffers, which the new data can be read into.

The size of the buffer cache is determined by the size of the **db_block_buffers** parameter in the init.ora file. Each buffer is the size of one Oracle block, defined by **db_block_size**. Therefore, each block within the database can be stored within each block of the buffer cache. Reading blocks from the buffer cache can be defined as being either a cache hit or a cache miss. A hit defines that the buffer needed is in the SGA (within memory and quick to read); a miss defines that the buffer is not in the SGA and, therefore, has to be read from the database. Collecting this type of information makes tuning the SGA easier. You will always have a number of cache misses in any instance, because the whole database cannot usually fit into the size of the SGA. The DBA's job is to minimize the number of cache misses.

Shared Pool

The *shared pool* contains three major segments:

- Library cache
- Dictionary cache
- Control structures

The shared pool is an area of the SGA that stores the shared SQL areas. These are used to execute and store all unique SQL statements issued to the database. Oracle can then remember how it executed a previous identical statement and execute all others in the same way. The main point to remember is that the size of the shared pool determines the number of SQL statements you can store within the shared pool. The more that SQL statements can be stored, the better the chance you have of finding an identical statement to the one issued. The size of the shared pool is determined by the parameter **shared_pool_size**. This value is in bytes and can be found in the init.ora file.

Library Cache

The *library cache* contains the shared SQL and PL/SQL areas. This is a part of the SGA, which contains all reusable SQL statements.

Dictionary Cache

As mentioned in previous chapters, the *data dictionary* is the collection of tables and views that contain information about the database. You generally use these tables and views when tuning the database, as they hold statistical information relevant to the execution and status of the database. The *dictionary cache* holds information on:

- All objects within the database
- The name and data types of all columns within the database

- Details of all indexes available to the database

- Statistical information on the database

- All of the security information

The information in the dictionary cache is useful to all administrators. By interrogating the dictionary cache, the administrator can find all database information—for example, the locations and sizes of all files belonging to the database. Oracle also accesses the data dictionary to enable the correct execution of statements and check statement validation. For example, if you issue a **SELECT** statement on three columns from a table, Oracle makes sure the columns exist by looking at the dictionary cache. If the cache does not know about a column, Oracle can issue an error message. Oracle automatically creates and maintains the dictionary cache—i.e., when you create a table, the dictionary cache is updated automatically.

Program Global Area (PGA)

The *program global area (PGA)*, also referred to as the process global area, is a portion of memory reserved for information regarding server processes. A PGA is created automatically when an Oracle process is started—for example, when a user logs in. Each PGA contains a stack space, which is just a piece of memory reserved for storing the variables and arrays, etc., the user has defined within the connection to the database. The PGA also contains information on the user's session. The PGA is only writable by the user who owns it; it is not shared with other users. A DBA cannot change the size of the PGA, which is operating-system specific.

Sort Area

The Oracle database performs sorts whenever required. The number of sorts can be high. Whenever it sorts any information, Oracle needs an area to execute the sort in. The *sort area* is available to each user and exists only when a user requests a sort. If the sort is large, the sort area will dynamically extend until it reaches a predefined threshold—in this case, the **sort_area_size** parameter in the init.ora file. If you need to sort a large amount of information (larger than **sort_area_size**), Oracle splits the sort into smaller portions and sorts them, merging them at the end.

Redo Log Buffer

The *redo log buffer* is where Oracle logs changes to the database. This enables you to perform recovery if the database crashes. The redo log entries can be applied to the database to re-create it. The redo log buffer is written to the online redo logs at a predefined interval, using the log writer (LGWR) process (LGWR is covered later in this chapter). The size of the redo log buffer is defined by the **log_buffer** parameter, in bytes.

PROCESSES

Oracle background processes are called by user processes to perform specific functions against the database. An Oracle database has two types of processes: server and background.

Server Processes

Server processes communicate between the user and Oracle, telling the database what actions to perform. Normally, one server process per user is connected to the database (user process). In some cases, server processes can be shared among many users. This type of configuration is called *multithreaded server*. It increases performance, because you do not have the overhead of controlling many server processes. In some cases—for example, the client-server architecture—the server process is associated with the Oracle instance, and the user process is on the PC.

Background Processes

Whenever an Oracle instance is started, a number of background processes also begin. They handle the running of the database. You need to understand their functions before tuning any database. For example, it would not benefit performance to let anyone write directly to the database at any time, so Oracle created the DBWR process to do this. This process only writes to the database, nothing else. With each process having a specific function, efficiency and reliability increase. The background processes that may be available at any one time include:

- SMON
- PMON
- DBWR
- LGWR
- ARCH
- CKPT
- RECO
- Dnnn
- LCKn

The following sections explain all of these processes.

System Monitor (SMON)

The primary function of the system monitor process is to perform recovery when the Oracle instance is started. SMON also cleans up temporary segments that have been created by other processes. As a part of this tidying up, SMON coalesces the free spaces created within the database (extents) when they are freed up. This creates contiguous free space that is easier to reallocate later. You can think of SMON as the process that tidies up after the other processes and, when needed, fixes the database.

Process Monitor (PMON)

Process monitor looks after all of the other processes. It checks that they are functioning correctly, and when one dies or fails, it performs process recovery. Process recovery involves freeing up all resources the process had locked. The process monitor also logs its actions to operating-system files to alert the DBA as to the action taken.

Database Writer (DBWR)

The database writer process, as previously mentioned, writes modified blocks from the database buffer back to the data files. It writes these modified blocks in batches, only when the database buffer needs more space. Therefore, DBWR frees up space in the SGA by writing modified blocks back to the database. When any modified blocks are written to the data files, those blocks are the ones at the end of the least recently used list—that is, the oldest modified blocks in the SGA. DBWR also performs the checkpointing of the database. A checkpoint provides a means of rolling forward after a database crash.

Log Writer (LGWR)

The log writer process performs the writes to the online redo logs. It writes what is currently in the redo log buffer of the SGA into the redo log files on disk. These are held on disk and form part of the database. The redo logs are used to perform recovery on the database. They are best used when the database is in Archivelog mode, where redo logs are copied and kept on the system. When the database is not in Archivelog mode, the redo logs are cycled.

Archiver (ARCH)

In Archivelog mode, the archiver process appears. It is responsible for the copying of the redo log file to an archive area, specified by the DBA, when the current redo log is full. These archive logs are then stored and used when database recovery is required. They provide the ability to restore the database to any point in time.

Checkpointer (CKPT)

As mentioned in the DBWR section, there is a process that tells DBWR to *checkpoint* the database—that is, to write all of the current information in the SGA back to the data files. This is the checkpointer process. The DBA can specify the number of checkpoints that should be performed; you should make the database checkpoint whenever a redo log file is switched. CKPT also looks after the checkpointing information held within the SGA, writing to it whenever a checkpoint occurs.

Recoverer (RECO)

The recoverer process is active in distributed databases only. It handles the resolution of distributed transactions that are pending. At specified times, RECO connects to the distributed databases and attempts either to commit or roll back any pending information for distributed transactions.

Multithreaded Server (Dnnn)

The Dnnn process, otherwise known as the dispatcher process, is used only within a multithreaded server architecture—that is, multiple user processes being handled by one server process. Normally, one dispatcher process is created for each communication protocol used. The dispatcher process handles the routing of the requests to the database and back to the user, using the available pool of server processes.

Lock (LCKn)

The lock process is seen only when you use the Oracle Parallel Server option, which allows you to have one database, yet multiple instances (on different machines). This configuration is generally available on high-end Unix machines only. LCKn handles the locking between the two, or more, instances. For example, suppose one instance has a block locked and the other one needs to modify some information within the locked block. The lock process allows for communication between the two instances, to release the modified block.

THE OPTIMIZER

The optimizer defines how to execute the query you give to Oracle. In some complex queries, you could choose from any number of ways to execute the statement, all giving the same result—but in a different fashion. The optimizer defines the quickest way to execute the statement. For example, changing the order of the tables in the **FROM** clause of a **SELECT** statement results in the query being processed in a different way. The optimizer chooses the quickest way (usually) to execute the SQL statement. It selects the execution path by evaluating a number of different access paths to the data you require. More often than not, the developer writing the SQL statements knows the structure of the data better than the optimizer and can give the optimizer hints about the best access path to the required data. Depending on which optimizer is running (Oracle gives you the option of two optimizers), access paths will be chosen in different ways.

Executing A SQL Statement

To execute any SQL statement, Oracle has to know the best way to retrieve the required data, which may involve the execution of many different steps. These steps are collectively known as the *execution plan.* For example, Listing 16.2 shows the execution plan for a SQL statement issued against the database (don't worry too much at this stage about how to view the execution plan).

Listing 16.2   A sample execution plan.

```
SQL> set timing on autotrace on explain
SQL> select p.product_name,
  2          p.unit_cost_price,
  3          o.order_id,
  4          o.unit_price
  5   from products p,
  6        order_details o
  7* where p.product_id = o.product_id
SQL> /

PRODUCT_NAME                            UNIT_COST_PRICE  ORDER_ID UNIT_PRICE
------------------------------------    ---------------  -------- ----------
B Nut                                                 2    100001          4
A Nut                                                 1    100001          2
1cm Screw                                             5    100001         10
A Nut                                                 1    100002          2
B Nut                                                 2    100003          4
A Nut                                                 1    100004          2
B Nut                                                 2    100004          4
1cm Nail                                              3    100005          6
1cm Screw                                             5    100005         10
B Nut                                                 2    100005          4
A Nut                                                 1    100006          2
1cm Nail                                              3    100003          6

12 rows selected.

 real: 770
```

```
Execution Plan
----------------------------------------------------------
   0      SELECT STATEMENT Optimizer=CHOOSE
   1   0    NESTED LOOPS
   2   1      TABLE ACCESS (FULL) OF 'ORDER_DETAILS'
   3   1      TABLE ACCESS (BY INDEX ROWID) OF 'PRODUCTS'
   4   3        INDEX (UNIQUE SCAN) OF 'SYS_C00804' (UNIQUE)
```

The SQL statement in Listing 16.2 selects from the **PRODUCTS** and **ORDER_DETAILS** tables all rows joined by a **Product_id**. The execution plan shows you exactly which route the optimizer took to retrieve the data. The execution in this case happened in five steps (0 to 4):

0. Shows the type of statement being performed and the optimizer being used. An optimizer is chosen when the database is started up, as defined by the DBA.

1. Explains that a nested loop is being executed. This means that all of the indentations below this line (child processes) are performed once for each occurrence of the loop.

2. Shows that the **ORDER_DETAILS** table was accessed. The identifier in parentheses shows the type of table access that occurred—in this case, a full table scan. You should normally avoid full table scans when issuing SQL statements, but because the **ORDER_DETAILS** table contains only a few rows, this was not a problem.

3. Shows that another table access occurred, this time against the **PRODUCTS** table. Instead of being a full table scan, it is accessed by **INDEX ROWID**, one of the quickest types of table access. Basically, it reads an index instead of reading all of the columns of the table.

4. Shows that the index read by the table access in Step 3 was a unique scan and the name of the index was **SYS_C00804**, a system-generated index.

Just to show the different paths the optimizer may take, Listing 16.3 has the same SQL statement issued, but with a subquery, picking off all orders placed in 1999.

Listing 16.3 *Execution plan for more complex SQL.*

```
 1  select p.product_name,
 2         p.unit_cost_price,
 3         o.order_id,
 4         o.unit_price
 5  from order_details o,
 6       products p
 7  where p.product_id = o.product_id
 8  and o.order_id in (select ord.order_id
 9                     from orders ord
10*                    where substr(order_date,8,2) = '99')
```

```
SQL> /

PRODUCT_NAME                              UNIT_COST_PRICE  ORDER_ID UNIT_PRICE
---------------------------------------- ---------------- --------- ----------
B Nut                                                   2    100001          4
A Nut                                                   1    100001          2
1cm Screw                                              5    100001         10
A Nut                                                   1    100002          2
1cm Nail                                               3    100005          6
1cm Screw                                              5    100005         10
B Nut                                                   2    100005          4
A Nut                                                   1    100006          2

8 rows selected.

 real: 660

Execution Plan
------------------------------------------------------------
   0       SELECT STATEMENT Optimizer=CHOOSE
   1    0    NESTED LOOPS
   2    1      NESTED LOOPS
   3    2        TABLE ACCESS (FULL) OF 'ORDER_DETAILS'
   4    2        TABLE ACCESS (BY INDEX ROWID) OF 'PRODUCTS'
   5    4          INDEX (UNIQUE SCAN) OF 'SYS_C00804' (UNIQUE)
   6    1      TABLE ACCESS (BY INDEX ROWID) OF 'ORDERS'
   7    6        INDEX (UNIQUE SCAN) OF 'SYS_C00794' (UNIQUE)
```

You can see that by adding another table to the SQL statement, the optimizer chooses a different path to execute the SQL statement. This just shows the extra table, **ORDERS**, being accessed using another unique index. The execution plan command is discussed in more detail in Chapter 18.

As mentioned earlier, Oracle gives you the choice of two optimizers: rule-based and cost-based.

Rule-Based Optimization

Rule-based optimization has been around longer than cost-based, which was introduced with Oracle7. The rule-based approach works like this: When a piece of SQL needs to be executed, the optimizer chooses an execution plan based on the available access paths it knows about; it then ranks these paths and chooses the one that best fits. This way, if the same SQL statement were executed a number of times, the optimizer would always choose the same execution path.

Cost-Based Optimization

Cost-based optimization is slightly more intelligent than rule-based. It works in a similar way to rule-based optimization, but also takes into account statistics gathered from previous executions about the objects it is accessing. It can then choose the best way to access and retrieve the data. Always use the cost-based optimizer for newly written applications; the rule-based optimizer is present only for applications written prior to Oracle7 (however, some applications require the rule-based optimizer; see the application's documentation for specific details). One of the advantages of using the cost-based optimizer is that you can write hints into your code to tell the optimizer what the access path should be. The cost-based optimizer follows these three steps for all SQL statements executed:

1. The optimizer generates all of the available access paths for the data, taking into account any hints in the SQL statement.

2. It then estimates the cost of each execution plan (that is, the cost of resource usage) against the statistics it has gathered in the past.

3. All of the available costs are compared, and the lowest-cost access path is executed.

ANALYZE

As mentioned in Step 2, the cost-based optimizer uses previously gathered statistics to generate an execution plan. These statistics are generated with the **ANALYZE** command. This command looks at the storage of data for whichever object you are analyzing and stores the results within the data dictionary for the optimizer to use. The following data dictionary views have these statistics:

- ALL_INDEXES
- ALL_IND_PARTITIONS
- ALL_PART_COL_STATISTICS
- ALL_TABLES
- ALL_TAB_COLUMNS
- ALL_TAB_PARTITIONS
- DBA_CLUSTERS
- DBA_INDEXES
- DBA_IND_PARTITIONS
- DBA_PART_COL_STATISTICS

- DBA_TABLES

- DBA_TAB_COLUMNS

- DBA_TAB_PARTITIONS

- USER_CLUSTERS

- USER_INDEXES

- USER_IND_PARTITIONS

- USER_PART_COL_STATISTICS

- USER_TABLES

- USER_TAB_COLUMNS

- USER_TAB_PARTITIONS

Histograms

The cost-based optimizer uses histograms to define the spread of data within a table. This enables the optimizer to take into account any differences in data storage within the table. The histograms are created when you use the **ANALYZE** command. If data is uniformly spread among columns, the optimization of the statement is fairly easy; in most databases, however, the data is not spread evenly among columns, making histograms extremely important to the optimizer.

Consider a column within a table that has 1,000 rows of data, with the values for the histogram split into 10 equal parts (known as *buckets*). If the data were uniformly spread over the columns, you would expect to see each bucket contain, on average, 100 rows. If the data within the columns is not uniformly spread, you could see the following:

- *Bucket 1*—Contains 500 rows

- *Bucket 2*—Contains 200 rows

- *Bucket 3*—Contains 100 rows

- *Bucket 4*—Contains 100 rows

- *Bucket 5*—Contains 50 rows

- *Bucket 6*—Contains 10 rows

- *Bucket 7*—Contains 10 rows

- *Bucket 8*—Contains 10 rows

- *Bucket 9*—Contains 10 rows

- *Bucket 10*—Contains 10 rows

If this were the case, you would find 80 percent of the data stored within the first three buckets (if uniformly spread, you would expect to see 30 percent of the data within the first three buckets). The optimizer uses this type of information to define the quickest access to the data required. To view histogram information for columns that have been analyzed, you can look in the following views:

- ALL_HISTOGRAMS

- ALL_PART_HISTOGRAMS

- DBA_HISTOGRAMS

- DBA_PART_HISTOGRAMS

- TAB_COLUMNS

- USER_HISTOGRAMS

- USER_PART_HISTOGRAMS

CONTROL FILES

All Oracle databases have one or more control files. These files store details about the makeup of the database—i.e., the physical structure. Control files contain the following information:

- Database name

- Locations of data files and log files

- Names of data files and log files

- Sizes of data files and log files

- Creation information about the database—i.e., when it was created, what parameters were given to create the database

- Database backup information

Oracle needs one control file to start the database. In reality, you should store multiple copies of the control file, in case of an emergency.

How And When Control Files Are Used

Whenever a database is started, Oracle first reads the control file, which tells it which files to open for the specific database. These are the data files (which make up the tablespaces) and the redo log files (which are used to perform recovery). If the database is altered physically—i.e., a new tablespace added—the control file is changed to reflect the new physical makeup of the database.

ROLLBACK SEGMENTS

Rollback segments are used within Oracle for storing all of the undo information. For each statement issued against the database that modifies either data or structure, an entry is made in the rollback segment. This entry tells Oracle how to undo the change. In effect, it stores the values that existed before the change to the data. For example, if you inserted a row into the **PRODUCTS** table, the rollback entry would define how to delete the row you just inserted. Therefore, when the **ROLLBACK** command is entered, Oracle knows how to perform the rollback.

You can use the information stored within the rollback segments in a number of different ways:

- For read consistency

- For use in database recovery

- For rolling back any uncommitted transactions

You cannot read the contents of any rollback segment; only Oracle can do this. Whenever an entry is made into a rollback segment, a data block within the rollback segment itself is changed. This information is also stored within the redo logs. Usually, more than one rollback segment is in operation at any one time. This allows for contention between transactions, because no two transactions can write to the rollback segment at any one time. Whenever a statement is issued against the database, the next free rollback segment is picked up and the rollback entries entered into it until a commit happens. Once a commit occurs, the rollback entries are released and the rollback segment is ready for another transaction.

You can specify which rollback segment to use within the SQL statement with the **SET TRANSACTION** *rollback_segment_name* command. This command defines the rollback segment to use for this transaction. It is useful when lots of processing is happening—for example, when large amounts of data are being inserted into the database; in this case, you will need to use a larger rollback segment. In general, all rollback segments should be the same size (all rollback segments are usually the same size except for one, which is used specifically for large imports of data).

Whenever you create a database from scratch, one rollback segment—SYSTEM—is always created automatically within the SYSTEM tablespace. Creating a tablespace specifically for use by rollback segments, storing all other rollback segments within this tablespace, is a good idea. Always create another three or four rollback segments. The SYSTEM rollback segment is used for specific system duties only and should not be used normally.

Types Of Rollback Segments

Rollback segments can be public or private. They are either public or private to the instance—that is, a public rollback segment can be accessed through any instance of the database, and a private rollback segment is private to the instance that acquired it. Private rollback segments are acquired when the instance is started and are named within the init.ora file. Public rollback segments form a pool that any instance can access.

Any rollback segment can be in any of the following states at any point in time:

- *OFFLINE*—The rollback segment has not currently been acquired by an instance and, therefore, cannot be used until it is brought ONLINE.

- *ONLINE*—The rollback segment has been acquired by an instance and is available to take part in transactions.

- *NEEDS RECOVERY*—The rollback segment holds data that has not been committed and cannot, for some reason, be rolled back. This normally occurs when a tablespace has been taken offline while transactions are still active for objects within the tablespace.

- *PARTLY AVAILABLE*—Rollback segments are in this state only when an in-doubt transaction is taking place; this normally occurs with distributed transactions, and the cause is usually a network failure.

- *INVALID*—The rollback segment has been dropped.

The state of a rollback segment determines which transactions it can take part in. The **DBA_ROLLBACK_SEGS** view holds all applicable details about rollback segments, shown in Listing 16.4. To access this view, you must have DBA privileges.

Listing 16.4 *Details of rollback segments.*

```
SQL> select segment_name,
  2         tablespace_name,
  3         status
  4  from dba_rollback_segs;
```

```
SEGMENT_NAME                TABLESPACE_NAME                 STATUS
-------------------------   -----------------------------   -------------
SYSTEM                      SYSTEM                          ONLINE
RB_TEMP                     SYSTEM                          OFFLINE
RB1                         ROLLBACK_DATA                   ONLINE
RB2                         ROLLBACK_DATA                   ONLINE
RB3                         ROLLBACK_DATA                   ONLINE
RB4                         ROLLBACK_DATA                   ONLINE
RB5                         ROLLBACK_DATA                   ONLINE
RB6                         ROLLBACK_DATA                   ONLINE
RB7                         ROLLBACK_DATA                   OFFLINE
RB8                         ROLLBACK_DATA                   OFFLINE
RB9                         ROLLBACK_DATA                   OFFLINE
RB10                        ROLLBACK_DATA                   OFFLINE
RB11                        ROLLBACK_DATA                   OFFLINE
RB12                        ROLLBACK_DATA                   OFFLINE
RB13                        ROLLBACK_DATA                   OFFLINE
RB14                        ROLLBACK_DATA                   OFFLINE
RB15                        ROLLBACK_DATA                   OFFLINE
RB16                        ROLLBACK_DATA                   OFFLINE

18 rows selected.
```

REDO LOGS

Each Oracle database has two or more redo log files, which record all changes to the data within the database. This ensures that work is never lost. Redo logs are a critical part of the database, because they prevent failures. Oracle allows you to store more than one copy of the redo logs within the database, similar to control files. This is known as *multiplexed redo logs* and prevents failures against the redo logs themselves. In larger systems, store each set of redo logs on a different disk.

Redo logs are used only to recover the database from a media or system crash. For example, suppose a disk crashes. This means that no data can be written from memory to the disk until the disk is fixed and the tablespace brought back online. When the database is restarted, the redo logs are used to perform recovery and write the changes to the disk. Redo logs are cycled—after one is written to and filled, Oracle starts writing to the next one, and so on, until all are filled. Then it starts overwriting the first again. As previously mentioned, you can run the database in Archivelog mode. Once a redo log has been filled, it is copied to another area on the disk and the next redo log written to. This allows you to perform recovery to any point in time by applying the archived redo logs to the database.

LOCKING

Locking is performed within any type of database. This discussion is related mainly to multiuser systems, where locking is more critical. Personal Oracle8 still performs locking in the same way. In any single-user system, the user is not worried about two users altering the same data at the same time; but in multiuser systems, this is frequently the case. Oracle uses locking to maintain the concurrency and consistency of the database. *Concurrency* is the ability of multiple users to access the data at the same time, and *consistency* is the ability of a database to present a consistent view of the data to the users.

All multiuser database systems use *implement locking*. For example, Oracle provides the user with row-level locking: If a user changes a row, only that user can see the changes until the user commits the transaction; once committed, all other users can see the data as well. If the transaction is not committed, other users still see the original data, but cannot change it, because the user who changed the data in the first place still holds a lock on the row. No other user can change the data associated with the row until the lock is released (a lock is released when the user either commits or rolls back the transaction). Locking occurs only when data is modified within an object. Users issuing **SELECT** statements do not need locking, because they are using the objects in a read-only mode.

In some cases, a deadlock occurs. This is when two users need to acquire locks, and each needs to lock a row that the other one already has a lock on. Oracle automatically detects these deadlock situations and rolls back one of the transactions, so one user can complete the transaction.

Oracle can perform a number of different types of locks, briefly described here (this is a large topic and beyond the scope of this book, but knowing which types of locks occur is a good idea):

- *DML locks*—Always protect data; examples are row-level and table-level locks.
- *DDL locks*—Always protect the data definitions, i.e., tables and views.
- *Distributed locks*—Locks the data between distributed transactions, e.g., in a parallel server environment.

PUTTING EVERYTHING TOGETHER

After reading this chapter, you should have all the information that allows you to understand the internal workings of Oracle8. To summarize, the Oracle8 database works in a series of steps as follows:

1. An Oracle instance is currently running.

2. A user has a connection into the database.

3. The server accepts the connection from the user—i.e., the username and password are correct. Oracle then creates a user process against the instance.

4. The user executes a SQL statement and commits the transaction. For example, the user changes a product name in the **PRODUCTS** table.

5. The server then receives the statement and checks the shared pool for an identical SQL statement. If one is found, the server process checks the user's privileges to the data, and the previously existing shared SQL area is used. If not, a new shared SQL area is allocated for the statement, so that it can be parsed and executed.

6. The server processes the necessary data from the actual data file.

7. The server process modifies data in the SGA. The DBWR process writes the modified blocks to disk when necessary. Because the transaction was committed, the LGWR process records the transaction in the redo logs.

8. If the transaction is successful, the server process sends a message to the user that the commit was successful. If it is not, an error message is produced.

9. Throughout these steps, the background processes execute, waiting for conditions that require their intervention. While all of this is going on, the database is also servicing other users in the same way, using locks where necessary.

In the next chapter, I will discuss the Oracle Server Manager software. Performance tuning your database is also addressed in a fair amount of detail, introducing you to the concept of putting traces against the database to see exactly what is going on. I would not attempt to implement any of the performance-tuning tips without first reading and understanding Chapter 17.

DATABASE ADMINISTRATION

CHAPTER 17

This chapter addresses the database administration (DBA) involved with keeping your Personal Oracle8 database up and running. It includes a discussion of the main tool used within any DBA function—Server Manager—as well as the setup and tuning of your database, indexing strategies, and an in-depth look at the init.ora file and its parameters.

Performing administration duties to keep the database running fast.

SERVER MANAGER

The Oracle Server Manager is a piece of software that helps you administer any Oracle database. In most cases, Server Manager is a graphical tool, but in the Personal Oracle8 implementation, it is a character-based system. Oracle's Server Manager can execute most database administration functions, including the following:

- Database creation
- Database startup
- Database shutdown
- Database backup and recovery
- SQL and PL/SQL commands

Server Manager can also be passed a file, so you can write your Server Manager commands into a file and have them executed by Server Manager; this is particularly useful when creating databases. The Server Manager commands are exactly the same no matter which platform you are using—Windows 95, Windows NT, or Unix. The command to enter the Server Manager administration tool is (on Personal Oracle8) **SVRMGR30**. Once the command to start Server Manager is entered, the database will be started automatically; if it is already running, you will be left at the Server Manager command-line prompt (**SVRMGR>**). You can get help at any time within Server Manager if, from the command line, you execute the following:

```
SVRMGR30 HELP=Y
```

This will display the help information for Server Manager and leave you at the Server Manager prompt, as shown in Listing 17.1.

Listing 17.1   Displaying help information with Server Manager.

```
C:\WINDOWS>svrmgr30

Oracle Server Manager Release 3.0.3.0.0 - Production

(c) Copyright 1997, Oracle Corporation.  All Rights Reserved.

Personal Oracle8 Release 8.0.3.0.0 - Production
With the Partitioning option
PL/SQL Release 8.0.3.0.0 - Production

The following are SIMPLIFIED syntax descriptions. For complete syntax
descriptions, please refer to the Oracle Server Manager User's Guide.

STARTUP       [DBA] [FORCE] [PFILE=filespec] [EXCLUSIVE | SHARED]
              [MOUNT dbname | OPEN dbname] [NOMOUNT]

SHUTDOWN      [NORMAL | IMMEDIATE | ABORT]

MONITOR       For graphical modes only, bring up a monitor

ARCHIVE LOG   [START] [STOP] [LIST] [NEXT] [<n>] [ALL] ['destination']

RECOVER       { [DATABASE [MANUAL] ] | [TABLESPACE ts-name [,tsname]] }

CONNECT       [username [/password] ] [INTERNAL] ['@'instance-spec]
DISCONNECT

SET           options: INSTANCE, ECHO, TERMOUT, TIMING, NUMWIDTH, CHARWIDTH
SHOW          LONGWIDTH, DATEWIDTH, AUTOPRINT and for SHOW: ALL, SPOOL
```

```
EXIT
REM
                SQL statements can also be executed.
SVRMGR>
```

Another way to obtain the same help information is to type "help" at the Server Manager prompt. Always remember when using Server Manager that you will need to log in when you first enter it or before you use any commands that access the database. If you are connecting as a database administrator (DBA), you can issue the command **CONNECT INTERNAL** to connect you to the DBA account; otherwise, you will have to use the **CONNECT** command with a username and password.

You can execute a file of either Server Manager or SQL commands through the Server Manager tool. To do so, just use the @ command, exactly as in SQL*Plus—for example, issuing **@example1** would execute the file *example1.sql*. If you just type the @ command by itself, Server Manager will prompt you for the name of the file to execute. One of the differences between Server Manager and SQL*Plus is that Server Manager has no buffer, so you cannot access your previous command.

Server Manager Commands

Once in Server Manager, you can use a number of commands, described in the following sections.

@

Use the @ sign to execute scripts within Server Manager. The scripts can include any SQL, PL/SQL, or Server Manager commands. The syntax for the @ command is:

```
@ [command_file_name]
```

The *command_file_name* is optional; if you do not enter it with the @ command, Server Manager will ask you which file to execute. When executing command files in this way, remember to use the full path name when the file to execute is not in the current directory or on the current path. If you wish to execute scripts within scripts, you must use the @@ command, which tells Server Manager that the second file is in the same directory as the first.

ARCHIVE LOG

You use the **ARCHIVE LOG** command to:

• Start automatic archive logging

• Stop automatic archive logging

- Manipulate automatic archive logging
- Show details of the archive logs

To use the **ARCHIVE LOG** command, you must first be connected as the **INTERNAL**, **SYSOPER**, or **SYSDBA** user. The syntax of the **ARCHIVE LOG** command is:

```
ARCHIVE LOG [LIST|STOP] [START|NEXT|ALL|n [TO destination]]
```

The options with this command are as follows:

- *LIST*—Shows all details of the redo logs, including the current state of the archiving process. An example of this can be seen in Listing 17.2, which shows that automatic archiving is not enabled on the database. This is the default.

- *STOP*—Disables automatic archiving. Use caution with this command. If the database is in Archivelog mode and the automatic archiving is stopped, the database will stop when all redo logs fill up, because no redo logs can be archived to disk. (The only way around this is to issue one of the following commands: **ARCHIVE LOG NEXT** or **ARCHIVE LOG ALL**, explained in more detail later.)

- *START*—Starts the automatic archiver running (the **ARCH** background process). By default, there is no automatic archiving on the database created by the Oracle Installer. The way to enable automatic archiving automatically is to set the **log_archive_start** parameter in the init.ora file to **TRUE**.

- *NEXT*—Manually archives the next online redo log file that has been filled.

- *ALL*—Manually archives all online redo log files that have not been filled.

- *n*—Causes the archiver to archive the redo log with the sequence number entered. Using this command, you can specify a sequence number for any redo log that is still online. This is useful for re-archiving redo logs.

- *TO destination*—Tells the archiver where to archive the redo logs to. The destination can be defaulted by using the **log_archive_dest** parameter in the init.ora file. This defaults to the C:\ORAWIN95\DATABASE\ARCHIVE directory.

Listing 17.2   Using ARCHIVE LOG LIST.

```
SVRMGR> archive log list
Database log mode        No Archive Mode
Automatic archival       Disabled
Archive destination      %RDBMS80%\
```

```
Oldest online log sequence      65
Current log sequence            66
SVRMGR>
```

Listing 17.3 demonstrates how to use Server Manager to manipulate archive log files. It shows archiving being started, switching to the next redo log file, and then being stopped.

Listing 17.3   Manipulating redo logs within Server Manager.

```
SVRMGR> startup mount
ORACLE instance started.
Total System Global Area        5508612 bytes
Fixed Size                        45584 bytes
Variable Size                   4529140 bytes
Database Buffers                 409600 bytes
Redo Buffers                     524288 bytes
Database mounted.
SVRMGR> alter database archivelog;
Statement processed.
SVRMGR> alter database open;
Statement processed.
SVRMGR> archive log start
Statement processed.
SVRMGR> archive log list
Database log mode               Archive Mode
Automatic archival              Enabled
Archive destination             C:\ORAWIN95\database\archive
Oldest online log sequence      65
Next log sequence to archive    66
Current log sequence            66
SVRMGR> alter system switch logfile;
Statement processed.
SVRMGR> archive log list;
Database log mode               Archive Mode
Automatic archival              Enabled
Archive destination             C:\ORAWIN95\database\archive
Oldest online log sequence      66
Next log sequence to archive    67
Current log sequence            67
SVRMGR> archive log stop
Statement processed.
SVRMGR> archive log list;
Database log mode               Archive Mode
Automatic archival              Disabled
Archive destination             C:\ORAWIN95\database\archive
Oldest online log sequence      66
Next log sequence to archive    67
Current log sequence            67
```

CONNECT

The **CONNECT** command logs into the database from Server Manager. You must use this command before the first access to the database for each Server Manager session. You can use any username that exists within the database. It is possible to connect to Server Manager using a specified role with the **AS** clause of the **CONNECT** command. This is normally used for a non-DBA user to connect—but with either the **SYSOPER** or **SYSDBA** role. The syntax for the **CONNECT** command is:

```
CONNECT [USERNAME/PASSWORD|INTERNAL] [@database] [AS [SYSOPER|SYSDBA]]
```

The clauses used within the **CONNECT** command are as follows:

- *USERNAME*—Must exist within the database. If no username is entered, Server Manager will prompt you for one.

- *PASSWORD*—Must be entered for the username; if not, Server Manager will prompt you for it.

- *INTERNAL*—Should really never be used, because it is needed for only some DBA operations. It is provided for backward compatibility. DBAs should use the **SYSDBA** role instead.

- *@database*—Specifies which database to connect to, allowing you to connect to remote databases. You do not need to use it if you wish to connect to the local database.

- *AS SYSOPER*—Connects to Server Manager, if the user has been granted the **SYSOPER** privilege.

- *AS SYSDBA*—Connects to Server Manager, if the user has been granted the **SYSDBA** privilege.

DESCRIBE

As it is in SQL*Plus, the **DESCRIBE** command is used to describe a function, package, procedure, table, or view. This command is useful when viewing the structure of the database. You must be connected to the database to issue a **DESCRIBE** command. Its syntax is as follows:

```
DESCRIBE [FUNCTION|PACKAGE|PROCEDURE|TABLE|VIEW] object_name
```

Listing 17.4 shows an example of the **DESCRIBE** command on the **PRODUCTS** table.

Listing 17.4   Using the **DESCRIBE** command.

```
C:\WINDOWS>svrmgr30

Oracle Server Manager Release 3.0.3.0.0 - Production

(c) Copyright 1997, Oracle Corporation.  All Rights Reserved.

Personal Oracle8 Release 8.0.3.0.0 - Production
With the Partitioning option
PL/SQL Release 8.0.3.0.0 - Production

SVRMGR> connect demo/demo
Connected.
SVRMGR> describe table products;
Column Name                         Null?     Type
------------------------------- -------- ----
PRODUCT_ID                          NOT NULL NUMBER(4)
SUPPLIER_ID                         NOT NULL NUMBER(4)
PRODUCT_NAME                        NOT NULL VARCHAR2(40)
UNIT_COST_PRICE                              NUMBER(5,2)
UNIT_RETAIL_PRICE                   NOT NULL NUMBER(5,2)
UNITS_IN_STOCK                      NOT NULL NUMBER(5)
REORDER_LEVEL                                NUMBER(4)
SVRMGR>
```

DISCONNECT

To disconnect from your current session within Server Manager, you use the **DISCON-NECT** command. For example, if you connected within Server Manager to the **DEMO** user, **DISCONNECT** would disconnect you from that user. To use this command, you must be connected to the database. The syntax for the **DISCONNECT** command is just **DISCONNECT**.

EXECUTE

The **EXECUTE** command is used to execute one-line PL/SQL routines. If you need to execute more than one line, the code must be formatted correctly—i.e., using **BEGIN** and **END**. The syntax for the **EXECUTE** command is as follows:

```
EXECUTE command
```

To execute a one-line PL/SQL command, you could issue the commands in Listing 17.5.

Listing 17.5   *Using the **EXECUTE** command.*

```
C:\WINDOWS>svrmgr30

Oracle Server Manager Release 3.0.3.0.0 - Production

(c) Copyright 1997, Oracle Corporation.  All Rights Reserved.

Personal Oracle8 Release 8.0.3.0.0 - Production
With the Partitioning option
PL/SQL Release 8.0.3.0.0 - Production

SVRMGR> variable greeting VARCHAR2
SVRMGR> EXECUTE :greeting := 'HELLO';
Statement processed.
SVRMGR> print greeting
GREETING
--------
HELLO
SVRMGR>
```

EXIT

The **EXIT** command quits the Server Manager session and returns you to the operating-system prompt. If you have any uncommitted work within Server Manager, the **EXIT** command automatically commits any outstanding transactions and leaves Server Manager immediately. The syntax for the **EXIT** command is just **EXIT**. Listing 17.6 shows an example of **EXIT**.

Listing 17.6   *Using the **EXIT** command.*

```
C:\WINDOWS>svrmgr30

Oracle Server Manager Release 3.0.3.0.0 - Production

(c) Copyright 1997, Oracle Corporation.  All Rights Reserved.

Personal Oracle8 Release 8.0.3.0.0 - Production
With the Partitioning option
PL/SQL Release 8.0.3.0.0 - Production

SVRMGR> exit
Server Manager complete.

C:\WINDOWS>
```

HELP

The **HELP** command displays the help information within Server Manager. This information gives you the simplified syntax for all of the commands that you can use within Server Manager. The syntax is just **HELP**. An example of the output from the **HELP** command is shown in Listing 17.7.

Listing 17.7   Using the HELP command.

```
SVRMGR> help
The following are SIMPLIFIED syntax descriptions. For complete syntax
descriptions, please refer to the Oracle Server Manager User's Guide.

STARTUP       [DBA] [FORCE] [PFILE=filespec] [EXCLUSIVE | SHARED]
              [MOUNT dbname | OPEN dbname] [NOMOUNT]

SHUTDOWN      [NORMAL | IMMEDIATE | ABORT]

MONITOR       For graphical modes only, bring up a monitor

ARCHIVE LOG   [START] [STOP] [LIST] [NEXT] [<n>] [ALL] ['destination']

RECOVER       { [DATABASE [MANUAL] ] | [TABLESPACE ts-name [,tsname]] }

CONNECT       [username [/password] ] [INTERNAL] ['@'instance-spec]
DISCONNECT

SET           options: INSTANCE, ECHO, TERMOUT, TIMING, NUMWIDTH, CHARWIDTH
SHOW          LONGWIDTH, DATEWIDTH, AUTOPRINT and for SHOW: ALL, SPOOL

EXIT
REM
              SQL statements can also be executed.
```

HOST

You can perform tasks outside of Server Manager without exiting first using the **HOST** command. You can use the command in two ways:

- By itself, which allows you to enter a host session, perform a number of tasks, and return to Server Manager by typing "exit".

- To perform a one off command from within Server Manager. To do this, you type in **HOST**, followed by the command you wish to perform. You can see an example in Listing 17.8, where I use the **HOST** command to view the contents of the init.ora file. (Using the **HOST** command to manipulate and view the init.ora file is a feature that is used regularly within Server Manager.)

The syntax for the **HOST** command is:

```
HOST [operating_system_command]
```

*Listing 17.8   Using the **HOST** command.*

```
SVRMGR>host type c:\orawin95\database\initorcl.ora
#
# $Header: init.ora 05-jun-97.14:56:46 hpiao Exp $
#
# Copyright (c) 1991, 1997 by Oracle Corporation
#
###############################################################################
# Example INIT.ORA file
#
# This file is provided by Oracle Corporation to help you customize
# your RDBMS installation for your site.  Important system parameters
# are discussed, and example settings given.
#
# Some parameter settings are generic to any size installation.
# For parameters that require different values in different size
# installations, three scenarios have been provided: SMALL, MEDIUM
# and LARGE.  Any parameter that needs to be tuned according to
# installation size will have three settings, each one commented
# according to installation size.
#
# Use the following table to approximate the SGA size needed for the
# three scenarios provided in this file:
#
#                       ------Installation/Database Size------
#                       SMALL           MEDIUM          LARGE
# Block         2K      4500K           6800K           17000K
# Size          4K      5500K           8800K           21000K
#
# To set up a database that multiple instances will be using, place
# all instance-specific parameters in one file, and then have all
# of these files point to a master file using the IFILE command.
# This way, when you change a public
# parameter, it will automatically change on all instances.  This is
# necessary, since all instances must run with the same value for many
# parameters. For example, if you choose to use private rollback segments,
# these must be specified in different files, but since all gc_*
# parameters must be the same on all instances, they should be in one file.
#
# INSTRUCTIONS: Edit this file and the other INIT files it calls for
# your site, either by using the values provided here or by providing
# your own.  Then place an IFILE= line into each instance-specific
# INIT file that points at this file.
###############################################################################
```

```
# replace "oracle" with your database name
db_name=oracle

db_files = 1024                                          # INITIAL
# db_files = 80                                            # SMALL
# db_files = 400                                           # MEDIUM
# db_files = 1000                                          # LARGE


control_files = C:\ORAWIN95\DATABASE\ctl1orcl.ora

db_file_multiblock_read_count =  8                      # INITIAL
# db_file_multiblock_read_count = 8                        # SMALL
# db_file_multiblock_read_count = 16                       # MEDIUM
# db_file_multiblock_read_count = 32                       # LARGE

db_block_buffers =  200                                 # INITIAL
# db_block_buffers = 100                                   # SMALL
# db_block_buffers = 550                                   # MEDIUM
# db_block_buffers = 3200                                  # LARGE

shared_pool_size = 3500000                              # INITIAL
# shared_pool_size = 3500000                               # SMALL
# shared_pool_size = 5000000                               # MEDIUM
# shared_pool_size = 9000000                               # LARGE

log_checkpoint_interval = 10000

processes =  50                                         # INITIAL
# processes = 50                                           # SMALL
# processes = 100                                          # MEDIUM
# processes = 200                                          # LARGE

parallel_max_servers = 5                                 # SMALL
# parallel_max_servers = 4 x (number of CPUs)              # MEDIUM
# parallel_max_servers = 4 x (number of CPUs)              # LARGE

log_buffer =  8192                                      # INITIAL
# log_buffer = 8192                                        # SMALL
# log_buffer = 32768                                       # MEDIUM
# log_buffer = 163840                                      # LARGE

sequence_cache_entries =  10                            # INITIAL
# sequence_cache_entries = 10                              # SMALL
# sequence_cache_entries = 30                              # MEDIUM
# sequence_cache_entries = 100                             # LARGE

sequence_cache_hash_buckets =  10                       # INITIAL
# sequence_cache_hash_buckets = 10                         # SMALL
# sequence_cache_hash_buckets = 23                         # MEDIUM
```

```
# sequence_cache_hash_buckets = 89                                    # LARGE

audit_trail = db                    # if you want auditing
# timed_statistics = true           # if you want timed statistics
max_dump_file_size = 10240          # limit trace file size to 5 Meg each

# Uncommenting the line below will cause automatic archiving if archiving has
# been enabled using ALTER DATABASE ARCHIVELOG.
log_archive_start = true
log_archive_dest = %ORACLE_HOME%\database\archive
log_archive_format = "%%ORACLE_SID%%T%TS%S.ARC"

# If using private rollback segments, place lines of the following
# form in each of your instance-specific init.ora files:
# rollback_segments = (name1, name2)

# If using public rollback segments, define how many
# rollback segments each instance will pick up, using the formula
#    # of rollback segments = transactions / transactions_per_rollback_segment
# In this example each instance will grab 40/10 = 4:
# transactions = 40
# transactions_per_rollback_segment = 10

# Global Naming -- enforce that a dblink has same name as the db it connects to
global_names = TRUE

# Edit and uncomment the following line to provide the suffix that will be
# appended to the db_name parameter (separated with a dot) and stored as the
# global database name when a database is created.  If your site uses
# Internet Domain names for e-mail, then the part of your e-mail address after
# the '@' is a good candidate for this parameter value.

# db_domain = us.acme.com
# global database name is db_name.db_domain

# Uncomment the following line if you wish to enable the Oracle Trace product
# to trace server activity.  This enables scheduling of server collections
# from the Oracle Enterprise Manager Console.
# Also, if the oracle_trace_collection_name parameter is non-null,
# every session will write to the named collection, as well as enabling you
# to schedule future collections from the console.

# oracle_trace_enable = TRUE

# define directories to store trace and alert files
background_dump_dest=%RDBMS80%\trace
user_dump_dest=%RDBMS80%\trace
```

```
db_block_size = 2048

job_queue_processes = 2

remote_login_passwordfile = shared

disk_asynch_io = false
SVRMGR>
```

MONITOR

You cannot use the **MONITOR** command within Server Manager with Personal Oracle8. This is because it is purely a line-mode interface, and the monitors are a graphical tool. On other systems, monitors are available and can be used to monitor the following:

- Circuits
- Dispatchers
- File I/O
- Latches
- Library cache
- Locking
- Processes
- Queues
- Rollback segments
- Sessions
- SGA
- System I/O
- Tables and tablespaces

PRINT

The **PRINT** command is used in conjunction with the **VARIABLE** command to print the values of variables. I already used the **PRINT** command in Listing 17.5, with the **EXECUTE** command, to print the value of the variable called *greeting*. If you do not specify a variable, the **PRINT** command will print all current variables. The syntax for **PRINT** is:

```
PRINT [variable]
```

RECOVER

You can recover tablespaces, data files, or the whole database with the **RECOVER** command. To issue the command, you must be connected to Server Manager as **INTERNAL**, **SYSDBA** (recommended), or **SYSOPER**. The syntax for **RECOVER** is:

```
RECOVER DATABASE [UNTIL] [USING BACKUP CONTROLFILE] [PARALLEL]
```

or

```
RECOVER TABLESPACE tablespace_name [PARALLEL clause]
```

or

```
RECOVER DATAFILE file_name [PARALLEL clause]
```

The syntax you use depends on what needs recovering. For example, if you need to recover the whole database because you have a corrupt control file, use the **RECOVER DATABASE USING BACKUP CONTROLFILE** option.

REMARK

The **REMARK** command, which is usually shortened to **REM**, documents SQL commands within a batch file. **REMARK** is ignored by Server Manager and SQL*Plus. It has to appear as the first word on a line within the batch file to be ignored. The syntax for **REMARK** is:

```
REMARK [text]
```

Listing 17.9 shows an example of the **REMARK** command to document a batch file of SQL statements.

Listing 17.9 *Using the **REMARK** command in a SQL batch file.*

```
REM START OF BATCH FILE
REM
REM This is a sample SQL batch file.
REM
REM First connect as the DEMO user
connect demo/demo
REM
REM The next SQL statement selects all details from the ORDERS table.
select * from orders
/
REM
REM The next SQL statement selects all details from the PRODUCTS table.
select * from products
```

```
/
REM
REM END OF BATCH FILE
```

SET

The **SET** command changes the environment for the Server Manager session. This command is similar to the **SET** command within SQL*Plus (see Chapter 8 for details) and can make a number of changes.

The syntax for the various **SET** commands is:

```
SET AUTORECOVERY [ON|OFF]
SET CHARWIDTH n
SET COMPATIBILITY [V6|V7|NATIVE]
SET DATEWIDTH n
SET ECHO [ON|OFF]
SET INSTANCE [path|LOCAL]
SET LOGSOURCE path
SET LONGWIDTH n
SET MAXDATA n
SET NUMWIDTH n
SET RETRIES [n|INFINITE]
SET SERVEROUTPUT [ON[SIZE n]|OFF]
SET STOPONERROR [ON|OFF]
SET TERMOUT [ON|OFF]
SET TIMING [ON|OFF]
```

An explanation of each of these commands follows:

- *AUTORECOVERY*—Allows Server Manager to automatically pick up the default file names for the redo logs to apply to recover the database when requested. The default file names and locations are specified in the init.ora file using the parameters **log_archive_dest** and **log_archive_format**. When set to **OFF** (the default), Server Manager prompts you for the location and name of the redo logs it needs to recover the database.

- *CHARWIDTH*—Sets the default display width for any columns defined with the **CHAR** data type. The default is 80.

- *COMPATIBILITY*—Allows you to change the compatibility of Server Manager—that is, it lets you use it against a version 6 or 7 database. When set to **NATIVE**, it matches the version of the current database.

- *DATEWIDTH*—Sets the default display width for any columns defined with the **DATE** data type. The default is 9.

- *ECHO*—When set to **ON**, echoes each command as it is executed from a command file. The valid values for this parameter are **ON** and **OFF**, the default being **OFF**. This parameter is effective only when executing commands from an operating-system file—i.e., using the @ command.

- *INSTANCE*—Changes the default instance for your session to the specified instance path. The default instance—the local one—is used for commands when no instance is specified. This parameter is used mainly with Net8 or SQL*Net.

- *LOGSOURCE*—Specifies the location of redo log files when used with the **RECOVER** command. The default for this parameter is set by the init.ora parameter **log_archive_dest**.

- *LONGWIDTH*—Sets the default display width for any columns defined with the **LONG** data type. The default is 20,480 bytes.

- *MAXDATA*—Specifies the maximum amount of data that can be retrieved with one fetch in a single **SELECT** statement. The default is 20,480 bytes.

- *NUMWIDTH*—Sets the default display width for any columns defined with the **NUM-BER** data type. The default is 10.

- *RETRIES*—Tells Server Manager the maximum number of retries that can be issued when a database is being started with the **RETRY** option. The default is **INFINITE**.

- *SERVEROUTPUT*—When set to **ON**, allows debug information to be shown on the Server Manager screen. This debug information is processed with the **DBMS_OUTPUT** package. You can also specify the size of the buffer Server Manager uses to output the information. When set to **OFF**, this parameter disables the output of the information to the screen.

- *STOPONERROR*—Useful when executing command files through Server Manager. Normally, when this parameter is set to **OFF** (the default) when command files are running, error messages are ignored, and the next command in the file is executed. When **STOPONERROR** is set to **ON**, the command file stops executing and exits whenever an error is encountered.

- *TERMOUT*—Controls the display of output while executing commands from an operating-system file. When using this parameter, you should remember that all commands executed through a file or Server Manager are affected—i.e., all commands entered interactively, at the **SVRMGR>** prompt, will not display output. When this parameter is set to **ON** (the default), output will be displayed as normal. When this parameter is set to **OFF**, **TERMOUT** will not allow output to be seen on screen. This is useful when executing large reports and spooling them to a file. (Spooling reports to a file is covered in Chapter 8.)

- *TIMING*—Displays the amount of time it took to execute the SQL statement after each execution of the statement. The time is given in elapsed time and CPU time. This parameter is useful when tuning SQL statements through Server Manager.

SHOW

The **SHOW** command displays all of the information currently set in the Server Manager environment as either default or changed using the **SET** command. The syntax for the **SHOW** command is:

```
SHOW parameter_name
```

Listing 17.10 shows an example output from this command.

Listing 17.10   Using the SHOW command.

```
SVRMGR> show
Instance                        local
Spool                           OFF
Timing                          ON
Termout                         ON
Echo                            OFF
Stoponerror                     OFF
Autorecovery                    OFF
Logsource                       <default>
Maxdata                         20480
Numwidth                        10
Charwidth                       80
Longwidth                       80
Datewidth                       9
Labwidth                        32
Compatibility                   NATIVE
Retries                         infinite
Server Output                   OFF
Autoprint                       OFF
Fetchrows                       infinite
Appinfo                         OFF (USERTEXT : Oracle Server Manager)
SVRMGR>
```

When using the **SHOW** command, you can show two parameters that cannot be set using the **SET** command:

- *PARAMETERS*—Interrogates the database to see which init.ora parameters are in effect for the database instance. Issue this command with the parameter name you wish to view. For example, to see all parameters containing the word *log*, you would issue the **SHOW PARAMETERS LOG** command, an example of which can be seen in Listing 17.11.

- *SGA*—Allows you to view the size and makeup of the System Global Area (SGA). You can use this command only to view the SGA; to alter it, you would need to make changes to the init.ora file. An example of the **SHOW SGA** command is shown in Listing 17.12.

Listing 17.11 *Using the **SHOW PARAMETERS LOG** command.*

```
SVRMGR> show parameters log
NAME                                 TYPE     VALUE
-----------------------------------  ------   ------------------------------
dblink_encrypt_login                 boolean  FALSE
delayed_logging_block_cleanouts      boolean  TRUE
log_archive_buffer_size              integer  127
log_archive_buffers                  integer  4
log_archive_dest                     string   %ORACLE_HOME%\database\archive
log_archive_duplex_dest              string
log_archive_format                   string   %%ORACLE_SID%%T%TS%S.ARC
log_archive_min_succeed_dest         integer  1
log_archive_start                    boolean  TRUE
log_block_checksum                   boolean  FALSE
log_buffer                           integer  8192
log_checkpoint_interval              integer  10000
log_checkpoint_timeout               integer  0
log_checkpoints_to_alert             boolean  FALSE
log_file_name_convert                string
log_files                            integer  255
log_simultaneous_copies              integer  0
log_small_entry_max_size             integer  80
mts_rate_log_size                    string
remote_login_passwordfile            string   SHARED
SVRMGR>
```

Listing 17.12 *Using the **SHOW SGA** command.*

```
SVRMGR> show sga
Total System Global Area        5508612 bytes
Fixed Size                        45584 bytes
Variable Size                   4529140 bytes
Database Buffers                 409600 bytes
Redo Buffers                     524288 bytes
SVRMGR>
```

SHUTDOWN

The **SHUTDOWN** command is used to shut down a Personal Oracle8 database. Only a user connected to Server Manager as the **INTERNAL, SYSOPER,** or **SYSDBA** can issue the **SHUTDOWN** command. Its syntax is:

```
SHUTDOWN [ABORT|IMMEDIATE|NORMAL]
```

As you can see from the syntax, three options are available with the **SHUTDOWN** command:

- *NORMAL*—Waits for all users to exit the database before starting the shutdown. While Oracle waits for users to log out of the database, it prevents any other user from logging in. This type of shutdown does not require any type of recovery when the database is started back up again. This is the preferred method—and the default if no option is supplied—to shut down your database.

- *IMMEDIATE*—Performs a similar task to the **NORMAL** option except that it does not wait for the currently connected users to log out of the database; it just disconnects them and shuts the database down. This type of shutdown, again, does not require any type of recovery when the database is restarted.

- *ABORT*—Performs the fastest shutdown possible. Avoid this option if possible; at times, however, it is unavoidable—for example, if a process terminates unexpectedly. Using this option requires recovery to take place the next time the database is started.

SPOOL

The **SPOOL** command stores the output from queries executed within Server Manager in operating-system files. If the **SPOOL** command is entered by itself, Server Manager will prompt you for the name of the file to spool to. The default file extension for the **SPOOL** command within Server Manager is .LOG. The syntax for the **SPOOL** command is:

```
SPOOL [[filename.ext] |OFF|OUT]
```

You can spool directly to a connected printer with the **SPOOL OUT** command. Remember, when spooling output from a command file, use the **set termout off** parameter.

STARTUP

You start a Personal Oracle8 database with the **STARTUP** command. This command can be issued only by a user connected to Server Manager as the **INTERNAL, SYSOPER,** or **SYSDBA** user. The syntax is:

```
STARTUP [FORCE|RESTRICT|PFILE=filename] [MOUNT|OPEN|NOMOUNT]
```

As you can see, six options are available with the **STARTUP** command:

- *FORCE*—Used only when a database is already running and you wish to reboot it. Oracle does a **SHUTDOWN ABORT** on the instance and then starts it back up again. Don't use this option in general day-to-day use, because doing a **SHUTDOWN ABORT** is never a really good idea.

- *RESTRICT*—Starts up the database and lets only those users with the **RESTRICTED SESSION** privilege log in.

- *PFILE*—Allows you to specify the init.ora file to be used when starting the database. See the "init.ora File" section of this chapter for more information on init.ora files.

- *MOUNT*—Lets you start up and mount the database, but not open it. This allows you to do administrative work on the database.

- *OPEN*—Allows you to open the database for normal use when administrative work has completed and the database has not been mounted.

- *NOMOUNT*—Gives you the option of not mounting the database when the instance is started.

VARIABLE

The **VARIABLE** command allows you to define variables within the current Server Manager session. These variables can be used in conjunction with the **EXECUTE** and **PRINT** commands, as described earlier. The syntax for the **VARIABLE** command is:

```
VARIABLE variable_name TYPE
```

INIT.ORA FILE

Whenever you start a database—either Personal Oracle8 or Oracle8—it begins with a number of parameters to tell Oracle exactly the environment the instance should run in. It does so by using a file—referred to as the *init.ora file*, even though this is not the name of the file. The file name depends on the name of the database it is used against. For example, if you have a database called *orcl*, the name of the init.ora file would be *initorcl.ora*. The name of the database comes directly after the *init* and before the *.ora*. This way, the database knows which file to use to set the environment.

The init.ora file is located in the C:\ORAWIN95\DATABASE directory by default. This is the place Personal Oracle8 looks for the file automatically. If the file is anywhere else, you must start the database using Server Manager with the **STARTUP PFILE=**fi*lename* option. The init.ora file is a plain text file and can be edited in the normal fashion.

Within the init.ora file are a number of parameters that are used when the database is started up. The file contains sections for each parameter. The sample file supplied by Oracle has default settings for small, medium, and large databases. Listing 17.13 shows the default init.ora file.

Listing 17.13   The default init.ora file.

```
#
# $Header: init.ora 05-jun-97.14:56:46 hpiao Exp $
#
# Copyright (c) 1991, 1997 by Oracle Corporation
#
##############################################################################
# Example INIT.ORA file
#
# This file is provided by Oracle Corporation to help you customize
# your RDBMS installation for your site.  Important system parameters
# are discussed, and example settings given.
#
# Some parameter settings are generic to any size installation.
# For parameters that require different values in different size
# installations, three scenarios have been provided: SMALL, MEDIUM
# and LARGE.  Any parameter that needs to be tuned according to
# installation size will have three settings, each one commented
# according to installation size.
#
# Use the following table to approximate the SGA size needed for the
# three scenarios provided in this file:
#
#                       ------Installation/Database Size------
#                       SMALL           MEDIUM          LARGE
#  Block        2K      4500K           6800K           17000K
#  Size         4K      5500K           8800K           21000K
#
# To set up a database that multiple instances will be using, place
# all instance-specific parameters in one file, and then have all
# of these files point to a master file using the IFILE command.
# This way, when you change a public
# parameter, it will automatically change on all instances.  This is
# necessary, since all instances must run with the same value for many
# parameters. For example, if you choose to use private rollback segments,
# these must be specified in different files, but since all gc_*
# parameters must be the same on all instances, they should be in one file.
#
# INSTRUCTIONS: Edit this file and the other INIT files it calls for
# your site, either by using the values provided here or by providing
# your own.  Then place an IFILE= line into each instance-specific
# INIT file that points at this file.
```

```
##############################################################################

# replace "oracle" with your database name
db_name=oracle

db_files = 1024                                              # INITIAL
# db_files = 80                                              # SMALL
# db_files = 400                                             # MEDIUM
# db_files = 1000                                            # LARGE

control_files = C:\ORAWIN95\DATABASE\ctl1orcl.ora

db_file_multiblock_read_count =  8 # INITIAL
# db_file_multiblock_read_count = 8                          # SMALL
# db_file_multiblock_read_count = 16                         # MEDIUM
# db_file_multiblock_read_count = 32                         # LARGE

db_block_buffers =  200                                      # INITIAL
# db_block_buffers = 100                                     # SMALL
# db_block_buffers = 550                                     # MEDIUM
# db_block_buffers = 3200                                    # LARGE

shared_pool_size =  3500000                                  # INITIAL
# shared_pool_size = 3500000                                 # SMALL
# shared_pool_size = 5000000                                 # MEDIUM
# shared_pool_size = 9000000                                 # LARGE

log_checkpoint_interval = 10000

processes =  50                                             # INITIAL
# processes = 50                                             # SMALL
# processes = 100                                            # MEDIUM
# processes = 200                                            # LARGE

parallel_max_servers = 5                                     # SMALL
# parallel_max_servers = 4 x (number of CPUs)                # MEDIUM
# parallel_max_servers = 4 x (number of CPUs)                # LARGE

log_buffer =  8192                                          # INITIAL
# log_buffer = 8192                                          # SMALL
# log_buffer = 32768                                         # MEDIUM
# log_buffer = 163840                                        # LARGE

sequence_cache_entries =  10                                # INITIAL
# sequence_cache_entries = 10                                # SMALL
# sequence_cache_entries = 30                                # MEDIUM
# sequence_cache_entries = 100                               # LARGE
```

```
sequence_cache_hash_buckets =  10              # INITIAL
# sequence_cache_hash_buckets = 10             # SMALL
# sequence_cache_hash_buckets = 23             # MEDIUM
# sequence_cache_hash_buckets = 89             # LARGE


audit_trail = db            # if you want auditing
# timed_statistics = true   # if you want timed statistics
max_dump_file_size = 10240  # limit trace file size to 5 Meg each


# Uncommenting the line below will cause automatic archiving if archiving has
# been enabled using ALTER DATABASE ARCHIVELOG.
log_archive_start = true
log_archive_dest = %ORACLE_HOME%\database\archive
log_archive_format = "%%ORACLE_SID%%T%TS%S.ARC"


# If using private rollback segments, place lines of the following
# form in each of your instance-specific init.ora files:
# rollback_segments = (name1, name2)


# If using public rollback segments, define how many
# rollback segments each instance will pick up, using the formula
#    # of rollback segments = transactions / transactions_per_rollback_segment
# In this example each instance will grab 40/10 = 4:
# transactions = 40
# transactions_per_rollback_segment = 10


# Global Naming -- enforce that a dblink has same name as the db it connects to
global_names = TRUE


# Edit and uncomment the following line to provide the suffix that will be
# appended to the db_name parameter (separated with a dot) and stored as the
# global database name when a database is created.  If your site uses
# Internet Domain names for e-mail, then the part of your e-mail address after
# the '@' is a good candidate for this parameter value.


# db_domain = us.acme.com
# global database name is db_name.db_domain


# Uncomment the following line if you wish to enable the Oracle Trace product
# to trace server activity.  This enables scheduling of server collections
# from the Oracle Enterprise Manager Console.
# Also, if the oracle_trace_collection_name parameter is non-null,
# every session will write to the named collection, as well as enabling you
# to schedule future collections from the console.


# oracle_trace_enable = TRUE
```

```
# define directories to store trace and alert files
background_dump_dest=%RDBMS80%\trace
user_dump_dest=%RDBMS80%\trace

db_block_size = 2048

job_queue_processes = 2

remote_login_passwordfile = shared

disk_asynch_io = false
```

As you can see from Listing 17.13, anything with a hash mark as the first character of the line is a comment; the file is fairly well documented. If you change the file, the changes will take effect only when the database is next started. You can use the init.ora file to do the following:

- Tune memory settings

- Tune database performance

- Change database settings

- Change the limits of the database

- Change default directory and naming conventions

You can alter most of the parameters within the init.ora file to change the way in which the database performs; some, however, should not be altered. When you alter parameters within the file, remember that all parameters have a default value. Just because the parameter does not appear within the file does not mean it has no value set.

Common Parameters In The init.ora File

This section lists some of the more common parameters within the init.ora file. Included with most of the parameters are the changes you can expect when these parameters are either increased or decreased.

audit_file_dest

The **audit_file_dest** parameter defines which directory any audit files that are created by Oracle should be written to. This parameter can be changed to any directory on the system, but it defaults to C:\ORAWIN95\RDBMS80\AUDIT.

audit_trail

The **audit_trail** parameter either enables or disables the writing of audit information to the audit trail. This parameter has three possible values:

- *NONE (or FALSE)*—No audit trail information is written to the audit trail. This is the default.

- *DB (or TRUE)*—Audit information is written to the database and stored in the **SYS.AUD$** table.

- *OS*—Audit information is written to the operating system's internal audit trail. This is not possible on Personal Oracle8 running under Windows 95.

background_core_dump

The **background_core_dump** parameter tells Oracle whether to include the SGA in any dump files it creates. The allowable values for this parameter are **FULL** (the default) and **PARTIAL**. When the parameter is set to **FULL**, the SGA is dumped along with the core file. When set to **PARTIAL**, the SGA is not dumped.

background_dump_dest

The **background_dump_dest** parameter specifies where to store any debug or trace information for the background processes. This directory includes an alert file showing all operations—such as shutdowns, startups, and log-file switches—that happen on the database.

compatible

With the **compatible** parameter, you can use a new release of the database, but ensure backward compatibility with previous releases. The default for this parameter is 8.0.0.

control_files

The **control_files** parameter specifies where on the system the database's control files are stored. This parameter expects a comma-separated list of file names with their relevant paths. A maximum of eight files can be specified within this parameter. Oracle always recommends that you have this parameter in the init.ora file, and with more than one file. This allows for multiple control files, giving you a means of recovery if one is corrupted. See Chapter 16 for more information on control files.

core_dump_dest

The **core_dump_dest** parameter specifies where any core dump files should be stored. These files are created when an error occurs within Oracle or the user process. The default for this parameter is C:\ORAWIN95\DBS.

cpu_count

The **cpu_count** parameter specifies how many CPUs are available for Oracle to use. This parameter should never be changed, because the value is automatically set by Oracle. On computers with only one CPU (running Personal Oracle8), the value for **cpu_count** is always set to 0.

cursor_space_for_time

To save time, the **cursor_space_for_time** parameter allows the database to give more space within the SGA to cursors. This parameter has two values: **TRUE** and **FALSE**, the default being **FALSE**. When the parameter is set to **TRUE**, you should notice an increase in the performance of PL/SQL when executed against a very busy database.

db_block_buffers

One of the most frequently changed parameters within the init.ora file is **db_block_buffers**. The value of this parameter defines the number of buffers within the buffer cache of the SGA. This value, when increased, will increase the size of the SGA, therefore increasing the amount of memory needed. The buffer cache is one of the primary areas of the SGA. The default for this parameter is 50; you will have to play around with it to find the optimal setting for your database, because this varies with the numbers and types of actions performed.

db_block_lru_extended_statistics

The **db_block_lru_extended_statistics** parameter is used either to enable or disable statistics that measure the effects of increasing the amount of buffers within the buffer cache. When this parameter is enabled, it logs the number of disk accesses that would have been saved if the buffer cache had been larger. By then interrogating the statistics, you can see how the effects of increasing the buffer cache will change performance. The default value for this parameter is 0, meaning no statistics are gathered. To start gathering statistics, set this parameter to the number of extra buffers for which you want to collect information. For example, if you wanted to see how the database would perform with an extra 50 buffers, set this parameter to 50. Running a database with this parameter set to anything above 0 will dramatically slow your database.

db_block_size

The **db_block_size** parameter specifies the size, in bytes, of each block within the database. It is effective only when the database is first created. The default value for this parameter is operating-system-dependent, but is usually in the range of 2,048 to 32,768. For normal databases, it is usually set to 2,048 or 4,096. For highly query-intensive databases, such as data warehouses, block sizes of around 32K are not uncommon.

db_files

The **db_files** parameter defines the maximum number of files that can be opened for the database. The default for this parameter is operating-system-dependent, but is usually set to 32. This should be more than enough, but for some very large databases, this value should be set to 255. Once the database has been created, you can change the value of the **db_files** parameter within the init.ora file.

db_name

The **db_name** parameter specifies the name of the database that the init.ora file is used against. The name can be any combination of eight characters. Because this parameter is optional, it has no default. If you specify the database name on the command line when starting the database, you do not need to specify this parameter in the init.ora file. You have to be careful when naming a database, because Oracle does not recognize some characters. The allowable characters are:

- All alphabetic characters
- All numeric characters
- The underscore character (_)
- The hash sign (#)
- The dollar sign ($)

disk_asynch_io

The **disk_async_io** parameter specifies whether any writes to the database are done using async I/O. If your platform supports async I/O, this parameter should be left as is. If your platform does not support async I/O (Windows 95), ignore this parameter.

fixed_date

With the **fixed_date** parameter, you can set **SYSDATE** to a constant. The format of the parameter is YYYY-MM-DD-HH24:MI:SS. It allows you to test features on the database without changing the system clock on the operating system. This is useful for year 2000 testing. The default for this parameter is NULL. This parameter should be used only when testing and never in a production database.

hash_area_size

The **hash_area_size** parameter specifies the maximum amount of memory, in bytes, to be used for hash joins. The default for this parameter is set to twice the value for **sort_area_size**.

ifile

The **ifile** parameter is used to embed another parameter file within the init.ora file. When the database comes across this parameter in the init.ora file, it is directed to another file to read. This is useful when you have one file that stores the parameters you may change regularly and one where the parameters are static. I normally use **ifile** and call a file called *config<database_name>.ora*. For example, if you wish the init.ora file to call a file called *configorcl.ora,* you would put the following line into the init.ora file:

```
IFILE=C:\orawin95\database\configorcl.ora
```

This would then call the config file when the database is being started. You can also insert another **ifile** parameter within the file being called, nesting these calls up to three deep. In addition, you can use multiple **ifile** parameters within the one init.ora file.

license_max_sessions

The **license_max_sessions** parameter regulates the maximum number of concurrent sessions allowed to connect to the database. Once this number is set, when the maximum number of sessions is reached, only users with the **RESTRICTED SESSION** privilege are allowed to connect to the database; other users receive a warning message that the maximum number of permitted sessions has been reached. A 0 value, the default, signifies that the maximum number of allowable concurrent sessions is disabled—i.e., no checking is done. If this parameter is set to 0, you should set the **license_sessions_warning** parameter (explained later in this section). Also, if **license_max_sessions** is set to 0, the **license_max_users** parameter should be set to a nonzero number.

license_max_users

The **license_max_users** parameter specifies the maximum number of users you can create in the database. Once this limit is reached, Oracle will not allow you to create any more users within the database. **license_max_users** and **license_max_sessions** should not both be set at the same time within any one database.

license_sessions_warning

The **license_sessions_warning** parameter specifies a warning threshold on the number of concurrent sessions. When this limit is reached, users can still connect, but Oracle writes a message to the alert file for each new connection.

log_archive_buffer_size

The **log_archive_buffer_size** parameter specifies the size of buffer used to write information to the archive logs, in blocks. You should not need to change this parameter; the default should be fine.

log_archive_buffers

The **log_archive_buffers** parameter defines the number of buffers used for archiving. You should not need to change the default value (it's operating-system-dependent) unless you experience problems with the speed of archiving.

log_archive_dest

You can specify the location for the archived redo logs with the **log_archive_dest** parameter. It is effective only if your database is running in Archivelog mode. This parameter accepts a directory path as a value.

log_archive_format

Use the **log_archive_format** parameter to specify the file-naming convention for all of your archived redo logs. This parameter, again, is effective only if your database is running in Archivelog mode. The value for this parameter is used along with the value for **log_archive_dest** to define the directory and file name for all archived redo log files. The makeup of the file name will include the log sequence number, specified in this parameter as *%s*. If used in uppercase *(%S)*, the number generated is of fixed length and padded with zeros. For example, to specify your archived redo logs to be in the C:\ORAWIN95\ARCH directory, with each one to be called *archive* followed by its sequence number, you should specify the following in the init.ora file:

```
LOG_ARCHIVE_DEST=C:\orawin\archive
LOG_ARCHIVE_FORMAT="archive%S.arch"
```

log_archive_start

The **log_archive_start** parameter defines whether the database should automatically archive redo logs. It is effective only if the database is in Archivelog mode. The default for this value is **FALSE**, meaning manual archiving is in operation. A **TRUE** value indicates that the database will automatically archive redo logs. If this parameter is set to **FALSE** and all archive logs fill, without being manually archived, the database will stop performing operations, because it cannot write to the redo log files. The only way to resume the database is to manually archive the redo logs. Automatic archiving is always best.

log_buffer

To define the amount of memory used when buffering redo information to the redo log files, use the **log_buffer** parameter. Remember, the LGWR background process writes redo log information. Increase this value to reduce the amount of I/O to the files.

log_files

The **log_files** parameter defines the maximum number of redo logs that can be used when a database starts up. The default for this parameter is 255—more than enough for the databases you will create using Personal Oracle8. You can reduce this value to free up more space within the SGA.

max_dump_file_size

You can use the **max_dump_file_size** parameter to specify the maximum size of any trace files written by Personal Oracle8. This is very useful, because large trace files can be generated if this parameter is not set. The default is 10,000, in blocks. If you append either a K or M to this figure, the value is then in either kilobytes (* 1,000) or megabytes (* 1,000,000). This parameter can also be set to **UNLIMITED**, which does not limit the size of the dump file.

max_enabled_roles

The **max_enabled_roles** parameter specifies the maximum number of roles a user can enable at any one time. The default is 20, which should be more than enough for all users.

max_rollback_segments

The **max_rollback_segments** parameter is used to define the maximum size of the rollback-segment cache within the SGA, or the maximum number of rollback segments that can be used in any one database. The default of 30 should be enough for most small databases, but if the database you are running is very large or has multiple users—more than 30 concurrent users—you should increase this parameter.

nls_currency

The **nls_currency** parameter specifies the local currency symbol. This parameter, which is derived from the value of the **nls_territory** parameter, is usually not altered.

nls_date_format

The **nls_date_format** parameter specifies which date format is used with the **TO_CHAR** and **TO_DATE** functions within SQL*Plus. The default value for this parameter is derived from the **nls_territory** parameter.

nls_date_language

The **nls_date_language** parameter specifies the language to use for the spelling of day and month names. The default value of this parameter is the language specified by the **nls_language** parameter.

nls_language

The **nls_language** parameter specifies the default language of the database. This is the language that will be used in displaying error messages and for all text derived from the database (used within such functions as **TO_DATE** and **TO_CHAR**). This parameter is used to define other parameters—for example, **nls_date_language** and **nls_sort**.

nls_numeric_characters

The **nls_numeric_characters** parameter specifies the characters to use as the group separator and decimal placeholder. The default for this parameter is usually a "." (period) followed by a "," (comma) and is derived from the value of the **nls_territory** parameter. The parameter is specified as follows:

```
NLS_NUMERIC_CHARACTERS = ".,"
```

open_cursors

You can specify the maximum number of cursors that can be open at any one time per user session with the **open_cursors** parameter. This allows the DBA some control over how much processing each user can do. The default for this parameter is 50. This parameter is one that is usually changed. Setting it high is not a problem, because you must make sure that enough cursors can be opened to allow your application to function.

optimizer_mode

The **optimizer_mode** parameter specifies which optimizer is used for your SQL and PL/SQL code. This parameter has a number of values:

- *CHOOSE*—Uses cost-based optimization, as long as at least one table in the query has statistics in the data dictionary (gathered using the **ANALYZE** command). This is the default.

- *RULE*—Uses rule-based optimization. This can be overridden if hints are used within the SQL code.

- *FIRST_ROWS*—Uses cost-based optimization, but executes statements to minimize the execution time.

- *ALL_ROWS*—Uses cost-based optimization, but executes statements to minimize the overall execution time.

partition_view_enabled

The **partition_view_enabled** parameter is used in conjunction with the cost-based optimizer to allow queries using partitioned views to use only the partitions that are needed. The default for this parameter is **FALSE**—i.e., uses all of the partitioned view.

rollback_segments

Upon instance startup, the **rollback_segments** parameter defines which rollback segments are to be used. This parameter accepts any number of rollback segments and should be specified as follows:

```
ROLLBACK_SEGMENTS=(rs01,rs02,rs03)
```

This would start the database with rollback segments rs01, rs02, and rs03 in use.

sequence_cache_entries

The **sequence_cache_entries** parameter specifies how many sequences should be kept within the SGA. This gives immediate access to them. The default is 10. This value should be set to the maximum number of sequences that will be used within the database.

sessions

The **sessions** parameter defines the maximum number of user and system sessions that are allowed within the database at any one time. The default value for this parameter is derived from the **processes** parameter.

shadow_core_dump

When a core dump is written, the **shadow_core_dump** parameter specifies whether the SGA should be included within the core dump file. The default value for this parameter is **FULL**, which includes the SGA information whenever a core dump is written. The only other allowable value for this parameter is **PARTIAL**, which does not include the SGA within any core dump files.

shared_pool_size

One of the most important init.ora parameters is **shared_pool_size**, which defines the size of the shared pool within the SGA. The default value for this parameter is 3,500,000 bytes

(3.5MB). The shared pool is the area of the SGA where all of the shared SQL and cursors are stored. The larger the value, the bigger the SGA gets. This improves performance in multiuser systems.

sort_area_size

Another well-used parameter is **sort_area_size**. It specifies the maximum size of the sort area for each user session. If this is exceeded, a sort is performed within the database. If you have an application that performs large sorts, you can improve performance by increasing this value.

sql_trace

The **sql_trace** parameter is used to turn the tracing facility of Personal Oracle8 on and off. The default value for this parameter is **FALSE**—i.e., no tracing. When this parameter is set to **TRUE**, tracing information is gathered, enabling you to tune the SQL statements that execute against the database. The trace files are collected in the C:\ORAWIN95\ RDBMS80\TRACE directory (specified by the **user_dump_dest** parameter).

timed_statistics

The database collects time-based information when the **timed_statistics** parameter is set to **TRUE** and disabled when set to **FALSE**. The default is **FALSE**.

user_dump_dest

The **user_dump_dest** parameter specifies where the database will write its trace files to. This is usually set to C:\ORAWIN95\RDBMS80\TRACE when using Personal Oracle8.

Changing Parameters Dynamically

In some cases, you can change these parameters without shutting down the database first. These are called *dynamic parameter changes*. They are performed by using three statements, each of which changes parameters in a different way.

ALTER SESSION

The **ALTER SESSION** command, which can be performed either through Server Manager or while logged into SQL*Plus, changes the values for the session it is specified in. You must remember that any parameters changed with the **ALTER SESSION** command are reset when you log out of the database. To change a parameter with the **ALTER SESSION** command, issue the following:

```
ALTER SESSION SET parameter_name=parameter_value
```

The parameters you can change with the **ALTER SESSION** command are as follows:

- allow_partial_sn_results
- b_tree_bitmap_plans
- db_file_multiblock_read_count
- global_names
- hash_area_size
- hash_multiblock_io_count
- max_dump_file_size
- nls_currency
- nls_date_format
- nls_date_language
- nls_iso_currency
- nls_language
- nls_numeric_characters
- nls_sort
- nls_territory
- object_cache_max_size_percent
- object_cache_optimal_size
- ops_admin_group
- optimizer_mode
- optimizer_percent_parallel
- optimizer_search_limit
- parallel_instance_group
- parallel_min_percent
- partition_view_enabled
- plsqlv2_compatibility
- remote_dependencies_mode

- sort_area_retained_size

- sort_area_size

- sort_direct_writes

- sort_read_fac

- sort_write_buffer_size

- sort_write_buffers

- spin_count

- star_transformation_enabled

- text_enable

- timed_statistics

ALTER SYSTEM

The **ALTER SYSTEM** command can be performed through Server Manager or SQL*Plus, but must be done by a user with a DBA responsibility. I usually use the **SYSTEM** user. To change a parameter with **ALTER SYSTEM**, issue the following command:

```
ALTER SYSTEM SET parameter_name=parameter_value
```

The **ALTER SYSTEM** command changes the parameter globally within the database. You can change the following parameters with the **ALTER SYSTEM** command:

- aq_tm_processes

- control_file_record_keep_time

- db_block_checkpoint_batch

- db_block_checksum

- db_block_max_dirty_target

- db_file_multiblock_read_count

- fixed_date

- freeze_db_for_fast_instance_recovery

- global_names

- hash_multiblock_io_count

- license_max_sessions
- license_max_users
- license_sessions_warning
- log_archive_duplex_dest
- log_archive_min_succeed_dest
- log_checkpoint_interval
- log_checkpoint_timeout
- log_small_entry_max_size
- max_dump_file_size
- mts_dispatchers
- mts_servers
- ops_admin_group
- parallel_instance_group
- parallel_transaction_resource_timeout
- plsql_v2_compatibility
- remote_dependencies_mode
- resource_limit
- spin_count
- text_enable
- timed_os_statistics
- timed_statistics
- user_dump_dest

ALTER SYSTEM DEFERRED

The **ALTER SYSTEM DEFERRED** command can be performed by entering Server Manager or SQL*Plus, but must be done by a user with a DBA responsibility. I usually use the **SYSTEM** user. To change a parameter with **ALTER SYSTEM DEFERRED**, issue the following command:

```
ALTER SYSTEM SET parameter_name=parameter_value DEFERRED
```

The **ALTER SYSTEM DEFERRED** command changes the parameter globally within the database for all users who connect after the command is issued. The following parameters can be changed with **ALTER SYSTEM DEFERRED**:

- allow_partial_sn_results
- backup_disk_io_slaves
- backup_tape_io_slaves
- db_file_direct_io_count
- object_cache_max_size_percent
- object_cache_optimal_size
- sort_area_retained_size
- sort_area_size
- sort_direct_writes
- sort_read_fac
- sort_write_buffer_size
- sort_write_buffers
- transaction_auditing

INDEXING

Indexes are special objects within an Oracle database. They allow you to gain access to the information you require faster than reading every value within a table. An index is really just a subset of a table that is read instead of the table itself. For example, normally when you join two tables together, you use a column in each. If this column is one of the primary or foreign keys, then the join could be done through an index. You could index the columns you are joining and increase the speed of the query.

Indexes created within any Oracle database are usually B-tree indexes. The advantage to this type of index is that no matter where in the index the value you require is, accessing it will take roughly the same amount of time, whether it is at the top of the list or at the end. The access time is usually independent of the size of the index. Once an index has been created, Oracle will try to use it wherever possible—i.e., wherever the column the index includes is referenced. This is done automatically and needs no intervention by the user, unless hints are specified.

As mentioned earlier, indexes are useful when joining tables, because one table must be searched for matches to each row in the other table. If tables are frequently joined, you should create indexes containing the column names for all tables in the join. This will increase query performance.

THE NEXT STEP IN TUNING

In this chapter, you earned what steps you can take to start diagnosing problems with your database, including the use of Server Manager and the makeup of the init.ora file. You can now use the information gained in this chapter to proceed to the next chapter, which discusses tuning SQL statements and other database functions.

Application And SQL Tuning

CHAPTER 18

Tuning your
application
to enhance
database and
SQL performance.

In the previous chapter, I discussed the Oracle Server Manager tool and init.ora file parameters. These should help you get the most out of your database configuration. In this chapter, I discuss getting the most out of your application. One of the primary ways in which this is accomplished is tuning your SQL statements. Among other topics, such as tuning I/O and memory, this chapter guides you through the maze of tuning SQL statements with the tools Oracle supplies.

As I demonstrated in the previous chapter, Personal Oracle8 is a very tunable product. You can alter the behavior of virtually every component. This is good in one sense, in that you can alter the performance to what you specify; but it can also be bad, in that you have so many options that you hardly know where to start. I will attempt to show the major obstacles to overcome in tuning any Oracle database.

All tuning is based on the following three areas (not in any particular order):

- Tuning I/O
- Tuning memory
- Tuning code

This chapter aims to cover these three areas, albeit in fairly brief detail. (I have books with thousands of pages dedicated solely to tuning Oracle databases.) First, you need to learn that Oracle has a fairly good script for producing database performance reports. The trick is knowing how to interpret the output. The first section of this chapter shows you how to run and read the results of this report. The remainder of this chapter describes the V$ performance views and explains how to tune your SQL code using Oracle utilities.

REPORTING DATABASE PERFORMANCE

Database performance statistics are gathered with two programs that Oracle has kindly supplied: utlbstat.sql and utlestat.sql, both of which can be found in the C:\ORAWIN95\ RDBMS80\ADMIN directory. These files are commonly referred to as the *bstat* and *estat* files. Before executing the bstat and estat report, you should check your init.ora file to see if the **timed_statistics** parameter is set to TRUE; if not, set it and restart the database. To gather statistics using these files, you first need to access the Server Manager software and connect as a DBA user—i.e., use the **CONNECT INTERNAL** database command. Once connected, run utlbstat.sql (begin statistics). This creates all of the required tables and initiates the collection of statistics. After a period of time, or when you have executed transactions for which you need statistics, you run utlestat.sql (end statistics), which gathers all of the statistics and produces a report called report.txt in the C:\ORAWIN95\RDBMS80\ADMIN directory.

Utlbstat And Utlestat Reporting

Once you have gathered the statistics and have the report, you need to interpret it and make any relevant changes. The following sections describe each section of the report and explain how each is used in tuning database and application performance, including which parameters, if any, can be used to gain the desired performance. Rather than use the whole report as an example, I have split it into 14 easily identifiable sections.

Section 1

This is one of the important sections of the report; all sections dealing with caches are important. This shows how the library cache is coping with the number of transactions that were passed through it in the interval defined for the report. Remember, the library cache is where all shared object information is stored. The main things to look at in this section are the values for the column **PinHitRatio**, which shows the percentage of times the required library was accessed within memory. As shown in Listing 18.1, the **PinHitRatio** is close to 100 percent in all cases except BODY and TABLE/PROCEDURE, where the hit ratios are 75 percent and 79.7 percent, respectively. This figure should be as close to 100 percent as possible. If you see values lower than, say, 90 percent, you should tune the library cache further by increasing the init.ora parameter **shared_pool_size**. This will allow for more of the library object to be held within the library cache and should reduce the number of reloads (the number of misses within the cache).

Listing 18.1   *Library cache statistics (Section 1).*

```
SVRMGR> Rem Select Library cache statistics.  The pin hit rate should be high.
SVRMGR> select namespace library,
    2>        gets,
    3>        round(decode(gethits,0,1,gethits)/decode(gets,0,1,gets),3)
    4>          gethitratio,
    5>        pins,
    6>        round(decode(pinhits,0,1,pinhits)/decode(pins,0,1,pins),3)
    7>          pinhitratio,
    8>        reloads, invalidations
    9>    from stats$lib;
```

LIBRARY	GETS	GETHITRATI	PINS	PINHITRATI	RELOADS	INVALIDATI
BODY	4	1	4	.75	1	0
CLUSTER	81	.988	123	.984	0	0
INDEX	2	.5	2	.5	0	0
OBJECT	0	1	0	1	0	0
PIPE	0	1	0	1	0	0
SQL AREA	511	.857	2143	.906	52	2
TABLE/PROCED	323	.935	561	.797	62	0
TRIGGER	0	1	0	1	0	0

```
8 rows selected.
```

Section 2

This section deals with the statistics generated by the database for the interval of the report. Listing 18.2 shows the total database activity for the interval of the report. The statistics in this section are provided for you to analyze the effectiveness of the data cache, known as the *hit ratio*. Because all objects have to pass through the data cache before they can be accessed, this ratio is a good pointer to how well the database is performing. The hit ratio is calculated as follows

```
HIT RATIO = ((LOGICAL READS - PHYSICAL READS)/LOGICAL READS) * 100
```

where

```
LOGICAL READS = CONSISTENT GETS + DB BLOCK GETS
```

The hit ratio for the figures shown in Listing 18.2 would be as follows:

```
HIT RATIO = (((3321 + 1004) - 374)/(3321 + 1004)) * 100
```

Therefore, the hit ratio for the listing would be 91.35 percent, which is not too bad. If this value drops below 80 percent, you should increase the value of the **db_block_buffers** init.ora parameter.

Another statistic to look for in this section is sorts (disk). In the example, this figure does not exist (meaning there were no sorts on disk). You should avoid sorts on disk; they should be done in memory. To avoid sorts on disk, increase the value of the **sort_area_size** parameter in the init.ora file.

Listing 18.2 Database statistics (Section 2).

```
SVRMGR> Rem The total is the total value of the statistic between the time
SVRMGR> Rem bstat was run and the time estat was run.  Note that the estat
SVRMGR> Rem script logs on as "internal" so the per_logon statistics will
SVRMGR> Rem always be based on at least one logon.
SVRMGR> select n1.name "Statistic",
    2>          n1.change "Total",
    3>          round(n1.change/trans.change,2) "Per Transaction",
    4>          round(n1.change/logs.change,2)  "Per Logon",
    5>          round(n1.change/(to_number(to_char(end_time,   'J'))*60*60*24 -
    6>                      to_number(to_char(start_time, 'J'))*60*60*24 +
    7>                      to_number(to_char(end_time,   'SSSSS')) -
    8>                      to_number(to_char(start_time, 'SSSSS')))
    9>                      , 2) "Per Second"
   10>     from stats$stats n1, stats$stats trans, stats$stats logs, stats$dates
   11>     where trans.name='user commits'
   12>       and  logs.name='logons cumulative'
   13>       and  n1.change != 0
   14>     order by n1.name;
```

Statistic	Total	Per Transact	Per Logon	Per Second
DBWR Flush object call foun	2	.33	.22	.01
DBWR Flush object cross ins	4	.67	.44	.03
DBWR buffers scanned	1118	186.33	124.22	7.71
DBWR checkpoint buffers wri	153	25.5	17	1.06
DBWR checkpoint write reque	25	4.17	2.78	.17
DBWR free buffers found	798	133	88.67	5.5
DBWR lru scans	76	12.67	8.44	.52
DBWR make free requests	52	8.67	5.78	.36
DBWR skip hot writes	10	1.67	1.11	.07
DBWR summed scan depth	1118	186.33	124.22	7.71
DBWR timeouts	37	6.17	4.11	.26
DBWR transaction table writ	28	4.67	3.11	.19
DBWR undo block writes	54	9	6	.37

SQL*Net roundtrips to/from	163	27.17	18.11	1.12
background checkpoints comp	1	.17	.11	.01
background checkpoints star	1	.17	.11	.01
background timeouts	144	24	16	.99
buffer is not pinned count	2005	334.17	222.78	13.83
buffer is pinned count	1450	241.67	161.11	10
bytes received via SQL*Net	17610	2935	1956.67	121.45
bytes sent via SQL*Net to c	10030	1671.67	1114.44	69.17
calls to get snapshot scn:	879	146.5	97.67	6.06
calls to kcmgas	50	8.33	5.56	.34
calls to kcmgcs	16	2.67	1.78	.11
calls to kcmgrs	397	66.17	44.11	2.74
cleanouts only - consistent	11	1.83	1.22	.08
cluster key scan block gets	812	135.33	90.22	5.6
cluster key scans	260	43.33	28.89	1.79
commit cleanout failures: b	13	2.17	1.44	.09
commit cleanout failures: b	2	.33	.22	.01
commit cleanouts	166	27.67	18.44	1.14
commit cleanouts successful	151	25.17	16.78	1.04
consistent gets	3321	553.5	369	22.9
cursor authentications	70	11.67	7.78	.48
db block changes	1070	178.33	118.89	7.38
db block gets	1004	167.33	111.56	6.92
deferred (CURRENT) block cl	59	9.83	6.56	.41
enqueue releases	326	54.33	36.22	2.25
enqueue requests	320	53.33	35.56	2.21
execute count	838	139.67	93.11	5.78
free buffer requested	473	78.83	52.56	3.26
immediate (CR) block cleano	11	1.83	1.22	.08
immediate (CURRENT) block c	73	12.17	8.11	.5
logons cumulative	9	1.5	1	.06
logons current	1	.17	.11	.01
messages received	117	19.5	13	.81
messages sent	117	19.5	13	.81
no buffer to keep pinned co	27	4.5	3	.19
no work - consistent read g	1689	281.5	187.67	11.65
opened cursors cumulative	451	75.17	50.11	3.11
opened cursors current	2	.33	.22	.01
parse count (hard)	135	22.5	15	.93
parse count (total)	515	85.83	57.22	3.55
physical reads	374	62.33	41.56	2.58
physical writes	269	44.83	29.89	1.86
recursive calls	9836	1639.33	1092.89	67.83
redo blocks written	298	49.67	33.11	2.06
redo buffer allocation retr	1	.17	.11	.01
redo entries	595	99.17	66.11	4.1
redo log space requests	1	.17	.11	.01
redo size	146028	24338	16225.33	1007.09
redo small copies	594	99	66	4.1

```
redo synch writes                  19      3.17      2.11        .13
redo wastage                     7272      1212       808       50.15
redo writes                        37      6.17      4.11        .26
rollback changes - undo rec         4       .67       .44        .03
session logical reads            4325    720.83    480.56      29.83
session pga memory             2428372  404728.67  269819.11  16747.39
session pga memory max         2428372  404728.67  269819.11  16747.39
session uga memory              69128   11521.33   7680.89     476.74
session uga memory max         260424     43404     28936     1796.03
sorts (memory)                    109     18.17     12.11        .75
sorts (rows)                      704    117.33     78.22       4.86
table fetch by rowid              479     79.83     53.22        3.3
table fetch continued row          83     13.83      9.22        .57
table scan blocks gotten           10      1.67      1.11        .07
table scan rows gotten              6         1       .67        .04
table scans (short tables)         11      1.83      1.22        .08
total file opens                   15       2.5      1.67         .1
user calls                        208     34.67     23.11       1.43
user commits                        6         1       .67        .04
write requests                     41      6.83      4.56        .28
82 rows selected.
```

Section 3

This section reports the average length of the queue for writes, as shown in Listing 18.3. The figure here should be as close to zero as possible. If you have a figure above zero, take a look at the value of the init.ora parameter **db_block_write_batch**, and compare it with the value you received. If the write queue length is higher than **db_block_write_batch**, then you should increase the parameter.

Listing 18.3   Queue length (Section 3).

```
SVRMGR> Rem Average length of the dirty buffer write queue.  If this is larger
SVRMGR> Rem than the value of:
SVRMGR> Rem  1. (db_files * db_file_simultaneous_writes)/2
SVRMGR> Rem  or
SVRMGR> Rem  2. 1/4 of db_block_buffers
SVRMGR> Rem which ever is smaller and also there is a platform specific limit
SVRMGR> Rem on the write batch size (normally 1024 or 2048 buffers). If the av-
SVRMGR> Rem erage length of the dirty buffer write queue is larger than the value
SVRMGR> Rem calculated before, increase db_file_simultaneous_writes or db_files.
SVRMGR> Rem Also check for disks that are doing many more IOs than other disks.
SVRMGR> select queue.change/writes.change "Average Write Queue Length"
     2>   from stats$stats queue, stats$stats writes
     3>  where queue.name  = 'summed dirty queue length'
     4>   and  writes.name = 'write requests';
Average Write Queue Length
--------------------------
                         0
1 row selected.
```

Section 4

This section is used for gathering statistics on all wait states within the database. The figures you are interested in are the buffer busy waits, which are used to calculate the buffer busy wait ratio as follows

```
BUFFER BUSY WAIT RATIO = (BUFFER BUSY WAITS / LOGICAL READS) * 100
```

where

```
LOGICAL READS = (CONSISTENT GETS + DB BLOCK GETS)
```

In our example from Listing 18.4,

```
BUFFER BUSY WAIT RATIO = ((1 / (3321 + 1004))) * 100
```

the ratio is 0.02 percent, which is fine. If the value for buffer busy waits exceeds 4 percent, some tuning is needed. To do so, find out what the waits are by looking at the **V$WAITSTAT** view. If you see lots of waits for undo information, this indicates that more rollback segments are needed.

Listing 18.4   Wait events (Section 4).

```
SVRMGR> Rem System wide wait events for non-background processes (PMON,
SVRMGR> Rem SMON, etc).  Times are in hundredths of seconds.  Each one of
SVRMGR> Rem these is a context switch which costs CPU time.  By looking at
SVRMGR> Rem the Total Time you can often determine what is the bottleneck
SVRMGR> Rem that processes are waiting for.  This shows the total time spent
SVRMGR> Rem waiting for a specific event and the average time per wait on
SVRMGR> Rem that event.
SVRMGR> select n1.event "Event Name",
          2> n1.event_count "Count",
          3> n1.time_waited "Total Time",
          4> round(n1.time_waited/n1.event_count, 2) "Avg Time"
     5>     from stats$event n1
     6>     where n1.event_count > 0
     7>     order by n1.time_waited desc;
Event Name                        Count        Total Time   Avg Time
-------------------------------   ----------   ----------   ----------
SQL*Net message from client         193               0            0
SQL*Net message to client           195               0            0
buffer busy waits                     1               0            0
control file sequential read         10               0            0
db file sequential read             398               0            0
file identify                         4               0            0
file open                            19               0            0
```

```
library cache pin                             3              0              0
log file switch completion                    1              0              0
log file sync                                17              0              0
rdbms ipc message                             2              0              0
rdbms ipc reply                               3              0              0
write complete waits                         10              0              0
SQL*Net break/reset to client                18              0              0
14 rows selected.
```

Section 5

This section looks at the wait events for the background processes, such as PMON, SMON, etc. It shows both the average and total time waiting. In Listing 18.5, you can see that even though a large number of total events is waiting, they are all waiting, on average, a zero amount of time. This is what you should expect to see.

Listing 18.5   Background process wait events (Section 5).

```
SVRMGR> Rem System wide wait events for background processes (PMON, SMON, etc)
SVRMGR> select n1.event "Event Name",
            2> n1.event_count "Count",
            3> n1.time_waited "Total Time",
            4> round(n1.time_waited/n1.event_count, 2) "Avg Time"
      5>    from stats$bck_event n1
      6>    where n1.event_count > 0
      7>    order by n1.time_waited desc;
Event Name                      Count        Total Time    Avg Time
------------------------------  -----------  ------------  ------------
control file parallel write          25              0              0
control file sequential read         26              0              0
db file parallel write               42              0              0
db file sequential read               4              0              0
db file single write                  4              0              0
file identify                         5              0              0
file open                             4              0              0
latch free                            1              0              0
log file parallel write              38              0              0
log file sequential read              6              0              0
log file single write                 2              0              0
log file sync                         3              0              0
pmon timer                      9432577              0              0
rdbms ipc message                   231              0              0
14 rows selected.
```

Section 6

Section 6 shows the latches present within the system. Remember that a latch is a lock held within the SGA. In Listing 18.6, the relevant figures in this section are **Hit_Ratio**, which should be as high as possible, and **Sleeps**, which should be as low as possible. The best possible result is to have all **Hit_Ratios** at 1 and **Sleeps** at 0.

Listing 18.6 *Latches (Section 6).*

```
SVRMGR> Rem Latch statistics. Latch contention will show up as a large value for
SVRMGR> Rem the 'latch free' event in the wait events above.
SVRMGR> Rem Sleeps should be low.  The hit_ratio should be high.
SVRMGR> select name latch_name, gets, misses,
     2>      round((gets-misses)/decode(gets,0,1,gets),3)
     3>        hit_ratio,
     4>      sleeps,
     5>      round(sleeps/decode(misses,0,1,misses),3) "SLEEPS/MISS"
     6>      from stats$latches
     7>      where gets != 0
     8>      order by name;
```

LATCH_NAME	GETS	MISSES	HIT_RATIO	SLEEPS	SLEEPS/MISS
Active checkpoint	102	0	1	0	0
Checkpoint queue l	1421	0	1	0	0
Token Manager	22	0	1	0	0
archive control	2	0	1	0	0
cache buffer handl	51	0	1	0	0
cache buffers chai	10067	0	1	0	0
cache buffers lru	530	0	1	0	0
dml lock allocatio	299	0	1	0	0
enqueue hash chain	608	0	1	0	0
enqueues	880	0	1	0	0
file number transl	4	0	1	0	0
library cache	11007	0	1	0	0
library cache load	186	0	1	0	0
list of block allo	103	0	1	0	0
loader state objec	2	0	1	0	0
messages	637	0	1	0	0
modify parameter v	9	0	1	0	0
ncodef allocation	47	0	1	0	0
process allocation	4	0	1	0	0
redo allocation	857	1	.999	1	1
row cache objects	2872	0	1	0	0
sequence cache	14	0	1	0	0
session allocation	4301	0	1	0	0
session idle bit	462	0	1	0	0
session switching	47	0	1	0	0
shared pool	5121	0	1	0	0

```
transaction alloca        204          0          1          0          0
undo global data          154          0          1          0          0
user lock                  14          0          1          0          0
29 rows selected.
```

Section 7

Section 7 is similar to Section 6. It looks at the amount of **no_wait** latches and the hit ratios associated with them. The optimum values for this section are 1 for all **Nowait_Hit_Ratio** figures and 0 for the **Nowait_Misses** figures. If you are experiencing problems with these figures, the reason is usually the redo copy and redo allocation latches (see Listing 18.7). You should decrease the value of the init.ora parameter **log_small_entry_max_size**.

Listing 18.7   No_wait latches (Section 7).

```
SVRMGR> Rem Statistics on no_wait gets of latches.  A no_wait get does not
SVRMGR> Rem wait for the latch to become free, it immediately times out.
SVRMGR> select name latch_name,
     2>      immed_gets nowait_gets,
     3>      immed_miss nowait_misses,
     4>      round((immed_gets/immed_gets+immed_miss), 3)
     5>       nowait_hit_ratio
     6>    from stats$latches
     7>    where immed_gets + immed_miss != 0
     8>    order by name;
LATCH_NAME            NOWAIT_GETS      NOWAIT_MISSES    NOWAIT_HIT_RATIO
----------------     ----------------  ---------------- ----------------
Token Manager                  35          0                1
cache buffers chai           4009          0                1
cache buffers lru             889          0                1
library cache                  38          0                1
multiblock read ob              1          0                1
process allocation              4          0                1
row cache objects              39          0                1
vecio buf des                  35          0                1
8 rows selected.
```

Section 8

This section describes the types of blocks that are experiencing buffer busy waits. If the values for this section are high for undo blocks, you should add more rollback segments. As you can see from Listing 18.8, the value is very low, because the only wait was for one data block.

Listing 18.8   Buffer busy wait (Section 8).

```
SVRMGR> Rem Buffer busy wait statistics.  If the value for 'buffer busy wait' in
SVRMGR> Rem the wait event statistics is high, then this table will identify
SVRMGR> Rem which class of blocks is having high contention.  If there are high
```

```
SVRMGR> Rem 'undo header' waits then add more rollback segments.  If there are
SVRMGR> Rem high 'segment header' waits then adding freelists might help.  Check
SVRMGR> Rem v$session_wait to get the addresses of the actual blocks having
SVRMGR> Rem contention.
SVRMGR> select * from stats$waitstat
     2>   where count != 0
     3>   order by count desc;
CLASS                 COUNT            TIME
----------------- ---------------- ----------------
data block                    1                0
1 row selected.
```

Section 9

This section gathers information about all rollback segments within the database, as shown in Listing 18.9. Because the listing is wrapped around and may be difficult to read, I have changed the layout to make it more readable. The values to look for in this section are **Trans Tbl_Waits**. If they are high, you need more rollback segments.

Listing 18.9   Rollback segments (Section 9).

```
SVRMGR> Rem Waits_for_trans_tbl high implies you should add rollback segments.
SVRMGR> select * from stats$roll;
UNDO        TRANS       TRANS       UNDO           SEGMENT
SEGMENT     TBL_GETS    TBL_WAITS   BYTES_WRITTEN  SIZE_BYTES   XACTS SHRINKS WRAPS
----------  ----------  ----------  -------------  ----------   ---- ------- ------
0           1           0           0              407552        0     0       0
2           26          0           3332           458752        0     0       0
3           16          0           11340          561152        0     0       0
4           18          0           4110           151552        0     0       0
5           16          0           3594           612352       -1     0       0
6           24          0           5916           151552        1     0       0
7           41          0           13980          1277952       0     0       0
7 rows selected.
```

Section 10

This section displays all information about the init.ora parameters that are in force for the current session. It displays only the information for all init.ora parameters that are different from the default—i.e., those you have changed. This section is useful when determining which parameters you have changed. It enables you to look down the list to check which parameters are in force. This section is for display purposes only. See Listing 18.10 for an example.

Listing 18.10   init.ora parameters (Section 10).

```
SVRMGR> Rem The init.ora parameters currently in effect:
SVRMGR> select name, value from v$parameter where isdefault = 'FALSE'
```

```
    2>    order by name;
NAME                                    VALUE
------------------------------------    -------------------------------------
audit_trail                             DB
background_dump_dest                    %RDBMS80%\trace
control_files                           C:\ORAWIN95\DATABASE\ctl1orcl.ora
db_block_size                           2048
db_files                                1024
db_name                                 oracle
disk_asynch_io                          FALSE
global_names                            TRUE
job_queue_processes                     2
log_archive_dest                        %ORACLE_HOME%\database\archive
log_archive_format                      %%ORACLE_SID%%T%TS%S.ARC
log_archive_start                       TRUE
log_buffer                              8192
log_checkpoint_interval                 10000
max_dump_file_size                      10240
processes                               50
remote_login_passwordfile               SHARED
sequence_cache_hash_buckets             10
shared_pool_size                        3500000
user_dump_dest                          %RDBMS80%\trace
20 rows selected.
```

Section 11

This section provides information on how the dictionary cache is performing, as in Listing 18.11. These values are useful in a number of calculations that determine the performance of the dictionary cache. The columns of this section are explained here:

- *Get_Reqs*—Displays how many times the particular type was requested from the dictionary cache.

- *Get_Miss*—Displays the number of times the particular type was requested and not found within the dictionary cache; remember, if it is not found within the dictionary cache, it must be loaded from disk.

- *Cur_Usage* —Displays the number of entries within the cache that are currently being used.

The best results are gained from the database where the **Get_Miss** and **Scan_Miss** statistics are as close to zero as possible. If the misses are more than 10 percent of the gets, the shared pool is not big enough. To rectify this, increase the value of the **shared_pool_size** init.ora parameter.

Listing 18.11   *Dictionary cache (Section 11).*

```
SVRMGR> Rem get_miss and scan_miss should be very low compared to the requests.
SVRMGR> Rem cur_usage is the number of entries in the cache that are being used.
SVRMGR> select * from stats$dc
      2>   where get_reqs != 0 or scan_reqs != 0 or mod_reqs != 0;
NAME             GET_REQS GET_MISS SCAN_REQ SCAN_MIS MOD_REQS COUNT    CUR_USAG
--------------   -------- -------- -------- -------- -------- -------- --------
dc_tablespaces        29        1        0        0        0        5        3
dc_free_extents       22       10        6        0       17       24       19
dc_segments          118       13        0        0       22       70       54
dc_used_extents       11       11        0        0       10       45       28
dc_tablespace_q       12        1        0        0        8       23        1
dc_users             127        4        0        0        3       21       17
dc_users               7        2        0        0        0       24        4
dc_user_grants        57        5        0        0        0       51       16
dc_objects           257       20        0        0       13      361      360
dc_synonyms           14        0        0        0        0       12       11
dc_usernames          62        3        0        0        0       21        8
dc_object_ids        195       18        0        0        4      202      201
dc_constraints         6        4        0        0        6       11        5
dc_sequences           2        0        0        0        1        5        4
dc_profiles            6        0        0        0        0       18        1
dc_histogram_de        0        0        3        0        0        1        0
16 rows selected.
```

Section 12

This section shows statistics for the spread of I/O across tablespaces. This should point out which tablespaces are doing the most processing. If you have more than one disk drive in your system, you should look at spreading the load of one of the tablespaces across other drives. This can be done with the **ALTER TABLESPACE ADD DATAFILE** command, which adds another data file to the tablespace on the other drive. As you can see from Listing 18.12, the SYSTEM tablespace has taken the most reads, but in this case, the number is rather low, so no action needs to be taken.

Listing 18.12   *Tablespace I/O (Section 12).*

```
SVRMGR> Rem Sum IO operations over tablespaces.
SVRMGR> select
      2>   table_space||'                                        '
      3>     table_space,
      4>   sum(phys_reads) reads,  sum(phys_blks_rd) blks_read,
      5>   sum(phys_rd_time) read_time,  sum(phys_writes) writes,
      6>   sum(phys_blks_wr) blks_wrt,  sum(phys_wrt_tim) write_time,
      7>   sum(megabytes_size) megabytes
      8> from stats$files
      9> group by table_space
```

```
    10>  order by table_space;
TABLE            BLKS  READ            BLKS    WRITE
SPACE      READS  READ  TIME  WRITES  WRT     TIME  MEGABYTES
-------------    ------ ----- ----- -------- -------- ----- ----------
ROLLBACK_DATA    15     15    0      88      88      0        5
SYSTEM           393    393   0      188     188     0       21
TEMPORARY_DATA   0      0     0      0       0       0        2
USER_DATA        5      5     0      9       9       0        3
4 rows selected.
```

Section 13

This section shows the number of accesses to the tablespaces by file position. Listing 18.13, which should be used in conjunction with Listing 18.12, shows the accesses by tablespace. When you add more data files to the tablespace, you should see the balancing of the I/O. Note that balancing I/O is one area where you can see large performance gains. If you are serious about running Oracle applications, you should really have more than one disk drive in your machine. This way, you can spread I/O evenly across all disk drives.

Listing 18.13 *Tablespace I/O (Section 13).*

```
SVRMGR> Rem I/O should be spread evenly across drives. A big difference between
SVRMGR> Rem phys_reads and phys_blks_rd implies table scans are going on.
SVRMGR> select table_space, file_name,
    2>        phys_reads reads, phys_blks_rd blks_read, phys_rd_time read_time,
    3>        phys_writes writes, phys_blks_wr blks_wrt,
    4>        phys_wrt_tim write_time, megabytes_size megabytes
    5>  from stats$files order by table_space, file_name;
TABLE          FILE                                  BLKS READ      BLKS WRI Mb
SPACE          NAME                       READS READ TIME WRTS WRT  TIM
-------------  -------------------------- ----- ---- ---- ---- ---- -- --
ROLLBACK_DATA  C:\ORAWIN95\DATABASE\RBS1ORCL.ORA   15   15   0   88   88   0  5
SYSTEM         C:\ORAWIN95\DATABASE\SYS1ORCL.ORA  393  393   0  188  188   0 21
TEMPORARY_DATA C:\ORAWIN95\DATABASE\TMP1ORCL.ORA    0    0   0    0    0   0  2
USER_DATA      C:\ORAWIN95\DATABASE\USR1ORCL.ORA    5    5   0    9    9   0  3
4 rows selected.
```

Section 14

This section displays all of the relevant version information for the database and any extra options installed. You can usually ignore this section of the report, because it does not contain any tuning information. I have included it for completeness. You can use it to check that you have installed everything correctly. Listing 18.14 is an example of this section.

Listing 18.14 *Version information (Section 14).*

```
SVRMGR> Rem Versions
SVRMGR> select * from v$version;
BANNER
------------------------------------------------------------
Personal Oracle8 Release 8.0.3.0.0 - Production
PL/SQL Release 8.0.3.0.0 - Production
CORE Version 4.0.3.0.0 - Production
TNS for 32-bit Windows: Version 8.0.3.0.0 - Production
NLSRTL Version 3.3.0.0.0 - Production
```

V$ VIEWS

The V$ views are used in performance tuning to view the statistics the database is generating for nearly all transactions that occur. You should be familiar with most of these views, especially the following:

- *V$ARCHIVED_LOG*—Gives details of all archived logs written to disk.

- *V$BACKUP*—Gives details of all backups that have occurred on the database.

- *V$BUFFER_POOL*—Used in calculation for buffer pool; also used in the bstat and estat reports.

- *V$CONTROLFILE*—Gives information regarding the control files currently in use.

- *V$DATABASE*—Gives information about the database.

- *V$DBFILE*—Gives information about all of the associated database files that make up the database.

- *V$LIBRARYCACHE*—Used in the bstat and estat reports to generate library cache statistics.

- *V$LOGFILE*—Gives information about all redo log files that the database is currently using.

- *V$NLS_PARAMETERS*—Provides information about all current NLS parameters.

- *V$NLS_VALID_VALUES*—Same as above.

- *V$PARAMETER*—Gives information on all init.ora parameters currently in force.

- *V$PROCESS*—Supplies information on all processes currently using the database.

- *V$ROLLNAME*—Provides rollback segment information; also used in the bstat and estat reports.

- *V$ROLLSTAT*—Same as above.

- *V$SESSION*—Gives information on all sessions currently connected to the database.

- *V$SESSTAT*—Gives statistics for the current session.

- *V$SGA*—Provides the current sizing for the SGA.

- *V$SGASTAT*—Gives current statistics for the SGA.

- *V$SQLAREA*—Provides current statistics and code held within the SGA.

- *V$STATNAME*—Provides the name and ID number for all statistics within the database.

- *V$SYSSTAT*—Gives the system statistics; also used in the bstat and estat reports.

- *V$TABLESPACE*—Provides information on all tablespaces within the database.

Examples of the V$ views follow in Listings 18.15 through 18.146.

Listing 18.15   *V$ACCESS* view.

```
Column Name                          Null?    Type
------------------------------ -------- ----
SID                                           NUMBER
OWNER                                         VARCHAR2(64)
OBJECT                                        VARCHAR2(1000)
TYPE                                          VARCHAR2(12)
```

Listing 18.16   *V$ACTIVE_INSTANCES* view.

```
Column Name                          Null?    Type
------------------------------ -------- ----
INST_NUMBER                                   NUMBER
INST_NAME                                     VARCHAR2(60)
```

Listing 18.17   *V$ARCHIVE* view.

```
Column Name                          Null?    Type
------------------------------ -------- ----
GROUP#                                        NUMBER
THREAD#                                       NUMBER
SEQUENCE#                                     NUMBER
CURRENT                                       VARCHAR2(3)
FIRST_CHANGE#                                 NUMBER
```

Listing 18.18   *V$ARCHIVED_LOG view.*

```
Column Name                       Null?    Type
-------------------------------   -------- ----
RECID                                      NUMBER
STAMP                                      NUMBER
NAME                                       VARCHAR2(513)
THREAD#                                    NUMBER
SEQUENCE#                                  NUMBER
RESETLOGS_CHANGE#                          NUMBER
RESETLOGS_TIME                             DATE
FIRST_CHANGE#                              NUMBER
FIRST_TIME                                 DATE
NEXT_CHANGE#                               NUMBER
NEXT_TIME                                  DATE
BLOCKS                                     NUMBER
BLOCK_SIZE                                 NUMBER
ARCHIVED                                   VARCHAR2(3)
DELETED                                    VARCHAR2(3)
COMPLETION_TIME                            DATE
```

Listing 18.19   *V$ARCHIVE_DEST view.*

```
Column Name                       Null?    Type
-------------------------------   -------- ----
ARCMODE                                    VARCHAR2(12)
STATUS                                     VARCHAR2(8)
DESTINATION                                VARCHAR2(256)
```

Listing 18.20   *V$BACKUP view.*

```
Column Name                       Null?    Type
-------------------------------   -------- ----
FILE#                                      NUMBER
STATUS                                     VARCHAR2(18)
CHANGE#                                    NUMBER
TIME                                       DATE
```

Listing 18.21   *V$BACKUP_CORRUPTION view.*

```
Column Name                       Null?    Type
-------------------------------   -------- ----
RECID                                      NUMBER
STAMP                                      NUMBER
SET_STAMP                                  NUMBER
SET_COUNT                                  NUMBER
PIECE#                                     NUMBER
FILE#                                      NUMBER
BLOCK#                                     NUMBER
BLOCKS                                     NUMBER
CORRUPTION_CHANGE#                         NUMBER
MARKED_CORRUPT                             VARCHAR2(3)
```

Listing 18.22 **V$BACKUP_DATAFILE** *view.*

```
Column Name                         Null?    Type
-------------------------------     -------- ----
RECID                                        NUMBER
STAMP                                        NUMBER
SET_STAMP                                    NUMBER
SET_COUNT                                    NUMBER
FILE#                                        NUMBER
CREATION_CHANGE#                             NUMBER
CREATION_TIME                                DATE
RESETLOGS_CHANGE#                            NUMBER
RESETLOGS_TIME                               DATE
INCREMENTAL_LEVEL                            NUMBER
INCREMENTAL_CHANGE#                          NUMBER
CHECKPOINT_CHANGE#                           NUMBER
CHECKPOINT_TIME                              DATE
ABSOLUTE_FUZZY_CHANGE#                       NUMBER
MARKED_CORRUPT                               NUMBER
MEDIA_CORRUPT                                NUMBER
LOGICALLY_CORRUPT                            NUMBER
DATAFILE_BLOCKS                              NUMBER
BLOCKS                                       NUMBER
BLOCK_SIZE                                   NUMBER
OLDEST_OFFLINE_RANGE                         NUMBER
COMPLETION_TIME                              DATE
```

Listing 18.23 **V$BACKUP_DEVICE** *view.*

```
Column Name                         Null?    Type
-------------------------------     -------- ----
DEVICE_TYPE                                  VARCHAR2(17)
DEVICE_NAME                                  VARCHAR2(513)
```

Listing 18.24 **V$BACKUP_PIECE** *view.*

```
Column Name                         Null?    Type
-------------------------------     -------- ----
RECID                                        NUMBER
STAMP                                        NUMBER
SET_STAMP                                    NUMBER
SET_COUNT                                    NUMBER
PIECE#                                       NUMBER
DEVICE_TYPE                                  VARCHAR2(17)
HANDLE                                       VARCHAR2(513)
COMMENTS                                     VARCHAR2(81)
MEDIA                                        VARCHAR2(65)
CONCUR                                       VARCHAR2(3)
TAG                                          VARCHAR2(32)
```

```
DELETED                            VARCHAR2(3)
START_TIME                         DATE
COMPLETION_TIME                    DATE
ELAPSED_SECONDS                    NUMBER
```

Listing 18.25   *V$BACKUP_REDOLOG* view.

```
Column Name                   Null?    Type
----------------------------- -------- ----
RECID                                  NUMBER
STAMP                                  NUMBER
SET_STAMP                              NUMBER
SET_COUNT                              NUMBER
THREAD#                                NUMBER
SEQUENCE#                              NUMBER
RESETLOGS_CHANGE#                      NUMBER
RESETLOGS_TIME                         DATE
FIRST_CHANGE#                          NUMBER
FIRST_TIME                             DATE
NEXT_CHANGE#                           NUMBER
NEXT_TIME                              DATE
BLOCKS                                 NUMBER
BLOCK_SIZE                             NUMBER
```

Listing 18.26   *V$BACKUP_SET* view.

```
Column Name                   Null?    Type
----------------------------- -------- ----
RECID                                  NUMBER
STAMP                                  NUMBER
SET_STAMP                              NUMBER
SET_COUNT                              NUMBER
BACKUP_TYPE                            VARCHAR2(1)
CONTROLFILE_INCLUDED                   VARCHAR2(3)
INCREMENTAL_LEVEL                      NUMBER
PIECES                                 NUMBER
START_TIME                             DATE
COMPLETION_TIME                        DATE
ELAPSED_SECONDS                        NUMBER
BLOCK_SIZE                             NUMBER
```

Listing 18.27   *V$BGPROCESS* view.

```
Column Name                   Null?    Type
----------------------------- -------- ----
PADDR                                  RAW(4)
NAME                                   VARCHAR2(5)
DESCRIPTION                            VARCHAR2(64)
ERROR                                  NUMBER
```

Listing 18.28   *V$BH* view.

```
Column Name                     Null?    Type
------------------------------- -------- ----
FILE#                                    NUMBER
BLOCK#                                   NUMBER
CLASS#                                   NUMBER
STATUS                                   VARCHAR2(4)
XNC                                      NUMBER
FORCED_READS                             NUMBER
FORCED_WRITES                            NUMBER
LOCK_ELEMENT_ADDR                        RAW(4)
LOCK_ELEMENT_NAME                        NUMBER
LOCK_ELEMENT_CLASS                       NUMBER
DIRTY                                    VARCHAR2(1)
TEMP                                     VARCHAR2(1)
PING                                     VARCHAR2(1)
STALE                                    VARCHAR2(1)
DIRECT                                   VARCHAR2(1)
NEW                                      CHAR(1)
OBJD                                     NUMBER
```

Listing 18.29   *V$BUFFER_POOL* view.

```
Column Name                     Null?    Type
------------------------------- -------- ----
ID                                       NUMBER
NAME                                     VARCHAR2(20)
LO_SETID                                 NUMBER
HI_SETID                                 NUMBER
SET_COUNT                                NUMBER
BUFFERS                                  NUMBER
LO_BNUM                                  NUMBER
HI_BNUM                                  NUMBER
```

Listing 18.30   *V$CIRCUIT* view.

```
Column Name                     Null?    Type
------------------------------- -------- ----
CIRCUIT                                  RAW(4)
DISPATCHER                               RAW(4)
SERVER                                   RAW(4)
WAITER                                   RAW(4)
SADDR                                    RAW(4)
STATUS                                   VARCHAR2(16)
QUEUE                                    VARCHAR2(16)
MESSAGE0                                 NUMBER
MESSAGE1                                 NUMBER
MESSAGES                                 NUMBER
BYTES                                    NUMBER
BREAKS                                   NUMBER
```

Listing 18.31   V$CLASS_PING view.

```
Column Name                       Null?    Type
---------------------------       -------- ----
CLASS                                      VARCHAR2(18)
X_2_NULL                                   NUMBER
X_2_NULL_FORCED_WRITE                      NUMBER
X_2_NULL_FORCED_STALE                      NUMBER
X_2_S                                      NUMBER
X_2_S_FORCED_WRITE                         NUMBER
X_2_SSX                                    NUMBER
X_2_SSX_FORCED_WRITE                       NUMBER
S_2_NULL                                   NUMBER
S_2_NULL_FORCED_STALE                      NUMBER
SS_2_NULL                                  NUMBER
NULL_2_X                                   NUMBER
S_2_X                                      NUMBER
SSX_2_X                                    NUMBER
NULL_2_S                                   NUMBER
NULL_2_SS                                  NUMBER
```

Listing 18.32   V$COMPATIBILITY view.

```
Column Name                       Null?    Type
---------------------------       -------- ----
TYPE_ID                                    VARCHAR2(8)
RELEASE                                    VARCHAR2(60)
DESCRIPTION                                VARCHAR2(64)
```

Listing 18.33   V$COMPATSEG view.

```
Column Name                       Null?    Type
---------------------------       -------- ----
TYPE_ID                                    VARCHAR2(8)
RELEASE                                    VARCHAR2(60)
UPDATED                                    VARCHAR2(60)
```

Listing 18.34   V$CONTROLFILE view.

```
Column Name                       Null?    Type
---------------------------       -------- ----
STATUS                                     VARCHAR2(7)
NAME                                       VARCHAR2(513)
```

Listing 18.35   V$CONTROLFILE_RECORD_SECTION view.

```
Column Name                       Null?    Type
---------------------------       -------- ----
TYPE                                       VARCHAR2(17)
RECORD_SIZE                                NUMBER
RECORDS_TOTAL                              NUMBER
RECORDS_USED                               NUMBER
```

```
FIRST_INDEX                                   NUMBER
LAST_INDEX                                    NUMBER
LAST_RECID                                    NUMBER
```

Listing 18.36   *V$COPY_CORRUPTION* view.

```
Column Name                     Null?    Type
------------------------------  -------- ----
RECID                                    NUMBER
STAMP                                    NUMBER
COPY_RECID                               NUMBER
COPY_STAMP                               NUMBER
FILE#                                    NUMBER
BLOCK#                                   NUMBER
BLOCKS                                   NUMBER
CORRUPTION_CHANGE#                       NUMBER
MARKED_CORRUPT                           VARCHAR2(3)
```

Listing 18.37   *V$DATABASE* view.

```
Column Name                     Null?    Type
------------------------------  -------- ----
DBID                                     NUMBER
NAME                                     VARCHAR2(9)
CREATED                                  DATE
RESETLOGS_CHANGE#                        NUMBER
RESETLOGS_TIME                           DATE
PRIOR_RESETLOGS_CHANGE#                  NUMBER
PRIOR_RESETLOGS_TIME                     DATE
LOG_MODE                                 VARCHAR2(12)
CHECKPOINT_CHANGE#                       NUMBER
ARCHIVE_CHANGE#                          NUMBER
CONTROLFILE_TYPE                         VARCHAR2(7)
CONTROLFILE_CREATED                      DATE
CONTROLFILE_SEQUENCE#                    NUMBER
CONTROLFILE_CHANGE#                      NUMBER
CONTROLFILE_TIME                         DATE
OPEN_RESETLOGS                           VARCHAR2(11)
VERSION_TIME                             DATE
```

Listing 18.38   *V$DATAFILE* view.

```
Column Name                     Null?    Type
------------------------------  -------- ----
FILE#                                    NUMBER
CREATION_CHANGE#                         NUMBER
CREATION_TIME                            DATE
TS#                                      NUMBER
RFILE#                                   NUMBER
STATUS                                   VARCHAR2(7)
ENABLED                                  VARCHAR2(10)
CHECKPOINT_CHANGE#                       NUMBER
```

```
CHECKPOINT_TIME                      DATE
UNRECOVERABLE_CHANGE#                NUMBER
UNRECOVERABLE_TIME                   DATE
LAST_CHANGE#                         NUMBER
LAST_TIME                            DATE
OFFLINE_CHANGE#                      NUMBER
ONLINE_CHANGE#                       NUMBER
ONLINE_TIME                          DATE
BYTES                                NUMBER
BLOCKS                               NUMBER
CREATE_BYTES                         NUMBER
BLOCK_SIZE                           NUMBER
NAME                                 VARCHAR2(513)
```

Listing 18.39   *V$DATAFILE_COPY* view.

```
Column Name                   Null?    Type
----------------------------- -------- ----
RECID                                  NUMBER
STAMP                                  NUMBER
NAME                                   VARCHAR2(513)
TAG                                    VARCHAR2(32)
FILE#                                  NUMBER
RFILE#                                 NUMBER
CREATION_CHANGE#                       NUMBER
CREATION_TIME                          DATE
RESETLOGS_CHANGE#                      NUMBER
RESETLOGS_TIME                         DATE
INCREMENTAL_LEVEL                      NUMBER
CHECKPOINT_CHANGE#                     NUMBER
CHECKPOINT_TIME                        DATE
ABSOLUTE_FUZZY_CHANGE#                 NUMBER
RECOVERY_FUZZY_CHANGE#                 NUMBER
RECOVERY_FUZZY_TIME                    DATE
ONLINE_FUZZY                           VARCHAR2(3)
BACKUP_FUZZY                           VARCHAR2(3)
MARKED_CORRUPT                         NUMBER
MEDIA_CORRUPT                          NUMBER
LOGICALLY_CORRUPT                      NUMBER
BLOCKS                                 NUMBER
BLOCK_SIZE                             NUMBER
OLDEST_OFFLINE_RANGE                   NUMBER
DELETED                                VARCHAR2(3)
COMPLETION_TIME                        DATE
```

Listing 18.40   *V$DATAFILE_HEADER* view.

```
Column Name                   Null?    Type
----------------------------- -------- ----
FILE#                                  NUMBER
STATUS                                 VARCHAR2(7)
ERROR                                  VARCHAR2(18)
```

```
FORMAT                          NUMBER
RECOVER                         VARCHAR2(3)
FUZZY                           VARCHAR2(3)
CREATION_CHANGE#                NUMBER
CREATION_TIME                   DATE
TABLESPACE_NAME                 VARCHAR2(30)
TS#                             NUMBER
RFILE#                          NUMBER
RESETLOGS_CHANGE#               NUMBER
RESETLOGS_TIME                  DATE
CHECKPOINT_CHANGE#              NUMBER
CHECKPOINT_TIME                 DATE
CHECKPOINT_COUNT                NUMBER
BYTES                           NUMBER
BLOCKS                          NUMBER
NAME                            VARCHAR2(513)
```

Listing 18.41   *V$DBFILE view.*

```
Column Name                     Null?    Type
------------------------------- -------- ----
FILE#                                    NUMBER
NAME                                     VARCHAR2(513)
```

Listing 18.42   *V$DBLINK view.*

```
Column Name                     Null?    Type
------------------------------- -------- ----
DB_LINK                                  VARCHAR2(128)
OWNER_ID                                 NUMBER
LOGGED_ON                                VARCHAR2(3)
HETEROGENEOUS                            VARCHAR2(3)
PROTOCOL                                 VARCHAR2(6)
OPEN_CURSORS                             NUMBER
IN_TRANSACTION                           VARCHAR2(3)
UPDATE_SENT                              VARCHAR2(3)
COMMIT_POINT_STRENGTH                    NUMBER
```

Listing 18.43   *V$DB_OBJECT_CACHE view.*

```
Column Name                     Null?    Type
------------------------------- -------- ----
OWNER                                    VARCHAR2(64)
NAME                                     VARCHAR2(1000)
DB_LINK                                  VARCHAR2(64)
NAMESPACE                                VARCHAR2(15)
TYPE                                     VARCHAR2(14)
SHARABLE_MEM                             NUMBER
LOADS                                    NUMBER
EXECUTIONS                               NUMBER
```

```
LOCKS                                      NUMBER
PINS                                       NUMBER
KEPT                                       VARCHAR2(3)
```

Listing 18.44   *V$DB_PIPES* view.

```
Column Name                   Null?     Type
----------------------------- -------- ----
OWNERID                                    NUMBER
NAME                                       VARCHAR2(1000)
TYPE                                       VARCHAR2(7)
PIPE_SIZE                                  NUMBER
```

Listing 18.45   *V$DELETED_OBJECT* view.

```
Column Name                   Null?     Type
----------------------------- -------- ----
RECID                                      NUMBER
STAMP                                      NUMBER
TYPE                                       VARCHAR2(13)
OBJECT_RECID                               NUMBER
OBJECT_STAMP                               NUMBER
```

Listing 18.46   *V$DISPATCHER* view.

```
Column Name                   Null?     Type
----------------------------- -------- ----
NAME                                       VARCHAR2(5)
NETWORK                                    VARCHAR2(128)
PADDR                                      RAW(4)
STATUS                                     VARCHAR2(16)
ACCEPT                                     VARCHAR2(3)
MESSAGES                                   NUMBER
BYTES                                      NUMBER
BREAKS                                     NUMBER
OWNED                                      NUMBER
CREATED                                    NUMBER
IDLE                                       NUMBER
BUSY                                       NUMBER
LISTENER                                   NUMBER
```

Listing 18.47   *V$DISPATCHER_RATE* view.

```
Column Name                   Null?     Type
----------------------------- -------- ----
NAME                                       VARCHAR2(5)
PADDR                                      RAW(4)
CUR_LOOP_RATE                              NUMBER
CUR_EVENT_RATE                             NUMBER
CUR_EVENTS_PER_LOOP                        NUMBER
```

CUR_MSG_RATE	NUMBER
CUR_SVR_BUF_RATE	NUMBER
CUR_SVR_BYTE_RATE	NUMBER
CUR_SVR_BYTE_PER_BUF	NUMBER
CUR_CLT_BUF_RATE	NUMBER
CUR_CLT_BYTE_RATE	NUMBER
CUR_CLT_BYTE_PER_BUF	NUMBER
CUR_BUF_RATE	NUMBER
CUR_BYTE_RATE	NUMBER
CUR_BYTE_PER_BUF	NUMBER
CUR_IN_CONNECT_RATE	NUMBER
CUR_OUT_CONNECT_RATE	NUMBER
CUR_RECONNECT_RATE	NUMBER
MAX_LOOP_RATE	NUMBER
MAX_EVENT_RATE	NUMBER
MAX_EVENTS_PER_LOOP	NUMBER
MAX_MSG_RATE	NUMBER
MAX_SVR_BUF_RATE	NUMBER
MAX_SVR_BYTE_RATE	NUMBER
MAX_SVR_BYTE_PER_BUF	NUMBER
MAX_CLT_BUF_RATE	NUMBER
MAX_CLT_BYTE_RATE	NUMBER
MAX_CLT_BYTE_PER_BUF	NUMBER
MAX_BUF_RATE	NUMBER
MAX_BYTE_RATE	NUMBER
MAX_BYTE_PER_BUF	NUMBER
MAX_IN_CONNECT_RATE	NUMBER
MAX_OUT_CONNECT_RATE	NUMBER
MAX_RECONNECT_RATE	NUMBER
AVG_LOOP_RATE	NUMBER
AVG_EVENT_RATE	NUMBER
AVG_EVENTS_PER_LOOP	NUMBER
AVG_MSG_RATE	NUMBER
AVG_SVR_BUF_RATE	NUMBER
AVG_SVR_BYTE_RATE	NUMBER
AVG_SVR_BYTE_PER_BUF	NUMBER
AVG_CLT_BUF_RATE	NUMBER
AVG_CLT_BYTE_RATE	NUMBER
AVG_CLT_BYTE_PER_BUF	NUMBER
AVG_BUF_RATE	NUMBER
AVG_BYTE_RATE	NUMBER
AVG_BYTE_PER_BUF	NUMBER
AVG_IN_CONNECT_RATE	NUMBER
AVG_OUT_CONNECT_RATE	NUMBER
AVG_RECONNECT_RATE	NUMBER
NUM_LOOPS_TRACKED	NUMBER
NUM_MSG_TRACKED	NUMBER
NUM_SVR_BUF_TRACKED	NUMBER
NUM_CLT_BUF_TRACKED	NUMBER

```
NUM_BUF_TRACKED                      NUMBER
NUM_IN_CONNECT_TRACKED               NUMBER
NUM_OUT_CONNECT_TRACKED              NUMBER
NUM_RECONNECT_TRACKED                NUMBER
SCALE_LOOPS                          NUMBER
SCALE_MSG                            NUMBER
SCALE_SVR_BUF                        NUMBER
SCALE_CLT_BUF                        NUMBER
SCALE_BUF                            NUMBER
SCALE_IN_CONNECT                     NUMBER
SCALE_OUT_CONNECT                    NUMBER
SCALE_RECONNECT                      NUMBER
```

Listing 18.48   V$DLM_CONVERT_LOCAL view.

```
Column Name                 Null?     Type
--------------------------  --------  ----
INST_ID                               NUMBER
CONVERT_TYPE                          VARCHAR2(64)
AVERAGE_CONVERT_TIME                  NUMBER
CONVERT_COUNT                         NUMBER
```

Listing 18.49   V$DLM_CONVERT_REMOTE view.

```
Column Name                 Null?     Type
--------------------------  --------  ----
INST_ID                               NUMBER
CONVERT_TYPE                          VARCHAR2(64)
AVERAGE_CONVERT_TIME                  NUMBER
CONVERT_COUNT                         NUMBER
```

Listing 18.50   V$DLM_LATCH view.

```
Column Name                 Null?     Type
--------------------------  --------  ----
LATCH_TYPE                            VARCHAR2(64)
IMM_GETS                              NUMBER
TTL_GETS                              NUMBER
```

Listing 18.51   V$DLM_MISC view.

```
Column Name                 Null?     Type
--------------------------  --------  ----
STATISTIC#                            NUMBER
NAME                                  VARCHAR2(64)
VALUE                                 NUMBER
```

Listing 18.52   V$ENABLEDPRIVS view.

```
Column Name                 Null?     Type
--------------------------  --------  ----
PRIV_NUMBER                           NUMBER
```

Listing 18.53   *V$ENQUEUE_LOCK view.*

```
Column Name                              Null?     Type
-------------------------------------    -------   ----
ADDR                                               RAW(4)
KADDR                                              RAW(4)
SID                                                NUMBER
TYPE                                               VARCHAR2(2)
ID1                                                NUMBER
ID2                                                NUMBER
LMODE                                              NUMBER
REQUEST                                            NUMBER
CTIME                                              NUMBER
BLOCK                                              NUMBER
```

Listing 18.54   *V$EVENT_NAME view.*

```
Column Name                              Null?     Type
-------------------------------------    -------   ----
EVENT#                                             NUMBER
NAME                                               VARCHAR2(64)
PARAMETER1                                         VARCHAR2(64)
PARAMETER2                                         VARCHAR2(64)
PARAMETER3                                         VARCHAR2(64)
```

Listing 18.55   *V$EXECUTION view.*

```
Column Name                              Null?     Type
-------------------------------------    -------   ----
PID                                                NUMBER
DEPTH                                              NUMBER
FUNCTION                                           VARCHAR2(10)
TYPE                                               VARCHAR2(7)
NVALS                                              NUMBER
VAL1                                               NUMBER
VAL2                                               NUMBER
SEQH                                               NUMBER
SEQL                                               NUMBER
```

Listing 18.56   *V$FILESTAT view.*

```
Column Name                              Null?     Type
-------------------------------------    -------   ----
FILE#                                              NUMBER
PHYRDS                                             NUMBER
PHYWRTS                                            NUMBER
PHYBLKRD                                           NUMBER
PHYBLKWRT                                          NUMBER
READTIM                                            NUMBER
WRITETIM                                           NUMBER
```

Listing 18.57   *V$FILE_PING* view.

```
Column Name                        Null?      Type
-------------------------------    --------   ----
FILE_NUMBER                                   NUMBER
FREQUENCY                                     NUMBER
X_2_NULL                                      NUMBER
X_2_NULL_FORCED_WRITE                         NUMBER
X_2_NULL_FORCED_STALE                         NUMBER
X_2_S                                         NUMBER
X_2_S_FORCED_WRITE                            NUMBER
X_2_SSX                                       NUMBER
X_2_SSX_FORCED_WRITE                          NUMBER
S_2_NULL                                      NUMBER
S_2_NULL_FORCED_STALE                         NUMBER
SS_2_NULL                                     NUMBER
WRB                                           NUMBER
WRB_FORCED_WRITE                              NUMBER
RBR                                           NUMBER
RBR_FORCED_WRITE                              NUMBER
RBR_FORCED_STALE                              NUMBER
CBR                                           NUMBER
CBR_FORCED_WRITE                              NUMBER
NULL_2_X                                       NUMBER
S_2_X                                         NUMBER
SSX_2_X                                       NUMBER
NULL_2_S                                      NUMBER
NULL_2_SS                                     NUMBER
```

Listing 18.58   *V$FIXED_TABLE* view.

```
Column Name                        Null?      Type
-------------------------------    --------   ----
NAME                                          VARCHAR2(30)
OBJECT_ID                                     NUMBER
TYPE                                          VARCHAR2(5)
TABLE_NUM                                     NUMBER
```

Listing 18.59   *V$FIXED_VIEW_DEFINITION* view.

```
Column Name                        Null?      Type
-------------------------------    --------   ----
VIEW_NAME                                     VARCHAR2(30)
VIEW_DEFINITION                               VARCHAR2(4000)
```

Listing 18.60   *V$GLOBAL_TRANSACTION* view.

```
Column Name                        Null?      Type
-------------------------------    --------   ----
FORMATID                                      NUMBER
GLOBALID                                      RAW(64)
```

```
BRANCHID                        RAW(64)
BRANCHES                        NUMBER
REFCOUNT                        NUMBER
PREPARECOUNT                    NUMBER
STATE                           VARCHAR2(18)
FLAGS                           NUMBER
COUPLING                        VARCHAR2(15)
```

Listing 18.61   *V$INDEXED_FIXED_COLUMN* view.

```
Column Name                  Null?     Type
---------------------------  --------  ----
TABLE_NAME                             VARCHAR2(30)
INDEX_NUMBER                           NUMBER
COLUMN_NAME                            VARCHAR2(30)
COLUMN_POSITION                        NUMBER
```

Listing 18.62   *V$INSTANCE* view.

```
Column Name                  Null?     Type
---------------------------  --------  ----
INSTANCE_NUMBER                        NUMBER
INSTANCE_NAME                          VARCHAR2(16)
HOST_NAME                              VARCHAR2(64)
VERSION                                VARCHAR2(17)
STARTUP_TIME                           DATE
STATUS                                 VARCHAR2(7)
PARALLEL                               VARCHAR2(3)
THREAD#                                NUMBER
ARCHIVER                               VARCHAR2(7)
LOG_SWITCH_WAIT                        VARCHAR2(11)
LOGINS                                 VARCHAR2(10)
SHUTDOWN_PENDING                       VARCHAR2(3)
```

Listing 18.63   *V$LATCH* view.

```
Column Name                  Null?     Type
---------------------------  --------  ----
ADDR                                   RAW(4)
LATCH#                                 NUMBER
LEVEL#                                 NUMBER
NAME                                   VARCHAR2(64)
GETS                                   NUMBER
MISSES                                 NUMBER
SLEEPS                                 NUMBER
IMMEDIATE_GETS                         NUMBER
IMMEDIATE_MISSES                       NUMBER
WAITERS_WOKEN                          NUMBER
WAITS_HOLDING_LATCH                    NUMBER
SPIN_GETS                              NUMBER
SLEEP1                                 NUMBER
```

```
SLEEP2                                    NUMBER
SLEEP3                                    NUMBER
SLEEP4                                    NUMBER
SLEEP5                                    NUMBER
SLEEP6                                    NUMBER
SLEEP7                                    NUMBER
SLEEP8                                    NUMBER
SLEEP9                                    NUMBER
SLEEP10                                   NUMBER
SLEEP11                                   NUMBER
```

Listing 18.64   *V$LATCHHOLDER view.*

```
Column Name                    Null?     Type
------------------------------ -------   ----
PID                                       NUMBER
SID                                       NUMBER
LADDR                                     RAW(4)
NAME                                      VARCHAR2(64)
```

Listing 18.65   *V$LATCHNAME view.*

```
Column Name                    Null?     Type
------------------------------ -------   ----
LATCH#                                    NUMBER
NAME                                      VARCHAR2(64)
```

Listing 18.66   *V$LATCH_CHILDREN view.*

```
Column Name                    Null?     Type
------------------------------ -------   ----
ADDR                                      RAW(4)
LATCH#                                    NUMBER
CHILD#                                    NUMBER
LEVEL#                                    NUMBER
NAME                                      VARCHAR2(64)
GETS                                      NUMBER
MISSES                                    NUMBER
SLEEPS                                    NUMBER
IMMEDIATE_GETS                            NUMBER
IMMEDIATE_MISSES                          NUMBER
WAITERS_WOKEN                             NUMBER
WAITS_HOLDING_LATCH                       NUMBER
SPIN_GETS                                 NUMBER
SLEEP1                                    NUMBER
SLEEP2                                    NUMBER
SLEEP3                                    NUMBER
SLEEP4                                    NUMBER
SLEEP5                                    NUMBER
SLEEP6                                    NUMBER
SLEEP7                                    NUMBER
```

```
SLEEP8                                        NUMBER
SLEEP9                                        NUMBER
SLEEP10                                       NUMBER
SLEEP11                                       NUMBER
```

Listing 18.67   V$LATCH_MISSES view.

```
Column Name                      Null?     Type
------------------------------   --------  ----
PARENT_NAME                                VARCHAR2(50)
WHERE                                      VARCHAR2(64)
NWFAIL_COUNT                               NUMBER
SLEEP_COUNT                                NUMBER
```

Listing 18.68   V$LATCH_PARENT view.

```
Column Name                      Null?     Type
------------------------------   --------  ----
ADDR                                       RAW(4)
LATCH#                                     NUMBER
LEVEL#                                     NUMBER
NAME                                       VARCHAR2(64)
GETS                                       NUMBER
MISSES                                     NUMBER
SLEEPS                                     NUMBER
IMMEDIATE_GETS                             NUMBER
IMMEDIATE_MISSES                           NUMBER
WAITERS_WOKEN                              NUMBER
WAITS_HOLDING_LATCH                        NUMBER
SPIN_GETS                                  NUMBER
SLEEP1                                     NUMBER
SLEEP2                                     NUMBER
SLEEP3                                     NUMBER
SLEEP4                                     NUMBER
SLEEP5                                     NUMBER
SLEEP6                                     NUMBER
SLEEP7                                     NUMBER
SLEEP8                                     NUMBER
SLEEP9                                     NUMBER
SLEEP10                                    NUMBER
SLEEP11                                    NUMBER
```

Listing 18.69   V$LIBRARYCACHE view.

```
Column Name                      Null?     Type
------------------------------   --------  ----
NAMESPACE                                  VARCHAR2(15)
GETS                                       NUMBER
GETHITS                                    NUMBER
GETHITRATIO                                NUMBER
PINS                                       NUMBER
```

```
PINHITS                            NUMBER
PINHITRATIO                        NUMBER
RELOADS                            NUMBER
INVALIDATIONS                      NUMBER
DLM_LOCK_REQUESTS                  NUMBER
DLM_PIN_REQUESTS                   NUMBER
DLM_PIN_RELEASES                   NUMBER
DLM_INVALIDATION_REQUESTS          NUMBER
DLM_INVALIDATIONS                  NUMBER
```

Listing 18.70 *V$LICENSE* view.

```
Column Name                     Null?    Type
------------------------------- -------- ----
SESSIONS_MAX                             NUMBER
SESSIONS_WARNING                         NUMBER
SESSIONS_CURRENT                         NUMBER
SESSIONS_HIGHWATER                       NUMBER
USERS_MAX                                NUMBER
```

Listing 18.71 *V$LOADCSTAT* view.

```
Column Name                     Null?    Type
------------------------------- -------- ----
READ                                     NUMBER
REJECTED                                 NUMBER
TDISCARD                                 NUMBER
NDISCARD                                 NUMBER
```

Listing 18.72 *V$LOADPSTAT* view.

```
Column Name                     Null?    Type
------------------------------- -------- ----
TABNAME                                  VARCHAR2(31)
PARTNAME                                 VARCHAR2(31)
LOADED                                   NUMBER
```

Listing 18.73 *V$LOADTSTAT* view.

```
Column Name                     Null?    Type
------------------------------- -------- ----
LOADED                                   NUMBER
REJECTED                                 NUMBER
FAILWHEN                                 NUMBER
ALLNULL                                  NUMBER
LEFT2SKIP                                NUMBER
PTNLOADED                                NUMBER
```

Listing 18.74 *V$LOCK* view.

```
Column Name                     Null?    Type
------------------------------- -------- ----
ADDR                                     RAW(4)
```

```
KADDR                              RAW(4)
SID                                NUMBER
TYPE                               VARCHAR2(2)
ID1                                NUMBER
ID2                                NUMBER
LMODE                              NUMBER
REQUEST                            NUMBER
CTIME                              NUMBER
BLOCK                              NUMBER
```

Listing 18.75 *V$LOCKED_OBJECT* view.

```
Column Name                     Null?    Type
----------------------------    -------- ----
XIDUSN                                   NUMBER
XIDSLOT                                  NUMBER
XIDSQN                                   NUMBER
OBJECT_ID                                NUMBER
SESSION_ID                               NUMBER
ORACLE_USERNAME                          VARCHAR2(30)
OS_USER_NAME                             VARCHAR2(15)
PROCESS                                  VARCHAR2(9)
LOCKED_MODE                              NUMBER
```

Listing 18.76 *V$LOCKS_WITH_COLISIONS* view.

```
Column Name                     Null?    Type
----------------------------    -------- ----
LOCK_ELEMENT_ADDR                        RAW(4)
```

Listing 18.77 *V$LOCK_ELEMENT* view.

```
Column Name                     Null?    Type
----------------------------    -------- ----
LOCK_ELEMENT_ADDR                        RAW(4)
INDX                                     NUMBER
CLASS                                    NUMBER
LOCK_ELEMENT_NAME                        NUMBER
MODE_HELD                                NUMBER
BLOCK_COUNT                              NUMBER
RELEASING                                NUMBER
ACQUIRING                                NUMBER
INVALID                                  NUMBER
FLAGS                                    NUMBER
```

Listing 18.78 *V$LOG* view.

```
Column Name                     Null?    Type
----------------------------    -------- ----
GROUP#                                   NUMBER
THREAD#                                  NUMBER
```

```
SEQUENCE#                              NUMBER
BYTES                                  NUMBER
MEMBERS                                NUMBER
ARCHIVED                               VARCHAR2(3)
STATUS                                 VARCHAR2(16)
FIRST_CHANGE#                          NUMBER
FIRST_TIME                             DATE
```

Listing 18.79   *V$LOGFILE* view.

```
Column Name                     Null?    Type
------------------------------- -------- ----
GROUP#                                   NUMBER
STATUS                                   VARCHAR2(7)
MEMBER                                   VARCHAR2(513)
```

Listing 18.80   *V$LOGHIST* view.

```
Column Name                     Null?    Type
------------------------------- -------- ----
THREAD#                                  NUMBER
SEQUENCE#                                NUMBER
FIRST_CHANGE#                            NUMBER
FIRST_TIME                               DATE
SWITCH_CHANGE#                           NUMBER
```

Listing 18.81   *V$LOG_HISTORY* view.

```
Column Name                     Null?    Type
------------------------------- -------- ----
RECID                                    NUMBER
STAMP                                    NUMBER
THREAD#                                  NUMBER
SEQUENCE#                                NUMBER
FIRST_CHANGE#                            NUMBER
FIRST_TIME                               DATE
NEXT_CHANGE#                             NUMBER
```

Listing 18.82   *V$MLS_PARAMETERS* view.

```
Column Name                     Null?    Type
------------------------------- -------- ----
NUM                                      NUMBER
NAME                                     VARCHAR2(64)
TYPE                                     NUMBER
VALUE                                    VARCHAR2(512)
ISDEFAULT                                VARCHAR2(9)
ISSES_MODIFIABLE                         VARCHAR2(5)
ISSYS_MODIFIABLE                         VARCHAR2(9)
ISMODIFIED                               VARCHAR2(10)
ISADJUSTED                               VARCHAR2(5)
DESCRIPTION                              VARCHAR2(64)
```

Listing 18.83   *V$MTS* view.

```
Column Name                       Null?     Type
------------------------------    --------  ----
MAXIMUM_CONNECTIONS                         NUMBER
SERVERS_STARTED                             NUMBER
SERVERS_TERMINATED                          NUMBER
SERVERS_HIGHWATER                           NUMBER
```

Listing 18.84   *V$MYSTAT* view.

```
Column Name                       Null?     Type
------------------------------    --------  ----
SID                                         NUMBER
STATISTIC#                                  NUMBER
VALUE                                       NUMBER
```

Listing 18.85   *V$NLS_PARAMETERS* view.

```
Column Name                       Null?     Type
------------------------------    --------  ----
PARAMETER                                   VARCHAR2(64)
VALUE                                       VARCHAR2(64)
```

Listing 18.86   *V$NLS_VALID_VALUES* view.

```
Column Name                       Null?     Type
------------------------------    --------  ----
PARAMETER                                   VARCHAR2(64)
VALUE                                       VARCHAR2(64)
```

Listing 18.87   *V$OBJECT_DEPENDENCY* view.

```
Column Name                       Null?     Type
------------------------------    --------  ----
FROM_ADDRESS                                RAW(4)
FROM_HASH                                   NUMBER
TO_OWNER                                    VARCHAR2(64)
TO_NAME                                     VARCHAR2(1000)
TO_ADDRESS                                  RAW(4)
TO_HASH                                     NUMBER
TO_TYPE                                     NUMBER
```

Listing 18.88   *V$OFFLINE_RANGE* view.

```
Column Name                       Null?     Type
------------------------------    --------  ----
RECID                                       NUMBER
STAMP                                       NUMBER
FILE#                                       NUMBER
OFFLINE_CHANGE#                             NUMBER
ONLINE_CHANGE#                              NUMBER
ONLINE_TIME                                 DATE
```

Listing 18.89   *V$OPEN_CURSOR view.*

```
Column Name                    Null?    Type
------------------------------ -------- ----
SADDR                                   RAW(4)
SID                                     NUMBER
USER_NAME                               VARCHAR2(30)
ADDRESS                                 RAW(4)
HASH_VALUE                              NUMBER
SQL_TEXT                                VARCHAR2(60)
```

Listing 18.90   *V$OPTION view.*

```
Column Name                    Null?    Type
------------------------------ -------- ----
PARAMETER                               VARCHAR2(64)
VALUE                                   VARCHAR2(64)
```

Listing 18.91   *V$PARAMETER view.*

```
Column Name                    Null?    Type
------------------------------ -------- ----
NUM                                     NUMBER
NAME                                    VARCHAR2(64)
TYPE                                    NUMBER
VALUE                                   VARCHAR2(512)
ISDEFAULT                               VARCHAR2(9)
ISSES_MODIFIABLE                        VARCHAR2(5)
ISSYS_MODIFIABLE                        VARCHAR2(9)
ISMODIFIED                              VARCHAR2(10)
ISADJUSTED                              VARCHAR2(5)
DESCRIPTION                             VARCHAR2(64)
```

Listing 18.92   *V$PQ_SESSTAT view.*

```
Column Name                    Null?    Type
------------------------------ -------- ----
STATISTIC                               VARCHAR2(30)
LAST_QUERY                              NUMBER
SESSION_TOTAL                           NUMBER
```

Listing 18.93   *V$PQ_SLAVE view.*

```
Column Name                    Null?    Type
------------------------------ -------- ----
SLAVE_NAME                              VARCHAR2(4)
STATUS                                  VARCHAR2(4)
SESSIONS                                NUMBER
IDLE_TIME_CUR                           NUMBER
BUSY_TIME_CUR                           NUMBER
CPU_SECS_CUR                            NUMBER
MSGS_SENT_CUR                           NUMBER
```

```
MSGS_RCVD_CUR                          NUMBER
IDLE_TIME_TOTAL                        NUMBER
BUSY_TIME_TOTAL                        NUMBER
CPU_SECS_TOTAL                         NUMBER
MSGS_SENT_TOTAL                        NUMBER
MSGS_RCVD_TOTAL                        NUMBER
```

Listing 18.94   *V$PQ_SYSSTAT* view.

```
Column Name                  Null?    Type
---------------------------- -------- ----
STATISTIC                             VARCHAR2(30)
VALUE                                 NUMBER
```

Listing 18.95   *V$PQ_TQSTAT* view.

```
Column Name                  Null?    Type
---------------------------- -------- ----
DFO_NUMBER                            NUMBER
TQ_ID                                 NUMBER
SERVER_TYPE                           VARCHAR2(10)
NUM_ROWS                              NUMBER
BYTES                                 NUMBER
OPEN_TIME                             NUMBER
AVG_LATENCY                           NUMBER
WAITS                                 NUMBER
TIMEOUTS                              NUMBER
PROCESS                               VARCHAR2(10)
INSTANCE                              NUMBER
```

Listing 18.96   *V$PROCESS* view.

```
Column Name                  Null?    Type
---------------------------- -------- ----
ADDR                                  RAW(4)
PID                                   NUMBER
SPID                                  VARCHAR2(9)
USERNAME                              VARCHAR2(15)
SERIAL#                               NUMBER
TERMINAL                              VARCHAR2(16)
PROGRAM                               VARCHAR2(64)
BACKGROUND                            VARCHAR2(1)
LATCHWAIT                             VARCHAR2(8)
LATCHSPIN                             VARCHAR2(8)
```

Listing 18.97   *V$PWFILE_USERS* view.

```
Column Name                  Null?    Type
---------------------------- -------- ----
USERNAME                              VARCHAR2(30)
SYSDBA                                VARCHAR2(5)
SYSOPER                               VARCHAR2(5)
```

Listing 18.98   *V$QUEUE* view.

```
Column Name                          Null?    Type
------------------------------       -------- ----
PADDR                                         RAW(4)
TYPE                                          VARCHAR2(10)
QUEUED                                        NUMBER
WAIT                                          NUMBER
TOTALQ                                        NUMBER
```

Listing 18.99   *V$RECOVERY_FILE_STATUS* view.

```
Column Name                          Null?    Type
------------------------------       -------- ----
FILENUM                                       NUMBER
FILENAME                                      VARCHAR2(513)
STATUS                                        VARCHAR2(13)
```

Listing 18.100   *V$RECOVERY_LOG* view.

```
Column Name                          Null?    Type
------------------------------       -------- ----
THREAD#                                       NUMBER
SEQUENCE#                                     NUMBER
TIME                                          DATE
ARCHIVE_NAME                                  VARCHAR2(513)
```

Listing 18.101   *V$RECOVERY_STATUS* view.

```
Column Name                          Null?    Type
------------------------------       -------- ----
RECOVERY_CHECKPOINT                           DATE
THREAD                                        NUMBER
SEQUENCE_NEEDED                               NUMBER
SCN_NEEDED                                    VARCHAR2(16)
TIME_NEEDED                                   DATE
PREVIOUS_LOG_NAME                             VARCHAR2(513)
PREVIOUS_LOG_STATUS                           VARCHAR2(13)
REASON                                        VARCHAR2(13)
```

Listing 18.102   *V$RECOVERY_FILE* view.

```
Column Name                          Null?    Type
------------------------------       -------- ----
FILE#                                         NUMBER
ONLINE                                        VARCHAR2(7)
ERROR                                         VARCHAR2(18)
CHANGE#                                       NUMBER
TIME                                          DATE
```

Listing 18.103   *V$REQDIST* view.

```
Column Name                       Null?    Type
------------------------------   --------  ----
BUCKET                                     NUMBER
COUNT                                      NUMBER
```

Listing 18.104   *V$RESOURCE* view.

```
Column Name                       Null?    Type
------------------------------   --------  ----
ADDR                                       RAW(4)
TYPE                                       VARCHAR2(2)
ID1                                        NUMBER
ID2                                        NUMBER
```

Listing 18.105   *V$RESOURCE_LIMIT* view.

```
Column Name                       Null?    Type
------------------------------   --------  ----
RESOURCE_NAME                              VARCHAR2(30)
CURRENT_UTILIZATION                        NUMBER
MAX_UTILIZATION                            NUMBER
INITIAL_ALLOCATION                         VARCHAR2(10)
LIMIT_VALUE                                VARCHAR2(10)
```

Listing 18.106   *V$ROLLNAME* view.

```
Column Name                       Null?    Type
------------------------------   --------  ----
USN                                        NUMBER
NAME                             NOT NULL  VARCHAR2(30)
```

Listing 18.107   *V$ROLLSTAT* view.

```
Column Name                       Null?    Type
------------------------------   --------  ----
USN                                        NUMBER
EXTENTS                                    NUMBER
RSSIZE                                     NUMBER
WRITES                                     NUMBER
XACTS                                      NUMBER
GETS                                       NUMBER
WAITS                                      NUMBER
OPTSIZE                                    NUMBER
HWMSIZE                                    NUMBER
SHRINKS                                    NUMBER
WRAPS                                      NUMBER
EXTENDS                                    NUMBER
AVESHRINK                                  NUMBER
AVEACTIVE                                  NUMBER
```

STATUS	VARCHAR2(15)
CUREXT	NUMBER
CURBLK	NUMBER

Listing 18.108   *V$ROWCACHE view.*

Column Name	Null?	Type
CACHE#		NUMBER
TYPE		VARCHAR2(11)
SUBORDINATE#		NUMBER
PARAMETER		VARCHAR2(32)
COUNT		NUMBER
USAGE		NUMBER
FIXED		NUMBER
GETS		NUMBER
GETMISSES		NUMBER
SCANS		NUMBER
SCANMISSES		NUMBER
SCANCOMPLETES		NUMBER
MODIFICATIONS		NUMBER
FLUSHES		NUMBER
DLM_REQUESTS		NUMBER
DLM_CONFLICTS		NUMBER
DLM_RELEASES		NUMBER

Listing 18.109   *V$SESSION view.*

Column Name	Null?	Type
SADDR		RAW(4)
SID		NUMBER
SERIAL#		NUMBER
AUDSID		NUMBER
PADDR		RAW(4)
USER#		NUMBER
USERNAME		VARCHAR2(30)
COMMAND		NUMBER
OWNERID		NUMBER
TADDR		VARCHAR2(8)
LOCKWAIT		VARCHAR2(8)
STATUS		VARCHAR2(8)
SERVER		VARCHAR2(9)
SCHEMA#		NUMBER
SCHEMANAME		VARCHAR2(30)
OSUSER		VARCHAR2(15)
PROCESS		VARCHAR2(9)
MACHINE		VARCHAR2(64)
TERMINAL		VARCHAR2(16)
PROGRAM		VARCHAR2(64)

```
TYPE                             VARCHAR2(10)
SQL_ADDRESS                      RAW(4)
SQL_HASH_VALUE                   NUMBER
PREV_SQL_ADDR                    RAW(4)
PREV_HASH_VALUE                  NUMBER
MODULE                           VARCHAR2(48)
MODULE_HASH                      NUMBER
ACTION                           VARCHAR2(32)
ACTION_HASH                      NUMBER
CLIENT_INFO                      VARCHAR2(64)
FIXED_TABLE_SEQUENCE             NUMBER
ROW_WAIT_OBJ#                    NUMBER
ROW_WAIT_FILE#                   NUMBER
ROW_WAIT_BLOCK#                  NUMBER
ROW_WAIT_ROW#                    NUMBER
LOGON_TIME                       DATE
LAST_CALL_ET                     NUMBER
PDML_ENABLED                     VARCHAR2(3)
FAILOVER_TYPE                    VARCHAR2(13)
FAILOVER_METHOD                  VARCHAR2(10)
FAILED_OVER                      VARCHAR2(3)
```

Listing 18.110   V$SESSION_CONNECT_INFO view.

```
Column Name                      Null?     Type
------------------------------   --------  ----
SID                                        NUMBER
AUTHENTICATION_TYPE                        VARCHAR2(15)
OSUSER                                     VARCHAR2(30)
NETWORK_SERVICE_BANNER                     VARCHAR2(4000)
```

Listing 18.111   V$SESSION_CURSOR_CACHE view.

```
Column Name                      Null?     Type
------------------------------   --------  ----
MAXIMUM                                    NUMBER
COUNT                                      NUMBER
OPENED_ONCE                                NUMBER
OPEN                                       NUMBER
OPENS                                      NUMBER
HITS                                       NUMBER
HIT_RATIO                                  NUMBER
```

Listing 18.112   V$SESSION_EVENT view.

```
Column Name                      Null?     Type
------------------------------   --------  ----
SID                                        NUMBER
EVENT                                      VARCHAR2(64)
```

```
TOTAL_WAITS                             NUMBER
TOTAL_TIMEOUTS                          NUMBER
TIME_WAITED                             NUMBER
AVERAGE_WAIT                            NUMBER
```

Listing 18.113   *V$SESSION_LONGOPS view.*

```
Column Name                 Null?       Type
--------------------------- --------    ----
SID                                     NUMBER
SERIAL#                                 NUMBER
UPDATE_COUNT                            NUMBER
COMPNAM                                 VARCHAR2(30)
OBJID                                   NUMBER
CONTEXT                                 NUMBER
STEPID                                  NUMBER
MSG                                     VARCHAR2(512)
STEPSOFAR                               NUMBER
STEPTOTAL                               NUMBER
SOFAR                                   NUMBER
TOTALWORK                               NUMBER
APPLICATION_DATA_1                      NUMBER
APPLICATION_DATA_2                      NUMBER
APPLICATION_DATA_3                      NUMBER
START_TIME                              DATE
CURRENT_TIME                            DATE
ELAPSED_SECONDS                         NUMBER
```

Listing 18.114   *V$SESSION_OBJECT_CACHE view.*

```
Column Name                 Null?       Type
--------------------------- --------    ----
PINS                                    NUMBER
HITS                                    NUMBER
TRUE_HITS                               NUMBER
HIT_RATIO                               NUMBER
TRUE_HIT_RATIO                          NUMBER
OBJECT_REFRESHES                        NUMBER
CACHE_REFRESHES                         NUMBER
OBJECT_FLUSHES                          NUMBER
CACHE_FLUSHES                           NUMBER
CACHE_SHRINKS                           NUMBER
CACHED_OBJECTS                          NUMBER
PINNED_OBJECTS                          NUMBER
CACHE_SIZE                              NUMBER
OPTIMAL_SIZE                            NUMBER
MAXIMUM_SIZE                            NUMBER
```

Listing 18.115   *V$SESSION_WAIT* view.

```
Column Name                             Null?      Type
------------------------------------   --------   ----
SID                                                NUMBER
SEQ#                                               NUMBER
EVENT                                              VARCHAR2(64)
P1TEXT                                             VARCHAR2(64)
P1                                                 NUMBER
P1RAW                                              RAW(4)
P2TEXT                                             VARCHAR2(64)
P2                                                 NUMBER
P2RAW                                              RAW(4)
P3TEXT                                             VARCHAR2(64)
P3                                                 NUMBER
P3RAW                                              RAW(4)
WAIT_TIME                                          NUMBER
SECONDS_IN_WAIT                                    NUMBER
STATE                                              VARCHAR2(19)
```

Listing 18.116   *V$SESSTAT* view.

```
Column Name                             Null?      Type
------------------------------------   --------   ----
SID                                                NUMBER
STATISTIC#                                         NUMBER
VALUE                                              NUMBER
```

Listing 18.117   *V$SESS_IO* view.

```
Column Name                             Null?      Type
------------------------------------   --------   ----
SID                                                NUMBER
BLOCK_GETS                                         NUMBER
CONSISTENT_GETS                                    NUMBER
PHYSICAL_READS                                     NUMBER
BLOCK_CHANGES                                      NUMBER
CONSISTENT_CHANGES                                 NUMBER
```

Listing 18.118   *V$SGA* view.

```
Column Name                             Null?      Type
------------------------------------   --------   ----
NAME                                               VARCHAR2(20)
VALUE                                              NUMBER
```

Listing 18.119   *V$SGASTAT* view.

```
Column Name                             Null?      Type
------------------------------------   --------   ----
POOL                                               VARCHAR2(11)
NAME                                               VARCHAR2(26)
BYTES                                              NUMBER
```

Listing 18.120 *V$SHARED_POOL_RESERVED* view.

```
Column Name                    Null?    Type
------------------------------ -------- ----
FREE_SPACE                              NUMBER
AVG_FREE_SIZE                           NUMBER
FREE_COUNT                              NUMBER
MAX_FREE_SIZE                           NUMBER
USED_SPACE                              NUMBER
AVG_USED_SIZE                           NUMBER
USED_COUNT                              NUMBER
MAX_USED_SIZE                           NUMBER
REQUESTS                                NUMBER
REQUEST_MISSES                          NUMBER
LAST_MISS_SIZE                          NUMBER
MAX_MISS_SIZE                           NUMBER
REQUEST_FAILURES                        NUMBER
LAST_FAILURE_SIZE                       NUMBER
ABORTED_REQUEST_THRESHOLD               NUMBER
ABORTED_REQUESTS                        NUMBER
LAST_ABORTED_SIZE                       NUMBER
```

Listing 18.121 *V$SHARED_SERVER* view.

```
Column Name                    Null?    Type
------------------------------ -------- ----
NAME                                    VARCHAR2(5)
PADDR                                   RAW(4)
STATUS                                  VARCHAR2(16)
MESSAGES                                NUMBER
BYTES                                   NUMBER
BREAKS                                  NUMBER
CIRCUIT                                 RAW(4)
IDLE                                    NUMBER
BUSY                                    NUMBER
REQUESTS                                NUMBER
```

Listing 18.122 *V$SORT_SEGMENT* view.

```
Column Name                    Null?    Type
------------------------------ -------- ----
TABLESPACE_NAME                         VARCHAR2(31)
SEGMENT_FILE                            NUMBER
SEGMENT_BLOCK                           NUMBER
EXTENT_SIZE                             NUMBER
CURRENT_USERS                           NUMBER
TOTAL_EXTENTS                           NUMBER
TOTAL_BLOCKS                            NUMBER
USED_EXTENTS                            NUMBER
USED_BLOCKS                             NUMBER
FREE_EXTENTS                            NUMBER
```

```
FREE_BLOCKS                           NUMBER
ADDED_EXTENTS                         NUMBER
EXTENT_HITS                           NUMBER
FREED_EXTENTS                         NUMBER
FREE_REQUESTS                         NUMBER
MAX_SIZE                              NUMBER
MAX_BLOCKS                            NUMBER
MAX_USED_SIZE                         NUMBER
MAX_USED_BLOCKS                       NUMBER
MAX_SORT_SIZE                         NUMBER
MAX_SORT_BLOCKS                       NUMBER
RELATIVE_FNO                          NUMBER
```

Listing 18.123   *V$SORT_USAGE* view.

```
Column Name                    Null?    Type
----------------------------   -------- ----
USER                                    VARCHAR2(30)
SESSION_ADDR                            RAW(4)
SESSION_NUM                             NUMBER
SQLADDR                                 RAW(4)
SQLHASH                                 NUMBER
TABLESPACE                              VARCHAR2(31)
CONTENTS                                VARCHAR2(9)
SEGFILE#                                NUMBER
SEGBLK#                                 NUMBER
EXTENTS                                 NUMBER
BLOCKS                                  NUMBER
SEGRFNO#                                NUMBER
```

Listing 18.124   *V$SQL* view.

```
Column Name                    Null?    Type
----------------------------   -------- ----
SQL_TEXT                                VARCHAR2(1000)
SHARABLE_MEM                            NUMBER
PERSISTENT_MEM                          NUMBER
RUNTIME_MEM                             NUMBER
SORTS                                   NUMBER
LOADED_VERSIONS                         NUMBER
OPEN_VERSIONS                           NUMBER
USERS_OPENING                           NUMBER
EXECUTIONS                              NUMBER
USERS_EXECUTING                         NUMBER
LOADS                                   NUMBER
FIRST_LOAD_TIME                         VARCHAR2(19)
INVALIDATIONS                           NUMBER
PARSE_CALLS                             NUMBER
DISK_READS                              NUMBER
BUFFER_GETS                             NUMBER
```

ROWS_PROCESSED	NUMBER
COMMAND_TYPE	NUMBER
OPTIMIZER_MODE	VARCHAR2(10)
OPTIMIZER_COST	NUMBER
PARSING_USER_ID	NUMBER
PARSING_SCHEMA_ID	NUMBER
KEPT_VERSIONS	NUMBER
ADDRESS	RAW(4)
TYPE_CHK_HEAP	RAW(4)
HASH_VALUE	NUMBER
CHILD_NUMBER	NUMBER
MODULE	VARCHAR2(64)
MODULE_HASH	NUMBER
ACTION	VARCHAR2(64)
ACTION_HASH	NUMBER
SERIALIZABLE_ABORTS	NUMBER

Listing 18.125 **V$SQLAREA** *view.*

Column Name	Null?	Type
SQL_TEXT		VARCHAR2(1000)
SHARABLE_MEM		NUMBER
PERSISTENT_MEM		NUMBER
RUNTIME_MEM		NUMBER
SORTS		NUMBER
VERSION_COUNT		NUMBER
LOADED_VERSIONS		NUMBER
OPEN_VERSIONS		NUMBER
USERS_OPENING		NUMBER
EXECUTIONS		NUMBER
USERS_EXECUTING		NUMBER
LOADS		NUMBER
FIRST_LOAD_TIME		VARCHAR2(19)
INVALIDATIONS		NUMBER
PARSE_CALLS		NUMBER
DISK_READS		NUMBER
BUFFER_GETS		NUMBER
ROWS_PROCESSED		NUMBER
COMMAND_TYPE		NUMBER
OPTIMIZER_MODE		VARCHAR2(25)
PARSING_USER_ID		NUMBER
PARSING_SCHEMA_ID		NUMBER
KEPT_VERSIONS		NUMBER
ADDRESS		RAW(4)
HASH_VALUE		NUMBER
MODULE		VARCHAR2(64)
MODULE_HASH		NUMBER
ACTION		VARCHAR2(64)
ACTION_HASH		NUMBER
SERIALIZABLE_ABORTS		NUMBER

Listing 18.126   V$SQLTEXT view.

```
Column Name                     Null?    Type
------------------------------- -------- ----
ADDRESS                                  RAW(4)
HASH_VALUE                               NUMBER
COMMAND_TYPE                             NUMBER
PIECE                                    NUMBER
SQL_TEXT                                 VARCHAR2(64)
```

Listing 18.127   V$SQLTEXT_WITH_NEWLINES view.

```
Column Name                     Null?    Type
------------------------------- -------- ----
ADDRESS                                  RAW(4)
HASH_VALUE                               NUMBER
COMMAND_TYPE                             NUMBER
PIECE                                    NUMBER
SQL_TEXT                                 VARCHAR2(64)
```

Listing 18.128   V$SQL_BIND_DATA view.

```
Column Name                     Null?    Type
------------------------------- -------- ----
CURSOR_NUM                               NUMBER
POSITION                                 NUMBER
DATATYPE                                 NUMBER
SHARED_MAX_LEN                           NUMBER
PRIVATE_MAX_LEN                          NUMBER
ARRAY_SIZE                               NUMBER
PRECISION                                NUMBER
SCALE                                    NUMBER
SHARED_FLAG                              NUMBER
SHARED_FLAG2                             NUMBER
BUF_ADDRESS                              RAW(4)
BUF_LENGTH                               NUMBER
VAL_LENGTH                               NUMBER
BUF_FLAG                                 NUMBER
INDICATOR                                NUMBER
VALUE                                    VARCHAR2(4000)
```

Listing 18.129   V$SQL_BIND_METADATA view.

```
Column Name                     Null?    Type
------------------------------- -------- ----
ADDRESS                                  RAW(4)
POSITION                                 NUMBER
DATATYPE                                 NUMBER
MAX_LENGTH                               NUMBER
ARRAY_LEN                                NUMBER
BIND_NAME                                VARCHAR2(30)
```

Listing 18.130   *V$SQL_CURSOR* view.

```
Column Name                      Null?    Type
------------------------------   ------   ----
CURNO                                     NUMBER
FLAG                                      NUMBER
STATUS                                    VARCHAR2(9)
PARENT_HANDLE                             RAW(4)
PARENT_LOCK                               RAW(4)
CHILD_LOCK                                RAW(4)
CHILD_PIN                                 RAW(4)
PERS_HEAP_MEM                             NUMBER
WORK_HEAP_MEM                             NUMBER
BIND_VARS                                 NUMBER
DEFINE_VARS                               NUMBER
BIND_MEM_LOC                              VARCHAR2(64)
INST_FLAG                                 VARCHAR2(64)
INST_FLAG2                                VARCHAR2(64)
```

Listing 18.131   *V$SQL_SHARED_MEMORY* view.

```
Column Name                      Null?    Type
------------------------------   ------   ----
SQL_TEXT                                  VARCHAR2(1000)
HASH_VALUE                                NUMBER
HEAP_DESC                                 RAW(4)
STRUCTURE                                 VARCHAR2(16)
FUNCTION                                  VARCHAR2(16)
CHUNK_COM                                 VARCHAR2(16)
CHUNK_PTR                                 RAW(4)
CHUNK_SIZE                                NUMBER
ALLOC_CLASS                               VARCHAR2(8)
CHUNK_TYPE                                NUMBER
SUBHEAP_DESC                              RAW(4)
```

Listing 18.132   *V$STATNAME* view.

```
Column Name                      Null?    Type
------------------------------   ------   ----
STATISTIC#                                NUMBER
NAME                                      VARCHAR2(64)
CLASS                                     NUMBER
```

Listing 18.133   *V$SUBCACHE* view.

```
Column Name                      Null?    Type
------------------------------   ------   ----
OWNER_NAME                                VARCHAR2(64)
NAME                                      VARCHAR2(1000)
TYPE                                      NUMBER
HEAP_NUM                                  NUMBER
```

```
CACHE_ID                                    NUMBER
CACHE_CNT                                   NUMBER
HEAP_SZ                                     NUMBER
HEAP_ALOC                                   NUMBER
HEAP_USED                                   NUMBER
```

Listing 18.134   *V$SYSSTAT* view.

```
Column Name                     Null?    Type
----------------------------    -------- ----
STATISTIC#                               NUMBER
NAME                                     VARCHAR2(64)
CLASS                                    NUMBER
VALUE                                    NUMBER
```

Listing 18.135   *V$SYSTEM_CURSOR_CACHE* view.

```
Column Name                     Null?    Type
----------------------------    -------- ----
OPENS                                    NUMBER
HITS                                     NUMBER
HIT_RATIO                                NUMBER
```

Listing 18.136   *V$SYSTEM_EVENT* view.

```
Column Name                     Null?    Type
----------------------------    -------- ----
EVENT                                    VARCHAR2(64)
TOTAL_WAITS                              NUMBER
TOTAL_TIMEOUTS                           NUMBER
TIME_WAITED                              NUMBER
AVERAGE_WAIT                             NUMBER
```

Listing 18.137   *V$SYSTEM_PARAMETER* view.

```
Column Name                     Null?    Type
----------------------------    -------- ----
NUM                                      NUMBER
NAME                                     VARCHAR2(64)
TYPE                                     NUMBER
VALUE                                    VARCHAR2(512)
ISDEFAULT                                VARCHAR2(9)
ISSES_MODIFIABLE                         VARCHAR2(5)
ISSYS_MODIFIABLE                         VARCHAR2(9)
ISMODIFIED                               VARCHAR2(8)
ISADJUSTED                               VARCHAR2(5)
DESCRIPTION                              VARCHAR2(64)
```

Listing 18.138   *V$TABLESPACE* view.

```
Column Name                     Null?    Type
-----------------------------   -------- ----
TS#                                      NUMBER
NAME                                     VARCHAR2(30)
```

Listing 18.139   *V$THREAD* view.

```
Column Name                     Null?    Type
-----------------------------   -------- ----
THREAD#                                  NUMBER
STATUS                                   VARCHAR2(6)
ENABLED                                  VARCHAR2(8)
GROUPS                                   NUMBER
INSTANCE                                 VARCHAR2(16)
OPEN_TIME                                DATE
CURRENT_GROUP#                           NUMBER
SEQUENCE#                                NUMBER
CHECKPOINT_CHANGE#                       NUMBER
CHECKPOINT_TIME                          DATE
ENABLE_CHANGE#                           NUMBER
ENABLE_TIME                              DATE
DISABLE_CHANGE#                          NUMBER
DISABLE_TIME                             DATE
```

Listing 18.140   *V$TIMER* view.

```
Column Name                     Null?    Type
-----------------------------   -------- ----
HSECS                                    NUMBER
```

Listing 18.141   *V$TRANSACTION* view.

```
Column Name                     Null?    Type
-----------------------------   -------- ----
ADDR                                     RAW(4)
XIDUSN                                   NUMBER
XIDSLOT                                  NUMBER
XIDSQN                                   NUMBER
UBAFIL                                   NUMBER
UBABLK                                   NUMBER
UBASQN                                   NUMBER
UBAREC                                   NUMBER
STATUS                                   VARCHAR2(16)
START_TIME                               VARCHAR2(20)
START_SCNB                               NUMBER
START_SCNW                               NUMBER
START_UEXT                               NUMBER
START_UBAFIL                             NUMBER
START_UBABLK                             NUMBER
```

START_UBASQN	NUMBER
START_UBAREC	NUMBER
SES_ADDR	RAW(4)
FLAG	NUMBER
SPACE	VARCHAR2(3)
RECURSIVE	VARCHAR2(3)
NOUNDO	VARCHAR2(3)
PTX	VARCHAR2(3)
PRV_XIDUSN	NUMBER
PRV_XIDSLT	NUMBER
PRV_XIDSQN	NUMBER
PTX_XIDUSN	NUMBER
PTX_XIDSLT	NUMBER
PTX_XIDSQN	NUMBER
DSCN-B	NUMBER
DSCN-W	NUMBER
USED_UBLK	NUMBER
USED_UREC	NUMBER
LOG_IO	NUMBER
PHY_IO	NUMBER
CR_GET	NUMBER
CR_CHANGE	NUMBER

Listing 18.142   V$TRANSACTION_ENQUEUE view.

Column Name	Null?	Type
ADDR		RAW(4)
KADDR		RAW(4)
SID		NUMBER
TYPE		VARCHAR2(2)
ID1		NUMBER
ID2		NUMBER
LMODE		NUMBER
REQUEST		NUMBER
CTIME		NUMBER
BLOCK		NUMBER

Listing 18.143   V$TYPE_SIZE view.

Column Name	Null?	Type
COMPONENT		VARCHAR2(8)
TYPE		VARCHAR2(8)
DESCRIPTION		VARCHAR2(32)
TYPE_SIZE		NUMBER

Listing 18.144   ***V$VERSION*** *view.*

```
Column Name                          Null?     Type
------------------------------------ --------  ----
BANNER                                         VARCHAR2(64)
```

Listing 18.145   ***V$WAITSTAT*** *view.*

```
Column Name                          Null?     Type
------------------------------------ --------  ----
CLASS                                          VARCHAR2(18)
COUNT                                          NUMBER
TIME                                           NUMBER
```

Listing 18.146   ***V$_LOCK*** *view.*

```
Column Name                          Null?     Type
------------------------------------ --------  ----
LADDR                                          RAW(4)
KADDR                                          RAW(4)
SADDR                                          RAW(4)
RADDR                                          RAW(4)
LMODE                                          NUMBER
REQUEST                                        NUMBER
CTIME                                          NUMBER
BLOCK                                          NUMBER
```

TUNING SQL STATEMENTS

One area in which most applications perform badly is SQL statements. You can tune these to execute in any way you wish. This section deals with using the Oracle tools available to tune your SQL statements to enhance performance. I will explain how to use the tracing facility and then tell you how to interpret the output, giving workarounds where possible to improve performance.

Oracle's Tracing Facility

A tracing facility is built into Personal Oracle8. It is normally turned off; you will have to change the init.ora parameter **sql_trace** to TRUE to turn Oracle's tracing on. Once it is on, the facility will trace all statements executed by the database. If, however, you want only SQL statements within your session to be traced, you can issue the **ALTER SESSION SET SQL_TRACE=TRUE** statement. This turns on tracing for your session only. All trace output files are generated in the directory specified by the init.ora parameter **user_dump_dest**. These trace files are then passed through the trace reporting program and the output read.

The trace reporting program is called *TKPROF80.EXE* and can be found in the C:\ORAWIN95\BIN directory. The TKPROF utility produces statistics for the following:

- Parse, execute, and fetch counts
- CPU and elapsed times
- Physical and logical reads
- Number of rows processed
- Misses on the library cache
- Username under which each parse occurred
- Each commit and rollback

This utility program is used to read the trace file generated through Oracle. If you type "TKPROF80" on the MS-DOS command line, you will see the help text displayed on your screen, showing you how to use the TKPROF80 utility. Listing 18.147 is an example of the help text.

Listing 18.147 TKPROF80 help text.

```
Usage: tkprof tracefile outputfile [explain= ] [table= ]
               [print= ] [insert= ] [sys= ] [sort= ]
  table=schema.tablename   Use 'schema.tablename' with 'explain=' option.
  explain=user/password    Connect to ORACLE and issue EXPLAIN PLAIN.
  print=integer       List only the first 'integer' SQL statements.
  aggregate=yes|no
  insert=filename     List SQL statements and data inside INSERT statements.
  sys=no              TKPROF does not list SQL statements run as user SYS.
  record=filename     Record non-recursive statements found in the trace file.
  sort=option         Set of zero or more of the following sort options:
    prscnt   number of times parse was called
    prscpu   cpu time parsing
    prsela   elapsed time parsing
    prsdsk   number of disk reads during parse
    prsqry   number of buffers for consistent read during parse
    prscu    number of buffers for current read during parse
    prsmis   number of misses in library cache during parse
    execnt   number of times execute was called
    execpu   cpu time spent executing
    exeela   elapsed time executing
    exedsk   number of disk reads during execute
    exeqry   number of buffers for consistent read during execute
    execu    number of buffers for current read during execute
    exerow   number of rows processed during execute
    exemis   number of library cache misses during execute
    fchcnt   number of times fetch was called
```

```
fchcpu  cpu time spent fetching
fchela  elapsed time fetching
fchdsk  number of disk reads during fetch
fchqry  number of buffers for consistent read during fetch
fchcu   number of buffers for current read during fetch
fchrow  number of rows fetched
userid  userid of user that parsed the cursor
```

Listing 18.148 shows an example of a trace file produced that just does a **SELECT** of everything from the **PRODUCTS** table as the **DEMO** user. The output file consists of a number of sections.

Listing 18.148   Using TKPROF80 to generate output files.

```
C:\ORAWIN95\RDBMS80\TRACE>tkprof80 ora14279.trc trace1.txt explain=demo/demo
sys=no

TKPROF: Release 8.0.3.0.0 - Production on Wed Mar 18 21:14:33 1998

(c) Copyright 1997 Oracle Corporation.  All rights reserved.

Trace file: ora14279.trc
Sort options: default


********************************************************************************
count    = number of times OCI procedure was executed
cpu      = cpu time in seconds executing
elapsed  = elapsed time in seconds executing
disk     = number of physical reads of buffers from disk
query    = number of buffers gotten for consistent read
current  = number of buffers gotten in current mode (usually for update)
rows     = number of rows processed by the fetch or execute call
********************************************************************************

alter session set SQL_TRACE=TRUE


call     count       cpu    elapsed       disk      query    current       rows
------  ------  --------  ---------  ---------  ---------  ---------  ---------
Parse        0      0.00       0.00          0          0          0          0
Execute      1      0.00       0.00          0          0          0          0
Fetch        0      0.00       0.00          0          0          0          0
------  ------  --------  ---------  ---------  ---------  ---------  ---------
total        1      0.00       0.00          0          0          0          0

Misses in library cache during parse: 0
Misses in library cache during execute: 1
Optimizer goal: CHOOSE
Parsing user id: 24  (DEMO)
********************************************************************************
```

```
select parameter, value
from
 v$nls_parameters     where (upper(parameter) in ('NLS_SORT','NLS_CURRENCY',
  'NLS_ISO_CURRENCY', 'NLS_DATE_LANGUAGE',
  'NLS_NUMERIC_CHARACTERS', 'NLS_LANGUAGE','NLS_TERRITORY'))
```

call	count	cpu	elapsed	disk	query	current	rows
Parse	1	0.00	0.00	0	0	0	0
Execute	1	0.00	0.00	0	0	0	0
Fetch	1	0.00	0.00	0	0	0	7
total	3	0.00	0.00	0	0	0	7

```
Misses in library cache during parse: 0
Optimizer goal: CHOOSE
Parsing user id: 24  (DEMO)
error during parse of EXPLAIN PLAN statement
ORA-01039: insufficient privileges on underlying objects of the view

parse error offset: 99
*******************************************************************************
select value
from
 v$nls_parameters          where (upper(parameter) = 'NLS_DATE_FORMAT')
```

call	count	cpu	elapsed	disk	query	current	rows
Parse	1	0.00	0.00	0	0	0	0
Execute	1	0.00	0.00	0	0	0	0
Fetch	1	0.00	0.00	0	0	0	1
total	3	0.00	0.00	0	0	0	1

```
Misses in library cache during parse: 0
Optimizer goal: CHOOSE
Parsing user id: 24  (DEMO)
error during parse of EXPLAIN PLAN statement
ORA-01039: insufficient privileges on underlying objects of the view

parse error offset: 92
*******************************************************************************
select *
from
products
```

call	count	cpu	elapsed	disk	query	current	rows
Parse	1	0.00	0.00	1	0	1	0
Execute	1	0.00	0.00	0	0	0	0
Fetch	2	0.00	0.00	1	2	3	10
total	4	0.00	0.00	2	2	4	10

Misses in library cache during parse: 1
Optimizer goal: CHOOSE
Parsing user id: 24 (DEMO)

Rows	Execution Plan
0	SELECT STATEMENT GOAL: CHOOSE
0	TABLE ACCESS (FULL) OF 'PRODUCTS'

****

commit

call	count	cpu	elapsed	disk	query	current	rows
Parse	1	0.00	0.00	0	0	0	0
Execute	1	0.00	0.00	0	0	0	0
Fetch	0	0.00	0.00	0	0	0	0
total	2	0.00	0.00	0	0	0	0

Misses in library cache during parse: 1
Optimizer goal: CHOOSE
Parsing user id: 24 (DEMO)

****

OVERALL TOTALS FOR ALL NON-RECURSIVE STATEMENTS

call	count	cpu	elapsed	disk	query	current	rows
Parse	4	0.00	0.00	1	0	1	0
Execute	5	0.00	0.00	0	0	0	0
Fetch	4	0.00	0.00	1	2	3	18
total	13	0.00	0.00	2	2	4	18

```
Misses in library cache during parse: 2
Misses in library cache during execute: 1


OVERALL TOTALS FOR ALL RECURSIVE STATEMENTS

call    count      cpu   elapsed      disk     query   current       rows
------   ------   ------  --------  --------  --------  --------  ----------
Parse       8     0.00      0.00         0         0         0           0
Execute     8     0.00      0.00         0         0         0           0
Fetch      17     0.00      0.00         6        35         0          14
------   ------   ------  --------  --------  --------  --------  ----------
total      33     0.00      0.00         6        35         0          14

Misses in library cache during parse: 0

     5  user  SQL statements in session.
     8  internal SQL statements in session.
    13  SQL statements in session.
     1  statement EXPLAINed in this session.
******************************************************************************
Trace file: ora14279.trc
Trace file compatibility: 7.03.02
Sort options: default

     1  session in tracefile.
     5  user  SQL statements in trace file.
     8  internal SQL statements in trace file.
    13  SQL statements in trace file.
    12  unique SQL statements in trace file.
     1  SQL statements EXPLAINed using schema:
        DEMO.prof$plan_table
           Default table was used.
           Table was created.
           Table was dropped.
   131  lines in trace file.
```

As you can see from Listing 18.148, the output file contains SQL statements that you have issued and SQL statements that have been issued by the database. The SQL statement we are interested in is

```
SELECT * FROM PRODUCTS;
```

which can be seen in Listing 18.149. This shows that the access path for the **SELECT** statement was a full table scan. Because all records need to be read from the table, this is okay. If all records do not need to be read, this could be a problem. The figures to look for in the listing are those in the **Disk** and **Query** columns. If these are high, then you should look at indexes to reduce and redefine the access path. You should be able to see the difference when executed again by looking at the execution plan information.

Listing 18.149 *Selecting from the **PRODUCTS** table.*
****

```
select *
from
products
```

call	count	cpu	elapsed	disk	query	current	rows
Parse	1	0.00	0.00	1	0	1	0
Execute	1	0.00	0.00	0	0	0	0
Fetch	2	0.00	0.00	1	2	3	10
total	4	0.00	0.00	2	2	4	10

```
Misses in library cache during parse: 1
Optimizer goal: CHOOSE
Parsing user id: 24  (DEMO)
```

Rows	Execution Plan
0	SELECT STATEMENT GOAL: CHOOSE
0	TABLE ACCESS (FULL) OF 'PRODUCTS'

****

OVERVIEW OF TUNING

This chapter has provided you with a start to tuning your database and applications code. For more information regarding tuning of applications code or database parameters, refer to the Oracle manuals on performance tuning. These are invaluable resources for information on performance tuning. The next chapter explains the concept of data warehousing and the special ways you can set up your database to handle this specific type of database.

DATA WAREHOUSING

This chapter is an introduction to the design and technology behind data warehousing for Oracle databases. Personal Oracle8 does have some data warehousing limitations, but by following this chapter, you should be able to plan and design an effective and efficient data warehouse.

Designing a data warehouse for use with Personal Oracle8.

WHAT IS A DATA WAREHOUSE?

What exactly is a data warehouse, and how does it differ from any other Oracle database? A *data warehouse* can be thought of as a very large database used, mainly by managers, to evaluate queries performed against it. This allows the managers to make faster (and, usually, more informed) decisions.

Data warehouses are updated, usually every night, from other systems that feed information into them. This way, the data warehouse is kept as a very large repository for all of a company's data. The data warehouse database is specially designed to allow users fast query access, as no **INSERT** or **UPDATE** statements should be issued by users. The data warehouse database is always kept separately from the other databases within the company. This allows the data warehouse to be in a *sterile* environment—i.e., no other systems are capable of interacting with the database during working hours.

Data warehouses have the added advantage of allowing the administrator to combine data from all of the company's information systems, thus forming new data (usually classified by subject). This, then, allows users to view the data by subject matter. This grouping of data allows users to easily produce reports on a particular subject matter. Once the data is grouped, users do not need to access several different systems to gather all of the information required, because it is all in one place. Furthermore, this can be done without access to any "live" data, therefore reducing the number of users on the "live" databases. All data warehouses have the following four key characteristics:

- *Subject-oriented*—Data warehouses are normally oriented around subjects, such as orders, deliveries, and people, rather than around specific applications, such as accounts, human resources, or stock control.

- *Integrated*—Data warehouses are usually used to combine all of the company's information in a centrally organized database, integrating the data of all company databases.

- *Time-based*—Data warehouses are usually used for time-based information. For example, reports are typically generated to show how information has changed over time. For this reason, data warehouses may contain years of company information.

- *Nonvolatile*—Data warehouses are usually nonvolatile—that is, the data does not change during normal working hours. All of the updating of the database is done during the night from other feeder systems. Figure 19.1 shows a typical data warehouse environment with its feeder systems updating nightly.

WHY USE ORACLE8 FOR A DATA WAREHOUSE?

Oracle8, with its added functionality, is suited to data warehousing for a number of reasons. As mentioned in previous chapters, many of Oracle8's new features are specifically designed for the data warehouse:

- Ease of data management

- Scalable applications and queries

- High availability

These are explained in detail in the following sections.

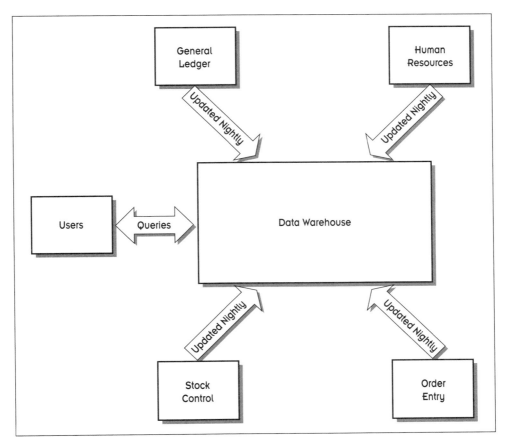

Figure 19.1 *Typical data warehouse environment.*

Ease Of Data Management

Oracle8 allows you the flexibility to handle large amounts of data fairly easily. In some cases, data warehouses have single tables in excess of 100GB. Not too many database providers will allow you to handle such large amounts of data. This scale of data is not usually associated with installations of Personal Oracle8, but it is possible to design and build your data warehouse with Personal Oracle8 and then scale the database up to another platform to run the live environment. This is covered in Chapter 21.

With the special needs of a data warehouse, Oracle provides a number of features that ease the management of such large amounts of data. The main feature for handling this amount of data is partitioning.

Data Partitioning

Data partitioning is the ability to spread your data within the database across several disks or, in the case of extremely large tables, disk arrays. This enables you to segment the data into sections. This type of partitioning enables the database to perform better and be administered more easily:

- Each partition of data can be stored on a different disk drive, increasing performance of the database and helping deal with disk failure problems. For example, if you have your data partitioned across three disk drives, and one drive fails, you can still access the data on the other two drives. If your data were not partitioned, you would not be able to access the table until the disk was replaced.

- By using data partitioning, you can treat each partition as a separate table, allowing you to perform parallel updates to the partition and relevant indexes. This has the advantage of performing the updates within tight time limits, required when updating lots of data overnight.

- Because the database knows the data within each partition, all query processing can take place against the relevant partitions. Queries against a specific partition will access only the specified partition and not the whole table.

Other advantages to using data partitioning are the parallel features within Oracle8. These features allow you to perform data administration functions in parallel, with the added functionality of implementing a fully parallel database. Some of the parallel functions performed with a data warehouse are:

- Nightly data loading

- Rebuilding indexes after data loads

- Enforcing constraints

- Generating optimizer statistics

- Backing up the database

- Recovering the database

All of these activities can be performed on the database as a whole or, with Oracle8, on the relevant data partition. All large-scale **INSERTs**, **UPDATEs**, and **DELETEs** can be performed in parallel. Within an Oracle8 database, there are a number of size restrictions (which you will probably never hit, even with an extremely large database). The maximum size for an Oracle database is now in the terabyte range. Personal Oracle8 is not designed to handle this much information; it is purely designed to allow you to get a feel for Oracle in a large system, without the expense and time associated with installing larger versions. I have always found that the best way to use Personal Oracle8 is as a prototyping tool. It is easy to use and create databases with, and it is very easy to scale up to larger Oracle environments.

Scalable Applications And Queries

Oracle8 has a new feature that allows you to process queries a lot faster than in other database providers: the ability to join all of the tables within the data warehouse using a star join. A *star join* increases the speed at which rows are returned and allows you to join tables more efficiently (for more information, see the section on star schemas later in this chapter).

Another Oracle8 feature that can be used within the data warehouse is the advanced parallel query architecture. This allows you to balance your processing across one or more partitions of the data, usually speeding up the time taken to perform most queries. As discussed in previous chapters, the cost-based optimizer is extremely flexible when defining execution paths for queries. Within the data warehouse, the cost-based optimizer can automatically take advantage of the new star join functions when a query is executed against the database. This is also true for executing parallel queries; the optimizer defines the best way to perform the query with the information it has stored in the database about the data.

The data warehouse, as I have discussed, is usually based upon only a few tables, but each one may have many millions of rows of data. With this type of implementation, indexes play a major role in the speed with which the data is transferred to the user when a query is executed. With Oracle8, you can efficiently use partitioned indexes (either B-tree or bitmapped) to index columns within the data warehouse. These partitioned indexes work in the same way as partitioned tables and views, as discussed in Chapters 11 and 13.

High Availability

As the data warehouse contains information transferred from the "live" databases, it is important that any data warehouse is available when needed, usually between 8 a.m. and 7 p.m. The use of data partitioning across several disks increases the availability of the data within the database; if one disk dies, then other partitions can still be used while the other disks are being replaced. This, along with the other features of Oracle, provides a very robust database.

Other problems normally associated with a high-availability database are backups and restores. These can be done online if need be. You should decide on the backup strategy for your data warehouse when you know the estimated usage and data load time. As with all of Oracle's database flavors, the backup and recovery facilities are all available with the standard product; you just have to decide which one is the right choice for your specific installation.

Now that Oracle8 has been released, all of the necessary backup and restore information is kept within the database. This helps when restoring data. In previous versions, no useful backup and restore information was kept within the database. Personal Oracle8 also provides you with the ability to use incremental backups for your data; this, then, backs up only the data that has changed and does not depend upon the size of the database. With data warehouses, the databases are very large, and most cannot physically be backed up in full overnight.

STAR SCHEMAS

Star schema refers to the way the schema looks when all of the tables are displayed on an entity-relationship diagram. Figure 19.2 shows the main (fact) table in the center and all of the other tables surrounding it (dimension tables), like a star. This is the model used for most data warehouses, with all of the information stored within the fact table.

The implementation of a star schema has a number of advantages:

- *Performance*—The performance of a data warehouse can be improved greatly by using a star schema. This, in effect, pre-joins all of the tables within the one fact table, increasing the speed of the database, because no join has to be performed by the optimizer.

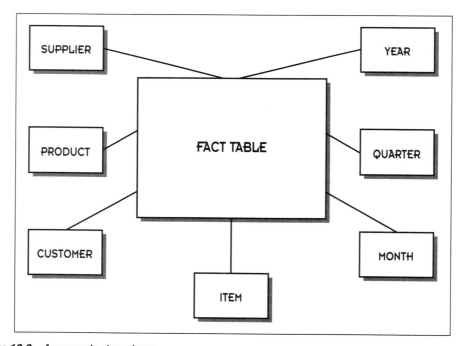

Figure 19.2   *An example star schema.*

Other performance improvements can be gained by using bitmapped indexes and parallel queries.

- *Flexibility*—With the use of bitmapped indexes (indexes that improve performance on columns with a high number of similar values), you can provide a data warehouse that is flexible in how the user queries the database. The DBA does not need to set up large amounts of concatenated indexes (indexes on more than one column of a table) to try to prejudge the way the user will query the database. Also, by using the star schema, you can integrate other star schemas. This is known as a *snowflake schema*, for obvious reasons.

- *Efficiency*—The Oracle database allows efficient storage of all data within the data warehouse. This is especially true of bitmapped indexes, where data compression techniques are used to store the data.

Star Joins

Star joins are used within Oracle8 to improve performance of queries against the data warehouse database. This is a new feature within Oracle8 and provides the database with an intelligent system for issuing queries against a star schema database. A star join works as follows:

1. First, the star join uses the indexes on the foreign-key columns of the fact table to retrieve rows quickly. Using bitmapped indexes makes this first step very quick.

2. Next, it joins the results from Step 1 to the relevant dimension tables to produce the required output.

By using star joins, you can make a number of improvements in the following areas:

- *Performance*—By using bitmapped indexes and parallel query execution, you can make vast improvements through star joins.

- *Scalability*—Using star joins means the database can cope with vast numbers of dimension tables.

- *Flexibility*—This approach to joining tables within the data warehouse via bitmapped indexes means that no concatenated indexes have to exist; therefore, you do not need to second-guess how the user is going to query the database. The star-join feature also allows the star schema to become more complicated by using snowflake schemas while still performing fast joins to the data.

DATA WAREHOUSING CONCLUSIONS

The intent of this chapter was to provide you with a basic understanding of the needs of a data warehouse. This knowledge will become important if you need to design a data warehouse within Personal Oracle8 to be scaled up to a larger system. Personal Oracle8 is an ideal place to start developing your data warehouse, because all routines can be checked and tested against a small database first. Many books are available that discuss data warehousing in much greater detail than I have. One of the best is Donald Burleson's *High Performance Oracle Data Warehousing*, published by The Coriolis Group. The next chapter covers a topic new to the information technology world: the network computer and how it can be related to the Oracle database.

ORACLE8 AND THE NETWORK COMPUTER

This chapter discusses the relationships between Oracle's new Network Computing Architecture (NCA) and Oracle8, and the advantages to using them both. I use a question and answer format to explain NCA.

NCA QUESTIONS AND ANSWERS

The advantages of Network Computing Architecture and Oracle8.

Q: What is Network Computing Architecture?
A: *Network Computing Architecture (NCA)* is an environment that is able to span many platforms for developing and deploying applications on a network. NCA is based on open standards and provides a framework that combines the client/server world, the Internet, and distributed objects.

Q: What is the structure of NCA?
A: NCA consists of three distinct levels:

- *Level 1*—The Oracle8 Universal Server for Network Computing (the database), which provides advanced data management, as explained earlier in this book.

- *Level 2*—Oracle's Web Application Server, which is an industry-standard application server. Web Application

Server provides an HTTP server for use in developing and deploying portable Web-related applications.

- *Level 3*—The universal client, which can be any client device used to access applications within NCA. Devices can include traditional PCs, Java- and/or browser-based clients, mobile devices, and network computers.

Q: What is network computing?

A: Network computing is Oracle's vision of the next generation of computing. It is really about moving the application and data from the desktop to an intelligent network of servers. This also includes the ability for a user to access any NCA application through any client device, such as a Web browser, with the added ability for the developer to create applications using reusable component-based technologies. Oracle's vision of network computing allows companies to use less of their budgets on computing infrastructure and worry more about the development of the application rather than the means of implementing the system.

Q: What is Oracle's network computing strategy, and what role does NCA play?

A: Network computing will be the direction of Oracle over the next three to five years. We are already seeing NCA-based applications, such as Oracle Web Employees.

Q: What benefits are offered through NCA?

A: The benefits of using NCA are:

- *Low cost*—All NCA applications are adaptable; this allows your infrastructure to be flexible and change over time.

- *Choice*—The NCA technology is based on existing open standards, thus protecting a company's investments.

Q: What are the elements behind NCA?

A: The elements behind NCA are:

- Cartridges, which can be developed and have the ability to plug in to the database

- Communication between components

- Extensible clients, application servers, and universal data servers

- Accepted open standards

Q: What are cartridges?

A: *Cartridges* are pieces of software or objects that combine small, well-defined objects into useful components. They may consist of full applications or parts of applications. They can be written in any number of languages, such as Java, PL/SQL, and C.

Q: What cartridges can be developed for NCA?

A: Three different types of cartridges can be developed for NCA:

- *Client cartridges*—These contain the presentation side of the application, such as the screen navigation and any pictures or graphics. They are for use on only the client level. Examples include Java applets and audio/video plug-ins.

- *Application server cartridges*—These contain application logic. Management, security, and load-balancing services are provided by the Oracle Web Application Server to the application server cartridges. These cartridges are available on any of the three levels, but are usually found on Level 2.

- *Data cartridges*—These can be used against Level 1 only. They provide the means to manipulate the data. These cartridges can be written in PL/SQL, C/C++, or Java. Data cartridges can register themselves with Oracle8 services, such as query optimization, access methods, and DBA utilities.

Q: How does NCA support existing client/server applications and the Internet?

A: With Oracle8, stored procedures can make external calls to application server cartridges interfaced to the Oracle Web Application Server. Application server cartridges can also make calls to PL/SQL stored procedures in the Oracle8 database. This creates a two-way conversation between the cartridge and the database, allowing applications to talk to each other across the Internet or intranet.

DATA CARTRIDGES

As already discussed in many chapters of this book, one of the main advantages to Oracle8 is its support for objects. The Oracle8 Universal Server, combined with NCA, provides a means for defining new object types (see Chapter 13 for more details on user-defined types). Data cartridges extend the object type support.

By using data cartridges, you can add enhanced support for all object data types (ODTs)—e.g., multimedia—for all of your applications. A data cartridge consists of one or more object types grouped into a package. Each object within the data cartridge holds information regarding the state of the object and the methods that can be used within the object. You can think of this as the object's behavior (see Chapter 13). The methods held within the object can range from simple (adding two numbers together) to complex (checking someone's creditworthiness). These methods can be written in any number of languages, including PL/SQL or C++.

The different types of data cartridges can be thought of as the various accounts a bank offers, such as checking and investment. These accounts may have different restrictions placed upon them—for example, with an investment account you may have to give 30 days' notice before withdrawing any money, and each account may have a different procedure for withdrawing money. This can all be built into different data cartridges, defining the behavior of the objects. The definition of these cartridges may be clear to someone with banking experience, but to others, it would be unclear. With data cartridges, you can allow the rules for objects to be spread across multiple applications.

Components Of Data Cartridges

A data cartridge must contain the definition for one or more related ODTs, which together provide the business rules to be implemented. Typically, a data cartridge will use the built-in data types, such as **INTEGER** and **VARCHAR2**, while defining most or all of the new ODTs it will need, and possibly referencing other ODTs defined in other data cartridges that it may depend upon. A data cartridge includes both the definition of ODTs and the code that implements their functionality.

Developing Data Cartridges

When developing data cartridges, you should use a predefined methodology for object design. One of the first steps you must take is to model the business processes. This will result in a list of objects that must be built. Once the objects on the list have been defined, along with the required methods for each object, the development can continue on three parallel paths:

- *Path 1*—Packages your existing 3rd Generation Language (3GL) code in a Dynamic Link Library (DLL) to be called by the SQL component of the object's method code. Where possible, this code should be tested in a standalone environment.

- *Path 2*—Defines and writes the object's type specifications and the PL/SQL components of the object's method code. Some methods may be written entirely in PL/SQL, whereas others may call into the external libraries. If external libraries are to be used, you must provide the libraries' definitions.

- *Path 3*—Uses the externally visible object definitions to write a sample test program. This will be helpful in the testing and debugging of the data cartridge.

Design Considerations

As always, you must bear in mind a number of considerations when designing data cartridges. One such item is security. Because all ODT data elements are available to those with the relevant privileges, there are no private or public methods. These should be available in the future. Another consideration is the use of a naming convention throughout the development cycle for data cartridges. This is essential, because some objects must have unique names to be able to operate. These objects are:

- Types

- Tables

- Directories

- Libraries

- Packages

A good way to achieve uniqueness in naming is to adopt a naming convention that uses a unique prefix.

You should also check that existing data cartridges could not be enhanced to perform the required options, rather than writing new ones from scratch. Sometimes, it is better to base data cartridges on other data cartridges. This conforms to the modular approach defined by most design methodologies.

Installing And Operating Data Cartridges

Before you can use a data cartridge, it must be installed. Installation is simply the process of putting the pieces in the right places and telling the server about the ODT's definitions. Putting the pieces in place involves putting dynamic link libraries, documentation, help files, and error message files in their correct locations. Telling the server about the ODTs involves running a SQL script that loads the individual ODTs defined by the cartridge. This step must be done from a privileged account. The users must then be granted the privileges to use the cartridge.

Building Data Cartridges

In this section, you will learn how to build a simple data cartridge. As with most languages, the way the ODT is specified is important. The order in which the components are specified is as follows:

- ODT specification

- ODT body code

- External library links

- External library

ODT Specification

The ODT specification is much like specifying a new class within C++. It names the object and defines the methods used within it. All of the data elements used within the ODT are listed, along with their type information.

ODT Body Code

The second component provides the body code for the methods defined within the ODT specification. The body code can be written in PL/SQL and may either perform the entire function or may call out to a 3GL library to perform part or all of the function.

External Library Links

If the ODT body code involves the use of 3GL code, the code must be kept in a sharable, runtime, or dynamic link library. This section defines the locations for the relevant libraries. This allows the Oracle8 server to invoke a separate process that calls into the shared library.

External Library

This section, where the external (usually 3GL) library code is written, can be interfaced with the Oracle8 Universal Server through the use of Oracle Call Interface (OCI) calls.

OVERVIEW OF NCA

I hope this chapter has given you insight into the design and uses of Oracle's new NCA ideas. A number of books are available on the development and use of NCA. This chapter is designed to give you an understanding and grounding on using NCA. Not much information is available at present (1998) on this subject, but a number of developer kits are undoubtedly on the way to support development of data cartridges and ODT methods.

Your Database And The Outside World

Interfacing and preparing your Personal Oracle8 database for the outside world— or, how to let others see your database.

In the last chapter, I discussed the use of Oracle's Network Computing Architecture. In this chapter, I will discuss how to let other users see your database through Net8 (Oracle's networking protocol). I will also explain how to prepare your database for a move to a larger system. Remember, Personal Oracle8 is an ideal prototyping tool, so at some point, you have to make it into a larger database. This chapter will show you the steps required to make the move to a larger system.

NETWORKING AND PERSONAL ORACLE8

As part of Personal Oracle8, Oracle supplies a networking product to allow you to connect and interact with remote databases across a network. The software included is called Oracle Net8. Net8 is an updated version of SQL*Net, a previous Oracle networking utility.

Oracle's networking product allows the user to establish sessions and transfer data to another computer system running an Oracle database. The networking software handles the transfers of data between the PC and the server. Every session with the server is established with the use of a *listener*, which listens for connections on the server from any user wishing to connect. The listener is a separate process that executes on the server, picking up the connections to the server and routing them to the relevant database.

Net8 is the networking layer. It uses the transparent network substrate (TNS) and other standard protocols, such as TCP/IP, to connect a client to a server.

The client-server relationship is handled by the Net8 connection. The client side always initiates the connection with the server (using SQL commands through an application, such as SQL*Plus). The application sends a request to Net8 to transport data to the required database. Once the listener accepts the connection, information can be transferred to the client from the server. The server side of the connection executes in the following fashion:

1. The server runs the Oracle8 database and a Net8 listener (which listens on the network for client connections).

2. The listener accepts connections for clients wishing to talk and transfer data to and from the required database.

3. The Net8 software acts as a chauffeur for the information that is being either sent or received from the server.

Net8

Net8 is a software layer that is required for communications between Oracle clients and Oracle servers. The role of Net8 is to establish and maintain a connection between the client and the server and exchange messages between the two. It provides client-to-server communications across most networks.

Oracle Protocol Adapters

Oracle protocol adapters map the functionality of TNS to the industry-standard protocols in use today. (A *protocol* is just a way of talking between applications.) Each adapter maps TNS to a specific protocol—for example, when you install the Net8 software, you also install Oracle TCP/IP Protocol Adapter, which maps the TNS functionality to the TCP/IP industry-standard protocol. Protocol adapters translate the following:

- Function calls of industry-standard protocols into function calls for Oracle TNS

- Oracle TNS function calls into function calls of industry-standard protocols

Oracle Net8 Easy Config

As with most networking applications, Net8 needs to be configured to work correctly against your network. Oracle provides an easy configuration utility—Oracle Net8 Easy Config—to ease the installation of Net8. Just follow these instructions to configure a simple network using the Oracle Net8 Easy Config utility:

1. From your PC, start the Oracle Net8 Easy Config application by selecting Start| Programs|Oracle for Windows 95|Oracle Net8 Easy Config. This will display a window similar to the one shown in Figure 21.1.

2. Enter a new service name (an alias for a database) in the New Service Name field. The service name can be any name you choose, but I suggest you keep this name fairly short; you may want to use a concatenation of the server and database name. Once you have done this, click on the Next button to display the next window, shown in Figure 21.2.

3. This screen displays the network protocols available for use with Net8. Select the one you require for your network (remember, the protocol must be installed on both the

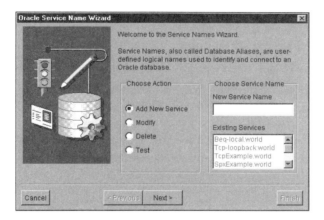

Figure 21.1   *Oracle Net8 Easy Config Screen 1.*

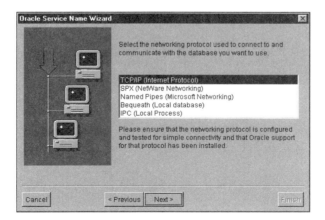

Figure 21.2   *Oracle Net8 Easy Config Screen 2.*

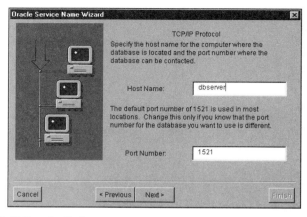

Figure 21.3   *Oracle Net8 Easy Config Screen 3.*

PC and the server). Once this has been completed, click on the Next button to display the next window, shown in Figure 21.3.

4. In this screen, you will need to know the name of the server you wish to attach to (the one the database is on). Enter the server name in the Host Name field (as you can see, I have used the host name *dbserver* as the server I wish to connect to). For the moment, leave the Port Number at 1521. This should be the port number for the server you wish to connect to (in some cases, this number may be 1525; check with your systems administrator or DBA if you have any problems). Once this is complete, click on the Next button to display the next screen, as shown in Figure 21.4.

5. In this screen, you need to enter the name of the database you wish to connect to, because a server may have more than one database on it. The name you enter here is the

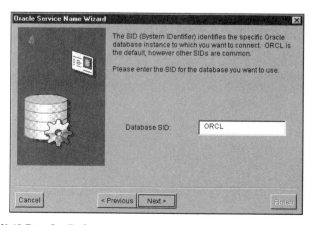

Figure 21.4   *Oracle Net8 Easy Config Screen 4.*

name of the database: ORACLE_SID. If you do not know what name to enter, please ask your DBA. The example in Figure 21.4 uses the default database name of ORCL. Once you've entered a name, click on the Next button to display the next screen, shown in Figure 21.5.

6. This screen allows you to test the setup you have defined within the previous four screens. You should test the setup whenever possible. When testing the connection, you must enter a valid username and password for the database you wish to connect to. Once the test has been completed, click on the Finish button to display the last screen of the Oracle Net8 Easy Config utility, as shown in Figure 21.6.

7. Click on Finish in this window to save your configuration and exit the Oracle Net8 Easy Config utility. If you reenter the Oracle Net8 Easy Config utility, you will see the

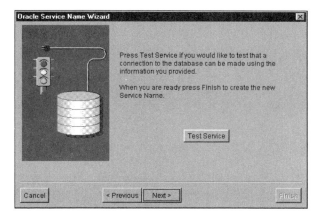

Figure 21.5   *Oracle Net8 Easy Config Screen 5.*

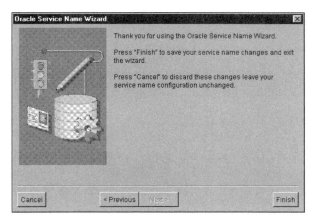

Figure 21.6   *Oracle Net8 Easy Config Screen 6.*

service you have just created in the Existing Services box of Figure 21.1. If your system supports more than one networking protocol, you will have to execute these steps once for each protocol, changing the protocol type in Step 3 each time.

The Easy Config utility is also useful for maintaining current network connections. Using the utility, you can easily perform any of the following functions:

- *Modify a service name*—Start the utility, select Modify, select the name to be modified, then select the network protocol to be used. Provide all of the relevant information for the network protocol selected; finally, test the connection and click on Finish if the test completes successfully.

- *Delete a service name*—Start the utility, select Delete, then select the service name you wish to delete. Click on Next, and a message will appear confirming the delete action. Click on Yes to confirm the delete, and click on Finish to delete the service name and exit the utility.

All of these changes perform actions against a file on your PC—tnsnames.ora, which can be found in the C:\ORAWIN95\NETWORK\ADMIN directory. You can edit this file directly (Oracle does not support editing this file directly). It is a lot quicker this way, but always make sure you have a backup of the file.

Oracle Net8 Assistant

Oracle also provides a means to administer your networking configurations once the files have been created: the Oracle Net8 Assistant. You can use this utility for manipulating your configuration files to:

- Add protocol addresses

- Delete protocol addresses

- Change naming methods—i.e., use a names server

For more details on how to accomplish these tasks using the Oracle Net8 Assistant, refer to the online documentation provided with the utility. Figure 21.7 shows an example of the Oracle Net8 Assistant window.

The tnsnames.ora file, which is created from the sessions with the Easy Config and Assistant utilities, will have a section for each connection you define. Listing 21.1 is an example of a section.

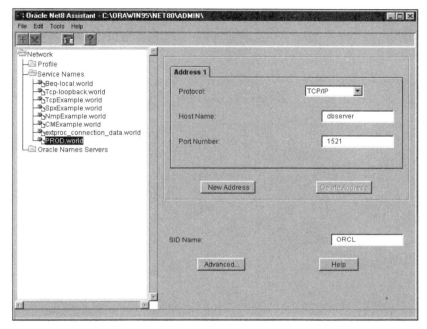

Figure 21.7   *The Oracle Net8 Assistant utility.*

Listing 21.1   *Example section from tnsnames.ora network file.*

```
PROD.world =
  (DESCRIPTION =
    (ADDRESS =
        (PROTOCOL = TCP)
        (HOST = dbserver)
        (PORT = 1521)
    )
    (CONNECT_DATA = (SID = ORCL)
    )
  )
```

CONNECTING USING ODBC

Another method of connecting to the Personal Oracle8 database is by using ODBC (open database connectivity). ODBC is an industry-standard interface that allows applications to talk to one another. This is a method of connecting to a database that is frequently used within Microsoft environments, such as Access. A database driver links the application to a specific database. A database driver is a dynamic link library (DLL) that an application can execute on demand to gain access to a particular database. The ODBC interface specifies the following:

- A library of ODBC function calls that allows an application to connect to a database, execute SQL statements, and retrieve results

- SQL syntax based on the X/Open specification

- A standard set of error codes

- A standard way of connecting to and logging on to a database

Installing ODBC

To install ODBC, follow these steps:

1. Use the Oracle Installer to install the Oracle8 ODBC Driver. The Oracle Installer automatically creates any necessary directories and icons.

2. In the Oracle8 ODBC Driver folder or in the Start bar option, the Installer creates the following icons: Oracle ODBC Test, Oracle ODBC Help, Oracle ODBC Readme, and Microsoft ODBC Administrator.

Many files are created when ODBC is installed on your PC. They are listed here for your reference:

- *sqora32.dll*—Oracle8 ODBC Driver dynamic link library (DLL)

- *sqoras32.dll*—Oracle8 ODBC Driver Setup DLL

- *squtl32.dll*—Oracle8 ODBC Utility Driver DLL

- *sqoci32.dll*—Oracle8 ODBC Database Access DLL

- *sqresus.dll*—Oracle8 ODBC Resource DLL

- *oraodbc.ini*—Oracle8 ODBC Driver initialization file

- *sqora.txt*—Oracle8 ODBC Driver release notes

- *sqora.hlp*—Oracle8 ODBC Driver for Windows 95 and Windows NT X86 help file

- *sqora.cnt*—Oracle8 ODBC Driver for Windows 95 and Windows NT X86 help contents file

- *odbctst.exes*—Oracle8 ODBC Test utility

To uninstall the Oracle8 ODBC Driver, use the Oracle Installer.

ODBC Setup

To set up the Oracle8 ODBC Driver to connect to a database, follow these steps:

1. First, make sure you have installed Net8 client on your PC. Next, enter the Microsoft ODBC Administrator utility, which enables you to set up a connection to the required database.

2. From within Microsoft ODBC Administrator, add a datasource for each Oracle database in which you want to access data.

3. Use the Oracle ODBC Test utility to try out your ODBC connection to a database.

SCALING UP YOUR PERSONAL ORACLE8 DATABASE

You must perform a number of tasks when moving your Personal Oracle8 database to another, usually bigger, system. Normally, a Personal Oracle8 database is used as a prototype and then moved to a larger development system. These development systems are usually based on the Oracle8 Universal Server. When this transition occurs, there are a number of points to consider:

- Extent sizing

- SGA sizing

- Tablespace placement (load balancing)

- Control file placement

Each of these topics is described in more detail in the following sections.

Extent Sizing

Normal practice is to check all of the tables you have created and size them for the amount of data you expect them to hold. This is done by calculating the amount of data you know they will hold and then sizing the initial extent to be that size, plus 10 percent. This allows all of your data within tables to be held in one place on the disk, rather than fragmenting data all around the database. Once the initial extent has been sized, you can size the next extent. This should be a figure big enough to hold about 20 percent of the expected data for the table. This way, if the table expands, you will not use up too many extents. This also allows you to check the number of extents daily; if you find that a table is using too many extents, the problem can be quickly identified and rectified.

SGA Sizing

The SGA must be sized according to the number of users who will be accessing the database and the number of SQL statements that will be held within the SGA. Overestimating the size of the SGA is usually better than underestimating. If the SGA is too large, you will not notice any major problems; if the SGA is too small, however, you will soon start experiencing problems. Many good tuning books are available that can help you in sizing and tuning the Oracle SGA.

Tablespace Placement

You must consider tablespace placement before the database is designed and implemented on the target machine. The placement of tablespaces can affect the performance of the database by causing I/O bottlenecks in the operating system. As a general rule, try to split apart tablespaces that are accessed together. Also, try to put all indexes in one tablespace and all tables in a different tablespace; then put these two tablespaces on different disk drives. Finally, try to put the SYSTEM tablespace, the ROLLBACK SEGMENT tablespace, and the redo logs all on their own disk drives.

Control File Placement

The control files—you should always be using more than one—should be placed on different disk drives. This is sometimes your only point of recovery if you corrupt a control file. Control files are the cornerstone of any database. Always keep them safe. You can specify where the control files should be stored by using the **control_files** parameter in the init.ora file.

Moving The Database

When moving a Personal Oracle8 database to the Oracle8 Universal Server, I have always found the best way is to use the export and import method. The steps involved are listed here:

1. Pre-create the database on the larger server, with exactly the same names for all of the tablespaces used in the Personal Oracle8 database (note that these tablespaces have to have the same name, but not necessarily the same size). Execute the catalog.sql file found in the RDBMS80 subdirectory of C:\ORAWIN95. This sets the database up so it's ready to accept your data.

2. Export the Personal Oracle8 database in Full mode; this way, when you import it back to the larger database, you will have created an exact copy of your database.

3. When importing your database to the pre-created database, always use the **COMMIT=Y** flag on the **IMP** command. This allows the database to commit after each array insert rather than after each table insert. This speeds up the insert when importing large tables to an Oracle database.

NEED TO KNOW MORE?

I hope this chapter has given you insight into the various ways of connecting to an Oracle database, whether remotely or locally. I provided a quick guide to networking; for more information, read the Oracle-supplied documentation, which is usually very good (if a bit complex). Using this chapter, you should be able to set up a connection to another database. You should also be able to create a larger Oracle8 database based on your original Personal Oracle8 database.

Appendix A

DBA_ Views

Listings A.1 through A.89 are all the DBA_ views that the database administrator should be able to access. These views are used to tune the database and provide vital information about how the database is performing. A subset of these views is referenced within this book.

Listing A.1   *DBA_2PC_NEIGHBORS view.*

```
Column Name                         Null?     Type
----------------------------------- --------  ----
LOCAL_TRAN_ID                                 VARCHAR2(22)
IN_OUT                                        VARCHAR2(3)
DATABASE                                      VARCHAR2(128)
DBUSER_OWNER                                  VARCHAR2(30)
INTERFACE                                     VARCHAR2(1)
DBID                                          VARCHAR2(16)
SESS#                                         NUMBER
BRANCH                                        VARCHAR2(128)
```

Listing A.2   *DBA_2PC_PENDING view.*

```
Column Name                         Null?     Type
----------------------------------- --------  ----
LOCAL_TRAN_ID                       NOT NULL  VARCHAR2(22)
GLOBAL_TRAN_ID                                VARCHAR2(169)
STATE                               NOT NULL  VARCHAR2(16)
MIXED                                         VARCHAR2(3)
ADVICE                                        VARCHAR2(1)
TRAN_COMMENT                                  VARCHAR2(255)
FAIL_TIME                           NOT NULL  DATE
```

FORCE_TIME		DATE
RETRY_TIME	NOT NULL	DATE
OS_USER		VARCHAR2(64)
OS_TERMINAL		VARCHAR2(255)
HOST		VARCHAR2(128)
DB_USER		VARCHAR2(30)
COMMIT#		VARCHAR2(16)

Listing A.3   DBA_ALL_TABLES view.

Column Name	Null?	Type
OWNER		VARCHAR2(30)
TABLE_NAME		VARCHAR2(30)
TABLESPACE_NAME		VARCHAR2(30)
CLUSTER_NAME		VARCHAR2(30)
IOT_NAME		VARCHAR2(30)
PCT_FREE		NUMBER
PCT_USED		NUMBER
INI_TRANS		NUMBER
MAX_TRANS		NUMBER
INITIAL_EXTENT		NUMBER
NEXT_EXTENT		NUMBER
MIN_EXTENTS		NUMBER
MAX_EXTENTS		NUMBER
PCT_INCREASE		NUMBER
FREELISTS		NUMBER
FREELIST_GROUPS		NUMBER
LOGGING		VARCHAR2(3)
BACKED_UP		VARCHAR2(1)
NUM_ROWS		NUMBER
BLOCKS		NUMBER
EMPTY_BLOCKS		NUMBER
AVG_SPACE		NUMBER
CHAIN_CNT		NUMBER
AVG_ROW_LEN		NUMBER
AVG_SPACE_FREELIST_BLOCKS		NUMBER
NUM_FREELIST_BLOCKS		NUMBER
DEGREE		VARCHAR2(10)
INSTANCES		VARCHAR2(10)
CACHE		VARCHAR2(5)
TABLE_LOCK		VARCHAR2(8)
SAMPLE_SIZE		NUMBER
LAST_ANALYZED		DATE
PARTITIONED		VARCHAR2(3)
IOT_TYPE		VARCHAR2(12)
TABLE_TYPE_OWNER		VARCHAR2(30)

```
TABLE_TYPE                                  VARCHAR2(30)
TEMPORARY                                   VARCHAR2(1)
NESTED                                      VARCHAR2(3)
BUFFER_POOL                                 VARCHAR2(7)
```

Listing A.4   *DBA_ANALYZE_OBJECTS* view.

```
Column Name                      Null?     Type
------------------------------   --------  ----
OWNER                            NOT NULL  VARCHAR2(30)
OBJECT_NAME                      NOT NULL  VARCHAR2(30)
OBJECT_TYPE                                VARCHAR2(7)
```

Listing A.5   *DBA_AUDIT_EXISTS* view.

```
Column Name                      Null?     Type
------------------------------   --------  ----
OS_USERNAME                                VARCHAR2(255)
USERNAME                                   VARCHAR2(30)
USERHOST                                   VARCHAR2(128)
TERMINAL                                   VARCHAR2(255)
TIMESTAMP                        NOT NULL  DATE
OWNER                                      VARCHAR2(30)
OBJ_NAME                                   VARCHAR2(128)
ACTION_NAME                                VARCHAR2(27)
NEW_OWNER                                  VARCHAR2(30)
NEW_NAME                                   VARCHAR2(128)
OBJ_PRIVILEGE                              VARCHAR2(16)
SYS_PRIVILEGE                              VARCHAR2(40)
GRANTEE                                    VARCHAR2(30)
SESSIONID                        NOT NULL  NUMBER
ENTRYID                          NOT NULL  NUMBER
STATEMENTID                      NOT NULL  NUMBER
RETURNCODE                       NOT NULL  NUMBER
```

Listing A.6   *DBA_AUDIT_OBJECT* view.

```
Column Name                      Null?     Type
------------------------------   --------  ----
OS_USERNAME                                VARCHAR2(255)
USERNAME                                   VARCHAR2(30)
USERHOST                                   VARCHAR2(128)
TERMINAL                                   VARCHAR2(255)
TIMESTAMP                        NOT NULL  DATE
OWNER                                      VARCHAR2(30)
OBJ_NAME                                   VARCHAR2(128)
ACTION_NAME                                VARCHAR2(27)
```

```
NEW_OWNER                                    VARCHAR2(30)
NEW_NAME                                      VARCHAR2(128)
SES_ACTIONS                                   VARCHAR2(19)
COMMENT_TEXT                                  VARCHAR2(4000)
SESSIONID                       NOT NULL NUMBER
ENTRYID                         NOT NULL NUMBER
STATEMENTID                     NOT NULL NUMBER
RETURNCODE                      NOT NULL NUMBER
PRIV_USED                                    VARCHAR2(40)
OBJECT_LABEL                                  MLSLABEL
SESSION_LABEL                                 MLSLABEL
```

Listing A.7 *DBA_AUDIT_SESSION view.*

```
Column Name                     Null?    Type
-------------------------------  -------- ----
OS_USERNAME                                  VARCHAR2(255)
USERNAME                                      VARCHAR2(30)
USERHOST                                      VARCHAR2(128)
TERMINAL                                      VARCHAR2(255)
TIMESTAMP                       NOT NULL DATE
ACTION_NAME                                   VARCHAR2(27)
LOGOFF_TIME                                   DATE
LOGOFF_LREAD                                  NUMBER
LOGOFF_PREAD                                  NUMBER
LOGOFF_LWRITE                                 NUMBER
LOGOFF_DLOCK                                  VARCHAR2(40)
SESSIONID                       NOT NULL NUMBER
RETURNCODE                      NOT NULL NUMBER
SESSION_LABEL                                 MLSLABEL
```

Listing A.8 *DBA_AUDIT_STATEMENT view.*

```
Column Name                     Null?    Type
-------------------------------  -------- ----
OS_USERNAME                                  VARCHAR2(255)
USERNAME                                      VARCHAR2(30)
USERHOST                                      VARCHAR2(128)
TERMINAL                                      VARCHAR2(255)
TIMESTAMP                       NOT NULL DATE
OWNER                                         VARCHAR2(30)
OBJ_NAME                                      VARCHAR2(128)
ACTION_NAME                                   VARCHAR2(27)
NEW_NAME                                      VARCHAR2(128)
OBJ_PRIVILEGE                                 VARCHAR2(16)
SYS_PRIVILEGE                                 VARCHAR2(40)
ADMIN_OPTION                                  VARCHAR2(1)
```

```
GRANTEE                                  VARCHAR2(30)
AUDIT_OPTION                             VARCHAR2(40)
SES_ACTIONS                             VARCHAR2(19)
COMMENT_TEXT                            VARCHAR2(4000)
SESSIONID                      NOT NULL NUMBER
ENTRYID                        NOT NULL NUMBER
STATEMENTID                    NOT NULL NUMBER
RETURNCODE                     NOT NULL NUMBER
PRIV_USED                               VARCHAR2(40)
SESSION_LABEL                           MLSLABEL
```

Listing A.9   *DBA_AUDIT_TRAIL* view.

Column Name	Null?	Type
OS_USERNAME		VARCHAR2(255)
USERNAME		VARCHAR2(30)
USERHOST		VARCHAR2(128)
TERMINAL		VARCHAR2(255)
TIMESTAMP	NOT NULL	DATE
OWNER		VARCHAR2(30)
OBJ_NAME		VARCHAR2(128)
ACTION	NOT NULL	NUMBER
ACTION_NAME		VARCHAR2(27)
NEW_OWNER		VARCHAR2(30)
NEW_NAME		VARCHAR2(128)
OBJ_PRIVILEGE		VARCHAR2(16)
SYS_PRIVILEGE		VARCHAR2(40)
ADMIN_OPTION		VARCHAR2(1)
GRANTEE		VARCHAR2(30)
AUDIT_OPTION		VARCHAR2(40)
SES_ACTIONS		VARCHAR2(19)
LOGOFF_TIME		DATE
LOGOFF_LREAD		NUMBER
LOGOFF_PREAD		NUMBER
LOGOFF_LWRITE		NUMBER
LOGOFF_DLOCK		VARCHAR2(40)
COMMENT_TEXT		VARCHAR2(4000)
SESSIONID	NOT NULL	NUMBER
ENTRYID	NOT NULL	NUMBER
STATEMENTID	NOT NULL	NUMBER
RETURNCODE	NOT NULL	NUMBER
PRIV_USED		VARCHAR2(40)
OBJECT_LABEL		MLSLABEL
SESSION_LABEL		MLSLABEL

Listing A.10 *DBA_CATALOG* view.

```
Column Name                      Null?     Type
---------------------------      --------  ----
OWNER                            NOT NULL  VARCHAR2(30)
TABLE_NAME                       NOT NULL  VARCHAR2(30)
TABLE_TYPE                                 VARCHAR2(11)
```

Listing A.11 *DBA_CLUSTERS* view.

```
Column Name                      Null?     Type
---------------------------      --------  ----
OWNER                            NOT NULL  VARCHAR2(30)
CLUSTER_NAME                     NOT NULL  VARCHAR2(30)
TABLESPACE_NAME                  NOT NULL  VARCHAR2(30)
PCT_FREE                                   NUMBER
PCT_USED                         NOT NULL  NUMBER
KEY_SIZE                                   NUMBER
INI_TRANS                        NOT NULL  NUMBER
MAX_TRANS                        NOT NULL  NUMBER
INITIAL_EXTENT                             NUMBER
NEXT_EXTENT                                NUMBER
MIN_EXTENTS                      NOT NULL  NUMBER
MAX_EXTENTS                      NOT NULL  NUMBER
PCT_INCREASE                     NOT NULL  NUMBER
FREELISTS                                  NUMBER
FREELIST_GROUPS                            NUMBER
AVG_BLOCKS_PER_KEY                         NUMBER
CLUSTER_TYPE                               VARCHAR2(5)
FUNCTION                                   VARCHAR2(15)
HASHKEYS                                   NUMBER
DEGREE                                     VARCHAR2(10)
INSTANCES                                  VARCHAR2(10)
CACHE                                      VARCHAR2(5)
BUFFER_POOL                                VARCHAR2(7)
```

Listing A.12 *DBA_CLUSTER_HASH_EXPRESSIONS* view.

```
Column Name                      Null?     Type
---------------------------      --------  ----
OWNER                            NOT NULL  VARCHAR2(30)
CLUSTER_NAME                     NOT NULL  VARCHAR2(30)
HASH_EXPRESSION                            LONG
```

Listing A.13 *DBA_CLU_COLUMNS* view.

```
Column Name                      Null?     Type
---------------------------      --------  ----
OWNER                            NOT NULL  VARCHAR2(30)
CLUSTER_NAME                     NOT NULL  VARCHAR2(30)
CLU_COLUMN_NAME                  NOT NULL  VARCHAR2(30)
```

```
TABLE_NAME                              NOT NULL VARCHAR2(30)
TAB_COLUMN_NAME                                  VARCHAR2(4000)
```

Listing A.14   *DBA_COLL_TYPES view.*

```
Column Name                     Null?     Type
------------------------------- --------  ----
OWNER                           NOT NULL  VARCHAR2(30)
TYPE_NAME                       NOT NULL  VARCHAR2(30)
COLL_TYPE                       NOT NULL  VARCHAR2(30)
UPPER_BOUND                               NUMBER
ELEM_TYPE_MOD                             VARCHAR2(7)
ELEM_TYPE_OWNER                           VARCHAR2(30)
ELEM_TYPE_NAME                            VARCHAR2(30)
LENGTH                                    NUMBER
PRECISION                                 NUMBER
SCALE                                     NUMBER
CHARACTER_SET_NAME                        VARCHAR2(44)
```

Listing A.15   *DBA_COL_COMMENTS view.*

```
Column Name                     Null?     Type
------------------------------- --------  ----
OWNER                           NOT NULL  VARCHAR2(30)
TABLE_NAME                      NOT NULL  VARCHAR2(30)
COLUMN_NAME                     NOT NULL  VARCHAR2(30)
COMMENTS                                  VARCHAR2(4000)
```

Listing A.16   *DBA_COL_PRIVS view.*

```
Column Name                     Null?     Type
------------------------------- --------  ----
GRANTEE                         NOT NULL  VARCHAR2(30)
OWNER                           NOT NULL  VARCHAR2(30)
TABLE_NAME                      NOT NULL  VARCHAR2(30)
COLUMN_NAME                     NOT NULL  VARCHAR2(30)
GRANTOR                         NOT NULL  VARCHAR2(30)
PRIVILEGE                       NOT NULL  VARCHAR2(40)
GRANTABLE                                 VARCHAR2(3)
```

Listing A.17   *DBA_CONSTRAINTS view.*

```
Column Name                     Null?     Type
------------------------------- --------  ----
OWNER                           NOT NULL  VARCHAR2(30)
CONSTRAINT_NAME                 NOT NULL  VARCHAR2(30)
CONSTRAINT_TYPE                           VARCHAR2(1)
TABLE_NAME                      NOT NULL  VARCHAR2(30)
SEARCH_CONDITION                          LONG
R_OWNER                                   VARCHAR2(30)
R_CONSTRAINT_NAME                         VARCHAR2(30)
DELETE_RULE                               VARCHAR2(9)
```

```
STATUS                              VARCHAR2(8)
DEFERRABLE                          VARCHAR2(14)
DEFERRED                            VARCHAR2(9)
VALIDATED                           VARCHAR2(13)
GENERATED                           VARCHAR2(14)
BAD                                 VARCHAR2(3)
LAST_CHANGE                         DATE
```

Listing A.18 DBA_CONS_COLUMNS view.

```
Column Name                  Null?     Type
---------------------------- --------  ----
OWNER                        NOT NULL VARCHAR2(30)
CONSTRAINT_NAME              NOT NULL VARCHAR2(30)
TABLE_NAME                   NOT NULL VARCHAR2(30)
COLUMN_NAME                           VARCHAR2(4000)
POSITION                              NUMBER
```

Listing A.19 DBA_DATA_FILES view.

```
Column Name                  Null?     Type
---------------------------- --------  ----
FILE_NAME                             VARCHAR2(513)
FILE_ID                      NOT NULL NUMBER
TABLESPACE_NAME              NOT NULL VARCHAR2(30)
BYTES                                 NUMBER
BLOCKS                       NOT NULL NUMBER
STATUS                                VARCHAR2(9)
RELATIVE_FNO                          NUMBER
AUTOEXTENSIBLE                        VARCHAR2(3)
MAXBYTES                              NUMBER
MAXBLOCKS                             NUMBER
INCREMENT_BY                          NUMBER
```

Listing A.20 DBA_DB_LINKS view.

```
Column Name                  Null?     Type
---------------------------- --------  ----
OWNER                        NOT NULL VARCHAR2(30)
DB_LINK                      NOT NULL VARCHAR2(128)
USERNAME                              VARCHAR2(30)
HOST                                  VARCHAR2(2000)
CREATED                      NOT NULL DATE
```

Listing A.21 DBA_DEPENDENCIES view.

```
Column Name                  Null?     Type
---------------------------- --------  ----
OWNER                        NOT NULL VARCHAR2(30)
NAME                         NOT NULL VARCHAR2(30)
TYPE                                  VARCHAR2(12)
```

REFERENCED_OWNER	VARCHAR2(30)
REFERENCED_NAME	VARCHAR2(64)
REFERENCED_TYPE	VARCHAR2(12)
REFERENCED_LINK_NAME	VARCHAR2(128)
DEPENDENCY_TYPE	VARCHAR2(4)

Listing A.22   *DBA_DIRECTORIES* *view.*

Column Name	Null?	Type
OWNER	NOT NULL	VARCHAR2(30)
DIRECTORY_NAME	NOT NULL	VARCHAR2(30)
DIRECTORY_PATH		VARCHAR2(4000)

Listing A.23   *DBA_ERRORS* *view.*

Column Name	Null?	Type
OWNER	NOT NULL	VARCHAR2(30)
NAME	NOT NULL	VARCHAR2(30)
TYPE		VARCHAR2(12)
SEQUENCE	NOT NULL	NUMBER
LINE	NOT NULL	NUMBER
POSITION	NOT NULL	NUMBER
TEXT	NOT NULL	VARCHAR2(4000)

Listing A.24   *DBA_EXP_FILES* *view.*

Column Name	Null?	Type
EXP_VERSION	NOT NULL	NUMBER(3)
EXP_TYPE		VARCHAR2(11)
FILE_NAME	NOT NULL	VARCHAR2(100)
USER_NAME	NOT NULL	VARCHAR2(30)
TIMESTAMP	NOT NULL	DATE

Listing A.25   *DBA_EXP_OBJECTS* *view.*

Column Name	Null?	Type
OWNER	NOT NULL	VARCHAR2(30)
OBJECT_NAME	NOT NULL	VARCHAR2(30)
OBJECT_TYPE		VARCHAR2(12)
CUMULATIVE		DATE
INCREMENTAL	NOT NULL	DATE
EXPORT_VERSION	NOT NULL	NUMBER(3)

Listing A.26   *DBA_EXP_VERSION* *view.*

Column Name	Null?	Type
EXP_VERSION	NOT NULL	NUMBER(3)

Listing A.27   *DBA_EXTENTS view.*

```
Column Name                          Null?    Type
------------------------------       -------- ----
OWNER                                         VARCHAR2(30)
SEGMENT_NAME                                  VARCHAR2(81)
PARTITION_NAME                                VARCHAR2(30)
SEGMENT_TYPE                                  VARCHAR2(17)
TABLESPACE_NAME                               VARCHAR2(30)
EXTENT_ID                            NOT NULL NUMBER
FILE_ID                              NOT NULL NUMBER
BLOCK_ID                             NOT NULL NUMBER
BYTES                                         NUMBER
BLOCKS                               NOT NULL NUMBER
RELATIVE_FNO                         NOT NULL NUMBER
```

Listing A.28   *DBA_FREE_SPACE view.*

```
Column Name                          Null?    Type
------------------------------       -------- ----
TABLESPACE_NAME                      NOT NULL VARCHAR2(30)
FILE_ID                              NOT NULL NUMBER
BLOCK_ID                             NOT NULL NUMBER
BYTES                                         NUMBER
BLOCKS                               NOT NULL NUMBER
RELATIVE_FNO                         NOT NULL NUMBER
```

Listing A.29   *DBA_FREE_SPACE_COALESCED view.*

```
Column Name                          Null?    Type
------------------------------       -------- ----
TABLESPACE_NAME                      NOT NULL VARCHAR2(30)
TOTAL_EXTENTS                                 NUMBER
EXTENTS_COALESCED                             NUMBER
PERCENT_EXTENTS_COALESCED                     NUMBER
TOTAL_BYTES                                   NUMBER
BYTES_COALESCED                               NUMBER
TOTAL_BLOCKS                                  NUMBER
BLOCKS_COALESCED                              NUMBER
PERCENT_BLOCKS_COALESCED                      NUMBER
```

Listing A.30   *DBA_FREE_SPACE_COALESCED_TMP1 view.*

```
Column Name                          Null?    Type
------------------------------       -------- ----
TS#                                  NOT NULL NUMBER
EXTENTS_COALESCED                             NUMBER
BLOCKS_COALESCED                              NUMBER
```

Listing A.31   *DBA_FREE_SPACE_COALESCED_TMP2 view.*

```
Column Name                       Null?     Type
------------------------------    --------  ----
TS#                               NOT NULL  NUMBER
TOTAL_EXTENTS                               NUMBER
TOTAL_BLOCKS                                NUMBER
```

Listing A.32   *DBA_INDEXES view.*

```
Column Name                       Null?     Type
------------------------------    --------  ----
OWNER                             NOT NULL  VARCHAR2(30)
INDEX_NAME                        NOT NULL  VARCHAR2(30)
INDEX_TYPE                                  VARCHAR2(12)
TABLE_OWNER                       NOT NULL  VARCHAR2(30)
TABLE_NAME                        NOT NULL  VARCHAR2(30)
TABLE_TYPE                                  VARCHAR2(11)
UNIQUENESS                                  VARCHAR2(9)
TABLESPACE_NAME                             VARCHAR2(30)
INI_TRANS                                   NUMBER
MAX_TRANS                                   NUMBER
INITIAL_EXTENT                              NUMBER
NEXT_EXTENT                                 NUMBER
MIN_EXTENTS                                 NUMBER
MAX_EXTENTS                                 NUMBER
PCT_INCREASE                                NUMBER
PCT_THRESHOLD                               NUMBER
INCLUDE_COLUMN                              NUMBER
FREELISTS                                   NUMBER
FREELIST_GROUPS                             NUMBER
PCT_FREE                                    NUMBER
LOGGING                                     VARCHAR2(3)
BLEVEL                                      NUMBER
LEAF_BLOCKS                                 NUMBER
DISTINCT_KEYS                               NUMBER
AVG_LEAF_BLOCKS_PER_KEY                     NUMBER
AVG_DATA_BLOCKS_PER_KEY                     NUMBER
CLUSTERING_FACTOR                           NUMBER
STATUS                                      VARCHAR2(8)
NUM_ROWS                                    NUMBER
SAMPLE_SIZE                                 NUMBER
LAST_ANALYZED                               DATE
DEGREE                                      VARCHAR2(40)
INSTANCES                                   VARCHAR2(40)
PARTITIONED                                 VARCHAR2(3)
TEMPORARY                                   VARCHAR2(1)
GENERATED                                   VARCHAR2(1)
BUFFER_POOL                                 VARCHAR2(7)
```

Listing A.33 *DBA_IND_COLUMNS view.*

Column Name	Null?	Type
INDEX_OWNER	NOT NULL	VARCHAR2(30)
INDEX_NAME	NOT NULL	VARCHAR2(30)
TABLE_OWNER	NOT NULL	VARCHAR2(30)
TABLE_NAME	NOT NULL	VARCHAR2(30)
COLUMN_NAME		VARCHAR2(4000)
COLUMN_POSITION	NOT NULL	NUMBER
COLUMN_LENGTH	NOT NULL	NUMBER

Listing A.34 *DBA_IND_PARTITIONS view.*

Column Name	Null?	Type
INDEX_OWNER	NOT NULL	VARCHAR2(30)
INDEX_NAME	NOT NULL	VARCHAR2(30)
PARTITION_NAME		VARCHAR2(30)
HIGH_VALUE		LONG
HIGH_VALUE_LENGTH	NOT NULL	NUMBER
PARTITION_POSITION	NOT NULL	NUMBER
STATUS		VARCHAR2(8)
TABLESPACE_NAME	NOT NULL	VARCHAR2(30)
PCT_FREE	NOT NULL	NUMBER
INI_TRANS	NOT NULL	NUMBER
MAX_TRANS	NOT NULL	NUMBER
INITIAL_EXTENT		NUMBER
NEXT_EXTENT		NUMBER
MIN_EXTENT	NOT NULL	NUMBER
MAX_EXTENT	NOT NULL	NUMBER
PCT_INCREASE	NOT NULL	NUMBER
FREELISTS		NUMBER
LOGGING		VARCHAR2(3)
BLEVEL		NUMBER
LEAF_BLOCKS		NUMBER
DISTINCT_KEYS		NUMBER
AVG_LEAF_BLOCKS_PER_KEY		NUMBER
AVG_DATA_BLOCKS_PER_KEY		NUMBER
CLUSTERING_FACTOR		NUMBER
NUM_ROWS		NUMBER
SAMPLE_SIZE		NUMBER
LAST_ANALYZED		DATE
BUFFER_POOL		VARCHAR2(7)

Listing A.35 *DBA_JOBS view.*

Column Name	Null?	Type
JOB	NOT NULL	NUMBER
LOG_USER	NOT NULL	VARCHAR2(30)
PRIV_USER	NOT NULL	VARCHAR2(30)

```
SCHEMA_USER                     NOT NULL VARCHAR2(30)
LAST_DATE                                DATE
LAST_SEC                                 VARCHAR2(8)
THIS_DATE                                DATE
THIS_SEC                                 VARCHAR2(8)
NEXT_DATE                       NOT NULL DATE
NEXT_SEC                                 VARCHAR2(8)
TOTAL_TIME                               NUMBER
BROKEN                                   VARCHAR2(1)
INTERVAL                        NOT NULL VARCHAR2(200)
FAILURES                                 NUMBER
WHAT                                     VARCHAR2(4000)
CURRENT_SESSION_LABEL                    MLSLABEL
CLEARANCE_HI                             MLSLABEL
CLEARANCE_LO                             MLSLABEL
NLS_ENV                                  VARCHAR2(4000)
MISC_ENV                                 RAW(32)
```

Listing A.36   *DBA_JOBS_RUNNING* view.

```
Column Name                     Null?    Type
------------------------------- -------- ----
SID                                      NUMBER
JOB                                      NUMBER
FAILURES                                 NUMBER
LAST_DATE                                DATE
LAST_SEC                                 VARCHAR2(8)
THIS_DATE                                DATE
THIS_SEC                                 VARCHAR2(8)
```

Listing A.37   *DBA_LIBRARIES* view.

```
Column Name                     Null?    Type
------------------------------- -------- ----
OWNER                           NOT NULL VARCHAR2(30)
LIBRARY_NAME                    NOT NULL VARCHAR2(30)
FILE_SPEC                                VARCHAR2(2000)
DYNAMIC                                  VARCHAR2(1)
STATUS                                   VARCHAR2(7)
```

Listing A.38   *DBA_LOBS* view.

```
Column Name                     Null?    Type
------------------------------- -------- ----
OWNER                           NOT NULL VARCHAR2(30)
TABLE_NAME                      NOT NULL VARCHAR2(30)
COLUMN_NAME                              VARCHAR2(4000)
SEGMENT_NAME                    NOT NULL VARCHAR2(30)
INDEX_NAME                      NOT NULL VARCHAR2(30)
CHUNK                                    NUMBER
PCTVERSION                      NOT NULL NUMBER
```

```
CACHE                                     VARCHAR2(3)
LOGGING                                   VARCHAR2(3)
IN_ROW                                    VARCHAR2(3)
```

Listing A.39   *DBA_METHOD_PARAMS* view.

```
Column Name                    Null?    Type
-----------------------------  -------- ----
OWNER                          NOT NULL VARCHAR2(30)
TYPE_NAME                      NOT NULL VARCHAR2(30)
METHOD_NAME                    NOT NULL VARCHAR2(30)
METHOD_NO                      NOT NULL NUMBER
PARAM_NAME                     NOT NULL VARCHAR2(30)
PARAM_NO                       NOT NULL NUMBER
PARAM_MODE                              VARCHAR2(6)
PARAM_TYPE_MOD                          VARCHAR2(7)
PARAM_TYPE_OWNER                        VARCHAR2(30)
PARAM_TYPE_NAME                         VARCHAR2(30)
CHARACTER_SET_NAME                      VARCHAR2(44)
```

Listing A.40   *DBA_METHOD_RESULTS* view.

```
Column Name                    Null?    Type
-----------------------------  -------- ----
OWNER                          NOT NULL VARCHAR2(30)
TYPE_NAME                      NOT NULL VARCHAR2(30)
METHOD_NAME                    NOT NULL VARCHAR2(30)
METHOD_NO                      NOT NULL NUMBER
RESULT_TYPE_MOD                         VARCHAR2(7)
RESULT_TYPE_OWNER                       VARCHAR2(30)
RESULT_TYPE_NAME                        VARCHAR2(30)
CHARACTER_SET_NAME                      VARCHAR2(44)
```

Listing A.41   *DBA_NESTED_TABLES* view.

```
Column Name                    Null?    Type
-----------------------------  -------- ----
OWNER                                   VARCHAR2(30)
TABLE_NAME                              VARCHAR2(30)
TABLE_TYPE_OWNER                        VARCHAR2(30)
TABLE_TYPE_NAME                         VARCHAR2(30)
PARENT_TABLE_NAME                       VARCHAR2(30)
PARENT_TABLE_COLUMN                     VARCHAR2(4000)
```

Listing A.42   *DBA_OBJECTS* view.

```
Column Name                    Null?    Type
-----------------------------  -------- ----
OWNER                                   VARCHAR2(30)
OBJECT_NAME                             VARCHAR2(128)
SUBOBJECT_NAME                          VARCHAR2(30)
OBJECT_ID                               NUMBER
DATA_OBJECT_ID                          NUMBER
```

```
OBJECT_TYPE                              VARCHAR2(15)
CREATED                                  DATE
LAST_DDL_TIME                            DATE
TIMESTAMP                                VARCHAR2(19)
STATUS                                   VARCHAR2(7)
TEMPORARY                                VARCHAR2(1)
GENERATED                                VARCHAR2(1)
```

Listing A.43   *DBA_OBJECT_SIZE* view.

```
Column Name                      Null?    Type
------------------------------   -------- ----
OWNER                            NOT NULL VARCHAR2(30)
NAME                             NOT NULL VARCHAR2(30)
TYPE                                      VARCHAR2(12)
SOURCE_SIZE                               NUMBER
PARSED_SIZE                               NUMBER
CODE_SIZE                                 NUMBER
ERROR_SIZE                                NUMBER
```

Listing A.44   *DBA_OBJECT_TABLES* view.

```
Column Name                      Null?    Type
------------------------------   -------- ----
OWNER                            NOT NULL VARCHAR2(30)
TABLE_NAME                       NOT NULL VARCHAR2(30)
TABLESPACE_NAME                  NOT NULL VARCHAR2(30)
CLUSTER_NAME                              VARCHAR2(30)
IOT_NAME                                  VARCHAR2(30)
PCT_FREE                                  NUMBER
PCT_USED                                  NUMBER
INI_TRANS                                 NUMBER
MAX_TRANS                                 NUMBER
INITIAL_EXTENT                            NUMBER
NEXT_EXTENT                               NUMBER
MIN_EXTENTS                               NUMBER
MAX_EXTENTS                               NUMBER
PCT_INCREASE                              NUMBER
FREELISTS                                 NUMBER
FREELIST_GROUPS                           NUMBER
LOGGING                                   VARCHAR2(3)
BACKED_UP                                 VARCHAR2(1)
NUM_ROWS                                  NUMBER
BLOCKS                                    NUMBER
EMPTY_BLOCKS                              NUMBER
AVG_SPACE                                 NUMBER
CHAIN_CNT                                 NUMBER
AVG_ROW_LEN                               NUMBER
AVG_SPACE_FREELIST_BLOCKS                 NUMBER
NUM_FREELIST_BLOCKS                       NUMBER
```

```
DEGREE                             VARCHAR2(10)
INSTANCES                          VARCHAR2(10)
CACHE                              VARCHAR2(5)
TABLE_LOCK                         VARCHAR2(8)
SAMPLE_SIZE                        NUMBER
LAST_ANALYZED                      DATE
PARTITIONED                        VARCHAR2(3)
IOT_TYPE                           VARCHAR2(12)
TABLE_TYPE_OWNER          NOT NULL VARCHAR2(30)
TABLE_TYPE                NOT NULL VARCHAR2(30)
TEMPORARY                          VARCHAR2(1)
NESTED                             VARCHAR2(3)
BUFFER_POOL                        VARCHAR2(7)
```

Listing A.45   *DBA_OBJ_AUDIT_OPTS* *view.*

```
Column Name                  Null?     Type
---------------------------- --------  ----
OWNER                                  VARCHAR2(30)
OBJECT_NAME                            VARCHAR2(30)
OBJECT_TYPE                            VARCHAR2(9)
ALT                                    VARCHAR2(3)
AUD                                    VARCHAR2(3)
COM                                    VARCHAR2(3)
DEL                                    VARCHAR2(3)
GRA                                    VARCHAR2(3)
IND                                    VARCHAR2(3)
INS                                    VARCHAR2(3)
LOC                                    VARCHAR2(3)
REN                                    VARCHAR2(3)
SEL                                    VARCHAR2(3)
UPD                                    VARCHAR2(3)
REF                                    VARCHAR2(3)
EXE                                    VARCHAR2(3)
CRE                                    VARCHAR2(3)
REA                                    VARCHAR2(3)
WRI                                    VARCHAR2(3)
```

Listing A.46   *DBA_PART_COL_STATISTICS* *view.*

```
Column Name                  Null?     Type
---------------------------- --------  ----
OWNER                        NOT NULL  VARCHAR2(30)
TABLE_NAME                   NOT NULL  VARCHAR2(30)
PARTITION_NAME                         VARCHAR2(30)
COLUMN_NAME                  NOT NULL  VARCHAR2(30)
NUM_DISTINCT                           NUMBER
LOW_VALUE                              RAW(32)
HIGH_VALUE                             RAW(32)
```

```
DENSITY                                  NUMBER
NUM_NULLS                                NUMBER
NUM_BUCKETS                              NUMBER
SAMPLE_SIZE                              NUMBER
LAST_ANALYZED                            DATE
```

Listing A.47   DBA_PART_HISTOGRAMS view.

```
Column Name                     Null?    Type
------------------------------  -------- ----
OWNER                                    VARCHAR2(30)
TABLE_NAME                               VARCHAR2(30)
PARTITION_NAME                           VARCHAR2(30)
COLUMN_NAME                              VARCHAR2(30)
BUCKET_NUMBER                            NUMBER
ENDPOINT_VALUE                           NUMBER
```

Listing A.48   DBA_PART_INDEXES view.

```
Column Name                     Null?    Type
------------------------------  -------- ----
OWNER                           NOT NULL VARCHAR2(30)
INDEX_NAME                      NOT NULL VARCHAR2(30)
PARTITIONING_TYPE                        VARCHAR2(7)
PARTITION_COUNT                 NOT NULL NUMBER
PARTITIONING_KEY_COUNT          NOT NULL NUMBER
LOCALITY                                 VARCHAR2(6)
ALIGNMENT                                VARCHAR2(12)
DEF_TABLESPACE_NAME                      VARCHAR2(30)
DEF_PCT_FREE                    NOT NULL NUMBER
DEF_INI_TRANS                   NOT NULL NUMBER
DEF_MAX_TRANS                   NOT NULL NUMBER
DEF_INITIAL_EXTENT              NOT NULL NUMBER
DEF_NEXT_EXTENT                 NOT NULL NUMBER
DEF_MIN_EXTENTS                 NOT NULL NUMBER
DEF_MAX_EXTENTS                 NOT NULL NUMBER
DEF_PCT_INCREASE                NOT NULL NUMBER
DEF_FREELISTS                   NOT NULL NUMBER
DEF_LOGGING                              VARCHAR2(7)
DEF_BUFFER_POOL                          VARCHAR2(7)
```

Listing A.49   DBA_PART_KEY_COLUMNS view.

```
Column Name                     Null?    Type
------------------------------  -------- ----
OWNER                                    VARCHAR2(30)
NAME                                     VARCHAR2(30)
COLUMN_NAME                              VARCHAR2(30)
COLUMN_POSITION                          NUMBER
```

Listing A.50   *DBA_PART_TABLES* view.

```
Column Name                    Null?    Type
---------------------------    -------- ----
OWNER                          NOT NULL VARCHAR2(30)
TABLE_NAME                     NOT NULL VARCHAR2(30)
PARTITIONING_TYPE                       VARCHAR2(7)
PARTITION_COUNT                NOT NULL NUMBER
PARTITIONING_KEY_COUNT         NOT NULL NUMBER
DEF_TABLESPACE_NAME            NOT NULL VARCHAR2(30)
DEF_PCT_FREE                   NOT NULL NUMBER
DEF_PCT_USED                   NOT NULL NUMBER
DEF_INI_TRANS                  NOT NULL NUMBER
DEF_MAX_TRANS                  NOT NULL NUMBER
DEF_INITIAL_EXTENT             NOT NULL NUMBER
DEF_NEXT_EXTENT                NOT NULL NUMBER
DEF_MIN_EXTENTS                NOT NULL NUMBER
DEF_MAX_EXTENTS                NOT NULL NUMBER
DEF_PCT_INCREASE               NOT NULL NUMBER
DEF_FREELISTS                  NOT NULL NUMBER
DEF_FREELIST_GROUPS            NOT NULL NUMBER
DEF_LOGGING                             VARCHAR2(7)
DEF_BUFFER_POOL                         VARCHAR2(7)
```

Listing A.51   *DBA_PENDING_TRANSACTIONS* view.

```
Column Name                    Null?    Type
---------------------------    -------- ----
FORMATID                                NUMBER
GLOBALID                                RAW(64)
BRANCHID                                RAW(64)
```

Listing A.52   *DBA_PRIV_AUDIT_OPTS* view.

```
Column Name                    Null?    Type
---------------------------    -------- ----
USER_NAME                               VARCHAR2(30)
PRIVILEGE                      NOT NULL VARCHAR2(40)
SUCCESS                                 VARCHAR2(10)
FAILURE                                 VARCHAR2(10)
```

Listing A.53   *DBA_PROFILES* view.

```
Column Name                    Null?    Type
---------------------------    -------- ----
PROFILE                        NOT NULL VARCHAR2(30)
RESOURCE_NAME                  NOT NULL VARCHAR2(32)
RESOURCE_TYPE                           VARCHAR2(8)
LIMIT                                   VARCHAR2(40)
```

Listing A.54   *DBA_RCHILD* view.

```
Column Name                            Null?     Type
------------------------------         --------  ----
REFGROUP                                         NUMBER
OWNER                                  NOT NULL  VARCHAR2(30)
NAME                                   NOT NULL  VARCHAR2(30)
TYPE#                                            VARCHAR2(30)
```

Listing A.55   *DBA_REFRESH* view.

```
Column Name                            Null?     Type
------------------------------         --------  ----
ROWNER                                 NOT NULL  VARCHAR2(30)
RNAME                                  NOT NULL  VARCHAR2(30)
REFGROUP                                         NUMBER
IMPLICIT_DESTROY                                 VARCHAR2(1)
PUSH_DEFERRED_RPC                                VARCHAR2(1)
REFRESH_AFTER_ERRORS                             VARCHAR2(1)
ROLLBACK_SEG                                     VARCHAR2(30)
JOB                                              NUMBER
NEXT_DATE                                        DATE
INTERVAL                                         VARCHAR2(200)
BROKEN                                           VARCHAR2(1)
PURGE_OPTION                                     NUMBER(38)
PARALLELISM                                      NUMBER(38)
HEAP_SIZE                                        NUMBER(38)
```

Listing A.56   *DBA_REFRESH_CHILDREN* view.

```
Column Name                            Null?     Type
------------------------------         --------  ----
OWNER                                  NOT NULL  VARCHAR2(30)
NAME                                   NOT NULL  VARCHAR2(30)
TYPE                                             VARCHAR2(30)
ROWNER                                 NOT NULL  VARCHAR2(30)
RNAME                                  NOT NULL  VARCHAR2(30)
REFGROUP                                         NUMBER
IMPLICIT_DESTROY                                 VARCHAR2(1)
PUSH_DEFERRED_RPC                                VARCHAR2(1)
REFRESH_AFTER_ERRORS                             VARCHAR2(1)
ROLLBACK_SEG                                     VARCHAR2(30)
JOB                                              NUMBER
NEXT_DATE                                        DATE
INTERVAL                                         VARCHAR2(200)
BROKEN                                           VARCHAR2(1)
PURGE_OPTION                                     NUMBER(38)
PARALLELISM                                      NUMBER(38)
HEAP_SIZE                                        NUMBER(38)
```

Listing A.57   *DBA_REFS* view.

```
Column Name                    Null?    Type
-----------------------------  -------- ----
OWNER                          NOT NULL VARCHAR2(30)
TABLE_NAME                     NOT NULL VARCHAR2(30)
COLUMN_NAME                             VARCHAR2(4000)
WITH_ROWID                              VARCHAR2(3)
IS_SCOPED                               VARCHAR2(3)
SCOPE_TABLE_OWNER                       VARCHAR2(30)
SCOPE_TABLE_NAME                        VARCHAR2(30)
```

Listing A.58   *DBA_REGISTERED_SNAPSHOTS* view.

```
Column Name                    Null?    Type
-----------------------------  -------- ----
OWNER                          NOT NULL VARCHAR2(30)
NAME                           NOT NULL VARCHAR2(30)
SNAPSHOT_SITE                  NOT NULL VARCHAR2(128)
CAN_USE_LOG                             VARCHAR2(3)
UPDATABLE                               VARCHAR2(3)
REFRESH_METHOD                          VARCHAR2(11)
SNAPSHOT_ID                             NUMBER(38)
VERSION                                 VARCHAR2(17)
QUERY_TXT                               LONG
```

Listing A.59   *DBA_RGROUP* view.

```
Column Name                    Null?    Type
-----------------------------  -------- ----
REFGROUP                                NUMBER
OWNER                          NOT NULL VARCHAR2(30)
NAME                           NOT NULL VARCHAR2(30)
IMPLICIT_DESTROY                        VARCHAR2(1)
PUSH_DEFERRED_RPC                       VARCHAR2(1)
REFRESH_AFTER_ERRORS                    VARCHAR2(1)
ROLLBACK_SEG                            VARCHAR2(30)
JOB                            NOT NULL NUMBER
PURGE_OPTION                            NUMBER(38)
PARALLELISM                             NUMBER(38)
HEAP_SIZE                               NUMBER(38)
```

Listing A.60   *DBA_ROLES* view.

```
Column Name                    Null?    Type
-----------------------------  -------- ----
ROLE                           NOT NULL VARCHAR2(30)
PASSWORD_REQUIRED                       VARCHAR2(8)
```

Listing A.61   *DBA_ROLE_PRIVS view.*

```
Column Name                      Null?     Type
------------------------------   --------  ----
GRANTEE                                    VARCHAR2(30)
GRANTED_ROLE                     NOT NULL  VARCHAR2(30)
ADMIN_OPTION                               VARCHAR2(3)
DEFAULT_ROLE                               VARCHAR2(3)
```

Listing A.62   *DBA_ROLLBACK_SEGS view.*

```
Column Name                      Null?     Type
------------------------------   --------  ----
SEGMENT_NAME                     NOT NULL  VARCHAR2(30)
OWNER                                      VARCHAR2(6)
TABLESPACE_NAME                  NOT NULL  VARCHAR2(30)
SEGMENT_ID                       NOT NULL  NUMBER
FILE_ID                          NOT NULL  NUMBER
BLOCK_ID                         NOT NULL  NUMBER
INITIAL_EXTENT                             NUMBER
NEXT_EXTENT                                NUMBER
MIN_EXTENTS                      NOT NULL  NUMBER
MAX_EXTENTS                      NOT NULL  NUMBER
PCT_INCREASE                     NOT NULL  NUMBER
STATUS                                     VARCHAR2(16)
INSTANCE_NUM                               VARCHAR2(40)
RELATIVE_FNO                     NOT NULL  NUMBER
```

Listing A.63   *DBA_SEGMENTS view.*

```
Column Name                      Null?     Type
------------------------------   --------  ----
OWNER                                      VARCHAR2(30)
SEGMENT_NAME                               VARCHAR2(81)
PARTITION_NAME                             VARCHAR2(30)
SEGMENT_TYPE                               VARCHAR2(17)
TABLESPACE_NAME                            VARCHAR2(30)
HEADER_FILE                                NUMBER
HEADER_BLOCK                               NUMBER
BYTES                                      NUMBER
BLOCKS                                     NUMBER
EXTENTS                                    NUMBER
INITIAL_EXTENT                             NUMBER
NEXT_EXTENT                                NUMBER
MIN_EXTENTS                                NUMBER
MAX_EXTENTS                                NUMBER
PCT_INCREASE                               NUMBER
```

```
FREELISTS                          NUMBER
FREELIST_GROUPS                    NUMBER
RELATIVE_FNO                       NUMBER
BUFFER_POOL                        VARCHAR2(7)
```

Listing A.64   DBA_SEQUENCES view.

```
Column Name                  Null?     Type
---------------------------  --------  ----
SEQUENCE_OWNER               NOT NULL  VARCHAR2(30)
SEQUENCE_NAME                NOT NULL  VARCHAR2(30)
MIN_VALUE                              NUMBER
MAX_VALUE                              NUMBER
INCREMENT_BY                 NOT NULL  NUMBER
CYCLE_FLAG                             VARCHAR2(1)
ORDER_FLAG                             VARCHAR2(1)
CACHE_SIZE                   NOT NULL  NUMBER
LAST_NUMBER                  NOT NULL  NUMBER
```

Listing A.65   DBA_SNAPSHOTS view.

```
Column Name                  Null?     Type
---------------------------  --------  ----
OWNER                        NOT NULL  VARCHAR2(30)
NAME                         NOT NULL  VARCHAR2(30)
TABLE_NAME                   NOT NULL  VARCHAR2(30)
MASTER_VIEW                            VARCHAR2(30)
MASTER_OWNER                           VARCHAR2(30)
MASTER                                 VARCHAR2(30)
MASTER_LINK                            VARCHAR2(128)
CAN_USE_LOG                            VARCHAR2(3)
UPDATABLE                              VARCHAR2(3)
REFRESH_METHOD                         VARCHAR2(11)
LAST_REFRESH                           DATE
ERROR                                  NUMBER
FR_OPERATIONS                          VARCHAR2(10)
CR_OPERATIONS                          VARCHAR2(10)
TYPE                                   VARCHAR2(8)
NEXT                                   VARCHAR2(200)
START_WITH                             DATE
REFRESH_GROUP                          NUMBER
UPDATE_TRIG                            VARCHAR2(30)
UPDATE_LOG                             VARCHAR2(30)
QUERY                                  LONG
MASTER_ROLLBACK_SEG                    VARCHAR2(30)
```

Listing A.66   DBA_SNAPSHOT_LOGS view.

```
Column Name                  Null?     Type
---------------------------  --------  ----
LOG_OWNER                    NOT NULL  VARCHAR2(30)
MASTER                       NOT NULL  VARCHAR2(30)
LOG_TABLE                    NOT NULL  VARCHAR2(30)
```

```
LOG_TRIGGER                         VARCHAR2(30)
ROWIDS                              VARCHAR2(3)
PRIMARY_KEY                         VARCHAR2(3)
FILTER_COLUMNS                      VARCHAR2(3)
CURRENT_SNAPSHOTS                   DATE
SNAPSHOT_ID                         NUMBER(38)
```

Listing A.67   *DBA_SNAPSHOT_LOG_FILTER_COLS* view.

```
Column Name                   Null?    Type
---------------------------   -------- ----
OWNER                         NOT NULL VARCHAR2(30)
NAME                          NOT NULL VARCHAR2(30)
COLUMN_NAME                   NOT NULL VARCHAR2(30)
```

Listing A.68   *DBA_SNAPSHOT_REFRESH_TIMES* view.

```
Column Name                   Null?    Type
---------------------------   -------- ----
OWNER                         NOT NULL VARCHAR2(30)
NAME                          NOT NULL VARCHAR2(30)
MASTER_OWNER                           VARCHAR2(30)
MASTER                                 VARCHAR2(30)
LAST_REFRESH                           DATE
```

Listing A.69   *DBA_SOURCE* view.

```
Column Name                   Null?    Type
---------------------------   -------- ----
OWNER                         NOT NULL VARCHAR2(30)
NAME                          NOT NULL VARCHAR2(30)
TYPE                                   VARCHAR2(12)
LINE                          NOT NULL NUMBER
TEXT                                   VARCHAR2(4000)
```

Listing A.70   *DBA_STMT_AUDIT_OPTS* view.

```
Column Name                   Null?    Type
---------------------------   -------- ----
USER_NAME                              VARCHAR2(30)
AUDIT_OPTION                  NOT NULL VARCHAR2(40)
SUCCESS                                VARCHAR2(10)
FAILURE                                VARCHAR2(10)
```

Listing A.71   *DBA_SYNONYMS* view.

```
Column Name                   Null?    Type
---------------------------   -------- ----
OWNER                         NOT NULL VARCHAR2(30)
SYNONYM_NAME                  NOT NULL VARCHAR2(30)
TABLE_OWNER                            VARCHAR2(30)
TABLE_NAME                    NOT NULL VARCHAR2(30)
DB_LINK                                VARCHAR2(128)
```

Listing A.72   *DBA_SYS_PRIVS* view.

```
Column Name                      Null?     Type
-----------------------------    --------  ----
GRANTEE                          NOT NULL  VARCHAR2(30)
PRIVILEGE                        NOT NULL  VARCHAR2(40)
ADMIN_OPTION                               VARCHAR2(3)
```

Listing A.73   *DBA_TABLES* view.

```
Column Name                      Null?     Type
-----------------------------    --------  ----
OWNER                            NOT NULL  VARCHAR2(30)
TABLE_NAME                       NOT NULL  VARCHAR2(30)
TABLESPACE_NAME                            VARCHAR2(30)
CLUSTER_NAME                               VARCHAR2(30)
IOT_NAME                                   VARCHAR2(30)
PCT_FREE                                   NUMBER
PCT_USED                                   NUMBER
INI_TRANS                                  NUMBER
MAX_TRANS                                  NUMBER
INITIAL_EXTENT                             NUMBER
NEXT_EXTENT                                NUMBER
MIN_EXTENTS                                NUMBER
MAX_EXTENTS                                NUMBER
PCT_INCREASE                               NUMBER
FREELISTS                                  NUMBER
FREELIST_GROUPS                            NUMBER
LOGGING                                    VARCHAR2(3)
BACKED_UP                                  VARCHAR2(1)
NUM_ROWS                                   NUMBER
BLOCKS                                     NUMBER
EMPTY_BLOCKS                               NUMBER
AVG_SPACE                                  NUMBER
CHAIN_CNT                                  NUMBER
AVG_ROW_LEN                                NUMBER
AVG_SPACE_FREELIST_BLOCKS                  NUMBER
NUM_FREELIST_BLOCKS                        NUMBER
DEGREE                                     VARCHAR2(10)
INSTANCES                                  VARCHAR2(10)
CACHE                                      VARCHAR2(5)
TABLE_LOCK                                 VARCHAR2(8)
SAMPLE_SIZE                                NUMBER
LAST_ANALYZED                             DATE
PARTITIONED                                VARCHAR2(3)
IOT_TYPE                                   VARCHAR2(12)
TEMPORARY                                  VARCHAR2(1)
NESTED                                     VARCHAR2(3)
BUFFER_POOL                                VARCHAR2(7)
```

Listing A.74   *DBA_TABLESPACES* view.

```
Column Name                      Null?    Type
------------------------------   -------- ----
TABLESPACE_NAME                  NOT NULL VARCHAR2(30)
INITIAL_EXTENT                            NUMBER
NEXT_EXTENT                               NUMBER
MIN_EXTENTS                      NOT NULL NUMBER
MAX_EXTENTS                      NOT NULL NUMBER
PCT_INCREASE                     NOT NULL NUMBER
MIN_EXTLEN                                NUMBER
STATUS                                    VARCHAR2(9)
CONTENTS                                  VARCHAR2(9)
LOGGING                                   VARCHAR2(9)
```

Listing A.75   *DBA_TAB_COLUMNS* view.

```
Column Name                      Null?    Type
------------------------------   -------- ----
OWNER                            NOT NULL VARCHAR2(30)
TABLE_NAME                       NOT NULL VARCHAR2(30)
COLUMN_NAME                      NOT NULL VARCHAR2(30)
DATA_TYPE                                 VARCHAR2(30)
DATA_TYPE_MOD                             VARCHAR2(3)
DATA_TYPE_OWNER                           VARCHAR2(30)
DATA_LENGTH                      NOT NULL NUMBER
DATA_PRECISION                            NUMBER
DATA_SCALE                                NUMBER
NULLABLE                                  VARCHAR2(1)
COLUMN_ID                        NOT NULL NUMBER
DEFAULT_LENGTH                            NUMBER
DATA_DEFAULT                              LONG
NUM_DISTINCT                              NUMBER
LOW_VALUE                                 RAW(32)
HIGH_VALUE                                RAW(32)
DENSITY                                   NUMBER
NUM_NULLS                                 NUMBER
NUM_BUCKETS                               NUMBER
LAST_ANALYZED                             DATE
SAMPLE_SIZE                               NUMBER
CHARACTER_SET_NAME                        VARCHAR2(44)
```

Listing A.76   *DBA_TAB_COL_STATISTICS* view.

```
Column Name                      Null?    Type
------------------------------   -------- ----
TABLE_NAME                       NOT NULL VARCHAR2(30)
COLUMN_NAME                      NOT NULL VARCHAR2(30)
NUM_DISTINCT                              NUMBER
LOW_VALUE                                 RAW(32)
```

```
HIGH_VALUE                          RAW(32)
DENSITY                             NUMBER
NUM_NULLS                           NUMBER
NUM_BUCKETS                         NUMBER
LAST_ANALYZED                       DATE
SAMPLE_SIZE                         NUMBER
```

Listing A.77   *DBA_TAB_COMMENTS view.*

```
Column Name                     Null?     Type
------------------------------  --------  ----
OWNER                           NOT NULL  VARCHAR2(30)
TABLE_NAME                      NOT NULL  VARCHAR2(30)
TABLE_TYPE                                VARCHAR2(11)
COMMENTS                                  VARCHAR2(4000)
```

Listing A.78   *DBA_TAB_HISTOGRAMS view.*

```
Column Name                     Null?     Type
------------------------------  --------  ----
OWNER                                     VARCHAR2(30)
TABLE_NAME                                VARCHAR2(30)
COLUMN_NAME                               VARCHAR2(4000)
ENDPOINT_NUMBER                           NUMBER
ENDPOINT_VALUE                            NUMBER
```

Listing A.79   *DBA_TAB_PARTITIONS view.*

```
Column Name                     Null?     Type
------------------------------  --------  ----
TABLE_OWNER                     NOT NULL  VARCHAR2(30)
TABLE_NAME                      NOT NULL  VARCHAR2(30)
PARTITION_NAME                            VARCHAR2(30)
HIGH_VALUE                                LONG
HIGH_VALUE_LENGTH               NOT NULL  NUMBER
PARTITION_POSITION              NOT NULL  NUMBER
TABLESPACE_NAME                 NOT NULL  VARCHAR2(30)
PCT_FREE                        NOT NULL  NUMBER
PCT_USED                        NOT NULL  NUMBER
INI_TRANS                       NOT NULL  NUMBER
MAX_TRANS                       NOT NULL  NUMBER
INITIAL_EXTENT                            NUMBER
NEXT_EXTENT                               NUMBER
MIN_EXTENT                      NOT NULL  NUMBER
MAX_EXTENT                      NOT NULL  NUMBER
PCT_INCREASE                    NOT NULL  NUMBER
FREELISTS                                 NUMBER
FREELIST_GROUPS                           NUMBER
LOGGING                                   VARCHAR2(3)
NUM_ROWS                                  NUMBER
BLOCKS                                    NUMBER
EMPTY_BLOCKS                              NUMBER
```

```
AVG_SPACE                        NUMBER
CHAIN_CNT                        NUMBER
AVG_ROW_LEN                      NUMBER
SAMPLE_SIZE                      NUMBER
LAST_ANALYZED                    DATE
BUFFER_POOL                      VARCHAR2(7)
```

Listing A.80   *DBA_TAB_PRIVS* view.

```
Column Name                   Null?    Type
----------------------------  -------- ----
GRANTEE                       NOT NULL VARCHAR2(30)
OWNER                         NOT NULL VARCHAR2(30)
TABLE_NAME                    NOT NULL VARCHAR2(30)
GRANTOR                       NOT NULL VARCHAR2(30)
PRIVILEGE                     NOT NULL VARCHAR2(40)
GRANTABLE                              VARCHAR2(3)
```

Listing A.81   *DBA_TRIGGERS* view.

```
Column Name                   Null?    Type
----------------------------  -------- ----
OWNER                         NOT NULL VARCHAR2(30)
TRIGGER_NAME                  NOT NULL VARCHAR2(30)
TRIGGER_TYPE                           VARCHAR2(16)
TRIGGERING_EVENT                       VARCHAR2(26)
TABLE_OWNER                   NOT NULL VARCHAR2(30)
TABLE_NAME                    NOT NULL VARCHAR2(30)
REFERENCING_NAMES                      VARCHAR2(87)
WHEN_CLAUSE                            VARCHAR2(4000)
STATUS                                 VARCHAR2(8)
DESCRIPTION                            VARCHAR2(4000)
TRIGGER_BODY                           LONG
```

Listing A.82   *DBA_TRIGGER_COLS* view.

```
Column Name                   Null?    Type
----------------------------  -------- ----
TRIGGER_OWNER                 NOT NULL VARCHAR2(30)
TRIGGER_NAME                  NOT NULL VARCHAR2(30)
TABLE_OWNER                   NOT NULL VARCHAR2(30)
TABLE_NAME                    NOT NULL VARCHAR2(30)
COLUMN_NAME                            VARCHAR2(4000)
COLUMN_LIST                            VARCHAR2(3)
COLUMN_USAGE                           VARCHAR2(17)
```

Listing A.83   *DBA_TS_QUOTAS* view.

```
Column Name                   Null?    Type
----------------------------  -------- ----
TABLESPACE_NAME               NOT NULL VARCHAR2(30)
USERNAME                      NOT NULL VARCHAR2(30)
```

```
BYTES                               NUMBER
MAX_BYTES                           NUMBER
BLOCKS                   NOT NULL   NUMBER
MAX_BLOCKS                          NUMBER
```

Listing A.84   *DBA_TYPES* view.

```
Column Name                   Null?     Type
-----------------------------  --------  ----
OWNER                                    VARCHAR2(30)
TYPE_NAME                     NOT NULL   VARCHAR2(30)
TYPE_OID                      NOT NULL   RAW(16)
TYPECODE                                 VARCHAR2(30)
ATTRIBUTES                               NUMBER
METHODS                                  NUMBER
PREDEFINED                               VARCHAR2(3)
INCOMPLETE                               VARCHAR2(3)
```

Listing A.85   *DBA_TYPE_ATTRS* view.

```
Column Name                   Null?     Type
-----------------------------  --------  ----
OWNER                                    VARCHAR2(30)
TYPE_NAME                     NOT NULL   VARCHAR2(30)
ATTR_NAME                     NOT NULL   VARCHAR2(30)
ATTR_TYPE_MOD                            VARCHAR2(7)
ATTR_TYPE_OWNER                          VARCHAR2(30)
ATTR_TYPE_NAME                           VARCHAR2(30)
LENGTH                                   NUMBER
PRECISION                                NUMBER
SCALE                                    NUMBER
CHARACTER_SET_NAME                       VARCHAR2(44)
```

Listing A.86   *DBA_TYPE_METHODS* view.

```
Column Name                   Null?     Type
-----------------------------  --------  ----
OWNER                         NOT NULL   VARCHAR2(30)
TYPE_NAME                     NOT NULL   VARCHAR2(30)
METHOD_NAME                   NOT NULL   VARCHAR2(30)
METHOD_NO                     NOT NULL   NUMBER
METHOD_TYPE                              VARCHAR2(6)
PARAMETERS                    NOT NULL   NUMBER
RESULTS                       NOT NULL   NUMBER
```

Listing A.87   *DBA_UPDATABLE_COLUMNS* view.

```
Column Name                   Null?     Type
-----------------------------  --------  ----
OWNER                         NOT NULL   VARCHAR2(30)
TABLE_NAME                    NOT NULL   VARCHAR2(30)
COLUMN_NAME                   NOT NULL   VARCHAR2(30)
```

```
UPDATABLE                           VARCHAR2(3)
INSERTABLE                          VARCHAR2(3)
DELETABLE                           VARCHAR2(3)
```

Listing A.88   *DBA_USERS view.*

```
Column Name                     Null?     Type
------------------------------  --------  ----
USERNAME                        NOT NULL  VARCHAR2(30)
USER_ID                         NOT NULL  NUMBER
PASSWORD                                  VARCHAR2(30)
ACCOUNT_STATUS                  NOT NULL  VARCHAR2(32)
LOCK_DATE                                 DATE
EXPIRY_DATE                               DATE
DEFAULT_TABLESPACE              NOT NULL  VARCHAR2(30)
TEMPORARY_TABLESPACE            NOT NULL  VARCHAR2(30)
CREATED                         NOT NULL  DATE
PROFILE                         NOT NULL  VARCHAR2(30)
EXTERNAL_NAME                             VARCHAR2(4000)
```

Listing A.89   *DBA_VIEWS view.*

```
Column Name                     Null?     Type
------------------------------  --------  ----
OWNER                           NOT NULL  VARCHAR2(30)
VIEW_NAME                       NOT NULL  VARCHAR2(30)
TEXT_LENGTH                               NUMBER
TEXT                                      LONG
TYPE_TEXT_LENGTH                          NUMBER
TYPE_TEXT                                 VARCHAR2(4000)
OID_TEXT_LENGTH                           NUMBER
OID_TEXT                                  VARCHAR2(4000)
VIEW_TYPE_OWNER                           VARCHAR2(30)
VIEW_TYPE                                 VARCHAR2(30)
```

GLOSSARY

ad-hoc query—A temporary query for which neither the specification nor the output are saved.

attribute—Describes a value that will be found in each tuple in a relation. Usually represented as a column of a relation.

base query—Same as ground query.

BCNF—See **Boyce-Codd Normal Form (BCNF)**.

Boyce-Codd dependency—A part of the key is dependent on a non-key attribute.

Boyce-Codd Normal Form (BCNF)—Relations are in BCNF if they are in third normal form and have no Boyce-Codd dependencies.

candidate key—One or more attributes that will uniquely identify one tuple in a relation. A candidate key is a potential primary key.

commit—The decision to proceed with the actual posting of a change to the database.

computed attribute—An attribute for which the value is calculated from other attributes. Although computed attributes may be stored in relations, they usually are not. Most often, they are produced as needed in the resolution of a query.

criterion (pl. criteria)—A characteristic or limitation applied to the values of an attribute to select some of the tuples of a relation during a query.

database—1. A collection of all the data needed by a person or organization to perform needed functions. 2. A collection of related files. 3. Any collection of data organized to answer queries. 4. A database management system (informally).

database management system—Also called a database manager. An integrated collection of programs designed to allow people to design databases, enter and maintain data, and perform queries.

database manager—1. The person with primary responsibility for the design, construction, and maintenance of a database. 2. A database management system (informally).

deadlock—A pathological state of a computer system reached when none of a group of competing processes can proceed, because each is waiting for resources locked by the other(s).

distributed database—A database in which the resources are stored on more than one computer system, often at different physical locations.

domain—The collection of all possible values of an attribute. The domain of an attribute may be finite or infinite.

entity—A real-world object, observation, transaction, or person about which data is to be stored in a database.

entity-relationship (ER) diagram—Design tool used primarily for relational databases in which entities are modeled as geometric shapes and the relationships between them are shown as labeled arcs.

field—Term used by Microsoft Access as a synonym for attribute.

fifth normal form—A relation is in fifth normal form if it is in fourth normal form and cannot be broken into smaller relations without loss of information.

file—1. The separately named unit of storage for all data and programs on most computers. For example, a relation or a whole database may be stored in one file. 2. Term used as a synonym for relation in some (particularly older) database managers, such as dBase.

filter—Microsoft Access term for persistent query.

first normal form—Relations in first normal form have no multiple-valued attributes.

fourth normal form—A relation is in fourth normal form if it is in Boyce-Codd normal form and it has, at most, only one independent multivalued dependency.

granularity—The size of the smallest unit that can be independently locked. A database may apply locks at the database level, the relation level, the tuple level, or on the value of a single attribute within a tuple.

ground query—A query in which all of the attributes are taken directly from relations; none is taken from the output of other queries.

index—1. A method used to reorder tuples or to display them in a specific order. 2. A data structure used to give rapid, random access to relations. Indexes are most often used with large relations.

inversion—An index from which the tuples in a main relation with a particular value for an attribute can be determined.

join—A query that uses data from more than one relation. The relations must have at least one attribute (called the *join* or *linking attribute*) in common.

key—An attribute or combination of attributes. A combination of their values will be used to select tuples from a relation.

locking—Reserving the use of a database, relation, tuple, or other collection of data for access by one user. This is a strategy to prevent anomalous behavior of a database, as would happen, for example, when one user reads data from a database that was being modified by another user.

many-to-many relationship—One or more tuples in one relation may be related to one or more tuples in a second relation by a common value of a join attribute. This implies that each value of the join attribute may appear any number of times in either relation or in both.

negation—Specifying that a query is to select all tuples except those with a particular value for a given attribute. Such queries are often unsafe, and many databases do not support negation.

normal form—1. A condition of relations and databases intended to reduce data redundancy and improve performance. 2. Rules and processes for putting relations and databases into normal form.

one-to-many relationship—Exactly one tuple in one relation is related by a common join attribute to many tuples in another relation. This implies that each value of the join attribute is unique in the first relation, but not necessarily in the second.

one-to-one relationship—Exactly one tuple in one relation is related by a common join attribute to exactly one tuple in another relation. This implies that each value of the join attribute appears no more than once in each of the relations.

partial dependency—The value of a non-key attribute is dependent on only part of the key (usually on one attribute of a multiattribute key).

persistent query—A query that is stored for reuse.

post—To make a change to the stored data. Posting may be done immediately or may be deferred until all related changes can be checked and verified.

primary key—A key such that the value of the key attribute(s) will uniquely identify any tuple in the relation. A relation must not have more than one primary key.

primary memory—The internal memory of a computer, usually consisting of RAM chips, on which the data and programs currently being used must reside.

project—A query in which only some of the attributes in the source relation appear in the output.

QBE—Query-By-Example, a tabular language for expressing queries, in which a query is specified by sketching an abbreviated schema of the output desired, along with any criteria that should be applied to the attributes desired.

query—1. A command, written in a query language, for the database to present a specified subset of the data in the database. 2. The subset of data produced as output in response to a query.

Query-By-Example—See **QBE**.

query language—A computer language that can be used to express queries.

query resolution—The process of collecting the data needed to answer a query.

read lock—A lock that allows the user receiving the lock to read all or part of a database, but not to modify it. Some database management systems will allow many users to have simultaneous read locks on a unit of data.

record—Term used as a synonym for *tuple* in some (particularly older) database management systems, such as dBase.

recursive query—A query in which the output of the query is then used as input for the same query.

relation—The basic collection of data in a relational database. Usually represented as a rectangular array of data, in which each row (tuple) is a collection of data about one entity.

row—Term used by Microsoft Access as a synonym for tuple.

running a query—Microsoft Access term for query resolution.

safe query—A query in which the output is guaranteed to be finite.

schema—1. A description of a database. It specifies (among other things) the relations, their attributes, and the domains of the attributes. In some database systems, the join attributes are also specified as part of the schema. 2. The description of one relation.

second normal form—Relations are in second normal form if they are in first normal form and have no partial dependencies.

secondary key—A key that is not the primary key for a relation.

secondary memory—The external storage of a computer, usually consisting of magnetic or optical disks, on which data and programs are held between the times they are actually in use.

select—A query in which only some of the tuples in the source relation appear in the output.

Sequel—See **SQL**.

Sequential Query Language—See **SQL**.

SQL—Pronounced "sequel," it stands for Sequential Query Language, the most common text-based database query language.

table—Term used by Microsoft Access as a synonym for relation.

third normal form—Relations are in third normal form if they are in second normal form and have no transitive dependencies.

transaction—1. The fundamental unit of change in many (transaction-oriented) databases. A single transaction may involve changes in several relations, all of which must be made simultaneously in order for the database to be internally consistent and correct. 2. The real-life event that is modeled by the changes to the database.

transitive dependency—The value of one non-key attribute is dependent on the value of one or more other non-key attributes.

tuple—Within a relation, a collection of all the facts related to one entity. Usually represented as a row of data.

two-phase commit—A strategy in which changes to a database are made temporarily to a buffered version of the database. Once it has been determined that all parts of an update can be made successfully, the changes are posted to the actual database.

unsafe query—A query in which the output is possibly infinite. This most often occurs in queries that are recursive or contain negation. Such queries are disallowed by many database management systems.

value—The computer representation of a fact about an entity.

write lock—A lock that allows the user receiving the lock to read and modify the database. Write locks almost always imply exclusive control of the database; no other users will be allowed to have either read or write locks as long as one write lock is active.

INDEX

P

Q Diagnostic Center™
for Oracle® and Client

Call Savant to activate the copy of Q provided on your CD.

Savant is extending a special 10% discount for the readers
of this book. Call for details.

Customer Support   800.956.9541
301.581.0511
qsupport@savant-corp.com

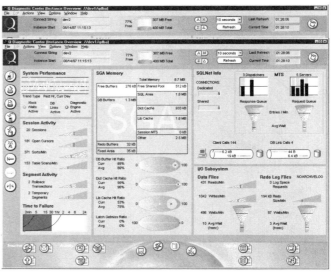

The Q™ Instance Overview Screen

S A V A N T®